SO-AIS-905

"ORDER UNDER LAW"

Fourth Edition

HV
9950
.O73
1992

"ORDER UNDER LAW"

Readings in criminal justice

Fourth Edition

Robert G. Culbertson
Northwest Missouri State University

Ralph Weisheit
Illinois State University

WAVELAND

PRESS, INC.

Prospect Heights, Illinois

KVCC KALAMAZOO VALLEY
COMMUNITY COLLEGE

SEP 3 0 1996

For information about this book, write or call:
Waveland Press, Inc.
P.O. Box 400
Prospect Heights, Illinois 60070
(708) 634-0081

Cover Design: Mark Tezak and John Stanicek

Copyright © 1992, 1988, 1984, 1981 by Waveland Press, Inc.

ISBN 0-88133-670-X

All rights reserved. No part of this book may be reproduced, stored in a retrieval system, or transmitted in any form or by any means without permission in writing from the publisher.

Printed in the United States of America

7 6 5 4 3 2

Contents

Preface

In the 1980s and 1990s the criminal justice system extended its reach, moving beyond its traditional concern with street crime to increase its focus on drug offenses, white collar crime, and organized crime. By the late 1980s, over one percent of Americans were either on probation or in prison. Courts, jails, and prisons have become increasingly overloaded. Added to the concern about crime in the 1960s has been a concern about the costs (both social and financial) of paying for a system which has grown out of control. Given these changes, it should not be surprising that criminal justice continues to hold the interest of students and researchers.

Part of the appeal of criminal justice as a field of study stems from the fact that the criminal justice system plays an important role in our lives. Rare is the individual who has never had contact with or has never witnessed the operation of the police. A smaller number of us have had occasion to view the courts and the corrections components of the criminal justice system. Criminal justice also generates widespread and intense interest due to the significance of the issues involved. When one studies criminal justice, he or she must come to grips with some of the most emotional and complex questions confronting our society. Do we have two standards of justice, one standard for the wealthy and another for the poor? Does our criminal justice system discriminate against minorities? What is the proper goal of punishment? Have moral and ethical issues been ignored in the "people changing" techniques used in rehabilitation? Is it proper for the state to take a life? One could continue to cite questions such as these—questions which reflect individual and collective value conflict.

A third explanation for our interest in criminal justice can be linked to the fact that much remains to be done in the field. Police organizations need reform and, many would claim, professionalization. Enormous caseloads demand that attention be devoted to the court process in order to improve both its efficiency and fairness. Corrections continues to function in an environment of confusion because of years of neglect and a lack of consensus regarding goals for this component of the criminal justice system. Ironically, the importance of these reforms has been recognized at precisely the time when federal, state, and local budgets are already strained.

The issues and controversies in the field of criminal justice have been closely scrutinized over the past twenty years and the result is a massive body of literature. In this publication we have attempted to focus on some of the major issues which have emerged from this body of literature. We have assembled a group of articles which we believe will facilitate understanding of the complexities of criminal justice for the general reader. Our primary interest, however, has been to provide a set of readings for the student commencing his or her study in criminal justice.

This fourth edition is necessary because of developments in knowledge about criminal justice. Further, while many problems persist, the issues on which our society focuses have shifted over time. The seven new articles (and two which have been updated) reflect a heightened awareness of issues related to victims, career criminals, female offenders, police practices, an overloaded court system, and current dilemmas facing prisons.

It is hoped that the reader will find this work to be both enjoyable and illuminating. In order to profit fully from the following selections, the reader should keep in mind the phrase which serves as our title—"Order Under Law." This phrase, coined by Jerome Skolnick in his landmark publication, *Justice Without Trial*, does much to explain the conflicts and controversies found in the criminal justice system. We demand that our police apprehend suspects, that our courts convict the accused, and that our correctional system, in some way, punish the convicted. We demand order. The tasks involved in insuring order would be relatively straightforward were it not for our simultaneous demand that the police, courts and correctional agencies operate within the constraints placed upon them by the law.

Robert G. Culbertson
Ralph A. Weisheit

Section I

Crime:
An American Institution

During the late 1960s crime was one of the most sensitive and emotional issues in our society. Increasing crime rates, generated in part by demographic factors, led many to conclude that our society was facing serious moral decay. Riots paralyzed a number of our major cities during a series of "long hot summers." Political and social movements were also influenced by assassins' bullets as we witnessed the deaths of President John F. Kennedy, Senator Robert Kennedy, and civil rights leader Rev. Martin Luther King. Politicians exploited the deep philosophical divisions in our society. Some politicians called for responses which placed additional demands on an already overburdened criminal justice system.

Richard Nixon's campaign for the Presidency in 1968 was based on the assumption that complex social problems could be solved with greater levels of crime control. As a part of the "war on crime," various groups pressured the courts to "stop handcuffing the police." At the same time, a number of Presidential Commissions described increased racial discrimination in our society and the special problems of the inner city resident—problems which could not be solved with crime control strategies. The 1960s also witnessed new rights for suspects, defendants and inmates in prisons as the U.S. Supreme Court delivered a number of landmark decisions which altered the operations of criminal justice agencies. Official abuses of power were condemned. For example, the Chicago Police Department was accused of "rioting" at the

1

1968 Democratic Convention. The study of criminal justice emerged from this climate of conflict and confrontation because traditional disciplines had ignored, for the most part, these overwhelming issues.

While politicians focused their attention on crime rates, they tended to ignore two basic problems. First, crime statistics, upon which crime rates are based, have never been very accurate. Published crime rates may or may not reflect the actual amount of crime at any particular time. Rather, these published rates reflect police activity and tend to rise and fall with changes in enforcement policies. Second, many politicians ignored the fact that American society has always been plagued by criminal activity of one kind or another. Youth gangs roamed the streets of our major cities in the early 1800s, and, by mid-century, New York's Central Park was dominated by young thugs during hours of darkness. Lynchings were a common feature in our society during the late 1800s and continued into the 1900s as racial strife permeated America. During the 1920s and 1930s criminals became heroes as John Dillinger and others pursued the American dream of wealth and affluence at a time when our economic system had failed. The 1960s were, therefore, not a departure from a pattern of lawfulness, but rather reflected the historical pattern of lawlessness.

In the 1980s, an era of conservative politics and public sentiment led to the unprecedented reliance on criminal punishments to tackle the crime problem. The focus was on making more arrests and making greater use of imprisonment. The crime crisis of the 1960s has been replaced in the 1990s by a crisis in the criminal justice system itself. This first section reflects many of the concerns facing criminal justice in the 1990s—the plight of victims, the problem of career offenders, the conflict between efficiency and fairness, and a concern with the rise of "new" offender groups.

In the first article, "The Rediscovery of Crime Victims," Andrew Karmen discusses many of the myths and realities about crime and its victims. He notes the increased attention given victims in recent years. He also demonstrates how the media both helps and harms victims in its coverage of crime. The concern with victims has also given rise to a large crime prevention industry and to a number of social movements which have pushed for changes in the way the criminal justice system responds to victims.

Controlling crime with limited resources has led to a focus on efficiency. This, in turn, has drawn attention to those few offenders who commit many crimes over a period of many years, the so-called "career criminals." In his article "Choosing Crime," Kenneth Tunnell uses interviews with repeat offenders to demonstrate that normal assumptions about using the law to stop crime may not fit these offenders. In general, they do not fear being caught, expect the punishment to be light, and find prison a relatively nonthreatening experience.

In the third article in this section, "Two Models of the Criminal Process," Herbert Packer addresses value conflicts in criminal justice. Packer's analysis of the Crime Control Model and the Due Process Model illustrates the philosophical differences between these models. On the one hand, we want persons who commit crimes to be apprehended, prosecuted, convicted and punished. And, we want these activities carried out effectively, efficiently and, on occasion, expediently. We want crime control. On the other hand, we have strong commitments to the Bill of Rights, and we insist that criminal justice officials act within Constitutional limits set by the courts which reinforce due process. We are both intense and emotional about these rights and their protection.

It is important to understand that because of these ideological differences, we have little consensus about what should be the goals for the criminal justice system. As a result, agencies often work from conflicting perspectives, the criminal justice system is generally ineffective, and, unfortunately, those public servants who run the operational agencies are criticized and condemned because they cannot resolve the crime problem.

In the final article in this section, "Patterns of Female Crime," Ralph Weisheit provides an overview of an important contemporary issue in criminal justice. He discusses changes in female crime since the 1960s, the types of crimes committed by women, and some of the explanations which have been used to account for female crime. Because of increases in their sheer number, female offenders have placed more demands on an already overworked system. A concern with female crime has also provided a fresh perspective on the factors which lead to crime for both sexes.

1

The Rediscovery of Crime Victims

Andrew Karmen

Laws create criminals and formally define persons as victims at the same time. The outlawing of specific harmful activities thus always marks, in a sense, the discovery of another set of victims. The laws prohibiting what are now called street crimes are among the very oldest on the books. Victims of murder, rape, robbery, assault, and theft were recognized and placed under the protection of the legal system centuries ago.

Some laws are controversial. People may disagree, for example, over whose interests are genuinely served by tax codes or which groups are actually protected by laws restricting drug use. But laws forbidding interpersonal violence and theft of property appear to be universal — present in all societies and necessary for every social system's survival. Everyone agrees that these kinds of victimizations can't be tolerated. If there is any lack of consensus about the laws governing violence and theft, it concerns how to handle the lawbreakers.

The Decline of Crime Victims

In colonial America, victims were the central figures in the criminal justice drama. Police forces and public prosecutors did not yet exist. Criminal acts

From *Crime Victims: An Introduction to Victimology*, 2nd Ed. by Andrew Karmen. Copyright © 1990 by Wadsworth, Inc. Reprinted by permission of Brooks/Cole Publishing Company, Pacific Grove, CA 93950.

were viewed primarily as harmful to the individuals involved. Victims conducted their own investigations, paid for warrants to have sheriffs make arrests, and hired private attorneys to indict and prosecute their alleged offenders. Convicts were forced to repay victims up to three times as much as they damaged or stole. The fates of offenders were closely tied to the wishes of their victims. Victims were key decision makers within and direct beneficiaries of the criminal justice process. But after the Revolutionary War and the framing of the Constitution, distinctions arose between offenses against the social order (crimes) and harmful acts inflicted on one individual by another (torts, or civil wrongs). Crimes were considered hostile attacks against the authority of the state, as the representative governing body of the people. Addressing the suffering of the victims was deemed to be less important than dealing with the symbolic threat posed by criminals to the society as a whole. Public prosecutors, as representatives of the government and of society, took over powers and responsibilities formerly assumed by victims. Federal, state, and district attorneys decided whether or not to press charges, what indictments to file, and what sanctions to ask judges to invoke against the guilty parties. Reimbursement of the victims became a minor concern as new priorities in sentencing took hold. The goals of deterring crime through punishment, rehabilitating troublemakers through treatment, and protecting society through the incarceration of dangerous persons began to overshadow the demands of victims that they be restored to financial, emotional, and physical health whenever possible. The state undertook the obligation of providing accused and convicted persons with lawyers, food, housing, medical care, recreational opportunities, schooling, job training, and psychological counseling, while leaving victims to fend for themselves. Victims lost control over their cases, and their role was reduced to initiating investigations by complaining to the police and testifying for the prosecution as just another piece of evidence in the state's presentation of damning facts against the accused. When the overwhelming majority of cases came to be resolved through confessions of guilt elicited in negotiated settlements, most victims lost their last opportunity to actively participate in the process—by telling their stories on the witness stand. Victims became so overlooked in criminal justice proceedings that they were rarely asked what actions the prosecution should take, and often were never informed of the outcome or the reasons for it. Many victims concluded that they had been harmed twice, the second time by a system ostensibly set up to help them but in reality more intent on satisfying the needs of its constituent agencies and officials (McDonald, 1977; Davis, Kunreuther, and Connick, 1984).

Renewed Interest

Social problems appear to have a natural history of their own and progress through stages in what can be termed a career or even a life-cycle (Fuller and Myers, 1941; Ross and Staines, 1972). In the case of the rediscovery of the plight of crime victims, the cycle was initiated in the late 1950s and early 1960s by a small number of self-help advocates, social scientists, crusading journalists, enlightened criminal justice officials, and responsive lawmakers. They started to make the public aware of what they defined as problematic: the historic and systematic inattention toward victim issues. Through writings, meetings, and events such as petition drives and demonstrations, these activists communicated to a wider audience their message that victims were forgotten persons who needed to be rediscovered. Discussion and debate emerged in the late 1960s and intensified throughout the 1970s and 1980s over why the situation existed and what could be done about it. Various groups with their own distinct interests formed coalitions and mobilized to campaign for changes. As a result, criminal justice policies are being reformed and new laws favorable to victims are being passed.

The major contributors to this process of rediscovery and to this critique of unjustifiable neglect have been the following: victims of rape and battering; survivors whose loved ones were murdered, or were killed in car crashes caused by drunk drivers; parents whose children were kidnapped; social scientists such as victimologists, criminologists, psychologists, and political scientists; criminal justice professionals such as judges, prosecutors, other lawyers, and police administrators; care givers such as doctors, nurses, and social workers; legislators on local, state, and federal levels; writers and investigative reporters; and inventors and entrepreneurs.

The leading institutional participants in this reawakening have been the news media, businesses selling security products and services, and the groups comprising the victims' movement in the political arena. Their participation has turned out to be a double-edged sword, however, with both promises and pitfalls. After routinely overlooking the plight of victims for many years, journalists within the news media now risk sensationalizing their descriptions of the impact of crime. After systematically ignoring the needs and wants of victims and of people afraid of being harmed by criminals, profit-oriented enterprises now are tapping a huge market of fearful customers who are vulnerable to commercial exploitation. After years of inattention, political figures are now addressing issues raised by the victims' rights movement in self-serving ways that can be manipulative and cynical in order to garner votes, campaign contributions, and endorsements.

The News Media: Portraying the Victim's Plight

The news media—newspapers, magazines, and radio and television stations—deserve a great deal of credit for contributing to the rediscovery of victims. Running accounts of crimes as front-page items, with prominent headlines and as the lead story in broadcasts, is a long-standing journalistic tradition. Today, everyone is familiar with America's crime problem—not because of firsthand experience but because of secondhand accounts relayed through the news media.

Since the media's historical preoccupation with violence and mayhem shows no sign of abating, however, two disturbing questions are being raised with increasing frequency: "How accurate is media coverage of the plight of street crime victims?" and "How ethical are journalists when they report on the harm suffered by victims?"

Questions about Accuracy

At its best, crime reporting can explain in precise detail just what happens to victims—how they are harmed, what losses they incur, what emotions they feel, what helps and hinders their recovery. By remaining faithful to the facts, journalists can enable their audiences to transcend their own limited experiences with criminals, and see emergencies, tragedies, triumphs, and dangers through the victims' eyes. Skillfully drafted accounts can convey a full picture of the consequences of lawless acts—from the raw emotion and drama of the situation to the institutional responses that make up the criminal justice process. Accurate information and well-grounded, insightful interpretations allow nonvictims to better understand and empathize with the actions and reactions of victims.

The news media's coverage of crime and its impact can be misleading instead of enlightening, however, and a source of fallacies and myths instead of the truth.

For example, media reporting practices can create the impression that a particular kind of crime is on the rise. The rediscovery of some group of victims by one news department can inspire competitors to search for additional newsworthy stories on the same theme. As editors and reporters scour the news releases of police departments for still more cases, a "crime wave" takes shape. Law enforcement officials and politicians who favor calling the public's attention to such cases can then use their news-making powers (for example, by holding press conferences or scheduling hearings) to keep the coverage going. The creation of a crime wave can be illustrated by describing events that took place in New York City for about seven weeks in 1976. The three daily newspapers and five local television stations all featured numerous stories describing an upsurge in crimes of violence against the elderly. In response, the mayor criticized lenient judges, the police commissioner beefed up the Senior Citizen's Robbery Squad, local precincts hosted victimization prevention demonstrations, and state legislators introduced bills mandating prison sentences for criminals who used force to subdue elderly victims. Opinion polls revealed that the public believed that assaults against the aged were on the rise; older people told interviewers that they were becoming more fearful. And yet, statistics released a few years later cast doubt on the impression that during the period when this theme was dominating the news media, the older generation was being abused by the younger generation like never before. Police reports of robberies of senior citizens did show a sharp increase, but statistics on the murder of older persons showed just as sharp a decrease. After the coverage of the alleged crime wave peaked, the number of such items per month dropped to levels somewhat higher than before the rediscovery of elderly victims, indicating a continuing interest in and sensitivity to this ongoing problem by news media editorial boards (Fishman, 1978).

Editors and journalists sift through an overwhelming number of real-life tragedies that come to their attention (largely through their contacts with the local police department) and select out the cases they anticipate will shock people out of their complacency or sear the public's social conscience. The stories that are featured strike a responsive chord in their audiences because the incidents symbolize some significant theme: for example, the potential for practically anyone to be chosen at random to be brutally victimized (simply for being at the wrong place at the wrong time); the depths to which contemporary society has sunk, especially in anonymous big city settings (as shown by the indifference of bystanders to the plight of a person under attack); or perhaps the potential dangers of interactions with complete strangers (as demonstrated by cases of betrayals of trust, such as those risked by women who frequent the singles-bar scene) (Roberts, 1989).

Unfortunately, the images depicted by the news media are often distortions of reality. Several kinds of obvious as well as subtle biases color most news reports about victimization. First of all, almost by definition, the items considered newsworthy must be attention grabbers; that is, some aspect of the crime, the offender, or the victim must be unusual, unexpected, strange, perverse, or shocking. What is typical, commonplace, or predictable is not news. As a result, as soon as some pattern of victimization becomes well known, it ceases to be "newsworthy." The media's roving eye has a notoriously short attention span. For example, victims of drive-by shootings who are caught in the cross fire between rival gang members might be the subject of lead stories for a week or so. Then this topic will disappear from the news, and a spate of incidents in which motorists get shot on congested highways might seize center stage. After that, a series of mysterious deaths among hospital patients might be featured. These events are then superseded by coverage of a rash of poisonings due to product tampering, or slayings of taxi drivers, or holdups of elderly women by teenage boys, or murders of children by abusive parents, or attacks on teachers by angry students. The procession of grisly, depressing, and infuriating tidbits never ceases, although eventually the subjects begin to be repeated. The question arises whether particular kinds of crime really break out and fade away in such patterns or whether such incidents occur at a fairly consistent rate, constituting a constant presence that news editors can choose to highlight or ignore.

Superficiality of coverage represents another bias within crime reporting. Space and time limitations dictate that items be short and quick, making fast-paced news more entertaining but less informative. Complex issues must be oversimplified, caricatured, reduced to stereotypes, edited out, or simply ignored. As a result, the intricacies of the victim-offender relationship, and the complicated reactions of victims to crimes, are rarely examined in any depth.

The third bias that colors media coverage is a tendency to accentuate the negative. Bad news sells better than good news. However, dwelling on defeat, destruction, and tragedy breeds cynicism, pessimism, even a sense of despair. The public is led to believe that victims suffer endless misery, that extreme reactions are typical responses, that problems are getting worse and worse, that crime is spiraling out of control, and that nothing positive is being done or ever can be done to counteract the damage inflicted by offenders.

At the root of the media's tendency to depart from accurate portrayals of victims' plights is a desire for financial gain. Newspapers, magazines, radio stations, and television networks are profit-oriented businesses. Shocking stories attract readers, listeners, and viewers. Blaring headlines, gripping accounts, colorful phrasing, memorable quotes, and other forms of media "hype" (hyperbole) build the huge audiences that permit media firms to charge sponsors high rates for advertising.

Questions about Ethics

Beneath the headline on the front page of the tabloid is a picture of the victim's smiling face. Next to it is a photo of her father, caught off guard by an enterprising photographer. The caption reads, "The tortured face of _____ displays the anguish of a father over the brutal murder of his 14-year-old daughter _____, who was found raped and bludgeoned to death in Queens [New York] yesterday" ("Queens Girl," 1988).

A woman is found murdered in a housing project. A camera crew arrives and starts filming as policemen carry the body into an ambulance. That night the six o'clock news shows a teenage girl pounding on the ambulance door, sobbing with disbelief and anguish, "That's my sister in there!" (Greenfield, 1987).

The remains of young women murdered by a serial killer begin to turn up. The cameras are rolling at the crime scene when the medical examiner picks up one of the victims' skulls and lets sand sift from the brain cavity. This footage is aired on all the local TV stations. The families of the missing young women, who have not been warned about the contents of the news broadcast, are horrified to see what has happened to their daughters (Barker, 1987).

These examples illustrate the kind of insensitivity to victims and survivors that raises questions of ethics and fairness in crime reporting. Overzealous journalists are frequently criticized for maintaining deathwatch vigils at kidnap victims' homes or for shoving microphones in the faces of bereaved, dazed, or hysterical persons. When reporters turn a personal tragedy into a media event, and thus into a public spectacle, their invasion of the victim's privacy represents a dismissal of the seriousness of the incident to the injured party (Briggs-Bunting, 1982; Karmen, 1989).[1]

Victims harbor many grievances against the press for what they consider to be "sensationalism" in the depiction of their plight. The kind of coverage that can be called "scandalmongering," "pandering," and "yellow journalism" occurs primarily because the news media that employ the journalists are commercial enterprises that seek to attract audiences for sponsors. But other factors are operating as well: considerations of personal gain (getting an "inside story" and "scooping" the competition, for example) and organizational imperatives (meeting inflexible deadlines and space limitations).

Journalistic sensationalism can take either of two forms: understating the victim's plight or overstating it. Understating occurs whenever the effects of the crime on the victim are overlooked, dismissed, minimized, or belittled. Those who understate the plight of victims seem to assume that victims can simply shrug off the emotional repercussions of a brush with disaster, a beating, or the death of a loved one. A more subtle and insidious form of downplaying the victim's plight occurs when reporters use the victim's suffering as a pretext for telling a much more "interesting" tale: the life story of the offender. This reduction of the victim to a minor character overshadowed by a powerful, albeit evil, central figure crops up in movies, plays, novels, and even ballads, as well as in news accounts of notorious arch-criminals.

The other tendency in sensationalism is to distort media coverage in the opposite direction and overstate the victim's plight. This can take several forms: overrating threats to safety and overestimating the risks of being victimized, exaggerating the degree to which the victim suffers, and overdramatizing the victim's reaction to the event.

Sensationalized coverage is exploitative whether the victim's plight is overstated or understated. Either way, certain details are highlighted to heighten interest or advance an argument. What the victim did or did not say or do may be used to prove some point. Any prior relationship the victim might have had with the offender will be scrutinized. The victim's lifestyle may be held up for criticism. Lies or half-truths may be presented as fact. In addition, when a story is splashed across the front page of the local newspaper or featured as the lead item in the evening news broadcast, the victim suffers an invasion of privacy that can damage his or her personal reputation and social standing. The victim experiences a loss of control as others comment on, interpret, draw lessons from, and impose judgments on the case.

And yet, this is a necessary evil. Criminal acts not only harm particular victims but threaten society as a whole. The public has a right and a need to know about the emergence of dangerous conditions and troublesome developments like outbreaks of theft and violence. The news media has a right, perhaps even a duty, to probe into, disclose fully, and disseminate widely all relevant details regarding significant violations of the law. Reporters and news editors have a constitutional right arising from the First Amendment protection of free speech to present the facts to the public without interference from the government. The problem is that the public's right to know the news and the media's right to report it clash with the victim's right to privacy in the face of unwanted publicity (Karmen, 1989).

Several remedies have been proposed to curb the abusive treatment of victims by insensitive journalists. One approach would be to enact new laws to protect victims from needless publicity, such as the unnecessary disclosure of their names and addresses. An alternative approach would be to rely on editors' self-restraint. The fact that most news accounts of rapes no longer reveal the victims' names is an example of this approach in action. A third remedy would be for the media to adopt a code of professional ethics. Journalists who abide by the code would "read victims their rights" at the outset of interviews just as police officers read suspects their Miranda rights when taking them into custody.

Of course, when victims know their rights in advance they can more effectively exercise them to protect their own interests. Empowering victims in this way could be accomplished by people serving as "victim advocates" (either as volunteers or as criminal justice professionals).

Victimologists can play an important role within this conflict between victims and the media, by studying how frequently and how seriously news reporters offend crime victims and by monitoring how successfully the various reform strategies limit and prevent abuses.

Businesses: Selling Products and Services to Victims

Businesses have discovered in victims an untapped market for goods and services. After suffering through an unpleasant experience, many victims become willing, even eager, consumers, searching for products that will protect them from any further harm. Potential victims—everyone else—constitute a far larger market, if they can be convinced that the personal security industry can increase their safety.

But the attention paid to the victim's plight by businesses may turn out, like media coverage, to be a mixed blessing. Along with the development of this new personal security market comes the possibility of commercial exploitation. Profiteers can engage in false advertising and fear mongering to cash in on the crime problem and capitalize on the legitimate concerns and needs of vulnerable and sometimes panicky customers.

Of equal significance, the development of a personal and home security industry (offering services such as bodyguards for rent and products ranging from guns to bulletproof clothing to burglar alarms) is imposing a commercial and private bias into efforts to reduce crime. Individuals and small groups equipped with the latest in technological gadgetry are becoming the troops in the "war on crime" as responsibility shifts away from the corporate and governmental sources of the problem.

From Crime Prevention to Victimization Prevention

The new interest in victims on the part of businesses has contributed to an evolution in crime prevention strategies. The term *crime prevention* refers to efforts taken to forestall or deter offenders before they strike, as opposed to *crime control* measures, which are taken in response to outbreaks of lawlessness.

Formerly, crime prevention strategies centered on government programs designed to get at the social roots of illegal behavior, such as poverty, unemployment, and discrimination. Crime prevention used to conjure up images of campaigns to improve the quality of education in inner city school systems, to provide decent jobs for all those seeking work, and to develop meaningful recreational outlets for idle youth. Now, however, crime prevention has come to mean "the anticipation, recognition, and appraisal of a crime risk, and the initiation of some action to remove or reduce it" (National Crime Prevention Institute, 1978). Crime prevention strategies are shifting toward individual and small-group actions rather than large-scale, even national, efforts. Perhaps a better term than *crime prevention* for these preemptive measures is *victimization prevention* (Cohn, Kidder, and Harvey, 1978). Victimization prevention is much more modest in intent than crime prevention. Its goal is simply to discourage criminals from attacking particular targets, such as a home, warehouse, store, car, or person. Like defensive driving, victimization prevention hinges on the dictum, "Watch and anticipate the other person's moves."

The first step in victimization prevention is to identify areas of vulnerability and assess all threats. The second step is to take precautions to reduce the risks of becoming a victim. Any measures that make a person look well protected and property well guarded will encourage potential offenders to look elsewhere for easier pickings (Moore, 1985).

Two strategies contribute to the prevention of victimization. The first involves educating likely victims about what they should and should not do to avoid trouble. The second calls for likely victims to enhance their safety through security hardware and protective services.

The shift from crime prevention on a societal and governmental level to victimization prevention on a group and individual level requires potential victims to become crime conscious, or "street smart." The responsibility for personal safety now falls on the would-be victims, who must outmaneuver the would-be offenders. Homeowners who would fend off burglars, for example, must observe certain basic precautions, such as installing security locks on all windows and outside doors and leaving lights on inside and outside the house at night. Of course, this new emphasis on being prepared sets the stage for finding fault with persons who fail to do so and wind up being harmed by offenders.

Clearly, victimization cannot be prevented solely through educational campaigns that simply stress following common sense do's and don'ts. A more comprehensive approach advocates a reliance on security hardware and protective services as well. As a result, the private security industry has come into being.

A major new focus in victimization prevention is on mechanical, or mechanistic, prevention, so named because it seeks to redesign the environment to reduce criminal opportunities, not because the approach necessarily relies on mechanical devices. Methods of mechanical prevention are supposed to reduce crime by increasing the risks of arrest, conviction, and punishment. One strategy is called "crime resistance," or "target hardening." It involves would-be victims (concerned, cautious individuals) in efforts to make the offender's task more difficult (the opposite of facilitating it through carelessness). Two examples of mechanical prevention are installing a burglar alarm in a home and wearing bulletproof clothing. The aim in both cases is to deter criminal attack by making property less vulnerable to theft or a person less subject to harm.

A "valve theory of crime-shifts" predicts that the number of crimes committed will not drop when targets are hardened, but that criminal activity will simply be deflected. If one area of illegal opportunity is "shut-off"— for example, if bus drivers are protected from robbery by the imposition of exact-fare requirements—criminals will shift their attention to more vulnerable targets—such as cabdrivers or storekeepers (National Commission on the Causes and Prevention of Violence, 1969). When crime is displaced, the risk of victimization goes down for some but rises for others, assuming that offenders are intent on committing crimes and that they are flexible in terms of time, place, target, and tactics (Allen, Friday, Roebuck, and Sagarin, 1981).

Whether or not these victimization prevention methods really work, on either an individual or a community-wide level, they lend themselves to commercial exploitation. Many new goods and services are being marketed to direct crime elsewhere.

Cashing in on Crime: Burglar Alarms

Intruders have always posed a threat. In ancient times, cities were surrounded by high walls to ward off invaders. Castles had moats as well as steep sides to keep unwanted visitors out. Fortresses had watchtowers in which lookouts could be posted. Today, electronic sensors warn homeowners if prowlers try to break in.

The FBI estimates that one out of every four residences is likely to be broken into in the next ten years. The average loss suffered by burglary victims approaches $1000 per incident ("U.S. Households," 1986). Worse yet, intruders intent on stealing things may also commit more serious acts of violence against anyone who is home at the time: robbery, assault, rape, or even murder. Even if no one is home, the invasion of one's personal space can be very upsetting. On the other hand, a substantial percentage of household burglaries are less unsettling, being unsuccessful attempts to break in, burglaries that result in minor property loss and damage, or burglaries committed by persons known or related to the victim. All such incidents are grouped together in police statistics (Rand, 1985).

Businesses selling home security hardware and monitoring services have zeroed in on burglary victims. Spokespersons for this industry boast that sales are booming, and predict that the day is fast approaching when alarm systems will be considered standard equipment for residences, stores, cars, and boats (Hager, 1981). Recognizing the considerable potential for growth, some manufacturers are trying to stimulate business by scaring the public with sales hype—overstatements similar to media hype. One company tried to trade on fear by falsely claiming in a full-page newspaper ad that "One Out of Every Four Homes in America Will Be Burglarized This Year" (Vertronix, 1981). Government figures revealed the actual burglary rate that year was closer to one out of every eleven homes (Bureau of Justice Statistics, 1983). A few years later, when government surveys estimated the burglary rate had dropped to about 5 percent—one home in twenty per annum (Bureau of Justice Statistics, 1987)—a security company claimed in a nationwide mail marketing campaign, "You've put a lot in your home. Too much to let it be the one out of six homes that will be hit by crime this year" (ADT Security Systems, 1987). An ad produced by another company cited a meaningless statistic: "The sad truth is that one out of five apartments is broken into sooner or later"—and continued, "Who's watching your apartment when you're not there? You may not like to think about it, but someone could be casing your apartment right now, looking for an easy way in. Chances are he'll find it" (Scandia Telecom, 1986). A competitor advertised its wares through the mail with unnerving messages like "Burglars are looking forward to your vacation as much as you are!" and "There are no safe neighborhoods . . . but there are safe homes." It portrayed its hardware as being "more than a security system, it's a 'peace of mind' system'' (Shelburne, 1982). A mail-order firm opened its pitch to potential customers by reminding them that "In the United States there is now one [burglary] every ten seconds!'' and noted that "A few poor souls simply shiver behind locked doors'' before it unveiled its product line (Watchdog Security Systems, 1987).

Has the discovery of burglary victims by home security companies been a positive or negative development? Are unsuspecting people being alerted to real dangers, or are businesses exploiting the fears they themselves feed?

Alarm company representatives now call themselves "security engineers'' — an effective impression management strategy. Depending on the customer, they draw on one of two different strategies of persuasion to clinch a sale. The first is fear accentuation, a sophisticated version of high-pressure scare tactics that plays upon the emotions of someone who might have been a victim in the past. The second is an aura-of-protection approach that stresses mechanical features and electronic wizardry in a more rational and technical vein (Siegal, 1978).

The most sophisticated systems set up an electronic barricade along the perimeter of the property to be protected. Low-light video cameras, electric eyes, heat sensors, and motion detectors warn of the approach of intruders. "Silent alarms'' with automatic dialers alert a central monitoring station and the local police precinct with a prerecorded message about a break-in in progress. Infrared, photoelectric, microwave, or ultrasonic detectors also trigger blaring alarms to alert neighbors.

The most likely purchasers of burglar alarm systems are persons who have recently been victimized. Among households that have suffered a break-in, 20 percent invest in an alarm system (Burden, 1984). A U.S. Department of Justice survey revealed that 7 percent of all households in the nation were equipped with alarms. But sharp differences in sales showed up when respondents were broken down into income groups. Only about 5 percent of poor and working class households were guarded by alarms, whereas in more affluent neighborhoods more than three times as many homes, 16 percent, were wired by security firms (Whitaker, 1986). But according to statistics collected by the FBI, low-income households experience break-ins more often than high-income households, apartments are struck more frequently than private homes, city dwellers are victimized more often than suburbanites or rural folks, and the homes of blacks are burglarized more often than those of whites (Rand, 1985). Hence, the people who need protection the most are less likely to have it.

It is not clear exactly how effective burglar alarms are. Are homes protected by alarm systems less likely to be targeted than comparable homes in comparable neighborhoods that are unprotected? Are homes with alarms ransacked less—do thieves cart off less loot because they are frightened by a blaring alarm? Are burglars more likely to be captured if they attack a home guarded by an alarm? Well-designed, methodologically sound scientific studies have not yet appeared in the professional literature of criminology and victimology. The value of alarm systems has not yet been firmly established (Mayhew, 1984), even though insurance companies encourage homeowners to buy them by offering those that have them discounts on their premiums.

The installation of an alarm (as evidenced by foil tape and decals in windows) does seem to have some value as a deterrent, however. Would-be trespassers and thieves may be warded off by the warning signs, which signal that their intended victims are prepared to detect and perhaps help capture them. Such deterrence is shown by statistics compiled by the police in the affluent, relatively safe, yet crime-conscious suburb of Scarsdale, New York, where over a quarter of the homes are guarded by electronic burglar alarms. From 1976 to 1982, the break-in rate ranged from around 0.5 percent a year to a little more than 2 percent a year for protected homes. During this period, residences without alarms were victimized from two to four times as often ("Alarm Systems," 1982).

A survey conducted in 1983 by the trade magazine of the security industry came up with similar results: only 2 percent of houses protected by alarms suffered losses from break-ins annually over a period of several years (Edersheim, 1986). However, if only deterrence is the goal, then there are much simpler and cheaper ways to scare away burglars. A dummy horn mounted outside the home and a sticker (falsely announcing that an alarm system is in operation) might be sufficient to ward off prowlers. Leaving lights on and a radio playing in strategic places provides an added measure of protection (Moore, 1985). Only about half of a nationwide sample of police chiefs reported (in a survey sponsored by the home security industry) that they had personally encouraged homeowners and business owners to install alarm systems. As many as 15 percent of police officials remain unconvinced that alarms decrease the chances of a residence being burglarized (Stat Resources, 1986). A government study concluded that no evidence could be found that the growing proliferation of security devices and alarms has had any demonstrable effect on the overall rates of either attempted or completed forcible entries. The researchers hypothesized, however, that would-be burglars might be avoiding homes with alarms (especially in communities with neighborhood patrols) and striking unprotected areas. If so, then the target-hardening precautions that some people have undertaken are shifting or deflecting offenders on to others (Rand, 1985).

Clearly, the private solution to the burglary problem promoted by the security hardware industry can cause hardships for neighbors, who might feel compelled to "keep up with the Joneses" for the sake of self-preservation rather than status seeking. If most nearby residences are protected by alarm systems, a prudent homeowner unwilling to be the only attractively vulnerable target on the block must purchase an alarm system too. The net effect of this "arms race" in security hardware is to deflect predatory street criminals from the well-guarded to the unguarded. To the extent that buying protective devices is more a question of income than of consumer priorities, the overall societal impact may be that the affluent will purchase security at the expense of those who can't afford to keep up with them. As alarm sales soar, the burden of victimization will be displaced, falling even more squarely on families that don't have much to lose but do have a great deal of trouble replacing stolen items.

Up to this point, several problems have been identified: alarm companies may be taking advantage of fears they stir up through their advertising slogans; alarm systems may not deliver all that the manufacturers promise, in terms of deterring intruders, limiting losses, and capturing burglars red-handed; and, if visible signs of protection do have a deterrent effect, the effect on society may be to deflect burglars from preying on the privileged to preying on the underprivileged. One further problem deserves attention: false alarms.

When burglar alarm sales began to take off, police departments enthusiastically agreed to coordinate their efforts with private security monitoring stations. The police anticipated increased opportunities to halt crimes in progress. But serious flaws in this scenario quickly became evident. Most of the time—in over 90 percent of all responses, in fact—the police find that they are answering false alarms. Investigating alarms that have malfunctioned or been tripped off innocently and accidently wastes police officers' time and taxpayers' money. For example, one district covered by the Metro-Dade County police in Florida reported that 229 out of 230 alarm calls were false (Clark, 1988). The Los Angeles Police Department estimated that 10 percent of all calls for assistance were responses to burglar alarms, of which 98 percent were false alarms, costing police two hundred thousand hours that could have been used for other services. In New York City, some midtown precincts waste more than 30 percent of their patrol car runs checking out false alarms. Local governments and law enforcement agencies have been forced to crack down on "alarm abusers" by adopting various measures: requiring a permit to own a home alarm system, requiring a license to install alarm devices, fining owners of chronically false alarm systems, and ignoring alarms that have "cried wolf" too many times in the past. Since these measures discourage people from purchasing alarm systems, the security hardware industry has set up a foundation to research ways of reducing false alarms (Duncan, 1985; "L.A. Police," 1982; Buder, 1981).

Clearly, the attention directed at burglary victims by businesses that sell alarm systems has had mixed effects. The proliferation of security devices has not yet been matched by a decrease in break-ins or alarm-related problems. Surely some intended victims have been spared from harm because blaring alarms frightened intruders away (these incidents would be classified as attempts, as opposed to successfully completed break-ins). A smaller number of victims have lost less because the commotion of the alarm drove burglars to rush through the premises and overlook valuables. An even smaller number of victims have enjoyed the satisfaction of knowing that the thieves who targeted them were caught red-handed by the police, thanks to alert neighbors or monitoring services or passing patrol officers. But these benefits must be weighed by policymakers (using studies conducted by criminologists and victimologists) against the social costs of this private solution to the crime problem: the unrealistically heightened fears due to exploitative advertising campaigns, the geographical and socioeconomic redistribution of the burden of burglary, and the wasting of scarce police resources.

Social Movements: Taking Up the Victim's Cause

Aside from having been harmed by criminals, victims have very little in common. They differ in age, gender, race, class, political orientation, and in many other important ways. Yet, as various kinds of victims gain recognition, sustained efforts are being made to organize them into self-help groups and to recruit these groups into a larger social movement. This victims' rights movement is now a large and diverse coalition of activists, self-help groups, and even government-financed organizations that act together to lobby for increased rights and expanded services. The movement's base is composed of over 2,000 private and independent projects, government-funded programs, and support groups that have sprung up across the country since the mid-1970s. The activities of its members include demonstrating at trials; lobbying for new rights; educating the public about the victim's plight; training criminal justice professionals and care givers; setting up research institutes and information clearinghouses; initiating experiments to improve advocacy, counseling, and emergency help; and meeting together at conferences to share ideas and experiences. The guiding principle holding this coalition together is that victims who otherwise would feel powerless, guilty, and enraged can regain a sense of control over their lives through practical assistance, mutual support, and involvement in the criminal justice process (Friedman, 1985). But, like any other social movement, this one has had its share of successes, defeats, rivalries, and factional fighting.

The emergence, growth, and development of the victims' rights movement has been fostered by campaigns conducted by members of other social movements whose aims coincided with the goals of particular groups of victims. The most important contributions to the progress of the victims' rights movement are being made by those in the law-and-order movement, the women's movement, and the civil rights and civil liberties movements.

The Law-and-Order Movement

The first social movement to rediscover crime victims was the conservative, hard-line law-and-order movement. Alarmed by an upsurge in street crime, the groups in this coalition launched a political campaign to convince public officials to support "get tough" policies toward offenders. The strength of this movement grows as people worry more about becoming a victim than about being falsely accused and unjustly punished (Hook, 1972). Law-and-order groups are particularly opposed to Supreme Court decisions that have restrained the state's (that is, the criminal justice system's) power to take action against individuals (as suspects, defendants, and prisoners). The rediscovery of crime victims provides the law-and-order movement with a symbolic lone individual (as a replacement for the government) to counterpose against the figure of the accused or convicted person when discussing questions of fairness and rights. Instead of arguing about the powers of the government versus the rights of the individual, law-and-order advocates equate the rights of the victim with the rights of the criminal. They charge that the scales of justice are unfairly tilted in favor of the wrongdoer at the expense of the innocent injured party. Once the victim of theft or violence is substituted for the government in the formulation, the issue appears to be one of undeserving offenders enjoying privileges while sympathetic figures must endure needless hardships, neglect, and restrictions.

In the victim-oriented criminal justice system that this movement seeks, punishment would be more heavily emphasized, and permissiveness — unwarranted leniency — rooted out. The imprisonment of convicted persons would be more certain, swift, and severe, and the granting of bail, probation, and parole would be restricted. Police, prosecutors, and prison officials would exercise greater power over offenders, to ensure that they would be punished more harshly as a way of vindicating victims.

Advocates of law-and-order policies that would enhance the government's ability to lock up troublemakers denounce their opponents as "pro-criminal" and "anti-victim" (see Carrington, 1975). At the same time, their opponents accuse them of seeking to undermine the fundamental principles of criminal justice within a democratic framework: the presumption that the accused is innocent unless proven guilty; the need for corroboration beyond the complainant's testimony in order to convict; and the exclusion of illegally obtained evidence from consideration in court. The assumption made by law-and-order advocates that all victims want harsh penalties to be imposed on their behalf also draws fire. Forcing the perpetrator to suffer does not really alleviate the victim's distress, nor does degrading the wrongdoer erase the humiliation felt by the injured party. Actually, under the guise of granting victims more rights to pursue what law-and-order advocates consider justice, the law-and-order movement extends the degree of control exercised by the administrators of the state machinery over all citizens (Fattah, 1986; Henderson, 1985).

The Women's Movement

The feminists of the 1800s and early 1900s fought primarily for the rights of women to own property, participate in political affairs, and vote. The contemporary movement began in the late 1960s by challenging the discrimination that women faced in education and employment. By the early 1970s, its focus had grown to encompass demands by women to control their own bodies. The silence that had shrouded the taboo subjects of abortion and rape (and later wife beating, sexual harassment, and incest) was shattered at consciousness-raising gatherings called "speak-outs," where victims shared their experiences with sympathetic audiences.

Both the anti-rape and the anti-battering movements were inspired by the feminist insight that all forms of violence unleashed by males against females are tools of domination intended to preserve the privileges males enjoy at the expense of females.

The anti-rape movement originated when radical feminists set up the first crisis centers for victims in Berkeley, California, and Washington, DC, in 1972. The volunteers who staffed the centers were often former victims of sexual assaults themselves. The centers offered a wide selection of services: hot lines for emergency advice, escorts to accompany victims to police stations and hospitals, peer counseling and support groups, self-defense classes, and referrals to other projects and agencies. But the centers were not only places of aid and comfort, they were also rallying sites for outreach efforts — public education campaigns and political organizing. Movement activists sought to counter the widely held notions that many used to try to justify the indifference or even hostile treatment to which sexual assault victims were subjected: the myths that women secretly longed to be raped, that females really meant "Yes" when they emphatically said "No!" and that rapists were merely misled by the allegedly provocative clothing, acts, words, and gestures of their victims. In fact sheets and pamphlets, anti-rape groups argued that rape ought to be reconceptualized: the act was not an impulsive outburst of uncontrollable desire and passion but rather a sign of contempt and an expression of a need to subjugate. Rape expresses violation rather than lust, and victims are innocent of any blame. Yet those who sought help from the criminal justice system were often accused of improper behavior, and in effect were put on trial and compelled to prove their innocence. To try to correct this injustice, anti-rape activists petitioned, lobbied, and demonstrated for reforms in laws and in police and court procedures. They achieved victories in nearly all states when certain anti-victim features were eliminated from rape statutes, especially double standards (compared to other crimes) concerning testimony (about the victim's past sexual experiences), evidence (requiring independent corroboration of the victim's testimony), and appropriate conduct (requiring the victim to prove that she physically resisted the rapist). Anti-rape activists also successfully pressured police departments to set up specialized and sensitized sex crimes squads, and hospitals to improve emergency room evidence-gathering procedures. A federally funded National Center for the Prevention and Control of Rape was established in 1976. A National Coalition against Sexual Assault facilitates communication between crisis centers and guides efforts to improve and coordinate services (Rose, 1977; Largen, 1981; Schechter, 1984).

Some anti-rape activists and groups went on to protest street harassment, uniting behind the slogan "Take back the night." This phrase expressed women's determination to regain the freedom to walk about without being considered "fair game" by men inclined toward verbal abuse or physical assault. Demonstrations were organized to discourage theaters from showing pornographic "snuff" films and horror movies that coupled graphic violence with explicit sex; to promote the boycotting of record companies that put out albums with covers glamorizing women in pain; and to protest other instances of the commercial exploitation of women's suffering. Activists argued that images that present violence against women as "entertainment" contribute to a climate in which too many people are indifferent to the ordeals endured by molested children, battered wives, and victims of rape. The prevalence of themes of sexual violence in popular culture—manifest in everything from cartoons and fairy tales to murder mysteries—is interpreted as evidence of the depth of woman hating in society as a whole. Marchers who want to "Take back the night" reject the well-meant advice that women should restrict their activities and observe self-imposed curfews to avoid harassment or sexual assault. They argue that any strategy that calls for women to rely on men to accompany them for protection is a self-defeating one that guarantees continued subordination (see Burgess, 1983; Lederer, 1980).

The movement to shelter battered women paralleled the pro-victim anti-rape movement in a number of ways. Both were initiated for the most part by former victims. Both developed a political position that rape and battering are societal and institutional problems rather than personal troubles and instances of individual failings. Both sought to empower victims by confronting established authority, challenging existing procedures, providing peer support and advocacy, and establishing alternative places to go for assistance. The "refuges," or "safe houses," for victims of wife beating provided services similar to those offered to rape victims at crisis centers: hotlines, advocates, consciousness-raising groups, counseling, and referrals, plus food and shelter. A federal Office on Domestic Violence coordinates activities, and a National Coalition against Domestic Violence, begun in 1978, lobbies for new administrative policies and legislation to assist battered women and their children (Capps and Myhre, 1982).

Activists in the battered women's movement argued that the time had come to reject the notion that the problem of wife beating was a family matter best handled behind closed doors. They traced the neglect and indifference shown women who have been beaten by their husbands back to beliefs about a husband's "right" to chastise, "correct," or "discipline" his wife, expressed throughout history, and in contemporary culture, religious teachings, and legal codes. As in cases of rape, those injured in domestic disturbances are often blamed for provoking their spouses' wrath, either by acting too aggressively or by acting too submissively. Like rape victims, battered women found the criminal justice system unresponsive to their needs, even though every state had laws against assault and battery long before activists focused attention on the problem. Activists groups argued that battered women were entitled to the same considerations as any other victim of violent crime: the police should respond, and make arrests, when called; prosecutors, recognizing the seriousness of the infractions, should press charges; and judges should grant orders of protection (called temporary injunctions or restraining orders in some jurisdictions) to prohibit further contacts that might endanger the victim. The movement also exposed that probation officers and family court judges were so concerned about keeping the marriage intact that they routinely sacrificed the victim's interests in regard to matters of marital counseling, mandatory therapy for the abuser, separation, divorce, child custody, visitation privileges, support payments, and attorney's fees. Through demonstrations, court-monitoring activities, and lawsuits, anti-battering advocates were able to change some policies and introduce new legal remedies and options. Yet some activists concluded from bitter experience that the problems victims of domestic battery had with criminal justice and social welfare agencies reflected deep-rooted sexist, racist, and classist features of the larger society. Attempts to bring about reform were necessary to alleviate needless suffering and even save lives, but consumed enormous amounts of time, energy, and money, and usually were either co-opted and rendered ineffective or abandoned and reversed when movement activists relaxed their vigilance and political pressure dissipated (Schechter, 1984).

Despite the prevalence of an ideology that blames victims of rape, battering, and harassment for their own plight, it is the fundamental institutions on which this social system is built that are the root causes of the crime problems women face. Offenses committed by men against women reflect a stubborn and pervasive sexism deeply embedded in the culture. With the bureaucratization and professionalization of anti-rape and anti-battering projects, however, much of the original impetus—the feminist critique that inspired these movements— has been lost: the recognition that preventing male violence against females requires profound changes in the ways boys and girls are raised, so that boys would no longer be socialized to be domineering and contemptuous of girls and women, nor girls to be passive and accommodating.

The Civil Rights and Civil Liberties Movements

For many years, the leading civil rights and civil liberties organizations have been working together to pursue common goals. The main focus of the civil rights movement has been a quest for racial equality and fair treatment in the face of deeply entrenched discriminatory practices. The central thrust of the civil liberties movement has been to preserve and extend constitutional rights and due process guarantees to all people, especially those who are poor, powerless, and unpopular.

As far as crime victims are concerned, the greatest achievements of the civil rights movement have been gained in the struggle against racist violence. In the past, the major problem was that the thousands of lynchings of minority males by racist mobs largely went unsolved and unpunished. Since local and state officials were ineffective in preventing lynchings or prosecuting the ringleaders, civil rights organizations campaigned for federal intervention. At present, their main concern centers upon hate-motivated *bias crimes*. These acts range from minor instances of vandalism and harassment (such as cross burnings) to major acts of violence (such as bombings and assassinations) that have the potential to foment intense racial and ethnic divisions. In a few jurisdictions across the country, civil rights groups have been instrumental in setting up anti-bias task forces and human rights commissions and in establishing special police squads and prosecutorial teams to deter or solve crimes that otherwise would polarize communities along racial and ethnic lines (Governor's Task Force, 1988).

Civil rights groups argue that a discriminatory double standard still infects the operations of the criminal justice system. Crimes by perpetrators who are black against victims who are white are handled as high-priority cases and are punished severely, whereas crimes by whites against blacks are routinely assigned a lower priority (unless the offenders were obviously motivated by bias and the incidents are likely to cause interracial conflict). "Black on black crime" also is apparently taken less seriously by the media, the general public, and criminal justice officials. For example, a gang rape and nearly fatal beating of a young white woman as she jogged through New York's Central Park one night by a group of teenage boys from minority backgrounds was the subject of headline stories for a week. Yet, during that same time period, the city's police were notified about 28 other first-degree rapes (those involving either violence or the threat of force). But nearly all of these attacks were committed against poor black or Hispanic women by poor minority males and therefore went largely unnoticed by the media and unsolved by the police (Terry, 1989). "Black on black crime" was rediscovered during the 1970s, when representatives of minority communities pointed out that blacks were victimized more often than whites in nearly every category of serious street crime; that fear levels were higher in minority ghettos than in more affluent neighborhoods; that intra-racial victimization was undermining the solidarity needed for progress; and that the problem of street crime and arson was destroying housing, driving away jobs, and closing down services (see *Ebony*, 1979).

Activists in the civil rights movement also point out that minority suspects may become victims of official misconduct, in the form of police brutality (or even worse, the unjustified use of deadly force), false accusations, frame-ups, and other miscarriages of justice.

Civil liberties organizations focus on the way government officials and agencies exercise their authority. The major contributions of the civil liberties movement to the welfare of crime victims has reformed the way in which complainants are handled by the criminal justice system.

Law-and-order groups calling for tougher measures against offenders have severely criticized civil rights and civil liberties groups for supporting policies that they claim "handcuff" the police and "coddle" criminals. What law-and-order groups call "loopholes" and "technicalities" that allow streetwise offenders to "beat the rap" are viewed by civil libertarians as procedural safeguards (for example, in obtaining confessions and physical evidence) that restrain the tendency of the government to overreact against individuals. Conservatives within the law-and-order movement condemn liberals and radical leftists within the civil liberties movement for allegedly showing excessive concern for the rights of suspects, defendants, and convicts at the expense of innocent victims and law-abiding citizens. Civil libertarians retort that the victims of official misconduct (like beatings) and abuses of authority (like unauthorized spying) by law enforcement agents, prosecutors, and prison administrators must be defended in court, not because they are sympathetic figures deserving of support but in order to prevent the development of a dictatorial police state, such as exists in many other countries.

Other Social Movements

Other social movements, besides those concerned with law and order, women's equality, civil rights, and civil liberties, have contributed to public awareness of the victim's plight. Most notable among the social movements that have rallied to the defense of specific kinds of street crime victims, starting in the 1960s and 1970s and continuing through the 1980s, are those that champion the causes of children's rights, senior citizens' rights, homosexual rights, and self-help.

Members of the children's rights movement campaign against the physical abuse, sexual abuse, and neglect of children. Their successes include more-effective parenting programs; stricter reporting requirements; less stringent requirements for arrest, prosecution, and conviction; greater sensitivity to the needs of victimized children as complaining witnesses; and enhanced protection and prevention services.

Activists in the senior citizens' movement are concerned about the abuse of older persons by care givers as well as street crimes committed against elderly victims. As a result of their campaigns in some jurisdictions, special police squads have been formed to protect older persons from younger persons, stiffer penalties apply when victims are over sixty, and extra benefits and forms of assistance are available to those who are harmed financially and physically.

The gay rights movement has called attention to the vulnerability of homosexuals and lesbians to robbery, blackmail, mobster exploitation, and police harassment. Gay anti-violence task forces have pointed out that street attacks against suspected homosexuals and lesbians have escalated since the outbreak of the AIDS epidemic and should be counted and prosecuted as serious bias-motivated crimes.

Groups loosely affiliated around the theme of self-help can be credited with some of the most dramatic advances on behalf of crime victims. They unite the participatory spirit of the grass roots protest movements of the 1960s and the self-improvement ideals of the human-potential movement of the 1970s. Self-help groups tend to be impatient with and distrustful of large distant bureaucracies and detached professional care givers. Their simple organizing principle is to bring together individuals who share the same problems. The groups provide mutual assistance and dependable support networks. Their underlying assumption is that the most-effective aid and insights come from people who have directly experienced and overcome similar hardships themselves. By accepting the role of helper and caring for others, victims facilitate their own recoveries. They empower themselves to cope with the distressing situations that arise in everyday life, and they engage in political activism to spare others such anguish in the future (Gartner and Riessman, 1980).

Victims' rights organizations, like any organization, risk losing sight of their original purposes. Further, within the movement itself, as in any movement, charismatic persons may wield disproportional influence. "Moral entrepreneurs" may lead crusades to enhance their own statuses, and in some situations, victims may end up exploited by the very persons who claim to champion their interests. Finally, as in all struggles for power, the gains won by groups and coalitions within the victims' movement might later be co-opted or erased by those with antagonistic (or simply different) interests, including administrators and professionals within the criminal justice system.

The social movements that have stimulated the growth of the victims' rights movement, and the self-help groups that comprise its base, need to be studied more closely by victimologists. The demographic characteristics of their membership and backers, and their alliances and rivalries, must be analyzed objectively, and their effectiveness as advocates for their constituents assessed. In addition, the meaningfulness of the changes they have brought about in terms of public consciousness of victims' plights and in the exercise of new rights by victims within the criminal justice process has to be evaluated (Smith, 1985).

The Continuing Process of Rediscovery

There is no end in sight to the process of discovering and rediscovering victims. All kinds of victims are beginning to receive the attention, concern, care, and assistance they deserve. They are being rediscovered by investigative journalists who put together feature stories, entrepreneurs who put out new lines of personal safety products, social scientists who explore their plight at conferences, legislators who introduce new laws to benefit them, and self-help groups that organize support networks to overcome the isolation that has divided them.

Since the late 1960s, and accelerating throughout the 1970s and 1980s, both in the United States and in other countries, victims of street crimes like murder, rape, robbery, assault, burglary, and auto theft have received most of the attention. Also in the public eye have been battered women, physically abused and sexually molested children, and neglected and frail elderly persons. During the 1980s, tremendous outpourings of concern were directed at missing and presumably kidnapped children, motorists injured or killed by drunk drivers, innocent persons singled out for attack because of their race or ethnicity, and hostages seized by terrorists.

A steady stream of fresh revelations appears daily in the popular press, on radio and TV talk shows, and in the professional literature about groups of people whose suffering has traditionally been overlooked, such as victims of crank phone calls, and college students, police officers wounded in the line of duty, or victims of credit card fraud. In this sense, it can be said that the process of rediscovering victims goes on and on.

References Cited

ADT Security Systems. 1987. *For Under $30 a Month You Can Protect Something Priceless*. North Amityville, NY: Author.
"Alarm Systems Cut Burglary Rate in Scarsdale, N.Y." 1982. *Alarm Signal*, March, p. 26.

Barker, L. 1987. "Quotes from the Symposium." In T. Thomason and A. Babbili (Eds.), *Crime Victims and the News Media* (p. 23). Fort Worth: Texas Christian University Department of Journalism.

Briggs-Bunting, J. 1982. "Behind the Headlines: News Media Victims." In J. Scherer and G. Shepherd (Eds.), *Victimization of the Weak: Contemporary Social Reactions* (pp. 80-97). Springfield, IL: Charles C Thomas.

Buder, L. 1981. "New York Police Moving to Curb False Automatic Burglar Alarms." *New York Times*, February 12, pp. A1, B6.

Burden, O. 1984. "Home Security: A Mixed Bag of Blessings?" *Law Enforcement News*, May 21, p. 9.

Bureau of Justice Statistics. 1983. *Technical Report: Criminal Victimization in the United States, 1981*. Washington, DC: U.S. Department of Justice.

_____. 1987. *Bulletin: Households Touched by Crime, 1986*. Washington, DC: U.S. Department of Justice.

Burgess, C. 1983. "Battered Chic: Fashion's Latest Assault." *Newsreport: Women Against Pornography*, 5(1) (Spring-Summer), p.9.

Capps, M. and D. Myhre. 1982. "Safe Space: A Strategy." *Aegis* 34 (Spring): pp. 8-13.

Carrington, F. 1975. *The Victims*. New Rochelle, NY: Arlington House.

Clark, J. 1988. "Use of 'force' analyzed in Dade County." *Law Enforcement News*, June 30, pp. 1, 7.

Cohn, E., L. Kidder and J. Harvey. 1978. "Crime Prevention vs. Victimization Prevention: The Psychology of Two Different Reactions." *Victimology*, 3(3), pp. 285-296.

Davis, R., F. Kunreuther and E. Connick. 1984. "Expanding the Victim's Role in the Criminal Court Dispositional Process: The Results of an Experiment." *Journal of Criminal Law and Criminology*, 75(2), pp. 491-505.

Duncan, J. 1985. "False Alarms Prove There Is No 'Free Lunch.'" *Police Chief*, May, p. 67.

Ebony Magazine. 1979. *Black on Black Crime* (Special issue, August).

Edersheim, P. 1986. "Making Sense of Alarms." *U.S. News and World Report*, August 4, pp. 49-50.

_____. (Ed.). 1986. *From Crime Policy to Victim Policy*. New York: St. Martin's Press.

Fishman, M. 1978. "Crime Waves as Ideology." *Social Problems* 25(5) (June), pp. 531-542.

Friedman, L. 1985. "The Crime Victim Movement at its First Decade." *Public Administration Review* 45(November), pp. 790-794.

Fuller, R. and R. Myers. 1941. "The Natural History of a Social Problem." *American Sociological Review*, 6(June), pp. 320-328.

Gartner, A. and F. Riessman. 1980. "Lots of Helping Hands." *New York Times*, February 19, p. A22.

Governor's Task Force on Bias-Related Violence. 1988. *Final Report*. Albany, NY: Author.

Greenfield, J. 1987. "TV: The Medium Determines Impact of Crime Stories." In
    T. Thomason and A. Babbili (Eds.), *Crime Victims and the News Media*
    (pp. 19-23). Fort Worth: Texas Christian University Department of Journalism.
Hager, S. 1981. "Do Be Alarmed." *New York Daily News*, July 15, p. 37.
Henderson, L. 1985. "The Wrongs of Victim's Rights." *Stanford Law Review*
    37(April), pp. 937-1021.
Hook, S. 1972. "The Rights of the Victims: Thoughts on Crime and Compassion."
    Encounter, April, pp. 29-35.
Karmen, A. 1989. "Crime Victims and the News Media: Questions of Fairness and
    Ethics." In J. Sullivan and J. Victor (Eds.), *Annual Editions: Criminal Justice
    1988-1989* (pp. 51-57). Guilford, CT: Dushkin Publishing Group.
"L.A. Police Imposing Fines for Excessive False Burglar Alarms." 1982. *Law
    Enforcement News*, January 25, p. 3.
Largen, M. 1981. "Grassroots Centers and National Task Forces: A Herstory of
    the Anti-rape Movement." *Aegis* 32(Autumn), pp. 46-52.
Lederer, L. 1980. *Take Back the Night*. New York: Morrow.
Mayhew, P. 1984. "Target Hardening: How Much of an Answer." In R. Clarke
    and T. Hope (Eds.), *Coping with Burglary* (pp. 29-44). Boston: Kluwer-Nijhoff.
McDonald, W. 1977. "The Role of the Victim in America." In R. Barnett and J.
    Hagel III (Eds.), *Assessing the Criminal: Restitution, Retribution, and the Legal
    Process* (pp. 295-307). Cambridge, MA: Ballinger.
Moore, L. 1985. "Your Home: Make it Safe." *Security Management*, March, pp.
    115-116.
National Commission on the Causes and Prevention of Violence. 1969. *Crimes of
    Violence*. Washington, DC: U.S. Government Printing Office.
National Crime Prevention Institute. 1978. *Understanding Crime Prevention*.
    Louisville, KY: Author.
"Queens Girl, 14, Slain." 1988. *New York Post*, February 8, p. 1.
Rand, M. 1985. *BJS Bulletin: Household Burglary*. Washington, DC: U.S.
    Department of Justice.
Roberts, S. 1989. "When Crimes Become Symbols." *New York Times*, March 7,
    Section 4, pp. 1, 28.
Rose, V. 1977. "Rape as a Social Problem: A By-product of the Feminist Movement."
    Social Problems 25(October), pp. 75-89.
Ross, R. and G. Staines. 1972. "The Politics of Analyzing Social Problems." *Social
    Problems*, 20(Summer), pp. 18-40.
Scandia Telecom. 1986. *Who's Watching Your Apartment When You're Not There?*
    Cambridge, MA: Author.
Schafer, S. 1968. *The Victim and His Criminal*. New York: Random House.
Schecter, S. 1984. *Women and Male Violence*. Boston: South End Press.
Shelburne. 1982. *There Are No Safe Neighborhoods . . . But There Are Safe Homes*.
    Owings Mills, MD: Author.
Siegal, G. 1978. "Cashing in on Crime: A Study of the Burglar Alarm Business."
    In J. Johnson and J. Douglas (Eds.), *Crime at the Top: Deviance in Business
    and the Professions* (pp. 69-89). Philadelphia: Lippincott.

Smith, B. 1985. "Trends in the Victims' Rights Movement and Implications for Future Research." *Victimology* 10(1-4), pp. 34-43.

Stat Resources. 1986. *Ninety Percent of Police Believe Security Systems Slow Down Burglars*. Boston: Author.

Terry D. 1989. "A Week of Rapes: The Jogger and 28 Not in the News." *New York Times*, May 29, p. 25.

"U.S. Households Lost About $13 Billion to Burglars So Far in the 1980s, FBI Report Says." 1986. *Crime Control Digest*, September 8, p. 1.

Vertronix. 1981. "One Out of Every Four Homes in America Will Be Burglarized this Year." *New York Times*, August 4, p. A20.

Watchdog Security Systems. 1987. *Watchdog, Now . . . Man's Best Friend*. Hauppauge, NY: Author.

Whitaker, C. 1986. *Special Report: Crime Prevention Measures*. Washington, DC: U.S. Department of Justice.

Notes

[1] To avoid exploiting victims in this way, the names of the victims will not be disclosed.

2

Choosing Crime: Close Your Eyes and Take Your Chances*

Kenneth D. Tunnell

Previous research on property crimes shows that a small group of repetitive offenders is responsible for a substantial percentage of index crimes (Blumstein 1986). One study found that 25 percent of a sample of 624 California inmates were ''career criminals'' who committed 60 percent of armed robberies and burglaries (Peterson, Braiker, and Polich 1980). A more recent study of recidivists informs us that at least ''80 percent of the men and women held in local jails in 1983 had a prior criminal conviction. About two-thirds had served time before in a jail or prison, and about a third had served a prior sentence at least twice'' (Beck and Shipley 1987, p. 1).

This group of chronic offenders is labeled a ''problem population'' because during their ''careers'' in crime they are responsible for the majority of thefts, burglaries, armed robberies, and forgeries. Still, little is known about the *nature* and the *incidence* of their offending and the way in which they incorporate the threat of punishment into their decisions to commit crimes. Researchers and policy makers have not determined ''whether those individuals who habitually make criminal decisions think in different ways from other

* An earlier version of this paper was presented to the American society of criminology in Reno in November 1989. This research was made possible by a grant from the National Institute of Justice (Grant –86-NIJ-CX0068). The interpretations here are the sole responsibility of the author and do not necessarily represent those of the National Institute of Justice.

Justice Quarterly, Vol. 7 No. 4, December 1990, © 1990 Academy of Criminal Justice Sciences.

people" (Clarke and Cornish 1985, p. 161). Despite calls for greater understanding of this population, little is known about what makes them tick (e.g., Clarke and Cornish 1985; Feeney 1986; Glassner and Carpenter 1985; Paternoster 1987).

Previous research on crime neglected to examine criminals' explanations and elaborations of their perceptions of the risks and rewards from crime commission, how they make decisions to engage in crime, and how they conceptualize the threat of sanction. This weakness remains despite the recognized need for studies that employ personal and qualitative measures of deterrent effects and of the offender's perspective (e.g., Clarke and Cornish 1985; Glassner and Carpenter 1985; Jacob 1979; Jensen, Erickson, and Gibbs 1978; Paternoster, Saltzman, Waldo, and Chiricos 1982; Piliavin, Thornton, Gardner, and Matsueda 1986; Tuck and Riley 1986).

Attempts have been made to learn the offender's perspective, but these attempts have suffered from certain limitations. Previous studies of individual criminals engaged in decision-making about crime focused only on *target selection* for various crimes rather than on the decision to commit a crime— a decision that precedes both target selection and the criminal act (e.g., Akerstrom 1985; Bennett and Wright 1984a, 1984b; Maguire 1980; Moe and Bennett 1982; Rengert and Wasilchick 1985). These studies ignore the individual's assessment of behavioral options, namely to commit or not to commit a crime. Doubtless these decisions are interrelated, but they involve different assessments of different decision-making problems.

In light of the recent research on target selection and the calls or further inquiry, I designed this research, in which the central objective was to learn how repetitive criminals make decisions about committing typical property crimes and how they incorporate the various sanction threats into their assessment of various behavioral options. As a way of situating this study within a broader theoretical explanation and of relying on previous research, I used deterrence and decision-making theories for theoretical and empirical guidance. This study is not a test of these theories; rather, it incorporates some of the theoretical suppositions into the types of questions posed to the individual respondents. As a result, the findings from this study have implications for these theories and for public policy.

The social science community has developed a greater understanding of minor illegality and of the decision-making processes among individuals facing risky legitimate decisions than among repetitive property criminals (e.g., Grasmick 1985; Grasmick and Milligan 1976; Jensen and Stitt 1982). In recent years, deterrence theorists have emphasized the importance of the psychological processes of individual criminals' decision making, which includes their perceptions of the risks and rewards of crime commission (e.g., Brown 1981; Carroll 1982; Cornish and Clarke 1987; Feeney 1986; Jacob 1979). This shift in focus has resulted in the development and use of perceptual deterrence theory—a rational-choice model of criminal decision making. It highlights the importance of the actor's assessment of the potential costs and benefits of various choices of behavior.

Perceptual deterrence and decision-making theories inform us that individuals, before acting, think about the potential positive and negative consequences of their actions (e.g., Cook 1980; Cornish and Clarke 1987). The decision whether to engage in a particular act is a product of the individual's rational calculation of the expected benefits and risks associated with that act. The logic of the theories, then, informs us that if the action is believed to produce greater positive than negative results, the actor is more than likely to proceed. In such a case it can be said that the rewards are believed to outweigh the risks. On the other hand, if the actor believes that the act will produce greater negative than positive consequences, he or she is more than likely not to engage in the act. In this case, the risks are believed to outweigh the benefits. Individual behavior is considered the product of *rational* deliberation about the expected risks and benefits of a particular course of action, compared to those of alternative courses of action (e.g., Brown and Reynolds 1973; Carroll 1978; Clarke and Cornish 1985).

Perceptual deterrence and decision-making theories emphasize the actor's ability to relate action to consequence, which is of the utmost importance in understanding how "risky" decision problems are resolved (e.g., Paternoster, et al. 1983; Rettig and Rawson 1963; Rim 1984; Sullivan 1973; Tversky and Kahneman 1981). Relating action to consequence is a result of the actor's *perceptions* of the likely outcome of actions, which propel him or her to act in one way or another.

Research Methods

The objective of this study was to obtain an insider's description of decision making among this overlooked and very important problem population (Petersilia, Greenwood, and Lavin 1978; Peterson et al. 1980)—repetitive property criminals—and to determine how they incorporate sanction threats into their criminal calculus.

To this end, I selected a sample of 60 "ordinary" repetitive male property offenders incarcerated in a state prison system, in cooperation with the State's Department of Corrections and Board of Parole (see Table 1 for demographics). I used this particular sample of offenders to learn how they decide to commit a crime and how the possibility of legal punishment is processed cognitively and socially in a problem population. Certainly repetitive property criminals are undeterred by the threat of legal and extralegal sanctions. They may not represent the average street criminal and certainly do not represent the average

Table 1

Demographics of the Sample (N=60)

	Mean
Age	34
Years of Education	10
Age at First Arrest	11

Racial composition: 38 white, 22 black.

citizen, but they belong to a population that society would like most to see deterred (see Table 2 for numbers of self-reported crimes).

I used three criteria in the sample selection. First, each respondent must have been serving at least his second prison incarceration for felony property crimes. Second, one of these incarcerations must have been for either burglary or armed robbery. Because these offenses represent the most "serious" types of index property crimes, it was important to select a sample of criminals who had histories of committing such crimes frequently. Third, each respondent had to be at least 25 years of age. I used this minimum age to eliminate younger participants from the sample for two reasons. First, this research depended on individual self-reflection of the kind that often eludes young adults. In addition, because sample members were required to be serving at least their second incarceration, they would have had opportunities to commit many more crimes than individuals below age 25.

The sample was limited to males because they represent ordinary property offenders more fully. Research shows that males account for the great majority of all serious property crimes and that females traditionally have not been involved actively in such crimes as burglary and armed robbery (Mann 1984; Morris 1987).

I contacted each of the 60 by letter, told him of the research, and said that I would visit him soon in prison. After agreeing to participate in the project, each respondent was interviewed in a private conference room that had been arranged by prison officials. Each participant and I had complete privacy; on those rare occasions when a prison official entered the room, we ceased our conversation immediately. This privacy further assured the participants of confidentiality. Each interview lasted from one to three hours. Much of the interview focused on one specific crime, the events leading up to that crime, the individual's description of his thoughts and conversations during the actual decision, and his thoughts of arrest and confinement. The crime itself and the target were only of peripheral interest. I asked each respondent to recall the most recent and most typical crime he had committed and could remember clearly. At that point we reconstructed

Table 2

Total Number of Self-Reported Crimes by Type and Number of Offenders

Crime Type	Number of Offenders	Total Number Committed*
Armed robbery	29	1,080
Strong-armed robbery	17	907
Residential burglary	43[a]	5,011
Business burglary	43[b]	2,441
Auto theft	37	3,400
Shoplifting	40	4,040
Dealing stolen goods	43	13,946
Forgery	24	6,441
Grand theft	41	7,581
Petty theft	38	3,879
Total number of crimes committed		48,626

* These figures represent self-report data. The participants were asked whether they had committed each of these crimes. If the answer was affirmative, they were asked how many they had committed as a juvenile, as a young adult, and as an adult. I also asked them about the frequency with which they had committed each of the self-reported crimes. The only possible validity check was to compare the types of crimes they reported committing with their official arrest and incarceration records. If they reported committing several burglaries, I expected to find some indication of burglary among their official arrest records. Again, such a method of data collection presents problems.

[a] nine of the 43 reported that they had committed no business burglaries;

[b] eight of the 43 reported that they had committed no residential burglaries.

in temporal order all events that occurred both before and during the crime. The emphasis, however, was on the individual's *decision* to commit the crime.

Because this research was informed by decision-making and deterrence theories, I gave attention to variables indicative of decision-making processes, namely the individual's knowledge and perceptions of the likely positive and negative consequences of his actions, the alternatives he considered in resolving the decision problem, and the neutralization technique (if applicable) that facilitated his decision to participate in the risky decision or event. The interviews were audiotaped and later were transcribed. Then I subjected the interview transcripts to qualitative analysis whereby I sought out patterns and constructed typologies from the indepth descriptions.

The interviews produced 60 detailed descriptions of how the offenders reached the decision to commit a crime. In other words, they yielded a retrospective description of the offenders' *criminal calculus*. I accomplished this by asking the participants to describe specifically 1) the most recent and most typical crime they had committed, 2) the context within which they reached the decision to commit the crime, and 3) their method of assessing the perceived risks and rewards of committing the crime. These three lines of inquiry produced the nucleus of the data for this study.

Findings and Theoretical Implications

Until this point in their lives, these offenders certainly had been undeterred by the threat of legal sanction. Only after having served at least two prison sentences and after suffering serious extralegal consequences did the majority claim that they would desist from committing property crimes. What aspect of the nature of their decision making and of their perceptions of legal punishment explains why the deterrent effect was lacking until now?

Three themes were most common in explaining the absence of deterrent effects on these respondents' actions. First, they believed that they would not be caught for their crimes (the most active criminals, high-rate offenders, knew from personal experience that the probability was low). Second, they believed that if they were caught, they would be imprisoned for a relatively short time. Third, they considered prison to be a nonthreatening environment. Each of these themes is explicated below; they suggest that the most active property offenders operate beyond the reach of the law and of policies designed to deter criminal behavior.

Getting Caught: Fat Chance

All 60 respondents reported that they (and nearly every thief they knew) simply do not think about the possible legal consequences of their criminal actions before committing crimes. This is especially true for criminals of grave concern to deterrence-minded policy makers—those who commit crimes at a very high rate. Rather than thinking of the possible negative consequences of their actions, those offenders reported thinking primarily of the anticipated positive consequences.

Deterrence and decision-making theories inform us that "risk" ideally is conceptualized and evaluated before acting. Again, however, contrary to decision-making theories, those few participants who conceptualized the possible negative consequences of their actions when deciding to commit a crime reported that they did not evaluate them. They managed to put thoughts of negative consequences out of their minds to complete the crime. Their fear was neutralized as they turned away from signs of danger. This finding suggests that the use of fear to influence behavior through punitive policies for repeat property criminals may be misplaced and may lack empirical support.

Even more important, the respondents reported that they rarely thought of the prison environment or their incarceration. Fifty-two reported that they simply believed they would not be caught and refused to think beyond that point. One 29-year-old rural burglar, who fancied himself an outlaw in the fashion of John Dillinger, reported the following during our conversation:

> Come on, now. You're not saying you didn't think about getting caught, are you?
>
> I never really thought about getting caught until, pow, you're in jail, you're in juvenile or something. That's when you go to think about it.

An inner-city hustler reported similar thoughts.

> So how much do you think you feared getting caught?
>
> I didn't. I never did think about it really. Not to a point that it would make me undecided or anything like that. I knowed I wasn't supposed to get caught. I just figured every time I wouldn't get caught. I never thought that I would get caught for nothing that I did.

During the crime, thinking of risks was distracting and interfered with performing well. I asked a 33-year-old burglar who specialized in stealing kitchen appliances from newly built apartment complexes about his thoughts of risks before committing a crime.

> As you did burglaries, what came first-the crime or thinking about getting caught for the crime?
>
> The crime comes first because it's enough to worry about doing the actual crime itself without worrying about what's going to happen if you get caught.

Even those who knew the possible consequences of their actions functioned with the belief that they would not be apprehended or suffer. The following conversation with a 29-year-old armed robber illustrates how he made the decision to commit a crime even though he was aware of the potential negative consequences.

> So, it sounds like as you were approaching an armed robbery you thought about going to prison.
>
> Yeah.
>
> And you said you also knew that your mama knew what you were into, and you said that bothered you.
>
> Yeah.
>
> And you also just now said you were worried about getting killed or killing somebody. So knowing all those things . . . how did you manage to go ahead and do the armed robberies?
>
> I was doing it just to get money. I didn't really . . . think about all the trouble . . . I'd end up in or anything.

Nearly all offenders claimed to have thought rarely of the potential legal consequences of criminality. Table 3 illustrates not only that thoughts of legal consequences were considered rarely, but that such thoughts changed with age (see, e.g., Shover 1985).

The decision-making process appears *not* to be a matter of rational evaluation or calculation of the benefits and risks that these criminals perceive as possible. Rather, they consider only the benefits; risks 1) are thought about only rarely or 2) are considered minimally but are put out of their minds. Risk was a distraction to those individuals. The decision was a matter of how to commit the crime. It was predicated on the anticipated benefits, *not* on the calculated expected outcome of the benefits versus the risks. The offenders put the possible negative consequences out of their minds; such perceptions of consequences distracted them from the act itself. A few reported that they could not commit a crime if negative thoughts lingered in their minds. If they were unable to rid themselves of these perceptions, they would not go through with the act. Thus in this sample, risk does not appear in the calculus of typical crimes. When perception of risk surfaces, it is evaluated (e.g., the individual asks whether it is instinctive or real) and acted upon. Typically the offender casts it aside and considers it a nuisance.

Table 3

Those Who Reported Not Worrying about Arrest and Incarceration by Percentage and Age Category

Response	Juvenile[a]	Young Adult[b]	Adult[c]
Never or occasionally worried about arrest	60	56.7	21.7
Never or occasionally worried about going to jail	66.7	60	28.3
Chances of arrest[d]	61.7	51.7	21.7
Chances of incarceration[d]	60	50	18.3

[a] Younger than age 18
[b] Ages 18 through 26
[c] Age 27 and older
[d] Responses are based on an eight-point Likert scale: 1 represents the belief that they had no chance of being arrested or incarcerated, and 8 represents a certain chance. The respondents were asked to state their perceptions of their chances for the three age periods. These figures represent cumulative percentages for numbers 1 through 4 on the eight-point scale.

Because this sample of repetitive property offenders believed that they would not be apprehended or punished for their crimes, they were undeterred.

Getting Caught: No Time

Many of the offenders had unrealistic or erroneous perceptions of the severity of the punishment for their crimes. Each participant reported that he knew his actions were illegal, and therefore did his best to avoid capture. Yet, a surprising number (N=32) did not know the severity of the punishment for their offenses before their arrest. Most learned the "going rate" *after* arrest (Walker 1985).

The respondents' perceptions of the severity of legal sanction were unrealistic. Therefore risk carried less weight than ideally it should have carried. One armed robber (the same as mentioned above) thought that his first conviction would yield a probationary sentence rather than a lengthy prison term. He never considered his chances of going to prison for a long time.

> So, before you learned the penalty for armed robbery, did you know that you could go to the penitentiary for it?
>
> I hadn't never got caught for robbery or nothing. I thought I'd go to jail and they'd put me on probation or something the first two times. So I really didn't pay too much attention to the penalty because I knew if I got caught that first time I might spend a few days in jail and I knew that my first time . . . I could get probation since it was my first offense. After my first conviction, five years for robbery, I really found out the penalty.

The offenders typically believed that the prison sentence for their actions would be less than the actual prescriptive punishment. I posed the following question to an inner-city offender who typically committed both armed robbery and strong-armed robbery.

> Did you have knowledge of the potential penalty for doing [strong-armed robbery]?
>
> In the state of _____, absolutely not. This Class X crime penalty that's supposed to be a deterrent . . . I wasn't aware of any Class X. I wasn't aware of any penalties whatsoever.

The rationality of the respondents' decisions is debatable because they could not have considered realistically the possible outcomes of their actions. They were predisposed to calculate erroneously because they assessed the degree of punishment unrealistically.

> I asked a participant who "specialized" in burglary about his worries of incarceration as a juvenile.

Did you know you could get some time as a juvenile for burglary?

Everybody told me, said, "Hey, all they're going to do is give you probation."

These offenders resolved problems about criminal decisions with less than full knowledge of the real possible outcomes of various decisions and actions.

Going to Prison: No Threat

Before their first incarceration, when considering a prison environment, these men thought of the same types of threats as nearly every other individual (e.g., physical and verbal abuse, threats of sexual assault, no contact with the outside world). During their first incarceration, however, they reached the conclusion that the state's punishment for committing property crimes was not as severe as they had feared. The worst punishment that the state could impose on them could be endured relatively easily; from that time on they viewed it as no great threat. The following dialogue with a 28-year-old burglar with a tenth-grade education illustrates how he came to define prison as a fairly insignificant threat and also to believe that it contributed to his manhood.

Prison must not be much of a threat to you.

It's not. Prison wasn't what I thought it was.

What do you mean by that?

When I went in . . . well, at that point in time it was kind of an awful thing to go to prison. That's what I had always heard, but when I got there and then found out the "Well hell, look who is here". . . "I didn't know he was here or they was here". . . And then I seen that I'm a man just like they are and I can make it, and I went and come back so quick.

These individuals learned the ins and outs of the correctional system (e.g., sentence reduction for "good and honor time"). They could rationalize their sentences more easily by knowing that actually they would not serve the full term. While committing crimes after they had learned the system, they calculated another prison sentence as a fairly insignificant threat. I held the following conversation with a 42-year-old who had committed dozens of residential burglaries and who also had served six prison sentences.

When I asked you how much time you did, you said "Nothing, 18 months." Did that not seem like much time to you?

I always thought it wasn't nothing because I went and did it and come on back here. But it really wasn't eighteen months, it was thirteen months and something. See they give me eighteen months . . . they give me so much off for good behavior. Just like this time I'm doing now. To you

> fifteen years would be a lot of time because you don't quite understand it, but after you get into the system here then they give you so many points for this and so many points for that . . . and when you get through looking at that you really don't have to stay as long as you might think.

Incarceration was no threat to many of these individuals (N=36), who calculated it as a less than serious negative consequence. Even those few who did consider the potential for legal punishment and those who had encountered it previously perceived it as not a great threat.

While serving their first prison sentence, these offenders acquired a typical education about prison lifestyles and learned for the first time about prison sentences. For most of them this knowledge was new. Afterward some offenders desisted from crime for a while. They attributed this decision to 1) their new knowledge of legal punishment and the threat it imposed and 2) extralegal factors in their lives (e.g., new family commitments, abstinence from drugs and alcohol, legitimate employment). During this period, some claimed to have considered and pursued legitimate alternatives to crime for the first time since they began to commit crimes frequently. They also reported going through phases of desistance which were not related to the threat of legal sanction. Rather, these phases were related to periods when conditions in their lives were positive and rewarding.

According to these findings, the most significant argument against deterrence theory and deterrence-guided policy is that the majority who desisted temporarily did so for reasons other than the threat of legal sanction. These findings give some support to "temporary deterrence," since the offenders desisted for a while because of the threat of legal punishment. Recent research suggests that desistance "is not necessarily permanent and may simply be part of a continuing process of lulls in the offending of persistent criminals" (Clarke and Cornish 1985, p. 173). Thus these respondents could be labeled cyclical or temporary desisters.

Those who did *not* desist for a time and who continued to commit crimes after their first incarceration changed their decision making in one of two ways. Some thought about the possibility of legal sanction much more than in the past. This thinking often led, at best, to a minimal increase in planning a crime. Others claimed that they simply chose not to think about the legal consequences of their actions. Such a choice was one of several neutralization techniques used by the participants to enable them to commit a crime even in the face of real consequences.

While committing crimes, most of the respondents (N=51) considered themselves immune from arrest and incarceration, although they believed that every habitual criminal eventually would be arrested. In their "profession" they internalized and exhibited what Tom Wolfe (1979) referred to among test pilots as the "right stuff." Their belief in their own immunity disallowed adequate consideration of the likelihood of legal consequences.

Although these participants had served several cumulative years in prison, few had served many years in a single prison term. Now, however, because of their habitual criminal involvement and their histories of repetitive incarcerations, they were faced with the threat of reincarceration as habitual criminals if they should be convicted of further property crimes. (States with "habitual criminal" statutes mandate that habitual criminal convictions result in a lifetime prison sentence.) Fifty-five percent of the sample (N=33) reported that they had been threatened with trial as habitual criminals. The respondents also said that they believed their chances of rearrest were greater now than at any point in their lives, and that their arrest on new criminal charges certainly would result in another prison sentence. This finding is similar to those of previous research efforts with chronic offenders (e.g., Petersilia et al. 1978; Shover 1985).

The participants also reported that they believed any future prison sentence would be long—given their age, too long for them at this point in their lives. (Table 3 illustrates the dynamics of their perceptions of the chance of arrest and imprisonment in relation to aging and the realities of long prison sentences.) All of those previously threatened with the "bitch" claimed that the severity of punishment posed too great a risk to justify continued commission of property crimes. This very severe penalty may act as a deterrent to these repetitive property offenders, who already have served several years in prison, who now perceive the threat of being tried as habitual criminals as real and consequential, and who realize that age is creeping up on them.

Even so, these responses may not indicate a deterrent effect. Prisoners, when talking of their plans for life after release from prison, construct such events rather questionably. They actually may believe that they will go straight until they are released and encounter the tribulations of being a two-time losing ex-con (e.g., stigma, reduced job marketability, loss of family trust). Again, when predicting their post-release behavior, they may be unable to separate the researcher from other members of "legitimate society" with whom they have had contact during their imprisonment, even if they can do so at other times. In other words, they may convey to researchers the same assertions that they make to prison counselors, parole board members, prison administrators, prospective employers, and family members—assertions that their life of crime is finished and that they are willing and eager to make a contribution to society. They may be telling us what they believe we want to hear, or they actually may be deterred by this severe punishment at this point in their lives; such a punishment would rob them of the remainder of their quickly passing years (see, e.g., Shover 1985). Although only 33 of these respondents have been threatened with this possibility, all now are potentially eligible for habitual criminal status and punishment—the most severe penalty the state can levy on property offenders.

Conclusion

For this sample of very active repeat offenders, deterrence theory and policy lack an adequate explanation. This sample represents a criminal population that commits a disproportionate number of street crimes, and does so with little concern for the law, arrest, or imprisonment. The implementation of harsher penalties may be adequate to deter those populations who either do not commit crime or do so infrequently, but it appears to be dubious when applied to frequent offenders. They view themselves as immune from criminal sanction, and hence are undeterred. They tend to believe that they simply will not be apprehended for their criminal actions; if they are caught, they will be imprisoned for a very short amount of time. Those who actually consider the possibilities of brief imprisonment view prison as a nonthreatening environment.

Further research using larger samples of active criminals would inform us further about perceptions of legal punishment and would allow generalizations to be made to other populations of offenders. Better yet, a participant observational research design (which may be impossible) using a sample of active property criminals would contribute invaluable insight on decision making in this problem population. Such research would allow data to be collected at the moment when decisions are made rather than retrospectively.

References Cited

Akerstrom, Malin. 1985. *Crooks and Squares*. New Brunswick, NJ: Transaction.

Beck, Allen J. and Bernard E. Shipley. 1987. "Recidivism of Young Parolees." *Criminal Justice Archive and Information Network*.

Bennett, Trevor and Richard Wright. 1984a. "What the Burglar Saw." *New Society*, 2: 162-163.

_____. 1984b. *Burglars on Burglary*. Hampshire, England: Gower.

Berk, Richard A. and Joseph M. Adams. 1970. "Establishing Rapport with Deviant Groups." *Social Problems*, 18: 102-118.

Blumstein, Alfred. 1986. *Criminal Careers and Career Criminals*. Washington, DC: National Academy Press.

Borcherding, K. and R.E. Schaefer. 1982. "Aiding Decision-Making and Information Processing." In Martin Irle (ed.), *Studies in Decision-Making*. Berlin: Walter de Gruyter, pp. 627-673.

Brown, Ivan D. 1981. "The Traffic Offense as a Rational Decision." In Sally Lloyd-Bostock (ed.), *Psychology in Legal Contexts*. London: Macmillan, pp. 203-222.

Brown, William and Morgan Reynolds. 1973. "Crime and Punishment Risk Implications." *Journal of Economic Theory*, 6: 508-514.

Carroll, John S. 1978. "A Psychological Approach to Deterrence: The Evaluation of Crime Opportunities." *Journal of Personality and Social Psychology*, 36: 1512-1520.

_____. 1982. "Committing a Crime: The Offender's Decision." In Vladimir J. Konecni and Ebbe B. Ebbesen (eds.), *The Criminal Justice System: A Social-Psychological Analysis*. San Francisco: Freeman, pp. 49-67.

Clarke, Ronald V. and Derek B. Cornish. 1985. "Modeling Offenders' Decisions: A Framework for Research and Policy." In Michael Tonry and Norval Morris (eds.), *Crime and Justice: An Annual Review of Research*, Volume 6. Chicago: University of Chicago Press, pp. 147-185.

Cook, Philip J. 1980. "Research in Criminal Deterrence: Laying the Groundwork for the Second Decade." In Norval Morris and Michael Tonry (eds.), *An Annual Review of Research*. Chicago: University of Chicago Press, pp. 211-268.

Cornish, Derek B. and Ronald V. Clarke. 1987. "Understanding Crime Displacement: An Application of Rational Choice Theory." *Criminology*, 25: 933-947.

Feeney, Floyd. 1986. "Robbers as Decision-Makers." In Derek B. Cornish and Ronald V. Clarke (eds.), *The Reasoning Criminal*. New York: Springer-Verlag, pp. 53-71.

Glassner, Barry and Cheryl Carpenter. 1985. *The Feasibility of an Ethnographic Study of Adult Property Offenders*. Washington, DC: U.S. Department of Justice.

Grasmick, Harold G. 1985. "The Application of a Generalized Theory of Deterrence to Income Tax Evasion." Paper presented to the Law and Society Conference.

Grasmick, Harold G. and Herman Milligan. 1976. "Deterrence Theory Approach to Socioeconomic/Demographic Correlates of Crime." *Social Science Quarterly*, 57: 608-617.

Jacob, Herbert. 1979. "Rationality and Criminality." *Social Science Quarterly*, 59: 584-585.

Jensen, Gary F., Maynard L. Erickson and Jack P. Gibbs. 1978. "Perceived Risk of Punishment and Self-Reported Delinquency." *Social Forces*, 57: 57-78.

Jensen, Gary and B. Grant Stitt. 1982. "Words and Misdeeds: Hypothetical Choices Versus Past Behavior as Measures of Deviance." In John Hagan (ed.), *Deterrence Reconsidered*. Beverly Hills: Sage, pp. 33-54.

Maguire, Mike. 1980. "Burglary as Occupation." *Home Office Research Bulletin*, 10: 6-9.

Maguire, Mike and Trevor Bennett. 1982. *Burglary in a Dwelling*. London: Heinemann.

Mann, Coramae. 1984. *Female Crime and Delinquency*. Birmingham: University of Alabama Press.

Morris, Allison. 1987. *Women, Crime, and Criminal Justice*. Oxford: Basil Blackwell.

Paternoster, Raymond. 1987. "The Deterrent Effect of the Perceived Certainty and Severity of Punishment: A Review of the Evidence and Issues." *Justice Quarterly*, 4: 173-217.

Paternoster, Raymond, L.E. Saltzman, G.P. Waldo and T.G. Chiricos. 1982. "Causal Ordering in Deterrence Research." In John Hagan (ed.), *Deterrence Reconsidered*. Beverly Hills: Sage, pp. 55-70.

_____. 1983. "Perceived Risk and Social Control: Do Sanctions Really Deter?" *Law and Society Review*, 17: 457-479.

Petersilia, Joan, Peter W. Greenwood and Marvin Lavin. 1978. *Criminal Careers of Habitual Felons*. Washington, DC: National Institute of Law Enforcement and Criminal Justice.

Peterson, Mark A., H.B. Braiker and Suzanne M. Polich. 1980. *Doing Crime: A Survey of California Prison Inmates*. Santa Monica: Rand.

Piliavin, Irving, C. Thornton, R. Gartner and R.L. Matsueda. 1986. "Crime, Deterrence and Rational Choice." *American Sociological Review*, 51: 101-119.

Rengert, George and John Wasilchick. 1985. *Suburban Burglary*. Springfield, IL: Charles C Thomas.

Rettig, S. and H.E. Rawson. 1963. "The Risk Hypothesis in Predictive Judgments of Unethical Behavior." *Journal of Abnormal and Social Psychology*, 66: 243-248.

Rim, Yeshayahu. 1964. "Social Attitudes and Risk Taking." *Human Relations*, 17: 259-265.

Shover, Neal. 1985. *Aging Criminals*. Beverly Hills: Sage.

Sullivan, Richard F. 1973. "The Economics of Crime: An Introduction to the Literature." *Crime and Delinquency*, 19: 138-149.

Sykes, Gresham M. and David Matza. 1957. "Techniques of Neutralization: A Theory of Delinquency." *American Sociological Review*, 22: 664-670.

Tuck, Mary and David Riley. 1986. "The Theory of Reasoned Action: A Decision Theory of Crime." In Derek B. Cornish and Ronald V. Clarke (eds.), *The Reasoning Criminal*. New York: Springer-Verlag, pp. 156-169.

Tversky, Amos and Daniel Kahneman. 1981. "The Framing of Decisions and the Psychology of Choice." *Science*, 211: 453-458.

Walker, Samuel. 1985. *Sense and Nonsense about Crime: A Policy Guide*. Monterey, CA: Brooks/Cole.

Wolfe, Tom. 1979. *The Right Stuff*. New York: Farrar, Strauss, and Giroux.

3

Two Models of the Criminal Process

Herbert L. Packer

Introduction

People who commit crimes appear to share the prevalent impression that punishment is an unpleasantness that is best avoided. They ordinarily take care to avoid being caught. If arrested, they ordinarily deny their guilt and otherwise try not to cooperate with the police. If brought to trial, they do whatever their resources permit to resist being convicted. And even after they have been convicted and sent to prison, their efforts to secure their freedom do not cease. It is a struggle from start to finish. This struggle is often referred to as the criminal process, a compendious term that stands for all the complexes of activity that operate to bring the substantive law of crime to bear (or to keep it from coming to bear) on persons who are suspected of having committed crimes. It can be described, but only partially and inadequately, by referring to the rules of law that govern the apprehension, screening, and trial of persons suspected of crime. It consists at least as importantly of patterns of official activity that correspond only in the roughest kind of way to the prescriptions of procedural rules.

At the same time, and perhaps in part as a result of this new accretion of knowledge, some of our lawmaking institutions—particularly the Supreme Court of the United States—have begun to add measurably to the prescriptions of law that are meant to govern the operation of the criminal

Reprinted from *The Limits of the Criminal Sanction* by Herbert L. Packer with the permission of the publishers, Stanford University Press. © 1968 by Herbert L. Packer.

process. This accretion has become, in the last few years, exponential in extent and velocity. We are faced with an interesting paradox: the more we learn about the Is of the criminal process, the more we are instructed about its Ought and the greater the gulf between Is and Ought appears to become. We learn that very few people get adequate legal representation in the criminal process; we are simultaneously told that the Constitution requires people to be afforded adequate legal representation in the criminal process. We learn that coercion is often used to extract confessions from suspected criminals; we are then told that convictions based on coerced confessions may not be permitted to stand. We discover that the police often use methods in gathering evidence that violate the norms of privacy protected by the Fourth Amendment; we are told that evidence obtained in this way must be excluded from the criminal trial. But these prescriptions about how the process ought to operate do not automatically become part of the patterns of official behavior in the criminal process. Is and Ought share an increasingly uneasy coexistence. Doubts are stirred about the kind of criminal process we want to have....

Two models of the criminal process will let us perceive the normative antinomy at the heart of the criminal law. These models are not labeled Is and Ought, nor are they to be taken in that sense. Rather, they represent an attempt to abstract two separate value systems that compete for priority in the operation of the criminal process. Neither is presented as either corresponding to reality or representing the ideal to the exclusion of the other. The two models merely afford a convenient way to talk about the operation of a process whose day-to-day functioning involves a constant series of minute adjustments between the competing demands of two value systems and whose normative future likewise involves a series of resolutions of the tensions between competing claims.

I call these two models the Due Process Model and the Crime Control Model. There is a risk in an enterprise of this sort that is latent in any attempt to polarize. It is, simply, that values are too various to be pinned down to yes-or-no answers. The models are distortions of reality. And, since they are normative in character, there is a danger of seeing one or the other as Good or Bad. The reader will have his preferences, as I do, but we should not be so rigid as to demand consistently polarized answers to the range of questions posed in the criminal process. The weighty questions of public policy that inhere in any attempt to discern where on the spectrum of normative choice the "right" answer lies are beyond the scope of the present inquiry. The attempt here is primarily to clarify the terms of discussion by isolating the assumptions that underlie competing policy claims and examining the conclusions that those claims, if fully accepted, would lead to.

Values Underlying the Models

Each of the two models we are about to examine is an attempt to give operational content to a complex of values underlying the criminal law. As I have suggested earlier, it is possible to identify two competing systems of values, the tension between which accounts for the intense activity now observable in the development of the criminal process. The actors in this development — lawmakers, judges, police, prosecutors, defense lawyers — do not often pause to articulate the values that underlie the positions that they take on any given issue. Indeed, it would be a gross oversimplification to ascribe a coherent and consistent set of values to any of these actors. Each of the two competing schemes of values we will be developing in this section contains components that are demonstrably present some of the time in some of the actors' preferences regarding the criminal process. No one person has ever identified himself as holding all of the values that underlie these two models. The models are polarities, and so are the schemes of value that underlie them. A person who subscribed to all of the values underlying one model to the exclusion of all of the values underlying the other would be rightly viewed as a fanatic. The values are presented here as an aid to analysis, not as a program for action. . . .

Crime Control Values. The value system that underlies the Crime Control Model is based on the proposition that the repression of criminal conduct is by far the most important function to be performed by the criminal process. The failure of law enforcement to bring criminal conduct under tight control is viewed as leading to the breakdown of public order and thence to the disappearance of an important condition of human freedom. If the laws go unenforced — which is to say, if it is perceived that there is a high percentage of failure to apprehend and convict in the criminal process — a general disregard for legal controls tends to develop. The law-abiding citizen then becomes the victim of all sorts of unjustifiable invasions of his interests. His security of person and property is sharply diminished, and, therefore, so is his liberty to function as a member of society. The claim ultimately is that the criminal process is a positive guarantor of social freedom. In order to achieve this high purpose, the Crime Control Model requires that primary attention be paid to the efficiency with which the criminal process operates to screen suspects, determine guilt, and secure appropriate dispositions of persons convicted of crime.

The model, in order to operate successfully, must produce a high rate of apprehension and conviction, and must do so in a context where the magnitudes being dealt with are very large and the resources for dealing with them are very limited. There must then be a premium on speed and finality. Speed, in turn, depends on informality and on uniformity; finality depends on minimizing the occasions for challenge. The process must not be cluttered up with ceremonious rituals that do not advance the progress of a case. Facts can be established more quickly through interrogation in a police station than through the formal process of examination and cross-examination in a court. It follows that extra-judicial processes should be preferred to judicial processes, informal operations to formal ones. But informality is not enough; there must also be uniformity. Routine, stereotyped procedures are essential if large numbers are being handled. The model that will operate successfully on these presuppositions must be an administrative, almost a managerial, model. The image that comes to mind is an assembly-line conveyor belt down which moves an endless stream of cases, never stopping, carrying the cases to workers who stand at fixed stations and who perform on each case as it comes by the same small but essential operation that brings it one step closer to being a finished product, or, to exchange the metaphor for the reality, a closed file. The criminal process, in this model, is seen as a screening process in which each successive stage — pre-arrest investigation, arrest, post-arrest investigation, preparation for trial, trial or entry of plea, conviction, disposition — involves a series of routinized operations whose success is gauged primarily by their tendency to pass the case along to a successful conclusion.

What is a successful conclusion? One that throws off at an early stage those cases in which it appears unlikely that the person apprehended is an offender and then secures, as expeditiously as possible, the conviction of the rest, with a minimum of occasions for challenge, let alone post-audit. By the application of administrative expertness, primarily that of the police and prosecutors, an early determination of probable innocence or guilt emerges. Those who are probably innocent are screened out. Those who are probably guilty are passed quickly through the remaining stages of the process. The key to the operation of the model regarding those who are not screened out is what I shall call a presumption of guilt. The concept requires some explanation, since it may appear startling to assert that what appears to be the precise converse of our generally accepted ideology of a presumption of innocence can be an essential element of a model that does correspond in some respects to the actual operation of the criminal process.

The presumption of guilt is what makes it possible for the system to deal efficiently with large numbers, as the Crime Control Model demands. The supposition is that the screening processes operated by police and prosecutors are reliable indicators of probable guilt. Once a man has been arrested and investigated without being found to be probably innocent, or, to put it differently, once a determination has been made that there is enough evidence of guilt to permit holding him for further action, then all subsequent activity directed toward him is based on the view that he is probably guilty. The precise point at which this occurs will vary from case to case; in many cases it will occur as soon as the suspect is arrested, or even before, if the evidence of probable guilt that has come to the attention of the authorities is sufficiently strong. But in any case the presumption of guilt will begin to operate well before the "suspect" becomes a "defendant."

The presumption of guilt is not, of course, a thing. Nor is it even a rule of law in the usual sense. It simply is the consequence of a complex of attitudes, a mood. If there is confidence in the reliability of informal administrative fact-finding activities that take place in the early stages of the criminal process, the remaining stages of the process can be relatively perfunctory without any loss in operating efficiency. The presumption of guilt, as it operates in the Crime Control Model, is the operational expression of that confidence.

It would be a mistake to think of the presumption of guilt as the opposite of the presumption of innocence that we are so used to thinking of as the polestar of the criminal process and that, as we shall see, occupies an important position in the Due Process Model. The presumption of innocence is not its opposite; it is irrelevant to the presumption of guilt; the two concepts are different rather than opposite ideas. The difference can perhaps be epitomized by an example. A murderer, for reasons best known to himself, chooses to shoot his victim in plain view of a large number of people. When the police arrive, he hands them his gun and says, "I did it and I'm glad." His account of what happened is corroborated by several eyewitnesses. He is placed under arrest and led off to jail. Under these circumstances, which may seem extreme but which in fact characterize with rough accuracy the evidentiary situation in a large proportion of criminal cases, it would be plainly absurd to maintain that more probably than not the suspect did not commit the killing. But that is not what the presumption of innocence means. It means that until there has been an adjudication of guilt by an authority legally competent to make such an adjudication, the suspect is to be treated, for reasons that have nothing whatever to do with the probable outcome of the case, as if his guilt is an open question.

The presumption of innocence is a direction to officials about how they are to proceed, not a prediction of outcome. The presumption of guilt, however, is purely and simply a prediction of outcome. The presumption of innocence is, then, a direction to the authorities to ignore the presumption of guilt in their treatment of the suspect. It tells them, in effect, to close their eyes to what will frequently seem to be factual probabilities. The reasons why it tells them this are among the animating presuppositions of the Due Process Model.

In this model, as I have suggested, the center of gravity for the process lies in the early, administrative fact-finding stages. The complementary proposition is that the subsequent stages are relatively unimportant and should be truncated as much as possible. This, too, produces tensions with presently dominant ideology. The pure Crime Control Model has very little use for many conspicuous features of the adjudicative process, and in real life works out a number of ingenious compromises with them. Even in the pure model, however, there have to be devices for dealing with the suspect after the preliminary screening process has resulted in a determination of probable guilt. The focal device, as we shall see, is the plea of guilty; through its use, adjudicative fact-finding is reduced to a minimum. It might be said of the Crime Control Model that, when reduced to its barest essentials and operating at its most successful pitch, it offers two possibilities: an administrative fact-finding process leading (1) to exoneration of the suspect or (2) to the entry of a plea of guilty.

Due Process Values. If the Crime Control Model resembles an assembly line, the Due Process Model looks very much like an obstacle course. Each of its successive stages is designed to present formidable impediments to carrying the accused any further along in the process. Its ideology is not the converse of that underlying the Crime Control Model. It does not rest on the idea that it is not socially desirable to repress crime, although critics of its application have been known to claim so. Its ideology is composed of a complex of ideas, some of them based on judgments about the efficacy of crime control devices, others having to do with quite different considerations. The ideology of due process is far more deeply impressed on the formal structure of the law than is the ideology of crime control; yet an accurate tracing of the strands that make it up is strangely difficult. What follows is only an attempt at an approximation.

The Due Process Model encounters its rival on the Crime Control Model's own ground in respect to the reliability of fact-finding processes. The Crime Control Model, as we have suggested, places heavy reliance on the ability of investigative and prosecutorial officers, acting in an informal setting in which their distinctive skills are given full sway, to elicit and reconstruct a tolerably accurate account of what actually took place in an alleged criminal event. The Due Process Model rejects this premise and substitutes for it a view of informal, nonadjudicative fact-finding that stresses the possibility of error. People are notoriously poor observers of disturbing events—the more emotion-arousing the context, the greater the possibility that recollection will be incorrect; confessions and admissions by persons in police custody may be induced by physical or psychological coercion so that the police end up hearing what the suspect thinks they want to hear rather than the truth; witnesses may be animated by a bias or interest that no one would trouble to discover except one specially charged with protecting the interests of the accused (as the police are not). Considerations of this kind all lead to a rejection of informal fact-finding processes as definitive of factual guilt and to an insistence on formal, adjudicative, adversary fact-finding processes in which the factual case against the accused is publicly heard by an impartial tribunal and is evaluated only after the accused has had a full opportunity to discredit the case against him. Even then, the distrust of fact-finding processes that animates the Due Process Model is not dissipated. The possibilities of human error being what they are, further scrutiny is necessary, or at least must be available, in case facts have been overlooked or suppressed in the heat of battle. How far this subsequent scrutiny must be available is a hotly controverted issue today. In the pure Due Process Model the answer would be: at least as long as there is an allegation of factual error that has not received an adjudicative hearing in a fact-finding context. The demand for finality is thus very low in the Due Process Model.

This strand of due process ideology is not enough to sustain the model. If all that were at issue between the two models was a series of questions about the reliability of fact-finding processes, we would have but one model of the criminal process, the nature of whose constituent elements would pose questions of fact not of value. Even if the discussion is confined, for the moment, to the question of reliability, it is apparent that more is at stake than simply an evaluation of what kinds of fact-finding processes, alone or in combination, are likely to produce the most nearly reliable results. The stumbling block is this: how much reliability is compatible with efficiency? Granted that informal fact-finding will make some mistakes that can be remedied if backed up by adjudicative fact-finding, the desirability of providing this backup is not affirmed or negated by factual demonstrations or predictions that the increase in reliability will be x per cent or x plus n per cent. It still remains to ask how much weight is to be given to the competing demands of reliability (a high degree of probability in each case that factual guilt has been accurately determined) and efficiency (expeditious handling of the large numbers of cases that the process ingests). The Crime Control Model is more optimistic about the improbability of error in a significant number of cases; but it is also, though only in part therefore, more tolerant about the amount of error that it will put up with. The Due Process Model insists on the prevention and elimination of mistakes to the extent possible; the Crime Control Model accepts the probability of mistakes up to the level at which they interfere with the goal of repressing crime, either because too many guilty people are escaping or, more subtly, because general awareness of the unreliability of the process leads to a decrease in the deterrent efficacy of the criminal law. In this view, reliability and efficiency are not polar opposites but rather complementary characteristics. The system is reliable *because* efficient; reliability becomes a matter of independent concern only when it becomes so attenuated as to impair efficiency. All of this the Due Process Model rejects. If efficiency demands shortcuts around reliability, then absolute efficiency must be rejected. The aim of the process is at least as much to protect the factually innocent as it is to convict the factually guilty. It is a little like quality control in industrial technology: tolerable deviation from standard varies with the importance of conformity to standard in the destined uses of the product. The Due Process Model resembles a factory that has to devote a substantial part of its input to quality control. This necessarily cuts down on quantitative output.

The combination of stigma and loss of liberty that is embodied in the end result of the criminal process is viewed as being the heaviest deprivation that government can inflict on the individual. Furthermore, the processes that culminate in these highly afflictive sanctions are seen as in themselves coercive, restricting, and demeaning. Power is always subject to abuse— sometimes subtle, other times, as in the criminal process, open and ugly. Precisely because of its potency in subjecting the individual to the coercive power of the state, the criminal process must, in this model, be subjected to controls that prevent it from operating with maximal efficiency. According to this ideology, maximal efficiency means maximal tyranny. And, although no one would assert that minimal efficiency means minimal tyranny, the proponents of the Due Process Model would accept with considerable equanimity a substantial diminution in the efficiency with which the criminal process operates in the interest of preventing official oppression of the individual.

The most modest-seeming but potentially far-reaching mechanism by which the Due Process Model implements these anti-authoritarian values is the doctrine of legal guilt. According to this doctrine, a person is not to be held guilty of crime merely on a showing that in all probability, based upon reliable evidence, he did factually what he is said to have done. Instead, he is to be held guilty if and only if these factual determinations are made in procedurally regular fashion and by authorities acting within competences duly allocated to them. Furthermore, he is not to be held guilty, even though the factual determination is or might be adverse to him, if various rules designed to protect him and to safeguard the integrity of the process are not given effect: the tribunal that convicts him must have the power to deal with his kind of case ("jurisdiction") and must be geographically appropriate ("venue"); too long a time must not have elapsed since the offense was committed ("statute of limitations"); he must not have been previously convicted or acquitted of the same or a substantially similar offense ("double jeopardy"); he must not fall within a category of persons, such as children or the insane, who are legally immune to conviction ("criminal responsibility"); and so on. None of these requirements has anything to do with the factual question of whether the person did or did not engage in the conduct that is charged as the offense against him; yet favorable answers to any of them will mean that he is legally innocent. Wherever the competence to make adequate factual determinations lies, it is apparent that only a tribunal that is aware of these guilt-defeating doctrines and is willing to apply them can be viewed as competent to make determinations of legal guilt. The police and the prosecutors are ruled out by lack of competence, in the first instance, and by lack of assurance of willingness, in the second. Only an impartial tribunal can be trusted to make determinations of legal as opposed to factual guilt.

Beyond the question of predictability this model posits a functional reason for observing the presumption of innocence: by forcing the state to prove its case against the accused in an adjudicative context, the presumption of innocence serves to force into play all the qualifying and disabling doctrines that limit the use of the criminal sanction against the individual, thereby enhancing his opportunity to secure a favorable outcome. In this sense, the presumption of innocence may be seen to operate as a kind of self-fulfilling prophecy. By opening up a procedural situation that permits the successful assertion of defenses having nothing to do with factual guilt, it vindicates the proposition that the factually guilty may nonetheless be legally innocent and should therefore be given a chance to qualify for that kind of treatment.

The possibility of legal innocence is expanded enormously when the criminal process is viewed as the appropriate forum for correcting its own abuses. This notion may well account for a greater amount of the distance between the two models than any other. In theory the Crime Control Model can tolerate rules that forbid illegal arrests, unreasonable searches, coercive interrogations, and the like. What it cannot tolerate is the vindication of those rules in the criminal process itself through the exclusion of evidence illegally obtained or through the reversal of convictions in cases where the criminal process has breached the rules laid down for its observance. And the Due Process Model, although it may in the first instance be addressed to the maintenance of reliable fact-finding techniques, comes eventually to incorporate prophylactic and deterrent rules that result in the release of the factually guilty even in cases in which blotting out the illegality would still leave an adjudicative fact-finder convinced of the accused person's guilt. Only by penalizing errant police and prosecutors within the criminal process itself can adequate pressure be maintained, so the argument runs, to induce conformity with the Due Process Model.

Another strand in the complex of attitudes underlying the Due Process Model is the idea—itself a shorthand statement for a complex of attitudes—of equality. This notion has only recently emerged as an explicit basis for pressing the demands of the Due Process Model, but it appears to represent, at least in its potential, a most powerful norm for influencing official conduct. Stated most starkly, the ideal of equality holds that "there can be no equal justice where the kind of trial a man gets depends on the amount of money he has."[1] The factual predicate underlying this assertion is that there are gross inequalities in the financial means of criminal defendants as a class, that in an adversary system of criminal justice an effective defense is largely a function of the resources that can be mustered on behalf of the accused, and that the very large proportion of criminal defendants who are, operationally speaking, "indigent" will thus be denied an effective defense. This factual premise has been strongly reinforced by recent studies that in turn have been both a cause and an effect of an increasing emphasis upon norms for the criminal process based on the premise.

The norms derived from the premise do not take the form of an insistence upon governmental responsibility to provide literally equal opportunities for all criminal defendants to challenge the process. Rather, they take as their point of departure the notion that the criminal process, initiated as it is by government and containing as it does the likelihood of severe deprivations at the hands of government, imposes some kind of public obligation to ensure that financial inability does not destroy the capacity of an accused to assert what may be meritorious challenges to the processes being invoked against him. At its most gross, the norm of equality would act to prevent situations in which financial inability forms an absolute barrier to the assertion of a right that is in theory generally available, as where there is a right to appeal that is, however, effectively conditional upon the filing of a trial transcript obtained at the defendant's expense. Beyond this, it may provide the basis for a claim whenever the system theoretically makes some kind of challenge available to an accused who has the means to press it. If, for example, a defendant who is adequately represented has the opportunity to prevent the case against him from coming to the trial stage by forcing the state to its proof in a preliminary hearing, the norm of equality may be invoked to assert that the same kind of opportunity must be available to others as well. In a sense the system as it functions for the small minority whose resources permit them to exploit all its defensive possibilities provides a benchmark by which its functioning in all other cases is to be tested: not, perhaps, to guarantee literal identity but rather to provide a measure of whether the process as a whole is recognizably of the same general order. The demands made by a norm of this kind are likely by their very nature to be quite sweeping. Although the norm's imperatives may be initially limited to determining whether in a particular case the accused was injured or prejudiced by his relative inability to make an appropriate challenge, the norm of equality very quickly moves to another level on which the demand is that the process in general be adapted to minimize discriminations rather than that a mere series of post hoc determinations of discrimination be made or makeable.

There is a final strand of thought in the Due Process Model that is often ignored but that needs to be candidly faced if thought on the subject is not to be obscured. This is a mood of skepticism about the morality and utility of the criminal sanction, taken either as a whole or in some of its applications. The subject is a large and complicated one, comprehending as it does much of the intellectual history of our times. It is properly the subject of another essay altogether. To put the matter briefly, one cannot improve upon the statement by Professor Paul Bator:

> In summary we are told that the criminal law's notion of just condemnation and punishment is a cruel hypocrisy visited by a smug society on the psychologically and economically crippled; that its premise of a morally autonomous will with at least some measure of choice whether to comply with the values expressed in a penal code is unscientific and outmoded; that its reliance on punishment as an educational and deterrent agent is misplaced, particularly in the case of the very members of society most likely to engage in criminal conduct; and that its failure to provide for individualized and humane rehabilitation of offenders is inhuman and wasteful.[2]

This skepticism, which may be fairly said to be widespread among the most influential and articulate contemporary leaders of informed opinion, leads to an attitude toward the processes of the criminal law that, to quote Mr. Bator again, engenders "a peculiar receptivity toward claims of injustice which arise within the traditional structure of the system itself; fundamental disagreement and unease about the very bases of the criminal law has, inevitably, created acute pressure at least to expand and liberalize those of its processes and doctrines which serve to make more tentative its judgments or limit its power." In short, doubts about the ends for which power is being exercised create pressure to limit the discretion with which that power is exercised.

There are two kinds of problems that need to be dealt with in any model of the criminal process. One is what the rules shall be. The other is how the rules shall be implemented. The second is at least as important as the first. The distinctive difference between the two models is not only in the rules of conduct that they lay down but also in the sanctions that are to be invoked when a claim is presented that the rules have been breached and, no less importantly, in the timing that is permitted or required for the invocation of those sanctions.

As I have already suggested, the Due Process Model locates at least some of the sanctions for breach of the operative rules in the criminal process itself. The relation between these two aspects of the process—the rules and the sanctions for their breach—is a purely formal one unless there is some mechanism for bringing them into play with each other. The hinge between them in the Due Process Model is the availability of legal counsel. This has a double aspect. Many of the rules that the model requires are couched in terms of the availability of counsel to do various things at various stages of the process—this is the conventionally recognized aspect; beyond it, there is a pervasive assumption that counsel is necessary in order to invoke sanctions for breach of any of the rules. The more freely available these sanctions are, the more important is the role of counsel in seeing to it that the sanctions are appropriately invoked. If the process is seen as a series of occasions for checking its own operation, the role of counsel is a much more nearly central one than is the case in a process that is seen as primarily concerned with expeditious determination of factual guilt. And if equality of operation is a governing norm, the availability of counsel to some is seen as requiring it for all. Of all the controverted aspects of the criminal process, the right to counsel, including the role of government in its provision, is the most dependent on what one's model of the process looks like, and the least susceptible of resolution unless one has confronted the antinomies of the two models.

I do not mean to suggest that questions about the right to counsel disappear if one adopts a model of the process that conforms more or less closely to the Crime Control Model, but only that such questions become absolutely central if one's model moves very far down the spectrum of possibilities toward the pure Due Process Model. The reason for this centrality is to be found in the assumption underlying both models that the process is an adversary one in which the initiative in invoking relevant rules rests primarily on the parties concerned, the state, and the accused. One could construct models that placed central responsibility on adjudicative agents such as committing magistrates and trial judges. And there are, as we shall see, marginal but nonetheless important adjustments in the role of the adjudicative agents that enter into the models with which we are concerned: For present purposes it is enough to say that these adjustments are marginal, that the animating presuppositions that underlie both models in the context of the American criminal system relegate the adjudicative agents to a relatively passive role, and therefore place central importance on the role of counsel.

One last introductory note before we proceed to a detailed examination of some aspects of the two models in operation. What assumptions do we make about the sources of authority to shape the real-world operations of the criminal process? Recognizing that our models are only models, what agencies of government have the power to pick and choose between their competing demands? Once again, the limiting features of the American context come into play. Ours is not a system of legislative supremacy. The distinctively American institution of judical review exercises a limiting and ultimately a shaping influence on the criminal process. Because the Crime Control Model is basically an affirmative model, emphasizing at every turn the existence and exercise of official power, its validating authority is ultimately legislative (although proximately administrative). Because the Due Process Model is basically a negative model, asserting limits on the nature of official power and on the modes of its exercise, its validating authority is judicial and requires an appeal to supra-legislative law, to the law of the Constitution. To the extent that tensions between the two models are resolved by deference to the Due Process Model, the authoritative force at work is the judicial power, working in the distinctively judicial mode of invoking the sanction of nullity. That is at once the strength and the weakness of the Due Process Model: its strength because in our system the appeal to the Constitution provides the last and the overriding word; its weakness because saying no in specific cases is an exercise in futility unless there is a general willingness on the part of the officials who operate the process to apply negative prescriptions across the board. It is no accident that statements reinforcing the Due Process Model come from the courts, while at the same time facts denying it are established by the police and prosecutors.

Notes

[1]Griffin vs. Illinois, 351 U.S. 12, 19 (1956).
[2]*Finality in Criminal Law and Federal Habeas Corpus for State Prisoners,* 76 Harvard Law Review 441, 442 (1963).

4

Patterns of Female Crime

Ralph A. Weisheit

Why study female crime? If female crime is infrequent compared with that of males, does that mean it's less important? There are several reasons why an understanding of female crime is vital to understanding and controlling crime more generally. First, a study of female crime is important precisely *because* it is less frequent than male crime. Consider the following (simplistic) explanation for crime: "Crime is the result of poverty." To defend this statement it is not only necessary to show that crime is higher in high poverty areas; it is also necessary to explain why women in high poverty areas are much less criminal than men in those same areas. Accounting for female crime thus compels us to more carefully scrutinize our explanations for crime, and hopefully make them more accurate. Second, whether it is desirable or not, women are the primary socializers of children in our society. Their criminality has a more direct impact on the criminality of future generations than does that of men. In addition, most women who enter prison leave young children behind, thus creating another set of problems for the children and for society.

Discovering Female Crime

Compared with men, women have traditionally committed few crimes, and what crimes they have committed were most often minor property offenses. For these reasons female offenders were an almost invisible offender population, neglected by both the media and the criminal justice system. In the mid-1970s, however, this was to change. Newspaper and television stories, often based on the first-hand accounts of police officers, judges, or prison officials reported a dramatic increase in female crime. They also told of a new breed of female offender whose violence and aggression rivaled that of males.

Scholars studying the crime problem also began to focus on the female offender. Dr. Freda Adler echoed the popular view that female crime was increasingly violent, and that much of this change could be traced directly to the rise of the women's movement. Liberation was a two-edged sword, freeing women to engage in both legitimate and illegitimate activities traditionally reserved for men. Women began to realize that a pressing need for money could be met by armed robbery or burglary, rather than by such "traditional" crimes as prostitution or writing bad checks.

A second researcher, Dr. Rita Simon, argued that female crime was on the rise, but only for property offenses. She suggested that increases in property crime were the result of more women entering the work force and having greater access to situations in which such crimes as embezzlement and theft were possible. Women simply could not have embezzled while they were denied jobs in which they were trusted with large sums of money.

In addition to the works of Adler and Simon, other explanations have been suggested. First, however, we turn to a description of crime committed by women, compare it with that committed by men, and see how it has changed over time.[1]

Nature of Female Crime

The major source of information about female crime is provided by official police records. Although the problems with official data are well known, such records are the only sources which: (1) provide basic information on characteristics of offenders, (2) are national in scope, and (3) have been routinely collected over a number of years. For these reasons, much of the discussion will be based on police files.

Each year the FBI collects information about criminal offenders from approximately 10,000 police agencies throughout the United States and publishes this information in the *Uniform Crime Reports* (UCR). For 1989, information was provided for 28 specific offenses, ranging in seriousness from vagrancy to murder. These data show how few women are arrested when compared with men. For all offenses combined, men are arrested 4½ times as often as women. Not only are women arrested less often than men, but in both absolute terms and when compared with males, female crime is overwhelmingly nonviolent. In fact, the crimes of murder and robbery combined account for only *six tenths of one percent* of all female arrests. The offenses for which females are most often arrested are theft (shoplifting, pick-pocketing, etc.), drug charges, and driving under the influence. In fact, only one of the ten crimes most committed by women is a violent crime, simple assault, and it's rate is less than half that of theft. Even the most frequent offenses by females are rare when compared with those of males. For example, while theft is the most common female crime and drug offenses are second, males are 2½ times more often arrested for theft and over 5 times more often arrested for drugs. In short, most crimes by women are nonviolent, and crimes by women are rare when compared with those of men.

What about serious crime? The FBI identifies eight offenses as "Index Crimes," which are among the most serious offenses. There are two major categories of index crime, violent crimes (murder, rape, robbery, aggravated assault) and property crimes (larceny-theft, burglary, motor vehicle theft, and arson). Table 1 compares male and female rates of arrest for each of these index crimes for 1989.[2] The table reveals several important points about serious crimes listed among the index offenses. First, both males and females are more likely to be arrested for property crimes than for violent crimes. Second, there is no serious crime for which females are more often arrested than males. In fact, for several of the offenses the differences between male and female rates are striking. For example, males are 11 times more often arrested for burglary or robbery, and are 7 times more often arrested for murder or aggravated assault. Even the most frequent female crime, larceny, is committed 2½ times more often by males. Third, index crimes by males are more likely to be violent crimes than are index crimes by females. For males, 26 percent of index offenses are for violent crimes, compared with only 12 percent of index offenses by women. Finally, those crimes for which males are most often arrested are also those for which females are most often arrested.

Changes Over Time

The interest in female criminality spawned in the mid-1970s was based partly on the belief that female crime was on the rise and might at some point equal the level and violence of male criminality. Has female crime become increasingly violent? Examining index offenses from 1965-1989 reveals that the percentage of index crimes which are crimes of violence remains surprisingly stable for both males and females.[3] About one of every eight index crimes committed by females is a crime of violence, while for males about one of every four is a crime of violence. Further, this difference between males and females has changed little over the past 25 years, providing little

Table I

Index Crimes for 1989, with Rates of Arrest for Each Sex

Offense	Adjusted Rate Per 100,000 (a)		
	Female Rate	Male Rate	Ratio of Males to Females
Violent Crimes			
Murder	2.4	19.2	1:8.0
Rape	.4	36.6	1:91.5
Robbery	13.0	148.4	1:11.4
Aggravated Assault	53.9	372.5	1:6.9
Property Crimes			
Burglary	34.7	394.6	1:11.4
Larceny-Theft (b)	434.0	1057.6	1:2.4
Motor Vehicle Theft	21.1	199.1	1:9.4
Arson	2.3	15.4	1:6.7

(a) Based on formula presented by Steffensmeier (1978) which takes into account the fact that UCR data does not include the entire population and that there are more females than males in the population.

(b) Includes shoplifting, pick-pocketing, and other kinds of theft which do not involve force or fraud.

support for the argument that female crime is increasingly violent (see also Simon and Landis, 1991).

A second question is whether the *amount* of female crime has changed over time, particularly regarding specific offenses. For example, Simon argued that the growing number of women in the workplace would lead to a rise in embezzlement, while Adler argued that they would more frequently engage in such crimes as robbery. An examination of these offenses for the years 1965-1989 is revealing.

The crime most directly linked to occupational roles, embezzlement, is among the most stable. Rates of embezzling change relatively little over the years, showing no dramatic increase among females, and certainly not during the 1960s, when the liberation of women is said to have begun. There were increases in the late 1980s, but these were more than matched by increases in crime by males. Robbery did increase until the early 1970s, but has since leveled off, and did not increase by nearly as much as robbery by males. Thus, for robbery and embezzlement there are serious doubts about the assumption that female crime is on a steady upward spiral. These patterns over time, particularly the fact that increased crime by women occurs during years when there are also increases in male crime, also raise questions about the impact of women's liberation. They suggest that changes in crime rates over time are due to changes in society which effect both sexes and, if anything, may have a greater impact on males than on females. Either the emancipation of women occurred on a much smaller scale than has been assumed by those who study women and crime, or emancipation has little impact on female crime.

The characteristics of female offenders also raise questions about the importance of emancipation for female crime. An examination of arrest files shows that the typical female offender is unemployed, without a high school diploma, unmarried but with dependent children (Wolf, Cullen and Cullen, 1984). These women are often petty property offenders for whom crime is one method of "getting by." This is hardly consistent with the public's image of what "new" or liberated women are like. Most female offenders are from those social classes least likely to have been affected by the women's liberation movement. The warden of an institution for juvenile female offenders has noted:

> They are the furthest from women's liberation that you can possibly imagine. They want a man to take care of them in most cases. And, they use their sex to get that for them. It's a resigned hopelessness. They haven't had hope in their lives. ("Special problems of female offenders," 1991, p. 7)

Explaining Female Crime

Through the years, researchers have had a variety of explanations for female criminality. For clarity of presentation these explanations will be divided into three categories, depending on whether they primarily focus on individual factors, small group processes, or the social structure.

I. Individual Factors

Some of the earliest explanations have seen female crime as evidence of some biological deficiency or flaw. For example, in 1916 Lombroso and Ferrero published a study arguing that biological factors led to unusually sinister forms of criminality in women. While "normal" women were gentle and kind, all women had the seeds of evil in them. When this evil emerged, it resulted in a criminal woman more monstrous than any man. They also questioned the large sex differences observed in official crime statistics, suggesting that female crime was more likely to be hidden and thus unrecorded.

Many of these biological arguments were restated in 1950 by Pollak, who shared the view that females were as criminal as males and that female criminality was in part biologically based. Pollak noted that their relative lack of physical strength could not account for the relatively low rate of female crime, since technology (guns, for example) allowed women to commit crimes requiring little physical strength—such as armed robbery or murder. He believed that women were as criminal as men, but were less often caught because of their unusual powers of deceit. This superior ability to trick and deceive was related to the fact that women are born without a penis and could therefore feign orgasms without their dishonesty ever being detected. He also traced the deceitfulness of women to social rules which required a woman to "conceal every four weeks the period of menstruation" (p. 10) and to conceal from her children the facts of life.

It can be seen that many of these explanations focus on "hidden" biological mechanisms within women. The existence of these "natural" or "innate" tendencies which motivate the female offender has never been proven. Until these biological mechanisms can be more clearly specified and more rigorous scientific procedures applied, such approaches are unlikely to yield much productive information about female criminality.

There are, however, several explanations which more clearly specify the biological factors to be examined. Dalton (1961) has focused on the link between crime and the stress experienced by women during menstruation. She found that nearly one-half of all crimes committed by a sample of inmates in a women's prison were committed during menstruation or in the premenstrual period, and this association was particularly strong for first offenders. Dalton's conclusions have been sharply criticized by Horney (1978), who argued that menstrual stress is difficult to identify as a single cause of crime because:

> studies have failed to isolate a unitary pattern of symptoms experienced just before or during menstruation; rather, the reports of particular symptoms vary from one woman to the next. In fact, some of the reported symptoms appear to be direct opposites: e.g., constipation and diarrhea, insomnia and sleeping all day, fatigue and bursts of energy. . . . The syndrome is not composed of symptoms uniquely associated with menstruation or even with women, but of symptoms often experienced by both sexes under stressful conditions. (p. 26)

Horney also argued that both the timing of the menstrual cycle and the nature of its accompanying symptoms are subject to social influence, so that it is premature to assume that menstruation directly causes criminal behavior. It is just as likely that the stress of arrest and imprisonment starts the menstrual cycle, and this is particularly likely for first offenders.

Whether menstruation leads to female crime is still highly controversial. In 1981, Dalton's testimony was instrumental in the release of two British women, one charged with murder and the other, who had nearly 30 previous arrests, with attempted murder. Each successfully argued that their violent episodes were triggered by menstruation-induced stress ("British Legal Debate," 1981). In the United States, however, defense attorneys dropped menstruation as a defense in a celebrated 1982 case because it seemed unlikely that it would succeed (Press and Clausen, 1982; Bird, 1982). It is unclear whether menstrual stress will eventually be accepted as a legitimate legal defense in the United States. Complicating matters is the fact that it is often used along with the insanity defense, which is not currently a popular defense strategy (D'Emilio, 1985). In 1986, the American Psychiatric Association announced that premenstrual syndrome (PMS) would be added to the next edition of their official diagnostic manual as a recognized disorder (Boffey, 1986). Such professional recognition of PMS would ordinarily pave the way for its use as a defense in court. However, PMS was included in the appendix of the diagnostic manual, making its usefulness in the courts questionable.

In addition to menstruation, several authors have discussed the possible importance of testosterone as a biological basis for explaining the lower crime rates for females compared with males. Testosterone is the main male hormone which is associated with the development of masculine physical characteristics and behavior. It is also produced in smaller quantities by women. Gove (1985), for example, notes that high testosterone levels are related to aggression among adolescents. Since the effects of testosterone decline with age and since testosterone levels are lower in females, testosterone is offered by Gove as one possible explanation for the decline in criminality with age and for the lower rates of crime for females. As Bruinsma et al. (1981) have noted, however, there are facts which cannot be accounted for by testosterone levels:

> Bearing in mind that testosterone production in women is relatively higher before puberty and after the climacterium [menopause] than during the fertile years, one might expect increased "aggressive" behavior precisely during these two periods. . . . On the contrary: female criminality is lowest during these two periods. (p. 47)

Further, as Sobel (1978) argues, the link between testosterone production and aggression is far from clear. It is just as likely, for example, that high levels of aggression may lead to the production of testosterone.

The fact that female crime remains less frequent than male crime across time and across a large number of cultures makes biological arguments particularly appealing. Before a biological basis for sex differences in crime can be established, it will be necessary to demonstrate a biological basis for differences in the general thinking and behavior of men and women. Proof of such differences remains elusive, but research continues at an accelerated pace (see Moir and Jessel, 1991). Although specific biological factors have not been identified which provide adequate explanations for female crime, these approaches promise to generate some of the most interesting and controversial research in the years ahead.

II. Small Group Processes

It is well known that people who commit crimes often have friends who commit crimes. Further, many crimes are committed in the company of others. Erickson and Jensen (1977) have shown that females are just as likely as males to commit their delinquent acts in the company of peers. In fact, for shoplifting, truancy, drinking and marijuana use, females were more likely than males to be with friends.

While it appears that friends are important in understanding female delinquency, few studies have examined this factor. Perhaps the major reason why so little research has been done is the absence of violent female gang activities. Both on the streets and in prisons female gangs are relatively rare and nonviolent.

In the first research of its kind, Frederick Thrasher's 1927 study of 1,313 Chicago gangs found only five or six female gangs, and most of these were more like clubs than criminal gangs (1927). Thrasher did note that girls were sometimes admitted as members to male gangs, but in these cases the girls took on masculine roles, and if they chose to adopt feminine characteristics they could no longer maintain their role in the gang.

It was not until a 1963 magazine article by Robert Rice that female gangs were again recognized in the literature. Rice noted that although the females in his study identified themselves as members of a female gang, the Persian Queens, "none of the members, as far as I know, has a police record or is conspicuously delinquent in any way except sexually" (1963, p. 153). Like Thrasher, Rice argued that these "gangs" were probably more appropriately described as clubs. Although the gang was small, the members seldom congregated and rarely undertook any activity as a group, except for weekly meetings at which attendance was sparse.

In his study of the Molls, Miller (1973) noted that status for female gang members came from affiliation with a male gang. Most of their "crime" was petty and nonviolent. Their most frequent crimes were truancy, minor theft (postcards, magazines, fountain pens, etc.), underage drinking, and vandalism. Members of the Molls were only about one-tenth as involved in illegal activity as were local male gang members. And, neither their behaviors nor their attitudes reflected support for the ideas of feminism.

Some studies have found that girls are most likely to get into trouble when in mixed-sex groups. These girls are not simply following the wishes of delinquent boyfriends, but use the boys as "educators" in the techniques of delinquency (Giordano, 1978; 1979). Others have found that when girls are with male gangs, the males are more likely to postpone or avoid delinquent acts. In most cases, females are excluded from the planning or carrying out of the delinquent activities of male gangs (Bowker, Gross, and Klein, 1980).

A more recent and detailed study of female gangs was undertaken by Campbell (1984a; 1984b) who spent time with three New York City female gangs. She spent six months each with: (1) Connie, leader of the Sandman Ladies, an auxiliary of a Puerto Rican male biker gang; (2) Weeza, leader of the Sex Girls, an auxiliary of a Puerto Rican male gang; and (3) Sun-Africa, member of The Five Percent Nation, a religious-cultural gang designed to teach young black males the correct ways of Islamic life. In each case, the woman was traditional in many ways. Connie and Weeza each had several children and had child care as their primary responsibility, and Sun-Africa was fully committed to serving the wishes of her male sponsor in the Five Percent Nation. None of the women were legally married, but all relied heavily on their relationships with male companions. The three lived in conditions of poverty in which violence was a common way of life. They all knew of close friends or other gang members who had been killed in fights or while committing crimes. The Sandman Ladies and the Sex Girls expected their members to be willing and able to fight for the honor of the gang. All three entered the gangs because of male companions, either brothers or boyfriends, who first exposed them to gang life and then persuaded them to become part of it. Unlike Bowker et al. (1980), Campbell's work suggests that females may often instigate fights between male gangs by making or receiving sexual advances from rival gang members. For these girls the gang provided some stability and harmony in their otherwise chaotic lives. Criminal activities and fighting sometimes went along with membership in the gang, but companionship and security always seemed to be the primary reason for remaining in the gang.

To summarize, females are rarely members of gangs and when female gangs are formed, they are often auxiliaries to male gangs. Female gangs are nonviolent compared with their male counterparts and there is little evidence of a growing problem of female gang activity. Two of the three gangs studied by Campbell, for example, were in decline and had only a few members left.

III. Social Structure

Most arguments surrounding female criminality have focused on larger structural issues and on the "convergence hypothesis," which assumes that "as the social roles of the sexes are equalized, the differences between the sexes in terms of crime rates is diminished" (Nettler, 1978, p. 124). As noted above, however, male and female criminality has not become more similar over time. Nevertheless, the *belief* that such convergence has taken place has led to a large body of research. Further, we are faced with the even more interesting dilemma of explaining why, if women's roles have become more similar to men's, their criminality has not followed suit.

From the assumption of convergence, two types of explanation have arisen. The first is that male and female crime rates differ because of structurally blocked opportunities, and the second is that differences arise from socialization practices and differing sex-role orientations.

A. *Structurally Blocked Opportunities.* From this approach it is argued that female crime is less frequent than male crime because females are less likely to have jobs or be in positions where they are able to commit such crimes as fraud or embezzlement. Simon (1975), for example, has argued that female criminality has been on the increase, but only for property crimes (larceny, fraud, embezzlement, etc.) which are directly tied to women's employment.

Although initially popular, the opportunity hypothesis has been difficult to support. Some have found that crimes by the young and crimes of violence increased at a greater rate than would be predicted by the opportunity hypothesis. Others have noted that the increases in property offenses by females had begun prior to the late 1960s and early 1970s when the women's movement should have had its greatest impact on changing work roles.

Bartel (1979) found that increases in female crime were less related to changes in women's work roles than to changes within their *family* role. The more preschool children there were, the *less* crime was committed by married females. These findings suggest that changes in the domestic role may be more significant in accounting for changes in female crime than changes in work roles outside the home.

Finally, Weisheit (1984) examined the records of female homicide offenders between 1940 and 1983 and found little evidence of a new breed of female offender. Women in the most recent years were just as likely as their predecessors to be unemployed and were even more likely to have dependent children. Both in their personal characteristics and in the characteristics of the offense there was little to suggest that changes in the social roles of women have had an impact on those women who commit crime.

B. *Socialization Practices and Sex-Role Orientation.* Some have suggested that female crime can better be explained by differing role orientations of males and females. As women adopt increasingly masculine roles and identities, they will become more like males in their criminal activity. Thus, it is suggested that female delinquents will have a more "masculine orientation" than other females and that both property and violent offenses will increase as sex roles converge (Adler, 1975).

Research on the impact of sex role orientation has yielded inconclusive results. Most studies have found no association between masculine orientation and female delinquency. Some have found that masculinity is related to delinquency, but more for males than females. More recently, researchers have begun to realize that the ideas of sex roles and liberation are complicated issues which have no simple relationship to crime. Naffin (1985) argues that this body of research has been flawed by relying on concepts (masculinity and femininity) which are so vague and imprecise that they are of little value for research. A female rated as "masculine" by one study, for example, might be found "feminine" by another. Thus, the way in which masculinity or femininity are defined significantly influences the conclusions reached. Further, social scientists have been unable to explain *why* or *how* masculinity and femininity should be related to crime. Until these fundamental problems are resolved, it is unlikely that studies of masculinity and crime will advance our understanding of female criminality.

Some of the most promising structural-level ideas about female crime have been developed by John Hagan and his associates (Hagan et al., 1979; 1985). They have argued that female criminality was related to the fact that in our society the behavior of men and women is controlled in different ways. This is largely the result of the way work is divided and can be traced far back into our history. As national and international markets developed, work for men came increasingly to take place outside the home. Women were entering the labor force at a much slower rate than males and still kept their ties to work in the home. Thus, males came more and more to work in public places and to be monitored by the criminal justice system while women continued to be controlled in the family setting. Hagan also found that youth from the upper classes were less likely to feel threatened by the risk of punishment. He noted that:

> The core assumption of our theory is that the presence of power [which comes from being in the upper classes] and the absence of control [which is more true for males] create conditions of freedom that permit common forms of delinquency. (1985, p. 1174)

Their theory is one of the few explanations for sex differences in crime which is based on a broad theoretical framework, has been successfully tested, and is consistent with many of the facts we have about female crime.

Summary

Although the study of female crime is relatively recent, understanding the problem is of great importance for understanding and controlling crime more generally. Since the mid-1970s, there has been a growing interest in female offenders and their criminal behavior. For a while some argued that female crime was increasing at a dramatic rate, and that these changes were particularly marked for violent crime. Although the popular press may have increased its coverage of female crime, arrest statistics from the FBI suggest that violent crime by women has increased little compared with that of men. Further, there is little evidence to suggest that male and female rates for either violent or property crime are converging. Crime in America was and continues to be a predominantly male activity. Any changes in the structure of our society brought about by women's liberation or the increased participation of women in the labor force have not led to dramatic increase in female crime or to a "new breed" of female offender. FBI statistics make it clear that the crimes for which women are most often arrested are minor offenses, such as writing bad checks or shoplifting.

While female crime has been studied from a variety of perspectives, none has proven completely satisfactory. Biological explanations are intriguing but are still too rudimentary. For example, they have not addressed the mechanisms by which a *biological* factor such as testosterone might produce a *social* action such as shoplifting. Even when focusing on aggressive crimes, studies based on testosterone or the premenstrual syndrome have not been able to determine the extent to which these factors are *causes* or *effects* of aggressive crime.

Small group studies focusing on females and gang behavior are interesting, but so little work has been done in this area that theoretical explanations have not yet surfaced. We do know that female gangs are rare, relatively nonviolent, and usually an auxiliary branch of a male gang.

Finally, those focusing on the social structure have approached female criminality from several perspectives. The idea that female crime is linked to changing work opportunities for women is appealing but has not been supported by most research. Either changing work roles have little to do with female crime or, as some have suggested, women's roles have really not changed that much over time. The evidence is also weak for the argument that "masculinity" or "femininity" are related to delinquency or adult crime. Conceptual and measurement issues raise serious questions about the possibility of explaining crime by examining sex-role orientation. A more fruitful approach has focused on the differences between men and women in the way they are regulated or controlled in our society.

Overall, the study of female crime has the potential for improving our understanding of crime in general. Just as importantly, the study of female criminality tells us a great deal about the noncriminal roles occupied by men and women in our society.

Notes

[1] A more extensive discussion of the issues covered here can be found in Weisheit and Mahan (1988).

[2] Simply comparing the *number* of males and females arrested for each crime may lead to inaccurate conclusions, since there are more females than males in the overall population.

To adjust for these differences, rates per 100,000 were computed for each offense. That is, the number of crimes are reported as if there were only 100,000 males and 100,000 females in the population.
[3] Rape is excluded because it is primarily a male offense and arson was excluded because it has only been included among index offenses since 1979.

References Cited

Adler, F. 1975 (reissued 1985). *Sisters in crime*. Prospect Heights, IL: Waveland Press.

Bartel, A.P. 1979. "Women and crime: An economic analysis." *Economic Inquiry*, 17(1), 29-51.

Bird, D. 1982. "Defense linked to menstruation dropped in case." *New York Times*, November 4, p. B4.

Boffey, P.M. 1986. "3 new psychiatric categories are accepted." *New York Times*, July 2, p. 11.

Bowker, L.H., H.S. Gross and M.W. Klein. 1980. "Female participation in delinquent gang activities." *Adolescence*, 15(59), 509-519.

"British legal debate: Premenstrual tension and criminal behavior." 1981. *New York Times*, December 29, p. C3.

Bruinsma, G.J.N., C.I. Dessaur and W.J.V. Van Hezewijk. 1981. In F. Adler (Ed.), *The incidence of female criminality in the contemporary world*. New York: New York University Press.

Campbell, A. 1984a. *The Girls in the Gang*. New York: Basil Blackwell.

————. 1984b. "Girls' talk: The social representation of aggression by female gang members." *Criminal Justice and Behavior*, 11(2), 139-156.

Dalton, K. 1961. "Menstruation and crime." *British Medical Journal*, December 30, 1752-1753.

D'Emilio, J. 1985. "Battered woman's syndrome and premenstrual syndrome: A comparison of their possible uses as defenses to criminal liability." *St. John's Law Review*, 59(3):558-587.

Erickson, M.L. and G.F. Jensen. 1977. "'Delinquency is still group behavior!': Toward revitalizing the group premise in the sociology of deviance." *Journal of Criminal Law and Criminology*, 68(2):262-273.

Giordano, P.C. 1978. "Girls, guys and gangs: The changing social context of female delinquency." *Journal of Criminal Law and Criminology*, 68(1), 126-132.

Giordano, P.C. and S.A. Cernkovich. 1979. "On complicating the relationship between liberation and delinquency." *Social Problems* 26(4), 467-481.

Gove, W. 1985. "The effect of age and gender on deviant behavior: A biopsychosocial perspective." In A.S. Rossi (Ed.), *Gender and the life course*. (pp. 115-144). New York: Aldine.

Hagan, J., A.R. Gillis and J. Simpson. 1985. "The class structure of gender and delinquency: Toward a power-control theory of common delinquent behavior." *American Journal of Sociology*, 90(6), 1151-1178.

Hagan, J., J.H. Simpson and A.R. Gillis. 1979. "The sexual stratification of social control: A gender-based perspective on crime and delinquency." *British Journal of Sociology*, 30(1), 25-38.

Horney, J. 1978. "Menstrual cycles and criminal responsibility." *Law and Human Behavior*, 2(1), 25-36.

Lombroso, C. and G. Ferrero. 1916. *The female offender*. New York: Appleton.

Miller, W.B. 1973. "The Molls." *Society*, 11(1), 32-35.

Moir, Anne and David Jessel. 1989. *Brain sex: The real difference between men and women*. London: Joseph.

Naffin, N. 1985. "The masculinity-femininity hypothesis: A consideration of gender-based personality theories of female crime." *British Journal of Criminology*, 25(4), 365-381.

Nettler, G. 1978. *Explaining Crime*, 2nd ed. New York: McGraw-Hill.

Pollak, O. 1950. *The criminality of women*. Westport, CT: Greenwood Press.

Press, A. and P. Clausen. 1982. "Not guilty because of PMS?" *Newsweek*, November 8, p. 111.

Rice, R. 1963. "The Persian Queens." *The New Yorker*, October 19, pp. 153-187.

Simon, R.J. 1975. *The contemporary woman and crime*. Washington, DC: U.S. Government Printing Office.

Simon, R.J. and J. Landis. 1991. *The crimes women commit, the punishments they receive*. Lexington, MA: Lexington Books.

Sobel, E. 1978. "The aggressive female." In I.L. Kutash, S.B. Kutash, L.B. Schlesinger and Associates (Eds.), *Violence: Perspectives on Murder and Aggression*. San Francisco: Jossey-Bass.

"Special problems of female offenders." 1991. *Insight into Corrections*, April, pp. 6-7.

Steffensmeier, D.J. 1978. "Changing patterns of female crime in rural America, 1962-75." *Rural Sociology*, 43(1), 87-102.

Thrasher, F.M. 1927 (reissued 1963). *The Gang*. Chicago: University of Chicago Press.

U.S. Department of Justice, Federal Bureau of Investigation. 1965-84. *Uniform crime reports*. Washington, DC: U.S. Government Printing Office.

Weisheit, R.A. 1984. "Female homicide offenders: Trends over time in an institutionalized population." *Justice Quarterly*, 1(4), 471-489.

Weisheit, R.A. and S. Mahan. 1988. *Women, crime, and criminal justice*. Cincinnati: Anderson.

Wolfe, N.T., F.T. Cullen and J.B. Cullen. 1984. "Describing the female offender: A note on the demographics of arrests." *Journal of Criminal Justice*, 12(5), 438-492.

Section II

Justice and Injustice in the Streets: The Police

The role of the police in American Society is undoubtedly one of the least understood aspects of the criminal justice system. Philosophical conflicts in the field of criminal justice are personified in the police officer. Handcuffed, according to crime control groups; riotous, according to due process groups, the police officer finds that the role he or she must play in the criminal justice system is wrought with conflicting expectations.

There are a variety of issues which contribute to the conflict and confusion in law enforcement. While most would agree that the police mission is to achieve "order under law," it is not always easy to apply this abstract concept to street situations. The officer does not have a lawyer by his or her side when making the decision to arrest a suspect who may have been involved in a crime. The officer may feel that probable cause exists for an arrest. However, in the days following the arrest, made perhaps in a crowded tavern after a fight in which the officer was injured, the decision will be subjected to intense scrutiny.

There are a variety of situations in which the legal basis for a decision to arrest is not always clear. In these situations the officer exercises considerable discretion. The authority to search, to arrest and to use deadly force constitutes enormous responsibility for the officer. The police officer is the "gatekeeper" of the criminal justice system. The police officer who sees the victim before the blood has been washed away must act while legal issues are unclear and must temper the use of force in the face of extreme provocation. The decision

73

as to whether a person will become an arrest statistic is ultimately left to the officer.

Study of the police role was ignored for many years. There are a number of factors that contributed to neglect of study in this area. First, considerable police behavior has low visibility. That is, the police officer is generally unsupervised in many areas of decision-making and the behavior is, therefore, difficult to study. Second, many persons believed that the prosecutor and the courts made the major decisions affecting the accused. Third, the "liberal bias" of academicians contributed to a focus on the offender, often ignoring those responsible for initial decisions regarding the offender. Fourth, police departments in many metropolitan centers have been intensely political. Police officers have not been considered "professionals" in this environment and, therefore, were not considered worthy of study.

The police response to the riots of the 1960s brought to the attention of American society a host of problems in the field of law enforcement. There has been considerable research on these law enforcement problems over the past ten years. It would be impossible to summarize this research. However, it is important to understand the socialization process for the individual officer as he or she moves from the status of civilian to that of police officer. It is equally valuable to understand the complexities of police work. Finally, it is important to understand what is often referred to as the "police subculture." It is in the context of this subculture that the values, attitudes and beliefs which ultimately affect police behavior are shaped. The articles in this section address these issues.

In "Observations on the Making of Policemen," John Van Maanen has presented an analysis of the processes involved in becoming a police officer. It is important to understand the expectations the police system has of the recruit and the socialization processes which bring about realization of those expectations. Van Maanen has provided a clear picture of both the expectations and the socialization process.

In "Making Neighborhoods Safe," James Q. Wilson and George Kelling argue that police work is much more than simply arresting criminals. It is also about maintaining order and community solidarity. A growing number of police departments recognize that high technology is not a solution to the crime problem. Technology may actually make citizens feel less secure if it takes officers off the street and reduces one-on-one interactions between police and the public.

Some crimes, such as drug use and prostitution have no complaining victim and few witnesses. Investigating these types of crime requires the police to take a more active stance, often using undercover techniques. In "Observations on Police Undercover Work," George Miller describes issues raised by this approach. Not only are there concerns about recruitment and training, but undercover work can easily set the stage for police corruption and unethical behavior.

Finally, in "Reflections on Police Corruption," James W. Birch examines one of the consequences of police work for some officers—corruption. Birch, a former Philadelphia police officer, provides a graphic account of his feelings of deep bitterness and disappointment in his fellow officers and their behavior. At the same time, Birch has also provided important insights on a number of factors which contribute to potentials for corruption and the extent to which the routine often borders on the corrupt.

5

Observations on the Making of Policemen

John Van Maanen*

In recent years the so-called "police problem" has become one of the more institutionalized topics of routine conversation in this society. Whether one views the police as friend or foe, virtually everyone has a set of "cop stories" to relate to willing listeners. Although most stories dramatize personal encounters and are situation-specific, there is a common thread running through these frequently heard accounts. In such stories the police are almost always depicted as a homogeneous occupational grouping somehow quite different from most other men.

Occupational stereotyping is, of course, not unknown. Professors, taxicab drivers, used-car salesmen, corporate executives all have

*I would like to gratefully acknowledge the generous cooperation and support of men like M.C., Dave, Doug, Leon, and Jim, who, like myself, learned what it means to live by the police culture. Their integrity, honesty, and defiance of popular stereotypes make this study a most enlightening and enjoyable experience. Also, I would like to thank my academic colleagues, in particular, Edgar H. Schein, Lyman W. Porter, Robert Dubin, and Mason Haire for their insightful suggestions and assistance during various phases of this research. Finally, I wish to express my appreciation to the Office of Naval Research, the Organizational Behavior Research Center at the University of California, Irvine, and the Organizational Studies Group at the Massachusetts Institute of Technology for partial support and total encouragement throughout this project.

Reproduced by permission of the Society for Applied Anthropology from *Human Organization* 32(4): 407-418, 1973.

mythological counterparts in the popular culture. Yet, what is of interest here is the recognition by the police themselves of the implied differences.

Policemen generally view themselves as performing society's dirty work. As such, a gap is created between the police and the public. Today's patrolman feels cut off from the mainstream culture and unfairly stigmatized. In short, when the policeman dons his uniform, he enters a distinct subculture governed by norms and values designed to manage the strain created by an outsider role in the community.[1]

To classify the police as outsiders helps us to focus on several important things: the distinctive social definitions used by persons belonging to such marginal subcultures (e.g., "everybody hates a cop"); the outsider's methods for managing the tension created by his social position (e.g., "always protect brother officers"); and the explicit delineation of the everyday standards of conduct followed by the outsider (e.g., "lay low and avoid trouble"). Furthermore, such a perspective forces a researcher to delve deeply into the subculture in order to see clearly through the eyes of the studied.

Context

While observation of the police in naturally occurring situations is difficult, lengthy, and often threatening, it is imperative. Unfortunately, most research to date relies almost exclusively upon interview-questionnaire data (e.g., Bayley and Mendelsohn 1969; Wilson 1968), official statistics (e.g., Webster 1970; President's Commission on Law Enforcement and the Administration of Justice 1967), or broad-ranging attitude surveys (e.g., Sterling 1972; McNamara 1967). The very few sustained observational studies have been concerned with specific aspects of police behavioral patterns (e.g., Skolnick 1966 — vice activities; Reiss 1971 — police-citizen contacts; Bittner 1967, Cicourel 1967 police encounters with "skid row alcoholics" and juveniles, respectively). This is not to say these diverse investigations are without merit. Indeed, without such studies we would not have even begun to see beneath the occupational shield. Yet, the paucity of in-depth police-related research — especially from the outsider perspective — represents a serious gap in our knowledge of a critical social establishment.[2]

In particular the process of becoming a police officer has been neglected.[3] What little data we presently have related to the police socialization process come from either the work devoted to certain hypothesized dimensions of the police personality (e.g., dogmatism, authoritarianism, cynicism, alienation, etc.) or cross-sectional snapshots of police attitudes toward their public audiences. Using a dramaturgic metaphor, these studies have concentrated upon the description of the actors, stage setting, and "on stage" performance of the police production. Little attention has been paid to the orientation of the performers to their particular role viewed from "backstage" perspective. Clearly, for any performance to materialize there must be casting sessions, rehearsals, directors, stagehands, and some form(s) of compensation provided the actors to insure their continued performance. Recognizing that to some degree organizational socialization occurs at all career stages, this paradigm focuses exclusively upon the individual recruit's entry into the organization. It is during the breaking-in period that the organization may be thought to be most persuasive, for the person has few guidelines to direct his behavior and has little, if any, organizationally based support for his "vulnerable selves" which may be the object of influence. Support for this position comes from a wide range of studies indicating that early organizational learning is a major determinant of one's later organizationally relevant beliefs, attitudes, and behaviors (Van Maanen 1972; Lortie 1968; Berlew and Hall 1966; Evan 1963; Hughes 1958; Dornbush 1955). Schein (1971) suggested perceptively that this process results in a "psychological contract" linking the goals of the individual to the constraints and purposes of the organization. In a sense, this psychological contract is actually a modus vivendi between the person and the organization representing the outcomes of the socialization process.

Method

The somewhat truncated analysis that follows was based upon the observation of novice policemen in situ. The study was conducted in Union City over a nine-month period.[4] Approximately three months of this time were spent as a fully participating member of one Union City Police Academy recruit class. Following the formal training phase of the initiation process, my fully participating role was modified. As a civilain, I spent five months (roughly eight to ten hours a day, six days a week) riding in patrol units operated by a recruit and his FTO (i.e., Field Training Officer charged with imputing "street sense" into the neophyte) as a back-seat observer.

From the outset, my role as researcher-qua-researcher was made explicit. To masquerade as a regular police recruit would not only have been problematic, but would have raised a number of ethical questions as well (particularly during the field training portion of the socialization sequence).[5]

The conversational data presented below are drawn primarily from naturally occurring encounters with persons in the police domain (e.g., recruits, veterans, administrators, wives, friends, reporters, court officials, etc.) While formal interviews were conducted with some, the bulk of the data contained here arose from far less-structured situations. (See Epilogue for a further discussion of the methods employed in this study — eds.)

The Making of a Policeman: A Paradigm

For purposes here, the police recruit's initiation into the organizational setting shall be treated as if it occurred in four discrete stages. While these stages are only analytically distinct, they do serve as useful markers for describing the route traversed by the recruit. The sequence is related to the preentry, admittance, change, and continuance phases of the organizational socialization process an are labeled here as choice, introduction, encounter, and metamorphosis, respectively.

Preentry: Choice

What sort of young man is attracted to and selected for a police career? The literature notes that police work seems to attract local, family-oriented, working-class whites interested primarily in the security and salary aspects of the occupation. Importantly, the authoritarian syndrome which has popularly been ascribed to persons selecting police careers has not been supported by empirical study. The available research supports the contention that the police occupation is viewed by the recruits as simply one job of many and considered roughly along the same dimensions as any job choice.

While my research can add little to the above picture, several qualifications are in order which perhaps provide a greater understanding of the particular choice process. First, the security and salary aspects of the police job have probably been overrated. Through interviews and experience with Union City recruits, a rather pervasive meaningful work theme is apparent as a major factor in job choice. Virtually all recruits alluded to the opportunity afforded by a police career to perform in a role which was perceived as consequential or important to society. While such altruistic motives may be subject to social desirability considerations, or other biasing factors, it is my feeling that these high expectations of community service are an important element in the choice process.

Second, the out-of-doors and presumably adventurous qualities of police work (as reflected in the popular culture) were perceived by the recruits as among the more influential factors attracting them to the job. With few exceptions, the novice policemen had worked several jobs since completing high school and were particularly apt to stress the benefits of working a nonroutine job.

Third, the screening factor associated with police selection is a dominating aspect of the socialization process. From the filling out of the application blank at City Hall to the telephone call which informs a potential recruit of his acceptance into the department, the individual passes through a series of events which serve to impress an aspiring policeman with a sense of being accepted into an elite organization. Perhaps some men originally take the qualifying examination for patrolman lightly, but it is unlikely many men proceed through the entire screening process—often taking up to six months or more—without becoming committed seriously to a police career. As such, the various selection devices, if successfully surmounted, increase the person's self-esteem, as well as buttress his occupational choice. Thus, this anticipatory stage tends to strengthen the neophyte's evaluation of the police organization as an important place to work.

Finally, as in most organizations, the police department is depicted to individuals who have yet to take the oath of office in its most favorable light. A potential recruit is made to feel as if he were important and valued by the organization. Since virtually all recruitment occurs via generational or friendship networks involving police officers and prospective recruits, the individual receives personalized encouragement and support which helps sustain his interest during the arduous screening procedure. Such links begin to attach the would-be policeman to the organization long before he actually joins.

To summarize, most policemen have not chosen their career casually. They enter the department with a high degree of normative identification with what they perceive to be the goals and values of the organization. At least in Union City, the police department was able to attract and select men who entered the organization with a reservoir of positive attitudes toward hard work and a strong level of organizational support. What happens to the recruit when he is introduced to the occupation at the police academy is where attention is now directed.

Admittance: Introduction

The individual usually feels upon swearing allegiance to the department, city, state, and nation that "he's finally made it." However, the department instantaneously and somewhat rudely informs him that until he has served his probationary period he may be severed from the membership rolls at any time without warning, explanation, or appeal. It is perhaps ironic that in a period of a few minutes, a person's position vis-a-vis the organization can be altered so dramatically. Although some aspects of this phenomenon can be found in all organizations, in the paramilitary environment of the police world, the shift is particularly illuminating to the recruit.

For most urban police recruits, the first real contact with the police subculture occurs at the academy. Surrounded by forty to fifty contemporaries, the recruit is introduced to the harsh and often arbitrary discipline of the organization. Absolute obedience to departmental rules, rigorous physical training, dull lectures devoted to various technical aspects of the occupation, and a ritualistic concern for detail characterize the academy. Only the recruit's classmates aid his struggle to avoide punishments and provide him an outlet from the long days. A recruit soon learns that to be one minute late to a class, to utter a careless word in formation, or to be caught walking when he should be running may result in a "gig" or demerit costing a man an extra day of work or the time it may take to write a long essay on, say, "the importance of keeping a neat appearance."

Wearing a uniform which distinguishes the novices from "real" policemen, recruits are expected to demonstrate group cohesion in all aspects of academy life. The training staff actively promotes solidarity through the use of group rewards and punishments, identifying garments for each recruit class, inter-class competition, and cajoling the newcomers—at every conceivable opportunity—to show some unity. Predictably, such stactics work—partial evidence is suggested by the well-attended academy class reunions held year after year in the department. To most veteran officers, their police academy experiences resulted in a career-long identification. It is no exaggeration to state that the "in-the-same-boat" collective consciousness which arises when groups are processed serially through a harsh set of experiences was as refined in the Union City Police Department as in other institutions such as military academies, fraternities, or medical schools.[6]

The formal content of the training academy is almost exclusively weighted in favor of the more technical aspects of police work. A few outside speakers are invited to the academy (usually during the last few weeks of training), but the majority of class time is filled by departmental personnel describing the more mundane features of the occupation. To a large degree, the formal academy may be viewed as a didactic sort of instrumentally oriented ritual passage rite. As such, feigning attention to lectures on, for example, "the organization of The Administrative Services Bureau" or "state and local traffic codes" is a major task for the recruits.

However, the academy also provides the recruit with an opportunity to begin learning or, more properly, absorbing the tradition which typifies the department. The novices' overwhelming eagerness to hear what police work is really like results in literally hours upon hours of war stories (alternately called "sea stories" by a few officers) told at the discretion of the many instructors. One recruit, when asked about what he hoped to learn in the academy, responded as follows:

> I want them to tell me what police work is all about. I could care less about the outside speakers or the guys they bring out here from upstairs who haven't been on the street for the last twenty years. What I want is for somebody who's gonna level with us and really give the lowdown on how we're supposed to survive out there.

By observing and listening closely to police stories and style, the individual is exposed to a partial organizational history which details certain personalities, past events, places, and implied relationships which the recruit is expected eventually to learn, and it is largely through war stories that the department's history is conveyed. Throughout the academy, a recruit is exposed to particular instructors who relate caveats concerning the area's notorious criminals, sensational crimes, social-geographical peculiarities, and political structure. Certain charismatic departmental personalities are described in detail. Past events — notably the shooting of police officers — are recreated and informal analyses passed on. The following excerpt from a criminal law lecture illustrates some of these concerns.

> I suppose you guys have heard of Lucky Baldwin? If not, you sure will when you hit the street. Baldwin happens to be the biggest burglar still operating in this town. Every guy in this department from patrolman to chief would love to get him and make it stick. We've busted him about ten times so far, but he's got an asshole lawyer and money so he always beats the rap. . . . If I ever get a chance to pinch the SOB, I'll do it my way with my thirty-eight and spare the city the cost of a trial.

The correlates of this history are mutually held perspectives toward certain classes of persons, places, and things which are the objective reality of police work. Critically, when war stories are presented, discipline within the recruit class is relaxed. The rookies are allowed to share laughter and tension-relieving quips with the veteran officers. A general atmosphere of comraderie is maintained. The near lascivious enjoyment accompanying these informal respites from academy routine serve to establish congeniality and solidarity with the experienced officers in what is normally a rather harsh and uncomfortable environment. Clearly, this is the material of which memories are made.

Outside the classroom, the recruits spend endless hours discussing nuances and implications of war stories, and collective understandings begin to develop. Via such experiences, the meaning and emotional reality of police work starts to take shape for the individual. In a sense, by vicariously sharing the exploits of his predecessors, the newcomer gradually builds a common language and shared set of interests which will attach him to the organization until he too has police experience to relate.

Despite these important breaks in formality, the recruits' early perceptions of policing are overshadowed by the submissive and often degrading role they are expected to play in the academy. Long, monotonous hours of class time are required, a seemingly eternal set of examinations are administered, meaningless assignments consume valuable off-duty time, various mortifying events are institutionalized rituals of academy life (e.g., each week, a class "asshole" was selected and received a trophy depicting a gorilla dressed as a policeman), and relatively sharp punishments enacted for breaches of academy regulations. The multitude of academy rules make it highly unlikely that any recruit can complete the training course unscathed. The following training division report illustrates the arbitrary nature of the dreaded gigs issued during the academy phase.

> You were observed displaying unofficerlike conduct in an academy class. You openly yawned (without making any effort to minimize or conceal the fact), (this happened twice), you were observed looking out the window constantly, and spent time with your arms lying across your desk. You will report to Sergeant Smith in the communications division for an extra three hours of duty on August 15 (parentheses theirs).

The main result of such stress training is that the recruit soon learns it is his peer group rather than the "brass" which will support him and which he, in turn, must support. For example, the newcomers adopt covering tactics to shield the tardy colleague, develop cribbing techniques to pass exams, and become proficient at constructing consensual ad hoc explanations of a fellow-recruit's mistake. Furthermore, the long hours, new friends, and ordeal aspects of the recruit school serve to detach the newcomer from his old attitudes and acquaintances. In short, the academy impresses upon the recruit that he must now identify with a new group—his fellow officers. That this process is not complete, however, is illustrated by the experience of one recruit during this last week of training before his introduction to the street. This particular recruit told his classmates the following:

> Last night as I was driving home from the academy, I stopped to get some gas. . . . As soon as I shut off the engine some dude comes running up flapping his arms and yelling like crazy about being robbed. Here I am sitting in my car with my gun on and the ole buzzer (badge) staring him right in the face. . . . Wow! . . . I had no idea what to do; so I told him to call the cops and got the hell away from there. What gets me is that it didn't begin to hit me that I WAS A COP until I was about a mile away (emphasis mine).

To this researcher, the academy training period serves to prepare the recruits to alter their initially high but unrealistic occupational expectations. Through the methods described above, the novices begin to absorb the subcultural ethos and to think like policemen. As a fellow recruit stated at the end of the academy portion of training:

> There's sure more to this job than I first thought. They expect us to be dog catchers, lawyers, marriage counselors, boxers, firemen, doctors, baby-sitters, race-car drivers, and still catch a crook occasionally. There's no way we can do all that crap. They're nuts!

Finally, as in other highly regulated social systems, the initiate learns that the formal rules and regulations are applied inconsistently. What is sanctioned in one case with a gig is ignored in another case. To the recruits, academy rules become behavioral prescriptions which are to be coped with formally, but informally dismissed. The newcomer learns that when The Department notices his behavior, it is usually to administer a punishment, not a reward. The solution to this collective predicament is to stay low and avoid trouble.

Change: Encounter

Following the classroom training period, a newcomer is introduced to the complexities of the "street" through his Field Training Officer (hereafter referred to as the FTO). It is during this period of apprenticeshiplike socialization that the reality shock encompassing full recognition of being a policeman is likely to occur. Through the eyes of his experienced FTO, the recruit learns the ins and outs of the police role. Here he learns what kinds of behavior are appropriate and expected of a patrolman within his social setting. His other instructors in this phase are almost exclusively his fellow patrolmen working the same precinct and shift. While his sergeant may occasionally offer tips on how to handle himself on the street, the supervisor is more notable for his absence than for his presence. When the sergeant does seek out the recruit, it is probably to inquire as to how many hazardous traffic violations the "green pea" had written that week or to remind the recruit to keep his hat on while out of the patrol car. As a matter of formal policy in Union City, the department expected the FTO to handle all recruit uncertainties. This traditional feature of police work — patrolmen training patrolmen — insures continuity from class to class of police officers regardless of the content of the academy instruction. In large measure, the flow of influence from one generation to another accounts for the remarkable stability of the pattern of police behavior.

It was my observation that the recruit's reception into the Patrol Division was one of consideration and warm welcome. As near as interviewing and personal experience can attest, there was no hazing or rejection of the recruit by veteran officers. In all cases, the recruits were fully accepted into the ongoing police system with good-natured tolerance and much advice. If anyone in the department was likely to react negatively to the recruits during their first few weeks on patrol, it was the supervisor and not the on-line patrolmen. The fraternal-like regard shown the rookie by the experienced officers stands in stark contrast to the stern greeting he received at the police academy. The newcomer quickly is bombarded with "street wise" patrolmen assuring him that the police academy was simply an experience all officers endure and has little, if anything, to do with real police work. Consequently, the academy experiences for the recruits stand symbolically as their rites de passage, permitting them access to the occupation. That the experienced officers confirm their negative evaluation of the academy heightens the assumed similarities among the rookies and veterans and serves to facilitate the recruit's absorption into the division. As an FTO noted during my first night on patrol:

> I hope the academy didn't get to you. It's something we all have to go through. A bunch of bullshit as far as I can tell.... Since you got through it all right, you get to find out what it's like out here. You'll find out mighty fast that it ain't nothing like they tell you at the academy.

During the protracted hours spent on patrol with his FTO, the recruit is instructed as to the real nature of police work. To the neophyte, the first few weeks on patrol is an extremely trying period. The recruit is slightly fearful and woefully ill-prepared for both the routine and eccentricities of real police work. While he may know the criminal code and the rudimentaries of arrest, the fledgling patrolman is perplexed and certainly not at ease in their application. For example, a two-day veteran told the following story to several of his academy associates.

> We were down under the bridge where the fags hang out and spot this car that looked like nobody was in it.... Frank puts the spot on it and two heads pop up. He tells me to watch what he does and keep my mouth shut. So I follow him up to the car and just kind of stand around feeling pretty dumb. Frank gives 'em a blast of shit and tells the guy sitting behind the wheel he's under arrest. The punk gets out of the car snivelling and I go up to him and start putting the cuffs on. Frank says, "just take him back to the car and sit on him while I get the dope on his boyfriend here." So I kind of direct him back to the car and stick him in the backseat and I get in the front.... While Frank's filling out a FIR (Field Investigation Report) on the other guy, the little pansy in the backseat's carrying on about his wife and kids like you wouldn't believe. I'm starting to feel sorta sorry for arresting him. Anyway, Frank finishes filling out the FIR and tells the other guy to get going and if he ever sees him again he'll beat the holy shit out of him. Then he comes back to the car and does the same number on the other fag. After we drove away, I told Frank I thought we'd arrested somebody. He laughed his ass off and told me that's the way we do things out here.

To a recruit, the whole world seems new, and from his novel point of view it is. Like a visitor from a foreign land, the daily events are perplexing and present a myriad of operational difficulties. At first, the squawk of the police radio transmits only meaningless static; the streets appear to be a maze through which only an expert could maneuver; the use of report forms seems inconsistent and confusing; encounters with a hostile public leave him cold and apprehensive; and so on. Yet, next to him in the patrol unit is his partner, a veteran. Hence, the FTO is the answer to most of the breaking-in dilemmas. It is commonplace for the rookie to never make a move without first checking with his FTO. By watching, listening, and mimicking, the neophyte policeman learns how to deal with the objects of his occupation — the traffic violator, the hippie, the drunk, the brass, and the criminal justice complex itself. One veteran reflected on his early patrol experiences as follows:

> On this job, your first partner is everything. He tells you how to survive on the job...how to walk, how to stand, and how to speak and how to think and what to say and see.

Clearly, it is during the FTO phase of the recruit's career that he is most susceptible to attitude change. The newcomer is self-conscious and truly in need of guidelines. A whole folklore of tales, myths, and legends surrounding the department is communicated to the recruit by his fellow officers — conspicuously by his FTO. Through these anecdotes — dealing largely with mistakes of "flubs" made by policemen — the recruit begins to adopt the perspectives of his more experienced colleagues. He becomes aware that nobody's perfect and, as if to reify his police academy experiences, he learns that to be protected from his own mistakes, he must protect others. One such yarn told to me by a two-year veteran illustrates this point.

> Grayson had this dolly he'd been balling for quite a while living over on the north side. Well, it seemed like a quiet night so we cruise out of our district and over to the girl's house. I baby-sit the radio while Grayson goes inside. Wouldn't you know it, we get an emergency call right away. ...I start honking the horn trying to get the horny bastard out of there; he pays me no mind, but the neighbors get kind of irritated at some cop waking up the nine-to-fivers. Some asshole calls the station and pretty soon Sparky and Jim show up to find out what's happening. They're cool but their Sergeant ain't, so we fabricate this insane story 'bout Sparky's girlfriend living there and how he always toots the horn when passing. Me and Grayson beat it back to our district and show up about 45 minutes late on our call. Nobody ever found out what happened, but it sure was close.

Critical to the practical learning porcess is the neophyte's own developing repertoire of experiences. These events are normally interpreted to him by his FTO and other veteran officers. Thus, the reality shock of being "in on the action" is absorbed and defined by the recruit's fellow officers. As a somewhat typical example, one newcomer, at the prodding of his patrol partner, discovered that to explain police actions to a civilian invited disrespect. He explained

> Keith was always telling me to be forceful, to not back down and to never try and explain the law or what we are doing to a civilian. I didn't really know what he was talking about until I tried to tell some kid why we have laws about speeding. Well, the more I tried to tell him about traffic safety, the angrier he got. I was lucky to just get his John

Hancock on the citation. When I came back to the patrol car, Keith explains to me just where I'd gone wrong. You really can't talk to those people out there, they just won't listen to reason.

In general, the first month or so on the street is an exciting and rewarding period for the recruit. For his FTO, however, it is a period of appraisal. While the recruit is busy absorbing many novel experiences, his partner is evaluating the newcomer's reaction to certain situations. Aside from assisting the recruit with the routines of patrol work, the training officer's main concern is in how the recruit will handle the "hot" or, in the contemporary language of the recruits, the "heavy" call (i.e., the in-progress, or on-view, or help the officer situation which the experienced officer knows may result in trouble). The heavy call represents everything the policeman feels he is prepared for. In short, it calls for police work. Such calls are anticipated by the patrolmen with both pleasure and anxiety, and the recruit's performance on such calls is in a very real sense the measure of the man. A Union City Sergeant described the heavy call to me as follows:

It's our main reason for being in business. Like when somebody starts busting up a place, or some asshole's got a gun, or some idiot tries to knock off a cop. Basically, it's the situation where you figure you may have to use the tools of your trade. Of course, some guys get a little shaky when these incidents come along, in fact, most of us do if we're honest. But, you know deep down that this is why you're a cop and not pushing pencils somewhere. You've got to be tough on this job and situations like these separate the men from the boys. I know I'd never trust my partner until I'd seen him in action on a hot one.

While such calls are relatively rare on a day-to-day basis, their occurrence signals a behavioral test for the recruit. To pass, he must have "balls." By placing himself in a vulnerable position and pluckily backing-up his FTO and/or other patrolmen, a recruit demonstrates his inclination to share the risks of police work. Through such events, a newcomer quickly makes a departmental reputation which will follow him for the remainder of his career.

At another level, testing the recruit's propensity to partake in the risks which accompany police work goes on continuously within the department. For example, several FTO's in Union City were departmental celebrities for their training techniques. One officer made it a ritual to have his recruit write parking citations in front of the local Black Panther Party headquarters. Another was prominent for requiring his recruit to "shake out" certain trouble bars in the rougher sections of town (i.e., check identifications, make cursory body searches, and possibly roust out customers, a la *The French Connection*). Less dramatic, but nonetheless as important, recruits are appraised as to their speed in getting out of the patrol car, their lack of hesitation when approaching a suspicious person, or their willingness to lead the way up a darkened stairwell. The required behaviors vary from event to event; however, contingent upon the ex post facto evaluation (e.g., Was a weapon involved? Did the officers have to fight the suspect? How many other patrolmen were on the spot?), a novice makes his departmental reputation. While some FTO's promote these climactic events, most wait quietly for such situations to occur. Certainly varying definitions of appropriate behavior in these situations exist from patrolman to patrolman, but the critical and common element is the recruit's demonstrated willingness to place himself in a precarious position while assisting a brother officer. In the police world, such behavior is demanded.

Although data on such instances are inherently difficult to collect, it appears that the behaviorally demonstrated commitment to one's fellow officers involved in such events is a particularly important stage in the socialization process. To the recruit, he has experienced a test and it provides him with the first of many shared experiences which he can relate to other officers. To the FTO, he has watched his man in a police work situation and now knows a great deal more about his occupational companion.

Aside from the backup test applied to all recruits, the other most powerful experience in a recruit's early days on patrol is his first arrest. Virtually all policemen can recall the individual, location, and situation surrounding their first arrest. One five-year veteran patrolman stated:

> The first arrest is really something. I guess that's because it's what we're supposedly out here for.... In my case, I'd been out for a couple of weeks but we hadn't done much.... I think we'd made some chippies, like stand-ups, or DWI's, but my partner never let me handle the arrest part. Then one night he tells me that if anything happens, Ive got to handle it. Believe me, I'll never forget that first arrest, even if it was only a scumbag horn (wino) who had just fallen through a window.... I suppose I can remember my first three or four arrests, but after that they just start to blur together.'

It is such occurrences that determine the recruit's success in the department. To some extent, both the back up test and the first arrest are beyond the direct control of the newcomer. The fact that they both take place at the discretion of the FTO underscores the orderliness of the socialization process. In effect, these climactic situations graphically demonstrate to the recruit his new status and role within the department. And after passing through this regulated sequence of events, he can say, "I am a cop!"

Continuance: Metamorphosis

This section is concerned broadly with what Becker et al. (1961) labeled the final perspective. As such, the interest is upon the characteristic response recruits eventually demonstrate regarding their occupational and organizational setting. Again, the focus is upon the perspectives the initiates come to hold for the backstage aspect of their career.

As noted earlier, one of the major motivating factors behind the recruit's decision to become a policeman was the adventure or romance he felt would characterize the occupation. Yet, the young officer soon learns the work consists primarily of performing routine service and administrative tasks—the proverbial clerk in a patrol car. This finding seems well-established in the pertinent literature and my observations confirm these reports (e.g., Wilson 1968; Webster 1970; Reiss 1971). Indeed, a patrolman is predominantly an order taker—a reactive member of a service organization. For example, most officers remarked that they never realized the extent to which they would be "married to the radio" until they had worked the street for several months.

On the other hand, there is an unpredictable side of the occupation and this aspect cannot be overlooked. In fact, it is the unexpected elements of working patrol that provides self-esteem and stimulation for the officers. This unpredictable feature of patrol work has too often been understated or disregarded by students of police behavior. To classify the police task as bureaucratically routine and monotonous ignores the psychological omnipresence of the potential "good pinch." It is precisely the opportunity to exercise his perceived police role that gives meaning to the occupational identity of patrolmen. Operationally, this does not imply patrolmen are always alert and working hard to make the "good pinch." Rather, it simply suggests that the unexpected is one of the few aspects of the job that helps maintain the patrolman's self-image of performing a worthwhile, exciting, and dangerous task. To some degree, the anticipation of the "hot call" allows for the crystallization of his personal identity as a policeman. One Union City patrolman with ten years' experience commented succinctly on this feature. He noted:

> Most of the time being a cop is the dullest job in the world...what we do is pretty far away from the stuff you see on Dragnet or Adam 12. But, what I like about this job and I guess it's what keeps me going, is that you never know what's gonna happen out there. For instance, me and my partner will be working a Sunday first watch way out in the north end and expecting everything to be real peaceful and quiet like; then all of a sudden, hell breaks loose...Even on the quietest nights, something interesting usually happens.

Reiss noted perceptually the atypical routine enjoyed by patrolmen. After examining the police "straight eight" — the tour of duty — he stated:

> No tour of duty is typical except in the sense that the modal tour of duty does not involve the arrest of a person (Reiss 1971:19).

Still, one of the ironies of police work is that recruits were attracted to the organization by and large via the unrealistic expectation that the work would be adventurous and exciting. In the real world such activities are few and far between. Once a recruit has mastered the various technical and social skills of routine policing (e.g., "learning the district," developing a set of mutual understandings with his partner, knowing how and when to fill out the myriad of various report forms) there is little left to learn about his occupation which can be transferred by formal or informal instruction. As Westley (1951) pointed out, the recruit must then sit back and wait, absorb the subjective side of police work and let his experiences accumulate. The wife of one recruit noted this frustrating characteristic of police work. She said:

> It seems to me that being a policeman must be very discouraging. They spend all that time teaching the men to use the gun and the club and then they make them go out and do very uninteresting work.

It has been suggested that for a newcomer to any occupation, "coping with the emotional reality of the job" is the most difficult problem to resolve (Schein 1963). In police work, the coping behavior appears to consist of the "learning of complacency." Since the vast majority of time is spent in tasks other than real police work, there is little incentive for performance. In other words, the young patrolman discovers that the most satisfying solution to the labyrinth of hierarchy, the red tape and paperwork, the plethora of rules and regulations and the "dirty work" which characterize the occupation is to adopt the group norm stressing staying out of trouble. And the best way in which he can stay out of trouble is to minimize the set of activities he pursues. One Union City veteran patrolman explained:

> We are under constant pressure from the public to account for why we did or did not do this or that. It's almost as if the public feels it owns us. You become supersensitive to criticisms from the public, almost afraid to do anything. At the same time, the brass around here never gives a straightforward answer about procedures to anyone and that creates a lot of discontent. All communication comes down. But, try and ask a question and it gets stopped at the next level up. It gets to the point where you know that if you don't do anything at all, you won't get in trouble.

In a similar vein, another veteran officer put it somewhat more bluntly. He suggested caustically:

> The only way to survive on this job is to keep from breaking your ass... if you try too hard you're sure to get in trouble. Either some civic-minded creep is going to get outraged and you'll wind up with a complaint in your file; or the high and mighty in the department will come down on you for breaking some rule or something and you'll get your pay docked.

These quotations suggest that patrolman disenchantment has two edges. One, the police with the general public—which has been well-substantiated in the literature—and two, the disenchantment with the police system itself. In short, a recruit begins to realize (through proverb, example, and his own experience) it is his relationship with his fellow officers (particularly those working the same sector and shift—his squad) that protects his interests and allows him to continue on the job—without their support he would be lost.[8]

To summarize, the adjustment of a newcomer in police departments is one which follows the line of least resistance. By becoming similar in sentiment and behavior to his peers, the recruit avoids censure by the department, his supervisor and, most important, his brother officers. Furthermore, since the occupational rewards are to be found primarily in the unusual situation which calls for "real" police work, the logical situational solution is for the officers to organize their activities in such a way as to minimize the likelihood of being sanctioned by *any* of their audiences. The low visibility of the patrolman's role vis-a-vis the department allows for such a response. Thus, the pervasive adjustment is epitomized in the "lie low, hang loose and don't expect too much" advice frequently heard within the Union City Police Department. This overall picture would indicate that the following tip given to me by a Union City veteran represents a very astute analysis of how to insure continuance in the police world. He suggested:

> There's only two things you gotta know around here. First, forget everything you've learned in the academy 'cause the street's where you'll learn to be a cop; and second, being first don't mean shit around here. Take it easy, that's our motto.

The above characterization of the recruit socialization process, while necessarily a drastic condensation of a much more complex and interdependent process, does delineate the more important aspects of becoming a policeman. Furthermore, this descriptive narrative hints that many of the recent attempts to alter or reform police behavior are likely to meet with frustration and failure.

A Coda For Reformers

Most police reformers view the behavior of individual patrolmen as a problem for the department or society, not vice versa. I have, in a small way, tried to correct this bias by describing the point of view of the entering recruit. This emphasizes the intelligibility of the newcomer's actions as he works out solutions to his unique problems. In short, we "looked up" at the nature of the network above the recruit rather than using the usual approach which, in the past, has "looked down" on the "outsider." Perhaps this approach indicates the dilemma in which our police are indeed trapped.

In a very real sense, this article suggests a limit upon the extent to which the police can be expected to solve their own problems. Regardless of how well-educated, well-equipped, or professional the patrolman may become, his normative position and task within society will remain unchanged. From this perspective, the characteristic response of police officers to their present situation is indeed both rational and functional. Clearly, the police subculture — like subcultures surrounding bricklayers, lawyers, or social workers — will probably exist in even the most reformed of departments. To change the police without changing the police role in society is as futile as the labors of Sisyphus.

The long-range goal should be a structural redefinition of the police task and a determination of ways in which the external control principle — so central to the rule of law — may be strengthened. Of course, ways must be found to make the policeman's lot somewhat more tolerable, both to him and to the general citizenry. Organizational change can aid this process by designing training programs which place less stress on the apprenticeship relationship. However, it is doubtful that without profound alterations in the definition and structural arrangement of the police task (and in the implied values such arrangements support), significant change is possible.

Thus, plans to increase the therapeutic and operational effectiveness of police institutions by "in-house" techniques must be judged in terms of what is being done now and what might be done — and, given the features of the police institution as described here, the difference is painfully small. The particular pattern of police practices is a response to the demands of the larger complex and, as such, reflects the values and norms prevalent throughout the society. The extent to which the police system undermines the rule of law; the extent to which the public is willing to alter the crime fighter image of police; the extent to which the police bureaucracy will allow change; and ultimately, the extent to which the police system as presently constructed can operate under strict public accounting — these are the major issues confronting the police, not the degree to which the individual policeman can be professionalized.⁹

Notes

[1] The use of the term "outsider" in the above context is not intended to invidiously portray the police. Rather, the term simply connotes the widespread conviction carried by the police themselves that they are, of necessity, somehow different, and set-off from the larger society. To most police observers, isolationism, secrecy, strong in-group loyalties, sacred symbols, common language, and a sense of estrangement are almost axiomatic subcultural features underpinning a set of common understandings among police in general which govern their relations with one another as well as with civilians (Bayley and Mendelsohn, 1969; President's Commission, 1967; Skolnick, 1966). Such a perspective emphasizes the necessity to view the world from the eyes of the outsider — a perspective which ideally is empathetic but neither sympathetic or judgmental.

[2] If one takes seriously research findings regarding esoteric subcultures, social scientists interested in police behavior are limited in their choice of methodological strategy. If we are to gain insight into the so-called police problem, researchers must penetrate the official smoke screen sheltering virtually all departments and observe directly the social action in social situations which, in the last analysis, defines police work.

[3] One exception is Westley's (1951) insightful observational study of a midwestern police department. However, his research was devoted mainly to the description of the more salient sociological features of the police occupation and was concerned only peripherally with the learning process associated with the police role.

[4] Union City is a pseudonym for a sprawling metropolitan area populated by more than a million people. The police department employs well over 1,500 uniformed officers, provides a salary above the national average, and is organized in the classic pyramidal arrangement (see Van Maanen, 1972). Based on interviews with police personnel from a number of different departments and, most importantly, critical readings of my work by policemen from several departments, the sequence of events involved in recruit socialization appears to be remarkably similar from department to department. This structural correspondence among recruit training programs has been noted by others (see Ahern, 1972; Berkeley, 1969; Neiderhoffer, 1967).

[5] While it cannot be stated categorically that my presence had little effect upon the behavior of the subjects, I felt I was accepted completely as a regular group member in my particular police academy class and little or no behavior was (or, for that matter, could be) altered explicitly. Furthermore, the lengthy, personal, and involving nature of my academy experiences produced an invaluable carry-over effect when I moved to the street work portion of the study. The importance of continuous observation and full participation as an aid for minimizing distortions and behavior change on the part of social actors has been strikingly demonstrated by a number of social scientists (e.g., see Whyte, 1943; Becker, 1963; Dalton, 1964; and, most recently, Schatzman and Strauss, 1973).

[6] Significantly, a recruit is not even allowed to carry a loaded weapon during the classroom portion of his academy training. He must wait until graduation night before being permitted to load his weapon. To the recruit, such policies are demeaning. Yet, the policies "stigmatizing" the recruits-as-recruits (e.g., different uniforms, old and battered batons, allocation of special parking spaces, special scarfs, and name plates) were exceedingly effective methods of impressing upon recruits that they were members of a particular class and were not yet Union City Police Officers.

[7] By "chippies," the officer was referring to normal arrests encountered frequently by patrolmen. Usually, a chippie is a misdemeanor arrest for something like drunkenness. The chippie crimes the officer noted in the quotation, "stand-up" and "DWI's" refer to drunk-in-public and driving-while-intoxicated, respectively.

[8] In most ways, the patrolmen represent what Goffman (1959) calls a team. In Goffmanesque, a team is "a set of individuals whose intimate co-operation is required if a given projected

definition of the situation is to be maintained" (1959:104). The situational definition to be sustained in the patrol setting is that "all-is-going-well-there-are-no-problems." The covert rule for patrolmen is to never draw attention to one's activities. An analysis I conducted on written weekly FTO progress reports illustrates this point convincingly. Of over 300 report forms, only one contained an even slightly negative evaluation. Uniformly, all forms were characterized by high praise for the recruit. The topics the FTO's chose to elaborate upon were typified by such concerns as the recruit's driving skill, the recruit's pleasing personality, the recruit's stable home life, and so on. The vast majority of reports contained no reference whatsoever to the types of activities engaged in by the recruits. The point is simply that in no case was an FTO Report filed which might result in departmental attention. It should be clear that such behavior does not pass unnoticed by the recruit. Indeed, he learns rapidly the importance and value of his team as well as the corresponding definition of the police situation. ⁹I have attempted to suggest in this article that the intelligibility of social events requires they be viewed in a context which extends both spatially and in time. Relatedly, social actors must be granted rationality for their behavior. Given the situational imperatives faced by patrolmen, is it any wonder our police recoil behind a blue curtain? Perhaps we have reached what R.D. Laing (1964) calls the "theoretical limit of institutions." According to Laing, this paradoxical position is characterized by a system which, when viewed as a collective, behaves irrationally, yet is populated by members whose everyday behavior is eminently rational.

References Cited

Ahern, J.F., (1972) *Police in Trouble.* New York: Hawthorn Books.

Bayley, P.H., and H. Mendelsohn, (1969) *Minorities and the Police.* New York: The Free Press.

Becker, H.S. (1963) *Outsiders: Studies in the Sociology of Deviance.* New York: The Free Press.

Becker, H.S., B. Greer, E.C. Hughes, and A. Strauss (1961) *Boys in White: Student Culture in Medical School.* Chicago: University of Chicago Press.

Berkeley, G.E. (1969) *The Democratic Policeman.* Boston: Beacon Press.

Berlew, D.E., and D.T. Hall, (1966) The socialization of managers; effects of expectations on performance. *Administrative Science Quarterly* 11:207-23.

Bittner, E., (1967) The police on skid row. *American Sociological Review* 32:699-715.

Cicourel, A.V., (1967) *The Social Organization of Juvenile Justice.* New York: John Wiley and Sons.

Dalton, M., (1964) Preconceptions and methods in men who manage. In *Sociologists at Work,* P. Hammond, ed. New York: Doubleday.

Dornbush, S.M., (1955) The military academy as an assimilating institution. *Social Forces* 33:316-21.

Evan, W.M., (1963) Peer group interaction and organizational socialization: a study of employee turnover. *American Sociological Review* 28:436-40.

Goffman, E., (1959) *The Presentation of Self in Everyday Life.* New York: Doubleday.

Greer, B., (1964) First days in the field. In *Sociologists at Work,* P. Hammond, ed. New York: Doubleday.

Hughes, E.C., (1958) *Men and their Work* Glencoe, Illinois: The Free Press.

Laing, R.D., (1964) The obvious. In *Dialectics of Liberation,* D. Cooper, ed. London: Institute of Phenomenological Studies.

Lortie, D.C., (1968) Shared ordeal and induction to work. In *Institutions and the Person,* H.S. Becker, B. Greer, D. Riesman, and R.T. Weiss, eds. Chicago: Aldine.

McNamara, J., (1967) Uncertainties in police work: the relevance of police recruits' background and training. In *The Police: Six Sociological Essays,* D.J. Bordura, ed. New York: John Wiley and Sons.

Neiderhoffer, A., (1967) *Behind the Shield.* New York: Doubleday.

President's Commission on Law Enforcement, *(1967)* Task Force Report: The Police. Washington, D.C.: Government Printing Office.

Reiss, A.J., (1971) *The Police and the Public.* New Haven: Yale University Press.

Schatzman, L., and A. Strauss, (1973) *Field Research: Strategies for a Natural Sociology.* Englewood Cliffs, New Jersey: Prentice-Hall.

Schein, E.H., (1963) Organizational socialization in the early career of industrial managers. Paper presented at the New England Psychological Association. Boston, Massachusetts. (1971) Organizational socialization and the profession of management. *Industrial Management Review* 2:37-45.

Skolnick, J., (1966) *Justice Without Trial: Law Enforcement in a Democratic Society.* New York: John Wiley and Sons.

Sterling, J.W., (1972) Changes in Role Concepts of Police Officers. Washington, D.C.: International Association of Chiefs of Police.

Van Maanen, J. (1972) Pledging the police: a study of selected aspects of recruit socialization in a large, urban police department. Ph.D. Dissertation, University of California, Irvine. (1976) Breaking-in: socialization to work. In *Handbook of Work, Organization, and Society,* R. Dubin, ed. Chicago: Rand-Mcnally.

Webster, J.A. (1970) Police task and time study. *Journal of Criminal Law, Criminology and Police Science* 61:94-100.

Westley, W.A., (1951) The police: a sociological study of law, custom and mortality. Ph.D. Dissertation, University of Chicago, Chicago, Illinois.

Whyte, W.F., (1943) *Street Corner Society.* Chicago: University of Chicago Press.

Wilson, J.Q., (1968) *Varieties of Police Behavior.* Cambridge, Massachusetts. Harvard University Press.

6

Making Neighborhoods Safe

James Q. Wilson
George L. Kelling

New Briarfield Apartments is an old run-down collection of wooden buildings constructed in 1942 as temporary housing for shipyard workers in Newport News, Virginia. By the mid-1980s it was widely regarded as the worst housing project in the city. Many of its vacant units provided hiding places for drug users. It had the highest burglary rate in Newport News; nearly a quarter of its apartments were broken into at least once a year.

For decades the police had wearily answered calls for assistance and had investigated crimes in New Briarfield. Not much came of this police attentiveness—the buildings went on deteriorating, the burglaries went on occurring, the residents went on living in terror. Then, in 1984, Detective Tony Duke, assigned to a newly created police task force, decided to interview the residents of New Briarfield about their problems. Not surprisingly, he found that they were worried about the burglaries—but they were just as concerned about the physical deterioration of the project. Rather than investigating only the burglaries, Duke spent some of his time investigating the *buildings*. Soon he learned that many city agencies—the fire department, the public-works department, the housing department—regarded New Briarfield as a major headache. He also discovered that its owners were in default on a federal loan and that foreclosure was imminent.

The report he wrote to Darrel Stephens, then the police chief, led Stephens to recommend to the city manager that New Briarfield be demolished and its tenants relocated. The city manager agreed. Meanwhile, Barry Haddix, the patrol officer assigned to the area, began working with members of other

Reproduced by permission of the Atlantic Monthly Company from *The Atlantic Monthly*, Vol. 263, No. 2, pp. 46-52, February 1989.

city agencies to fix up the project, pending its eventual replacement. Trash was carted away, abandoned cars were removed, potholes were filled in, the streets were swept. According to a study recently done by John E. Eck and William Spelman, of the Police Executive Research Forum (PERF), the burglary rate dropped by 35 percent after Duke and Haddix began their work.

Stephens, now the executive director of PERF tells the story of the New Briarfield project as an example of "problem-oriented policing," a concept developed by Professor Herman Goldstein, of the University of Wisconsin Law School, and sometimes also called community-oriented policing. The conventional police strategy is "incident-oriented"—a citizen calls to report an incident, such as a burglary, and the police respond by recording information relevant to the crime and then trying to solve it. Obviously, when a crime occurs, the victim is entitled to a rapid, effective police response. But if responding to incidents is all that the police do, the community problems that cause or explain many of these incidents will never be addressed, and so the incidents will continue and their number will perhaps increase.

This will happen for two reasons. One is that a lot of serious crime is adventitious, not the result of inexorable social forces or personal failings. A rash of burglaries may occur because drug users have found a back alley or an abandoned building in which to hang out. In their spare time, and in order to get money to buy drugs, they steal from their neighbors. If the back alleys are cleaned up and the abandoned buildings torn down, the drug users will go away. They may even use fewer drugs, because they will have difficulty finding convenient dealers and soft burglary targets. By the same token, a neglected neighborhood may become the turf of a youth gang, whose members commit more crimes together in a group than they would if they were acting alone. If the gang is broken up, former members will still commit some crimes but probably not as many as before.

Most crime in most neighborhoods is local: the offenders live near their victims. Because of this, one should not assume that changing the environmental conditions conducive to crime in one area will displace the crime to other areas. For example, when the New York City police commissioner, Ben Ward, ordered Operation Pressure Point, a crackdown on drug dealing on the Lower East Side, dealing and the criminality associated with it were reduced in that neighborhood and apparently did not immediately reappear in other, contiguous neighborhoods. Suburban customers of the local drug dealers were frightened away by the sight of dozens of police officers on the streets where these customers had once shopped openly for drugs. They could not—at least not right away—find another neighborhood in which to buy drugs as easily as they once had on the Lower East Side. At the same time, the local population included some people who were willing to aid and abet the drug dealers. When the police presence made drug dealing unattractive, the dealers could not—

again, at least not for the time being—find another neighborhood that provided an equivalent social infrastructure.

The second reason that incident-oriented police work fails to discourage neighborhood crime is that law-abiding citizens who are afraid to go out onto streets filled with graffiti, winos, and loitering youths yield control of these streets to people who are not frightened by these signs of urban decay. Those not frightened turn out to be the same people who created the problem in the first place. Law-abiding citizens, already fearful, see things occurring that make them even more fearful. A vicious cycle begins of fear-induced behavior increasing the sources of that fear.

A Los Angeles police sergeant put it this way: "When people in this district see that a gang has spray-painted its initials on all the stop signs, they decide that the gang, not the people or the police, controls the streets. When they discover that the Department of Transportation needs three months to replace the stop signs, they decide that the city isn't as powerful as the gang. These people want Us to help them take back the streets." Painting gang symbols on a stop sign or a storefront is not, by itself, a serious crime. As an incident, it is trivial. But as the symptom of a problem, it is very serious.

In an earlier article in *The Atlantic* (March, 1982) we called this the problem of "broken windows": If the first broken window in a building is not repaired, then people who like breaking windows will assume that no one cares about the building and more windows will be broken. Soon the building will have no windows. Likewise, when disorderly behavior—say, rude remarks by loitering youths—is left unchallenged, the signal given is that no one cares. The disorder escalates, possibly to serious crime.

The sort of police work practiced in Newport News is an effort to fix the broken windows. Similar projects are under way in cities all over America. This pattern constitutes the beginnings of the most significant redefinition of police work in the past half century. For example:

- When a gunfight occurred at Garden Village, a low-income housing project near Baltimore, the Baltimore County police responded by investigating both the shooting and the housing project. Chief Cornelius Behan directed the officers in his Community Oriented Police Enforcement (COPE) unit to find out what could be done to alleviate the fears of the project residents and the gang tensions that led to the shooting. COPE officers worked with members of other agencies to upgrade street lighting in the area, trim shrubbery, install door locks, repair the roads and alleys, and get money to build a playground. With police guidance, the tenants organized. At the same time, high-visibility patrols were started and gang members were questioned. When both a suspect in the shooting and a particularly troublesome parole violator were arrested, gang tensions eased. Crime rates dropped. In bringing about this change, the police dealt with eleven different public agencies.

• When local merchants in a New York City neighborhood complained to the police about homeless persons who created a mess on the streets and whose presence frightened away customers, the officer who responded did not roust the vagrants but instead suggested that the merchants hire them to clean the streets in front of their stores every morning. The merchants agreed, and now the streets are clean all day and the customers find the stores more attractive.

• When people in a Los Angeles neighborhood complained to the police about graffiti on walls and gang symbols on stop signs, officers assigned to the Community Mobilization Project in the Wilshire station did more than just try to catch the gang youths who were wielding the spray cans; they also organized citizens' groups and Boy Scouts to paint over the graffiti as fast as they were put up.

• When residents of a Houston neighborhood became fearful about crime in their area, the police not only redoubled their efforts to solve the burglaries and thefts but also assigned some officers to talk with the citizens in their homes. During a nine-month period the officers visited more than a third of all the dwelling units in the area, introduced themselves, asked about any neighborhood problems, and left their business cards. When Antony Pate and Mary Ann Wycoff, researchers at the Police Foundation, evaluated the project, they found that the people in this area, unlike others living in a similar area where no citizen-contact project occurred, felt that social disorder had decreased and that the neighborhood had become a better place to live. Moreover, and quite unexpectedly, the amount of property crime was noticeably reduced.

These are all examples of community-oriented policing, whose current popularity among police chiefs is as great as the ambiguity of the idea. In a sense, the police have always been community-oriented. Every police officer knows that most crimes don't get solved if victims and witnesses do not cooperate. One way to encourage that cooperation is to cultivate the good will of both victims and witnesses. Similarly, police-citizen tensions, over racial incidents or allegations of brutality or hostility, can often be allayed, and sometimes prevented, if police officers stay in close touch with community groups. Accordingly, most departments have at least one community-relations officer, who arranges meetings between officers and citizens' groups in church basements and other neutral locales.

But these commonplace features of police work are add-ons, and rarely alter the traditional work of most patrol officers and detectives: responding to radio calls about specific incidents. The focus on incidents works against a focus on problems. If Detective Tony Duke had focused only on incidents in New Briarfield, he would still be investigating burglaries in that housing project; meanwhile, the community-relations officer would be telling outraged residents that the police were doing all they could and urging people to call in any useful leads. If a tenant at one of those meetings had complained about stopped-up drains, rotting floorboards, and abandoned refrigerators, the community-relations officer would have patiently explained that these were not "police matters."

And of course, they are not. They are the responsibility of the landlord, the tenants themselves, and city agencies other than the police. But landlords are sometimes indifferent, tenants rarely have the resources to make needed repairs, and other city agencies do not have a twenty-four-hour emergency service. Like it or not, the police are about the only city agency that makes house calls around the clock. And like it or not, the public defines broadly what it thinks of as public order, and holds the police responsible for maintaining order.

Community-oriented policing means changing the daily work of the police to include investigating problems as well as incidents. It means defining as a problem whatever a significant body of public opinion regards as a threat to community order. It means working with the good guys, and not just against the bad guys.

The link between incidents and problems can sometimes be measured. The police know from experience what research by Glenn Pierce, in Boston, and Lawrence Sherman, in Minneapolis, has established: fewer than 10 percent of the addresses from which the police receive calls account for more than 60 percent of those calls. Many of the calls involve domestic disputes. If each call is treated as a separate incident with neither a history nor a future, then each dispute will be handled by police officers anxious to pacify the complainants and get back on patrol as quickly as possible. All too often, however, the disputants move beyond shouting insults or throwing crockery at each other. A knife or a gun may be produced, and somebody may die.

A very large proportion of all killings occur in these domestic settings. A study of domestic homicides in Kansas City showed that in eight out of ten cases the police had been called to the incident address at least once before; in half the cases they had been called *five times* or more. The police are familiar with this pattern, and they have learned how best to respond to it. An experiment in Minneapolis, conducted by the Police Foundation, showed that men who were arrested after assaulting their spouses were much less likely to commit new assaults than those who were merely pacified or asked to leave the house for a few hours. Research is now under way in other cities to test this finding. Arrest may prove always to be the best disposition, or we may learn that some kind of intervention by a social agency also helps. What is indisputable is that a domestic fight—like many other events to which the police respond — is less an "incident" than a problem likely to have serious, long-term consequences.

Another such problem, familiar to New Yorkers, is graffiti on subway cars. What to some aesthetes is folk art is to most people a sign that an important public place is no longer under public control. If graffiti painters can attack cars with impunity, then muggers may feel they can attack the people in those cars with equal impunity. When we first wrote in these pages about the problem of broken windows, we dwelt on the graffiti problem as an example of a minor crime creating a major crisis.

The police seemed powerless to do much about it. They could arrest youths with cans of spray paint, but for every one arrested ten more went undetected, and of those arrested, few were punished. The New York Transit Authority, led by its chairman, Robert Kiley, and its president, David Gunn, decided that graffiti-free cars were a major management goal. New, easier-to-clean cars were bought. More important, key people in the Authority were held accountable for cleaning the cars and keeping them clean. Whereas in the early 1980s two out of every three cars were covered with graffiti, today fewer than one in six is. The Transit Police have played their part by arresting those who paint the cars, but they have been more successful at keeping cars from being defaced in the first place than they were at chasing people who were spraying already defaced ones.

While the phrase "Community-oriented policing" comes easily to the lips of police administrators, redefining the police mission is more difficult. To help the police become accustomed to fixing broken windows as well as arresting window-breakers requires doing things that are very hard for many administrators to do.

Authority over at least some patrol officers must be decentralized, so that they have a good deal of freedom to manage their time (including their paid overtime). This implies freeing them at least partly from the tyranny of the radio call. It means giving them a broad range of responsibilities: to find and understand the problems that create disorder and crime, and to deal with other public and private agencies that can help cope with these problems. It means assigning them to a neighborhood and leaving them there for an extended period of time. It means backing them up with department support and resources.

The reason these are not easy things for police chiefs to do is not simply that chiefs are slaves to tradition, though some impatient advocates of community-oriented policing like to say so. Consider for a moment how all these changes might sound to an experienced and intelligent police executive who must defend his department against media criticisms of officer misconduct, political pressure to cut budgets, and interest-group demands for more police protection everywhere. With decentralized authority, no one will know precisely how patrol officers spend their time. Moreover, decentralized authority means that patrol officers will spend time on things like schmoozing with citizens, instead of on quantifiable tasks like issuing tickets, making arrests, and clearing cases.

Making the community-oriented officers generalists means letting them deal with other city agencies, a responsibility for which few officers are well trained and which cuts across sensitive questions of turf and public expectations.

If officers are left in a neighborhood, some of them may start taking money from the dope dealers and after-hours joints. To prevent that, officers are frequently moved around. Moreover, the best people are usually kept in the detective squad that handles the really big cases. Few police executives want their best people settling into a neighborhood, walking around the bus stops and shopping malls.

The enthusiasts for community-oriented policing have answers for all these concerns, but sometimes in their zeal they forget that they are contending with more than mere bureaucratic foot-dragging—that the problems are real and require thoughtful solutions. Many police executives get in trouble not because the crime rate goes up but because cops are accused of graft, brutality, laziness, incivility, or indifference.

In short, police management is driven more by the constraints on the job than by the goals of the job. You cannot cope with those constraints without understanding them. This may be why some of the biggest changes toward community-oriented policing have occurred in cities where a new chief has come in from the outside with a mandate to shake up a moribund department. Lee Brown brought a community orientation to the Houston Police Department under precisely those circumstances—the reputation of the department was so bad that almost any change would have been regarded as an improvement.

What can we say to the worried police chief who is already running a pretty good department? Start with corruption: For decades police executives and reformers have believed that in order to prevent corruption, you have to centralize control over personnel and discourage intimacy between police officers and citizens. Maybe. But the price one pays for this is very high. For example, many neighborhoods are being destroyed by drug dealers, who hang out on every street corner. The best way to sweep them off the streets is to have patrol officers arrest them for selling drugs and intimidate their customers by parking police cars right next to suspected drug outlets. But some police chiefs forbid their patrol officers to work drug cases, for fear they will be corrupted. When the citizens in these cities see police cars drive past scenes of open drug dealing, they assume the police have been paid off. Efforts to prevent corruption have produced the appearance of corruption.

Police Commissioner Ben Ward, in New York, decided that the price of this kind of anti-corruption strategy was too high. His Operation Pressure Point put scores of police officers on the streets to break up the drug-dealing bazaar. Police corruption is no laughing matter, especially in New York, but some chiefs now believe that it will have to be fought in ways that do not require police officers to avoid contact with people.

Consider the problem of getting police resources and managing political pressures: resources can be justified with statistics, but statistics often become ends in themselves. One police captain we interviewed said that his department was preoccupied with "stacking widgets and counting beans." He asked his superior for permission to take officers out of radio cars and have them work on community problems. The superior agreed but warned that he would be watching to see what happened to "the stats." In the short run the stats—for example, calls answered, average response time—were likely to get worse, but if community problems were solved, they would get better as citizens had fewer incidents to report. The captain worried, however, that he would not be given enough time to achieve this and that the bean counters would cut off his program.

A better way to justify getting resources from the city is to stimulate popular demand for resources devoted to problem-solving. Properly handled, community-oriented policing does generate support for the department. When Newark police officers, under orders from Hubert Williams, then the police director, began stopping city buses and boarding them to enforce city ordinances against smoking, drinking, gambling, and playing loud music, the bus patrons often applauded. When Los Angeles police officers supervised the hauling away of abandoned cars, onlookers applauded. Later, when some of the officers had their time available for problem-solving work cut back, several hundred citizens attended a meeting to complain.

In Flint, Michigan, patrol officers were taken out of their cars and assigned to foot beats. Robert Trojanowicz, a professor at Michigan State University, analyzed the results and found big increases in citizen satisfaction and officer morale, and even a significant drop in crime (an earlier foot-patrol project in Newark had produced equivalent reductions in fear but no reductions in crime). Citizen support was not confined to statements made to pollsters, however. Voters in referenda twice approved tax increases to maintain the foot-patrol system, the second time by a two-to-one margin. New Briarfield tenants unquestionably found satisfaction in the role the police played in getting temporary improvements made on their housing project and getting a commitment for its ultimate replacement. Indeed, when a department experiments with a community-oriented project in one precinct, people in other precincts usually want one too.

Politicians, like police chiefs, hear these views and respond. But they hear other views as well. One widespread political mandate is to keep the tax rate down. Many police departments are already stretched thin by sharp reductions in spending that occurred in the lean years of the 1970s. Putting *one* additional patrol car on the streets around the clock can cost a quarter of a million dollars or more a year.

Change may seem easier when resources are abundant. Ben Ward could start Operation Pressure Point because he had at his disposal a large number of new officers who could be thrown into a crackdown on street-level drug dealing. Things look a bit different in Los Angeles, where no big increases in personnel are on the horizon. As a result, only eight officers are assigned to the problem-solving Community Mobilization Project in the Wilshire district—an economically and ethnically diverse area of nearly 300,000 residents.

But change does not necessarily require more resources, and the availability of new resources is no guarantee that change will be attempted. One temptation is to try to sell the public on the need for more policemen and decide later how to use them. Usually when that script is followed, either the public turns down the spending increase or the extra personnel are dumped into what one LAPD captain calls the "black hole" of existing commitments, leaving no trace and producing no effects.

What may have an effect is how the police are deployed and managed. An experiment jointly conducted by the Washington, D.C., Police Department and the Police Foundation showed that if a few experienced officers concentrate on known repeat offenders, the number of serious offenders taken off the streets grows substantially. The Flint and Newark experiences suggest that foot patrols in certain kinds of communities (but not all) can reduce fear. In Houston problem-oriented tactics seem clearly to have heightened a sense of citizen security.

The problem of interagency cooperation may, in the long run, be the most difficult of all. The police can bring problems to the attention of other city agencies, but the system is not always organized to respond. In his book *Neighborhood Services*, John Mudd calls it the "rat problem": "If a rat is found in an apartment, it is a housing inspection responsibility; if it runs into a restaurant, the health department has jurisdiction; if it goes outside and dies in an alley, public works takes over." A police officer who takes public complaints about rats seriously will go crazy trying to figure out what agency in the city has responsibility for rat control and then inducing it to kill the rats.

Matters are almost as bad if the public is complaining about abandoned houses or school-age children who are not in school. The housing department may prefer to concentrate on enforcing the housing code rather than go through the costly and time-consuming process of getting an abandoned house torn down. The school department may have expelled the truant children for making life miserable for the teachers and the other students; the last thing it wants is for the police to tell the school to take the kids back.

All city and county agencies have their own priorities and face their own pressures. Forcing them to cooperate by knocking heads together at the top rarely works; what department heads promise the mayor they will do may bear little relationship to what their rank-and-file employees actually do. From his experiences in New York City government Mudd discovered that if you want agencies to cooperate in solving neighborhood problems, you have to get the neighborhood-level supervisors from each agency together in a "district cabinet" that meets regularly and addresses common concerns. This is not an easy task (for one thing, police district lines often do not match the district boundaries of the school, housing, traffic, and public-works departments), but where it has been tried it has made solving the "rat problem" a lot easier. For example, Mudd reports, such interagency issues as park safety and refuse-laden vacant lots got handled more effectively when the field supervisors met to talk about them than when memos went up the chain of command of one agency and then down the chain of command of another.

Community organizations along the lines of Neighborhood Watch programs may help reduce crime, but we cannot be certain. In particular, we do not know what kinds of communities are most likely to benefit from such programs. A Police Foundation study in Minneapolis found that getting effective community organizations started in the most troubled neighborhoods was very difficult. The costs and benefits of having patrol officers and sergeants influence the delivery of services from other city agencies has never been fully assessed. No way of wresting control of a neighborhood from a street gang has yet been proved effective.

And even if these questions are answered, a police department may still have difficulty accommodating two very different working cultures: the patrol officers and detectives who handle major crimes (murders, rapes, and robberies) and the cops who work on community problems and the seemingly minor incidents they generate. In every department we visited, some of the incident-oriented officers spoke disparagingly of the problem-oriented officers as "social workers," and some of the latter responded by calling the former "ghetto blasters." If a community-service officer seems to get too close to the community, he or she may be accused of "going native." The tension between the two cultures is heightened by the fact that in many departments becoming a detective is regarded as a major promotion, and detectives are often selected from among those officers who have the best record in making major arrests—in other words, from the ranks of the incident-oriented. But this pattern need not be permanent. Promotion tracks can be changed so that a patrol officer, especially one working on community problems, is no longer regarded as somebody who "hasn't made detective." Moreover, some police executives now believe that splitting the patrol force into two units—one oriented to incidents, the other to problems—is unwise. They are searching for ways to give all patrol officers the time and resources for problem-solving activities.

Because of the gaps in our knowledge about both the results and the difficulties of community-oriented policing, no chief should be urged to accept, uncritically, the community-oriented model. But the traditional model of police professionalism—devoting resources to quick radio-car response to calls about specific crime incidents—makes little sense at a time when the principal threats to public order and safety come from *collective*, not individual, sources, and from *problems*, not incidents: from well-organized gangs and drug traffickers, from uncared-for legions of the homeless, from boisterous teenagers taking advantage of their newfound freedom and affluence in congested urban settings.

Even if community-oriented policing does not produce the dramatic gains that some of its more ardent advocates expect, it has indisputably produced one that the officers who have been involved in it immediately acknowledge: it has changed their perceptions of the community. Officer Robin Kirk, of the Houston Police Department, had to be talked into becoming part of a neighborhood fear-reduction project. Once in it, he was converted. In his words, "Traditionally, police officers after about three years get to thinking that everybody's a loser. That's the only people you're dealing with. In community policing you're dealing with the good citizens, helping them solve problems."

7

Observations on Police*
Undercover Work

George I. Miller

Municipal police, like all formal organizations are characterized by a division of labor. At the patrol officer level alone there are at least 50 separate forms of work to which an officer may be assigned (Van Maanen, 1984). While duties such as property clerk, jailer, or dispatcher are necessary for police departments to function, they rarely make headlines or inspire television or theater dramatizations. In contrast, undercover police work, because of its utilization of deception, improvisation, and entrepreneurship does generate such attention. Undercover work is arguably the most problematic form of policing undertaken by municipal police departments and little is known about it in operation. This paper focuses on police undercover work and examines it as a contribution to a sociology of work.

Most policing depends upon the authority of a uniform. It is empowering (Joseph and Alex, 1972; Bickman, 1974; Wilson, 1978). But, for obvious reasons, a uniform limits an officer's ability to gather information. When the police want to know about crimes or conduct not commonly brought to their attention and where the presence of a uniform is an impediment to acquiring that knowledge, they must initiate that inquiry. That form of investigation is often referred to as proactive policing (Reiss, 1971).

* An earlier version of this paper was presented at the 1983 annual meeting of the American Society of Criminology. Support for this paper was provided in part by Grant MH15123 from the National Institute of Mental Health. A number of people made helpful comments on earlier drafts: Kai T. Erikson, Virginia H. Fallon, Robert P. Gandossy, Gary T. Marx, Diane L. Pike, Albert J. Reiss, Jr., David V. Summers, Diane Vaughan, Jay R. Williams, and Paul Root Wolpe. Helpful comments were also provided by several anonymous reviewers.

George I. Miller, "Observations on Police Undercover Work," *Criminology*, 25(1): 27-46, Copyright © 1987. Reprinted with permission from The American Society of Criminology.

Like any intelligence-gathering organization, the police have a limited number of options: surveillance, eavesdropping, the recruiting of informants, and espionage. In police organizations, the practice of engaging in espionage is often called undercover work. The term "undercover" has been applied generically to much of nonuniform police work. Marx (1980), for instance, includes decoys, sting operations, and the use of informants as police agents. Undercover police work is defined herein as instances when a sworn officer, for organizationally approved investigative purposes, adopts an encompassing but fictitious civic identity and maintains it as a total identity over a defined and considerable period of time. The officer's new identity and private life are merged with the police identity in an attempt to discover and police conduct not commonly reported. While violations being investigated may include drugs, gambling, prostitution, or sales of illegal goods, false identities may also be adopted to investigate law-abiding citizens merely regarded as suspicious (for example, those advocating "radical" political views; see also Dix, 1975). They also may be adopted for "general fishing expeditions" (Iverson, 1967: 1,109). Officers who work undercover, like espionage agents, are useful only to the extent that their activities remain secret.

Even within the definition used here, two types of undercover work may be distinguished: light-cover and deep-cover.[1] The difference between them is the degree to which the officer's private life merges with the fictitious civic identity. Officers assigned to light-cover often work a regular daily tour of duty and otherwise maintain their private identity. Light-cover is limited in its investigatory scope since it allows the officer to only partially embrace a fictitious identity. For that reason, light-cover officers frequently depend upon the assistance of informants who provide introductions or pass information while going about their everyday business, which is frequently of a criminal nature. In contrast, officers assigned to deep-cover work become entirely submerged in the new identity for the duration of the assignment, and the work most fully approximates the definition of undercover. Deep-cover work is open-ended and may last for months or years (Girodo, 1984). The usefulness and ultimate power of the disguise is that the officer is able to circulate in areas where the police would not otherwise be welcome (Reiss, 1974).

Data and Methodology

This paper reports a pilot study on the police use of fictitious identities in gathering information about conduct external to the organization. The particular data for this paper are drawn from interviews with erstwhile undercover officers and supervisors of undercover operations. Some of the more general observations are informed by the personal experiences of the author, who was employed by a municipal police department as a sworn officer for over 8 years, the first 16 months of which were in a deep-cover capacity. Eighteen interviews, ranging from one to three and one-half hours in duration, were conducted. Those interviewed are or were sworn police personnel acting in or directing undercover activities[2] at the municipal police level. Some of those interviewed are no longer members of police departments, but in no instance did the undercover assignment constitute their entire police career. Others are still police officers; some are patrol officers, others are detectives, and still others are supervisors or members of the command staff. The interviews were informal and open-ended, and took place in police departments, public places, or private homes.

A sample of this sort is very difficult to draw. Since undercover work, particularly deep-cover work, may not occur regularly in municipal police departments, the names and number of officers assigned to these duties is not always well known. For that reason, a snowball technique was employed to locate individuals. Before the snowball came to a rest, subjects had been drawn from six municipal police departments in two states in the Northeast. The officers had been assigned to undercover work at different times covering a 20-year period from the early 1960s to the early 1980s. Ten of the 18 officers interviewed had served in a deep-cover capacity. Only one of the officers interviewed was a female.[3]

Forms of Undercover Work

The first strategy of deep undercover work treats the officer as an intelligence agent whose job it is to keep certain groups of individuals under surveillance and gather information about their activities rather than prepare criminal cases or make arrests. These assignments, by their very nature, do not involve any specific length of time. One officer, who spent 18 months infiltrating "subversive groups," said, "They told me I could stay undercover for as long as I wanted, for years, but if I felt I had to come out I could." That officer's work, however, did not place him in contact with criminal violators but primarily with otherwise respectable citizens and no arrests resulted from his investigation.[4]

The second deep undercover strategy involves "making cases"—that is, gathering intelligence for prosecution. The operation may not be focused on one violator but may be seeking to uncover a hierarchy of offenders (at least ideally) or a group of similar offenders at the same level (for example, street drug dealers). In that mode officers gather evidence of an individual's criminal violation by purchasing drugs, weapons, or by placing wagers, for example, and become the complainant seeking an arrest warrant (Hellman, 1975; Daley,

1971). The officer may secure arrest warrants for dozens of individuals for a variety of violations, and these warrants are served when the officer's official identity is revealed.

Light-cover strategies fall into the same two classifications as deep-cover but with one significant difference: the former involves the active participation of an informant. This strategy is far more common in municipal police departments than is deep-cover; it is more focused in time, activity, and intent. As Wilson (1978:42) notes, "the dominant strategy of these investigations is not that of detecting or randomly observing a crime but of instigating one under controlled circumstances." The participation of an informant who is known and proven in the criminal milieu becomes part of the "cover" and affords officers easier access to violators without first having to fully establish their own credentials (Manning, 1980). One officer explained the plan:

> I was told to go out and attempt to buy drugs from known dealers who the informant knew and from whoever else was out there dealing. I worked mostly in the East Side of town buying heroin and coke . . . it was strictly through the informant who was right there 75% to 80% of the time acting as a go-between. . . . It resulted in 57 individual warrants for sales in 7 months.

A variant of the light-cover strategy involves using an informant for general introductions and establishment of a desired identity and then distancing oneself from that informant. Doing so is desirable for at least two reasons: it protects the informant's identity when arrests are later made and it removes the informant from possible participation in the illegal transaction. Only the female officer reported using that technique.

> I worked with an informant for a couple of months posing as his girlfriend but then I cut him loose. They brought in a male officer who then posed as my boyfriend. But I made the buys. . . . I made 59 arrests for heroin sales.

When the undercover officer is engaged in accumulating arrest warrants, time becomes a factor governing the length of the operation. One officer noted that

> The prosecutor made the decision [to end the operation]. He felt you damaged cases if you wait too long. The early cases would be jeopardized. The people had a legitimate right to be brought to trial.

The longer the elapsed time between the offense and the serving of the warrant, the more difficult it becomes for the arrested person to recall their activities and prepare a defense. The police, of course, maintain a daily log while citizens may not own an appointment book. And since legal questions involving the right to a speedy trial and other factors may become relevant, supervisors prefer to terminate operations of this type about one year after the first case is "made."

The decision to end an undercover operation, however, may be independent of the relative effectiveness of the officer. In a study of undercover operations in two different cities in the late 1960s and in 1970, Malkin (1971) showed that each operation could have been ended earlier with no appreciable loss of suspects. That is, the officer's effectiveness had peaked well before a year was up and suspects could have been brought to trial, or at least apprised of the charges against them, earlier than was done.

Selection

Deciding who will be chosen to join the department is a major problem for police administrators and the selection of who to assign to undercover work is a subset of that larger problem. The undercover officer is generally new to the organization and untrained. Of the 14 officers interviewed who worked undercover assignments, only two had any previous police experience.[5] Six were selected even before a civil service eligibility list was established and six were chosen at the beginning of their police training.[6] One officer said,

> I had no academy training. The Personnel Officer offered me the undercover assignment after I submitted my application. I took the civil service exam alone...and received mailed notification a week later that I had passed. I met with the Chief and [my supervisor] in a hotel room to get sworn in.

In the case of the single female in the study, undercover work was a way to get in the organization: Before she was assigned undercover, the leaders of the department had refused even to accept her application for employment.

> The police department came up with an informant but he would only work with a woman — he refused to introduce a strange man. The police department squeezed the informant and the informant squeezed the department. At the time they knew I wanted to get on the job (the department had no women and was not interested in hiring any). And the head of the drug unit said, "No, she won't work, she doesn't fit the mold." But they gave in and said they would try me out for one month — but not sworn. They said if it works they would make me a provisional police officer. I made a heroin buy my first night on the street.

This female officer was the only officer interviewed beginning her police career without being a sworn officer.

Undercover work may be perceived as a prerequisite for police employment for male officers as well — particularly when there are many applicants for new positions. When municipalities give preference to local residents for hiring, candidates from out of town may find the offered assignment a way to circumvent that policy. One officer reported,

> Hopefully they chose me because I'm bright. Probably they chose me because I didn't know [City A]. But I thought that if I turned [the assignment] down I might not have gotten onto the police department at all.

Police administrators select undercover officers based on the type of cases officers will investigate, the physical appearance of the officer, and the person's personality. One supervisor remarked, "We would never choose a guy six-six (6'6''), he'd stand out like a sore thumb." The black officers interviewed reported their selection was motivated by their race, and another supervisor observed that if he wanted to send someone to work in a Hispanic area he would need an Hispanic officer. The female officer, for example, was initially rejected because she did not fit a supervisor's notion of what a heroin user should look like. The use of such criteria is hardly a surprise, of course, as police in other assignments often rely on physical cues to evaluate suspects (Black, 1971). Another officer said,

> I was picked because I was Italian and looked like a gambler. I looked like a guinea punk. I never had a problem. I was always taken for a gangster and I have a "look of larceny" about me.

Not all of the supervisors agreed that mere appearance governed selection. One said, "It's a question of character," noting that what he was really looking for was the type of person "who doesn't really need anybody and can work, alone" (Girodo, 1984). He went on to say, with sincerity, that the undercover, particularly the deep-cover "must have the ability to improvise" because "there are no rules" to deep-cover work and the person must he "basically deceitful."

Other supervisors took the position that how the officer felt about the work itself was more consequential than external factors. A supervisor asked, "Is the nature of the work contrary to what they believe? Are they afraid? These individuals have no expertise in law enforcement." Girodo (1984: 171) indicated that the supervisor must spend "considerable time detailing the hazards and range of difficulty the prospective candidate will have to endure. Occasionally, he may even try to dissuade the applicant from volunteering." Among the officers interviewed for this study, no such discussion was reported. If anything, conversations which took place prior to beginning an undercover assignment only stressed the positive—what a successful operation could mean for the officer's career, for instance.

The officers in this study accepted undercover assignments for two primary reasons: it assured them of selection to the department, or it promised a later benefit such as choice of assignment or preference at promotion time. The female officer previously mentioned was told that if she did a good job she would later get a desired plainclothes assignment. Another officer was assured that he would be assigned to the precinct of his choice; several were promised immediate promotion to detective. Not all of these promises were kept, however. Few of the supervisors involved were truly in a position to keep the promises they made, and what a "good" job is becomes subject to interpretation. None of the promises, of course, were in writing. But, for some officers, the assignment itself—to "pass" in a new identity—was sufficient to secure cooperation. To quote one officer, whose comments were similar to those of three others, "Someone is offering me a chance to become a spy—really a neat thing."

Training

Formal academy training, which includes socialization into the police occupation as well as technical instruction, and which ranges from two months to one year in duration depending upon the municipality (Pike, 1981), is an experience the officer may not benefit from until the undercover assignment has ended. Police organizations that were observed evidence a preference for assigning newly recruited members to undercover work—particularly deep-cover work.[7]

> The rationale for this is that the Department does not want to have an agent identified while entering or leaving the academy or participating in training activities; further, as [the officer interviewed] said, "We don't want our undercover agents to react to situations like a cop" (Malkin, 1971: 14; also see Manning, 1989, especially pp. 49-52).

The undercover assignment, in this view, is more civilian than police, and it would be counterproductive to socialize a person to be a police officer and then ask them to adopt a false identity. Although instruction about rules of evidence, rights of suspects, and chains of custody would certainly be relevant for the undercover officer, the absence of that and other instruction is argued to be justified. One very experienced supervisor observed, "Maybe the training was inadequate, but if you want somebody to operate as an effective undercover person, do you really want them to have police training? I don't think so."

One of the officers interviewed as well as several supervisors provided a different explanation for the failure to provide police training, related more to organizational structure than to socialization. The officer contended that assigning trained personnel to undercover work would be sabotaged by other police officers. When asked about the benefits of training the officers in the academy before assigning them undercover, he said,

> If you did that you would probably get fucked by the other cops. Somebody who has a good informant would probably protect [the informant] by selling out the undercover.

A good informant, of course, keeps the police officer productive by generating information and arrests, and if the police department evaluates or rewards officers for making arrests (Miller, 1983), this suspicion is worth taking seriously. The fact may be that police solidarity, the vaunted "closed fraternity" often noted in police studies (Ahern, 1972), may not include new officers or those in organizationally marginal roles.[8]

The kind of investigation to which an undercover officer is assigned also affects whether training and socialization may be seen as dysfunctional to the work. Informants generally agreed that entry into the illegal drug market, for example, particularly at the level of street sales, involved fewer problems than other types of investigations. Most undercover officers assigned to street-level drug traffic were simply told to "hang around" specified areas and let themselves be seen. One officer observed, "Everybody was suspicious...but they dealt with a lot of people," so making drug purchases wasn't particularly difficult. Investigating "subversive" groups is seen as being more difficult and requiring a more detailed "cover story." Gambling investigations are seen as the most difficult to conduct as the structures of the enterprise are more formalized and durable. A supervisor pointed out that

> Gamblers are smarter. They question more. "Where are you from? Where are your parents from? What are you doing here?" So [your] cover has to be more solid than for drugs—the structure of gambling operations is tighter.

Officers were told to create their own cover stories utilizing as much of their identity as possible. A complete set of fictitious credentials was prepared for only two of the 14 officers interviewed.

The extent to which the officer receives training prior to assuming the fictitious identity varies from deep- to light-cover work. All of the officers interviewed who had worked deep-cover (eight) reported structured training of less than one day. As one officer remembered,

> I began on a Monday, hooked up with another more experienced undercover and was told what the job was like, what it consisted of, what you could do—should do—to make gambling cases. We rode around a few places...where they believed gambling activities were taking place. The training lasted only a day. The next day I went on the street alone.

This officer, like the other seven, did not enter the police academy until the undercover assignment ended. Those assigned to purchasing narcotics reported "training" for about two hours, focusing on identifying different drugs, packaging, terminology, and prices. The work, progressing on a moment-to-moment schedule, gets its momentum from the officer's success in gaining confidence and confidences (Manning, 1980: Chapter Six). The officer is further taught through a series of informal and unstructured conversations and learns to adjust and improvise rather than to follow strict guidelines (Dix, 1975).

Supervision

It is difficult to supervise undercover operations since direct control over the officer's activities is precluded by the nature of the work, and the "deeper" the cover the more limited the supervision possible (Williams and Guess, 1981). One officer said,

> They might tell me something to do, but the supervision was really minimal. They didn't have a real clear idea of what was going on — but that is what they had me out there for.

The supervisors reported that they were always aware of what their officers were doing, but there were general indications in the interviews that supervision was considered less important as undercover officers gained experience. A supervisor explained,

> . . . as the operation got going, surveillance lessened. The supervisors learned to trust the officer's competence and integrity — that they were doing what they were supposed to do.

The ideal model of how an undercover operation should be organized and supervised and the reality of how they actually run may be far apart.

The supervisor is also a counselor and stresses the law-enforcement orientation of the assignment: the officers must be constantly reminded that they are on the street and in the masquerade precisely because it is a masquerade and part of the job. In the undercover assignment, officers appear to sometimes lose sight of that fact. If the officer fails to maintain perspective, the police department's integrity is compromised. An officer in light-cover noted that the supervisor "keeps you from getting too close [emotionally]; he reminds you that the guy is a scum-bag."

Maintaining perspective may require close supervision, and the interviewed officers report exceptional independence which is all the more remarkable given their general inexperience. Two of the officers reported meeting with their police contact only once a week, although telephone contact was more frequent. One of those officers, however, was actively buying drugs and cases were being prepared for prosecution on the basis of the information and evidence supplied. This type of casual supervision of untrained operatives is especially questionable in terms of evidentiary chain of custody (Malkin, 1971). Evidence in the possession of the officers accumulates and is turned over en masse: it may be lost, misplaced, or mixed with contraband acquired from another source (Manning, 1980). It may also become a temptation for the officer to use, sell, or give away evidence. Novice officers, uninstructed in the correct procedures for handling evidence and writing reports, may ruin a case. The remainder of the undercover officers reported contact with their supervisors once a day, still an infrequent occurrence if multiple illegal transactions occur.

Undercover officers may not receive much feedback from their supervisors, and a one-way flow of information combined with a wholly new occupation and a fictitious identity can be problematic indeed. The officers, particularly those in deep-cover, are a valuable source of oftentimes unique information for the department, but rarely are they privy to organizational plans or analyses. As one supervisor remarked, there are

> no rewarding experiences. You don't know how your work is being received. You don't know what happens as a result of your work. [You] may work hard and get a guy good but then see him back on the street quickly—because supervisors can just turn him into an informant and you don't know what is going on.

The supervisors, however, felt that the officers had enough to worry about just concentrating on their day-to-day street activity and rejected the idea of including undercover officers in the formulation of strategy. The result, then, was that undercover officers reported little supervision in general and virtually none in the field. One informant stated that "I was supervised only to the extent [I] went back to headquarters and did paper work." Infrequent meetings with supervisors, ostensibly done to protect the officer's official identity, unintentionally exposes the novice officer to additional pressures and temptations.

Danger

Except in the very well-planned and organized light-cover assignment, there is almost no way to protect undercover officers in the field in the event their true identity is suspected or becomes known (see Girodo, 1984, for an examination of a well-planned undercover operation). The untrained officer is mainly left to his or her own devices. A supervisor explained,

> You can't have surveillance unless you are running multiple agents, one in deep-cover and one in light as a back-up. Plus there is no need to as they are there for information only (while in deep-cover). In this case the undercover becomes the known, reliable informant (who detectives reference when applying for search or arrest warrants).

The difficulty in providing field security for the officer does not prevent the promise of coverage, however. An officer said,

> I was not scared in the beginning because I was lied to. I was told there would be at least two policemen watching me at all times and I believed it for two weeks. When I realized there was no one watching I asked about it and the supervisor told me that there was surveillance but I

> couldn't see them. But then I got hold of a gun and carried it with me
> for protection—first a .22 [caliber] and then a .25 automatic.

Several of the undercover officers carried handguns, some privately owned
and some issued by the police department. But only in two cases were these
officers trained in the use of those weapons. All, however, carried guns with
the knowledge and tacit approval of their supervisors. A supervisor said he
provided "weapons but no identification" and that the weapons were ones
they had confiscated and were "private handguns not [police] service connected
revolvers." What might happen if an untrained officer shot a citizen remains
unknown and problematic.

Undercover work is seen by police officers as something akin to a game.
The officers are playing a part and if they do it well, they believe they will
do fine. In the beginning, the main problem is being thought to be a police
officer.

> I was called a cop on my first day [on the street] because of being a new
> person. I laughed at the guy. After hanging around awhile I managed
> to fit in.

As a new person in an environment likely to be wholly new to the officer,
and if no informant is used to provide an introduction, the undercover may
feel uncomfortable and conspicuous. An officer remarked,

> Everybody is looking at you and can tell you are a cop. How could they
> not know it? That was what was in my mind. But I didn't think they would
> do anything—beat me up or anything—just tell me to get out of there.

The thought that the work might be dangerous does occur to the officers,
but the threat is not regarded as being particularly credible. As one officer
observed, "I was too stupid to be scared." But the threat and danger is quite
real; five officers reported shooting incidents involving undercover officers
and two reported the shooting deaths of colleagues.

After a short period of settling in and establishing a cover story, the officers
under deep-cover cease to believe "cop" is written across their forehead.
An officer with 18 months of deep-cover experience said,

> I could not have been more securely established than I was. I was well
> liked—trusted. I didn't need a partner, surveillance, or anything. I simply
> couldn't have been more secure than I was.

The female officer, too, felt secure. There had never been a female undercover
in the city before and no one ever suggested she might constitute a threat.
She reported taking chances and constantly trying to extend herself in ways
which she now looks back upon in amazement. A light-cover officer, with
substantial police experience prior to his undercover assignment, felt that
routine patrol work was more dangerous than undercover work. He said,

> In patrol you come upon the unexpected. Here you knew you were dealing with felonies and individuals with guns. The awareness of what you were doing made it less dangerous.

The greater the penetration of an undercover officer into illicit activities, the greater the risk or threat was in reality but the perception was the opposite. The officer gets comfortable with the fictitious identity, feels secure, and, correspondingly, may take greater and perhaps unnecessary risks. Several officers, for example, noted they were constantly trying to test themselves to see how much they could get away with. None of the officers interviewed recognized the magnitude of the risk they took while the assignment was in progress. One officer stated, "Police work was all new to me—it seemed exciting and dangerous but I didn't know—like I do now—how dangerous it was." During the course of the interviews, all but one officer paused at some point to express astonishment at some aspect of what they had done in some situation.

In addition to situationally dangerous interactions, undercover assignments in general are extremely taxing emotionally on the officer; this is especially true for the deep-cover officer who is constantly "on" (Marx, 1982), always an actor on the stage.

> I was getting tired and was looking for a few days off. I called my supervisor to explain it. Instead of just asking for the time off straight out I began by telling him that I go to bed at night and dream of buying drugs. He got very excited—thought "this is great." He said he dreams of search warrants. He thought I was getting into it. I didn't get the time off.

For the officer infiltrating groups alleged to be "subversive," the strain can be enormous. Not only does the assignment require officers to work 24 hours a day, but they are not "making cases" and thus are unable to see a concrete product resulting from their work. Even relating feelings several years old was difficult:

> In order to be effective, I had to live and breathe socialism. And all my old friends are gone. You can live on your police contacts but you have to have friends and they are the ones I was writing reports about. But I knew they weren't [really friends]. So I asked to get out [of the assignment].

The effective intelligence operative clearly is subject to psychological strain and may be "turned" by those under investigation (Marx, 1974; Girodo, 1984). But, despite a general recognition of these problems, none of the officers in the study had been the subject of any special psychological evaluation prior to selection, after selection, or upon terminating the assignment.

Temptation

Undercover officers face a variety of temptations since they are posing as and interacting with violators and doing so with little supervision (Williams and Guess, 1981; Wilson, 1978; Marx, 1974, 1982). Using, selling, or simply giving away[9] the drugs they come in contact with (Girodo, 1984) is one such problem. Undercover officers posing as users may be maneuvered into situations where their failure to inhale, ingest, or inject substances places them in grave danger. Supervisors offered no real recommendations to guide the officers beyond encouraging them to arrange transactions, meetings, and other activities in public places. One supervisor, however, said he would rather see the officer "shoot up" than get hurt for failing to do so and would cover up the act and make sure the officer did not become addicted. None of the officers involved in buying drugs admitted any personal use during their operations, but two of the three deep-cover "intelligence" operatives reported smoking marijuana. The nature of their assignments, of course, made the suggestion to remain in public places largely impossible.

Another temptation involves how cases are "made" or activity reports are written (Marx, 1982). Entrapment is always a possibility when police adopt a fictitious identity in the undercover assignment. While one supervisor remarked, "It's always better not to commit perjury," it is clear both that exculpatory information is not included in warrant applications emanating from undercover operations and, given the supervisor's observation, at least some forms of perjury may be deemed "acceptable." In other studies (Manning, 1974; Skolnick, 1975), it has been observed that officers' reports adhere to the letter of the law even if their actions do not. The interviews reported here indicate that officers' official reports may differ from those originally submitted.

The undercover officer, like the researcher, faces the problem of "going native." Citizens are not only candidates for arrest, they are social companions, confidants to some extent, and perhaps lovers. Moreover, given the nature of the work, a distinct possibility exists that friendships may develop with those same individuals the officer has made a case against. In other instances, officers can experience changing values and grow to identify with a "radical" point of view. As an officer said,

> I started with drugs and [the relationships were] clearly evident—white hats and black hats. Then I switched to subversive activities and it was more like white hats and grey hats. And my hat got grey. But they were my only friends. I didn't have any other friends. [You] develop a closeness that is psychologically difficult to close off.

Since undercover officers must spend a lot of time trying to blend into their new environment and open a circle of acquaintances, they need "tremendous self-discipline and self-awareness,'' according to supervisors. The extent to which the officers selected for this work are capable of handling the associated difficulties is reasonably open to question, and incidents where former undercover officers are later found to have become violators themselves are common (Marx, 1982; Girodo, 1984). As Donner (1971, quoted in Marx, 1974:421) argues, "The infiltrator's secret knowledge that he alone in the group is immune from accountability for his acts dissolves all restraints on his zeal." Given the amount of contact these officers have with their "criminal" environment and the fact that they maintain this contact while misrepresenting their true identity with a modicum of supervision and training, it is surprising that more problems do not appear.

Coming Out

Undercover assignments end when the officer can no longer continue the work (for example, they "burn out" or become identified as police officers) or when the officer's services have ceased to be necessary (for example, the "case has been made"). For light-cover officers there may be few or no problems attached to ending the masquerade as the style of work did not greatly intrude on their private identity. But, for the officer in a deep-cover assignment, the completion of an often lengthy masquerade may be intensely emotional (Girodo, 1984).

The deep-cover assignments of the officers interviewed averaged more than one year in duration; the range was 8 to 18 months. Its end required abruptly abandoning the fictitious identity they had lived and embracing a police identity with which they were largely unfamiliar. The officers looked forward to becoming a "regular" member of the police department, although they largely did not know what that meant, and to resuming "normal lives" with greater separation between work and private life. They were glad to "surface" and sought to renew old friends and acquaintances long abandoned. One officer reported,

> At the end I felt good, I felt real good. I went out and bought an M.G. — didn't change my appearance — and went to people [I had been friends with before the undercover assignment] with a badge and a gun to tell them what I had been doing for the past year and a half — to make friends again.

Only one of the officers reported any difficulty reestablishing abandoned relationships; this was an officer whose investigation involved bookmaking arrests. But as novice officers often go directly into the police academy for conventional training after the undercover assignment ends, they have an opportunity to establish a new circle of friends, which minimizes transition problems.[10]

For officers whose work activities involved "making cases," the end of the assignment coincided with a "round-up" of accused individuals for whom arrest warrants had been prepared. As all officers interviewed were employed by municipal police organizations and their work was primarily done within that municipality, the arrests generated focused hostility toward them for "tricking" those arrested. As a result, the former undercover officer was instructed to take unusual safety precautions upon shedding the fictitious identity. In addition to altering physical appearances (for example, cutting hair, shaving beards, growing mustaches), they were told to be alert for someone following them while driving to and from work. If they had used their own car during the assignment, they were encouraged to purchase a new automobile, although at their own expense. One officer, who had infiltrated the highest levels of a local organized crime group, was assigned a bodyguard. The officer was still living with his parents and the bodyguard, armed with a shotgun, stayed in the house during the evening hours. The female officer noted she received far more protection and attention after the assignment ended than while it was ongoing. She said,

> For almost a year afterwards, I drove to another officer's house in the morning and I rode into work with him. Later they put a police radio in my personal car. They checked my gun [for cartridges] and the battery in my [portable] radio every day. They were very protective. This is not because they felt I wasn't capable, they weren't sure what to do so they were careful.

Finally, the supervisors must, in some fashion, "debrief" outgoing undercover officers and help them adjust to their new public identity as police officers. As a supervisor noted,

> They come to feel they are special and...are not treated specially. This is the biggest drawback. They feel they deserve things like promotion and very quickly get bitter when they do not get promoted.

Recall, however, that promises of promotion and other special treatment were reported by officers to have been among the inducements offered for undertaking the masquerade to begin with. Additionally, officers leave a rather unstructured setting for perhaps the most structured of all police settings, the academy. That socializing experience may be even more extreme for those officers with undercover experience. These interviews, albeit limited in number, indicate that former police undercover officers do face significant and immediate disappointments often due to inflated expectations of what awaits them upon termination. It may be true that the more successful the officer is in the undercover assignment, the greater will be the problems of readjustment.

Discussion

Municipal police departments continue to assign police officers to undercover investigations as a strategy to learn about criminal and other activities of citizens. While police departments also use covert tactics internally, this paper has focused only on investigations external to the organization. The intent here has been to seek understanding of a particular form of police work through the experiences of knowledgeable practitioners.

Undercover police work is used to locate and arrest persons involved in illegal activity. It is also used for intelligence gathering purposes, which means investigating persons even when there exists no intention or expectation of initiating any criminal prosecution. In that latter form, undercover operations are frequently questioned as they extend police activity to perhaps unreasonable lengths and directly threaten constitutionally protected behaviors (Dix, 1975; Lundy, 1969). Importantly, police departments do not initiate undercover operations only when other investigative techniques fail: agencies that use them tend to do so regularly. Thus, undercover operations may not be bounded by time and events; when one officer's masquerade ends, another officer's begins.

As opposed to being an investigation assigned to the most highly trained, competent, and knowledgeable officers in the organization, undercover work tends to be carried out by newly recruited and inexperienced members.[11] The undercover assignment, problematic as a police enforcement strategy, is even more problematic as an introduction and technique for newly appointed members. While Manning (1980:52) pointed out that narcotic officers' freedom from the constraints of law "loosens the commitment of the officer to both the law and the police role," the even greater freedom afforded the undercover operative, as yet untrained and a police officer in name only, is even more troublesome.

Supervisors, although experienced police officers, may be no more knowledgeable of undercover tactics and problems than are the novice officers. One supervisor, commenting on an undercover operation in which one of the two novice officers was shot and killed, observed, "We had never done anything like this before. We were flying by the seat of our pants." The officer's death terminated only one part of the undercover project and did not prompt changes in supervision, selection, or training. The supervisors merely sought to salvage the cases yielded by the operation without questioning policies which contributed to the officer's death.

These interviews revealed that officers learn one of the most questionable police tactics principally through informal and unstructured conversations which address only specific immediate problems and work-related concerns. Undercover work constitutes a problematic introduction to law enforcement as it stresses flexibility and creativity (Girodo, 1984) which are at odds with the bureaucratic and quasi-military orientation of the enterprise. The most important characteristic of the successful undercover operative, according to supervisors, is to dissemble. As one officer said, one must be

> a good liar—actor. This goes without saying. You wouldn't get to step one if you weren't. I guess I don't think of myself so much as a liar as an actor because I think of myself as basically a trustworthy person. You know they can't trust you but they think they can trust you and do.

The freedom and creativity inherent in the work, however, is potentially at odds with legal guidelines and leads to an investigatory-centered operation (Manning, 1980) run by untrained officers. With virtually no guidelines or standards to refer to, untrained officers may not know the standard against which their conduct must be judged (Dix, 1975).

Although undercover policing appears to be a useful strategy, officers and supervisors indicate several problems. There are few standards governing selecting and qualifying "agents," supervision may be lax, informants may assume wholly inappropriate responsibilities, and inexperienced officers are exposed to significant dangers with little preparation. There is little information about how effective undercover investigations are, what they cost (economically, psychologically, or constitutionally), or why they fail. Similarly, the extent to which police departments use the strategy is unknown. And there is a general absence of information regarding the adjustment problems officers experience either during an assignment or after the assignment has ended (but see Marx, 1982; Girodo, 1984), what these adjustment problems mean to the employing organization, or to what extent they result in damaging innocent citizens (Dix, 1975).

Hellman (1975: 69) notes that "once the use of undercover agents is accepted as a legitimate tool of law enforcement, distinctions among crimes tend to be forgotten." Successful operations encourage repetitions and foster a reliance on a tactic which becomes a regular investigative tool as opposed to a strategy of last resort. As an operation which relies on deception, an adherence to rules and careful supervision and oversight is imperative because the lives of inexperienced police officers and the rights of citizens hang in the balance.

References Cited

Ahern, James F. 1972. *Police in Trouble*. New York: Hawthorn.
Bickman, Leonard. 1974. "Social roles and uniforms: Clothes make the person." *Psychology Today*, 7: 49-51.
Black, Donald. 1971. "The social organization of arrest." *Stanford Law Review*, 23: 1,087-1,111.

Daley, Robert. 1971. *Target Blue*. New York: Dell.

Dix, George E. 1975. "Undercover investigations and police rule making." *Texas Law Review*, 53: 203-294.

Donnelly, Richard C. 1951. "Judicial control of informants, spies, stool pigeons, and agent provocateurs." *Yale Law Journal*, 60: 1,091-1,131.

Girodo, Michel. 1984. "Entry and re-entry strain in undercover agents." In Vernon L. Allen and Evert van de Vliert (eds.), *Role Transitions*. New York: Plenum.

Hellman, Arthur D. 1975. *Laws Against Marijuana*. Chicago: University of Illinois Press.

Iverson, William D. 1967. "Judicial control of secret agents." *Yale Law Journal*, 76: 994-1,019.

Joseph, Nathan and Nicholas Alex. 1972. "The uniform: A sociological perspective." *American Journal of Sociology*, 77: 719-730.

Lundy, Joseph P. 1969. "Police undercover agents: New threat to first amendment freedoms." *George Washington Law Review*, 37: 634-668.

Malkin, Joseph. 1971. *Justice before trial: Undercover narcotics investigations*. Unpublished manuscript, New Haven, CT: Yale University Law School.

Manning, Peter K. 1974. "Police lying." *Urban Life and Culture*, 3: 283-306.

_____. 1980. *The Narcs' Game*. Cambridge, MA: MIT Press.

Martin, Susan Ehrlich. 1980. *Breaking and Entering: Policewomen on Patrol*. Berkeley: University of California Press.

Marx, Gary T. 1974. "Thoughts on a neglected category of social movement participants: The agent provocateur and the informant." *American Journal of Sociology*, 80: 402-442.

_____. 1980. "The new undercover police work." *Urban Life* 8: 399-446.

_____. 1981. "Ironies of social control: Authorities as contributors to deviance through escalations, non-enforcement and covert facilitation." *Social Problems*, 28: 221-246.

_____. 1982. "Who really gets stung: Some issues raised by the new police undercover work." *Crime and Delinquency*, 8: 165-193.

Miller, George I. 1983. "On the construction and production of ideology: The question of police civility." Presented at the annual meeting of the American Society of Criminology.

Pike, Diane L. 1981. "Making rookies: The social organization of police academy training." Unpublished Ph.D. dissertation, New Haven, CT: Yale University.

Reiss, Albert J., Jr. 1971. *The Police and the Public*. New Haven, CT: Yale University Press.

_____. 1974. "Citizen access to criminal justice." *The British Journal of Law and Society*, 1: 50-74.

Seedman, Albert A. 1974. *Chief*. New York: Arthur Fields.

Skolnick, Jerome. 1975. *Justice Without Trial*. New York: Wiley.

Van Maanen, John. 1984. "Making rank: Becoming an American police sergeant." *Urban Life* 3: 155-176.

Williams, Jay R. and L. Lynn Guess. 1981. "The informant: A narcotics enforcement dilemma." *Journal of Psychoactive Drugs*, 13:235-245.

Wilson, James Q. 1978. *The Investigators*. New York: Basic Books.

Notes

[1] Williams and Guess (1981) have used a similar distinction of "partial" and "deep" cover.

[2] In one case the officer did both, but at different times.

[3] Two other women with undercover experience of the type explored here were located but declined to be interviewed. The absence of females in this study should come as no surprise; females only entered conventional police roles in the early 1970s and their main function outside of uniform assignments most frequently was in decoy type work (Martin, 1980). The number of female police officers in any police department remains small even in the mid-1980s, and the likelihood of women being assigned to undercover work at the municipal police level is smaller still.

[4] Marx (1974; 1981) argues that police involvement in political intelligence situations may serve to increase or even instigate violations. But there was no indication of such provocative behavior on the part of the officers in this study. Intelligence-based investigations are also commented on by Lundy, 1969; Hellman, 1975; and Dix, 1975.

[5] One officer was selected when his recruit training class ended and one had worked in uniform patrol for four years.

[6] This mode of selection apparently occurs in the New York City Police Department also (Seedman, 1974).

[7] Girodo's (1984) study indicates an exception. Still, since this research is principally exploring municipal police departments carrying out undercover operations largely within their own boundaries, recruitment of newly appointed members may continue to be the norm.

[8] Officers assigned to "internal affairs," for example, may also be excluded.

[9] Giving narcotics or controlled drugs is technically viewed as a sale at law.

[10] Girodo's (1984) more experienced operatives lacked this type of support.

[11] The most recent undercover operation reported in these interviews (1982) indicates some movement away from this practice. See also Girodo, 1984.

8

Reflections on Police Corruption

James W. Birch

I've given a great deal of thought to policing since leaving the Philadelphia Police Department four years ago. So many questions still go unanswered, and I often wonder if any of the inequities and corrupt ways will ever change — or if anyone really wants them to change.

For seven years I worked uniform patrol in a high crime district in a major metropolitan area and met some of the best and worst police officers society has to offer. We shared many good times, some bad times, and, of course, we shared the everyday sacrifices of loss of privacy and identity so common to police work. Being a cop was like living in a fish bowl with everyone watching and judging your every move. The public was consistently ready to forget the good job you did the minute they saw what they thought was a bad job. The public was so quick to condemn!

But the hardest feelings to reconcile are the feelings of deep bitterness and disappointment I still feel toward many of my former fellow officers and supervisors. Why did so many of the police seem to feel that sleeping, drinking, and on-duty sexual activity were perquisites of the job? It always dumbfounded me that cops would resent those few supervisors who actually tried to run straight squads. And why was the ward leader always the one to see for favored assignments and transfers, rather than having the assignments and transfers awarded on merit — that is, on earning them?

Birch, James, "Reflections on Police Corruption," in *Criminal Justice Ethics.* 1983, Vol. 2.2, beginning on page 2. Reprinted by permission.

If the public only knew how much the marriage between local politics and police really cost them in inefficiency and quality of service! And corruption—why did city officials keep talking about the few "rotten apples" when every officer and citizen knew police corruption was a system problem? Didn't the city hear everyone laughing?

It's corruption that I found hardest to endure. Always the daily decisions of whether to take or not to take. The free coffee and meals, formal pads, and peer pressure all worked to blur ethics. Why did it seem that every citizen had something a little extra they wanted you to do or to overlook? I can remember headlines of corruption investigations, especially the Knapp Commission, which identified the "meat-eaters"—those corrupt, greedy cops in city after city who always wanted more and finally got caught. I was prepared for the big bribes; it would be easy to turn those down. An old adage I believe in states, "A man thinking about committing a sin would do well to first imagine reading about it as if it were public." I had no intention of making those headlines. But somebody should have emphasized the "grass eaters"—those legions of cops who simply take what comes their way. Somebody should have mentioned that from the moment you hit the street, you're faced with decisions regarding corruption.

Corruption starts with the free cup of coffee and slowly builds into a ladder of opportunities, with each rung becoming more and more serious. I remember all the little tests everyone had for you. Your partners, supervisors, and the public were constantly watching and making assumptions about what kind of cop you were going to be based on which favors you accepted and which you turned down.

I remember well my first day on the street, working a wagon with a veteran copy—I remember all the questions I wanted to ask, all the pride and enthusiasm that swelled inside me. What would we do first? Where would we patrol? For two weeks we worked together and for two weeks our first stop was always at the same diner. After all, you never began a tour without first getting some coffee! My partner always "bought" the coffee, but one day, after much persistence on my part (and reluctance on his) he said, "OK kid, you go this time." I walked to the counter, ordered two to go, and handed the owner some money. "That's OK officer, no charge." "No, I insist, how much is it?" "Really, officer, don't worry about it." I pushed the change toward him and he pushed it back. The scene was comical, yet absurd. I finally got in the last push and turned to leave. I couldn't believe it when he actually threw the coins at me. By this time everyone in the diner was looking and I felt absolutely ridiculous. Would I ever get used to being in the fish bowl? My partner laughed hysterically when I told him what happened. I wasn't sure if I'd passed my first test or not!

Coffee, free meals, haircuts—everywhere you went the public insisted on giving a special "police discount." No police solicitation; just enter a store, offer to pay full price and wait for the inevitable discount. It was so common that even the most idealistic, straight guys would secretly resent the few stores which didn't participate. Everyone had their own reasons for giving. Some had relatives who were cops, some were police buffs, some were intimidated by the uniform and felt they had to do something. But most were buying "insurance"; they expected a quick response if they ever needed the police. I don't know any officer who didn't feel comfortable taking at least some of these minor favors. But this is precisely what makes the coffee, etc., a problem — the vast police participation tends to legitimize the behavior to both the police and the public. Also, it sets the stage for increased involvement on the corruption ladder.

Maybe this is why I wasn't completely offended or caught off-guard when it was my turn to make some club checks and found the owners willing to barter for letting them stay open. By then I was aware that members of the public offered things for their own self-interest. It was obvious that few bars or private clubs in any area were ready to close at the legally prescribed hour. The public didn't want to leave their favorite watering holes by such unrealistic hours and, in many cases, off-duty cops were doing the drinking which prompted the old double standard rule. However, when you were working midnights, it was a requirement to make "appearances" at these establishments to ensure that all customers were gone, and to complete a report saying so. It didn't take a genius to quickly figure out that the emphasis was on those "appearances." Seldom were the places actually closed. As long as the report was submitted stating the customers were gone and the door was locked, no one would verify it.

I remember, when I was still considered a rookie, working a sector for the first time where I was required to close a club. I decided I'd better do it by the book in spite of all the advice from my fellow cops just to stick my head in the door and then write a report saying the club was closed. At the prescribed time I made the first of two required visits just to let the club owner know that I would be back in thirty minutes to be sure all customers had gone. The bartender seemed cooperative — "Sure, Officer, don't worry, we always close on time." The problem occurred when I returned and found more customers than before and a much brisker business. The bartender was still cordial, "What can I get you — a beer? mixed drink?" Everybody was always trying to give you something and change the subject! When I strongly suggested he immediately stop sales and close the club, and when he knew I wasn't kidding, he suggested I'd better get a supervisor right away. It was really hard to do things by the book....After relating the events to a supervisor, he gave me the typical "Good job" and sent me away. He would handle the situation personally. I never did go back to see if the club actually closed. It was just amazing to realize the extent of the barter system in which police operate. Each day brought new opportunities to compromise ideals and principles. "I'll give you free drinks and x amount of dollars and you give me under-enforcement of all laws regarding my customers!" Anyway, it was a long time before I worked a route that had a club on it.

When I joined the police department in 1971, all eyes were on the problems New York City was having relative to the Knapp Commission. Police were always watching other departments to compare pay, benefits, and working conditions. But this was a little different. Could that type of major corruption investigation ever happen here? I don't remember any Serpicos in my department. Few cops would ever risk exposing the system the way Serpico did. More often than not, a live and let live attitude existed. By the time I, or any cop, got a steady car or beat, ground rules would already have been established. Without ever having to say anything, it was known which cops would and which wouldn't get involved with any of the unofficial arrangements between the public and police. Supervisors had a good idea of which run you were on and how high on the corruption ladder you were likely to climb. But it was interesting to compare departments. We spent many an hour assigning "meat eater" and "grass eater" labels to cops we knew. Even though we couldn't think of any Serpicos, it was easy to identify the other career paths cops followed. You participated in the unofficial arrangements either by actively soliciting or simply taking what the public offered; or you didn't participate at all, but in that case, you also didn't tell. It was always clearcut. Obviously the choice Serpico made was out of the question, and resigning from the department because of ideals was laughable. "Don't make waves" seemed to be the cop's favorite cliche.

It still amazes me when I think how difficult it was to avoid corrupt situations. You could always be sure that some citizen would find you and make you an offer you couldn't refuse. I could stop a car for running a light, for instance, and have the operator beg me to take $20 to forget the ticket. Or, better yet, the driver might throw the $20 in my window because he knows it's the going rate in the district. So many things can go through an officer's mind, so many ways to rationalize the corruption. If I saw nothing wrong with the free coffee or in allowing clubs to stay open beyond legal closing times, then why not make this motorist happy too? After all, he made the offer and, in essence, I'm here to serve the community. Then again, I could arrest him for bribery—but who wants to face the inside crew? The grief you receive from some cops for making such a petty arrest is merciless. Or, I could really make the guy angry by telling him what to do with his $20 and give him the ticket. What a system!

The magnitude of the problem really hit home one day when I was working a car with a young cop who had spent about two years on the force and who had acquired the reputation of being really aggressive. A supervisor "gave us a meet" at a certain intersection and, naturally, we responded supposing we were to have our log signed. Instead, the cop was summoned into the supervisor's car and they talked for a long time. Later that day the young cop told me how happy he was to have been finally accepted by the squad. The supervisor had told him he was a good cop, trustworthy, made good arrests and showed up at most squad parties. In fact, he fit in so much that he was now officially in on those unofficial arrangements which guaranteed him a second income. He was so happy to be accepted that he had to tell someone and he figured it was OK to tell me because he knew I wasn't the Serpico type!

I didn't know many greedy "meat eater" cops. There really weren't that many. There was no need to break away and get involved with high risk vices like narcotics when the public was so willing to provide everything from free coffee up to formal payments to overlook gambling and liquor violations. My department was the target of a corruption investigation in 1973. It was embarrassing and humiliating to read about how the city refused to cooperate and how they kept insisting that corruption wasn't a system problem — just a problem of a few "rotten apples." I agree that the "meat eaters" are the "rottenest" of the apples. But why does everyone ignore how they became that way? They didn't become cops one day and start dealing narcotics the next. They were weaned through their careers by a public willing to pay for favors, cops willing to take, and public officials refusing to admit that these "rotten apples" actually live in a very "rotten barrel"!

I wish police departments and city officials would admit that police corruption results from a system where honest police recruits are placed into a dishonest police subculture. The police system is typical of the bartering and favor-peddling which pervades the entire justice system and society as well. Public officials would only be telling the public what they already know, but in admitting to the extent of the problem, officials could also share responsibility for it with the public, as they properly should. Why shouldn't the public be told that they are part of the problem and that corruption in the police department will only end when the public wants it to end? Let the police department identify and eliminate the greedy "meat eaters," but tell the public they are responsible for eliminating "minor perks," payments for bar closing, ticket-fixing, and formalized pads — that is, for eliminating the minor bribes that create the climate for "meat eaters."

The hypocrisy that exists now is pitiful. I marvel at the mentality behind some of the ways departments attempt to pacify the public. For instance, as one boss told me, it is a well-known fact that if vice arrest quotas aren't assigned to officers, then few if any vice arrests will be made because police officers are citizens who also enjoy playing numbers and drinking after hours and don't really view these activities as illegal. So, given the choice, they wouldn't make arrests for this type of vice activity. Typically, the department responds by assigning a fixed number of arrests each month for vice. They fear that without the quota the total vice arrests will be so low that the public, knowing vice exists, will assume the police are taking pay-offs and are corrupt. Consequently, each month the required arrests are made to try to persuade the public that the department isn't corrupt. Unbelievable!

I often wonder if we need vice units at all. The level of corruption in any area is determined by the community, not police enforcement. Just take two cops, give them a small office, and tell the public that due to limited man-power and their obvious desire for some corruption, the police will only respond to citizen complaints. Then we could take the squads currently assigned to vice and place them in activities where they have public support.

We must stop worrying about appearances and politics. Tell the people they are responsible for much of the corruption, and the police will not expend any more manpower fighting a losing battle. We must also admit to ourselves that a system of vice opportunities presents itself to all officers at all ranks. We should start with new police applicants and explain to them that inherent in the job is the constant temptation to make "little extras" ranging from free meals to regular monthly payoffs. We must tell the appli-cant that some officers can't take the pressure and some end up behind bars. We must continually emphasize to police academy classes that as soon as they receive their first assignments, they will be unofficially and officially watched and tested by the community and their peers alike to see how they do on the ladder of corruption. I remember vividly the instructors at my police academy stating "there is no systematic corruption in this department — only those few 'rotten apples'"! If the instructors had told the truth, perhaps hundreds of new officers would have been prepared for the rude awakening of the real world. We must continually have in-service classes for veteran officers and supervisors so that the veterans can learn about and discuss the findings of the various commission investigations throughout the country. We should formulate programs which continually educate both the public and police that corruption is a system problem.

There is so much that needs to be done. Wouldn't it be refreshing if police departments would finally do something innovative, and finally stand up and admit that each department has a corruption problem — rather than repeating the traditional "rotten apple" rhetoric?

I will continue giving a great deal of thought to policing. Since leaving the department I've had the opportunity to soul-search and to work with many police departments in many states. These experiences, plus personal research, have increased my desire to see change. While operations may differ among departments, I've found the basics are always evident — a system of public and police corruption, police politics, and an aversion to innovation. I'm looking forward to and will work toward the day when the public and police will overcome this system.

Section III

Confrontation and Compromise: The Courts

The criminal courts are steeped in myth and surrounded by controversy. Myths abound because many citizens have ignored their rights and neglected their duties in regard to the courts. Ignored has been the potential for access, recognized in the U.S. Constitution, which extends to each citizen the opportunity to observe the criminal process in open court. Neglected has been the duty to participate in and contribute to a more efficient and effective court system through service on grand and petit juries. The notice to appear for jury duty often results in the development of a host of excuses why one cannot serve. Without first hand experiences then, we should not be surprised that most Americans have relied on the media for information about the court process. For the most part, contributions made by movies, television and popular novels have not been positive and constructive in that reality is often distorted. Although ''Perry Mason'' and ''L.A. Law'' have entertained us, they have deceived us as well.

We have been led to believe that the criminal trial is a frequent and highly dramatic event which takes place in an emotion-filled courtroom packed by spectators and the press. We are surprised when we learn that most cases do not go to trial. Courtrooms are often empty or are utilized by a very few individuals engaged in the tedious business that makes up everyday reality for judges and lawyers. Contrary to popular conception, most cases are plea bargained, a somewhat complex process through which a charge against the defendant is reduced in exchange for a plea of guilty, thereby avoiding a costly and time-consuming trial. Nothing in our media experience has prepared us for the attorney who is incompetent or so terribly disinterested in a case that justice is denied. The wise and dispassionate judge we see on television cannot always be found in the courtroom. Sometimes the judge we observe seems to be ignorant and prejudiced. Finally, we often overlook the fact that it is the prosecutor who ultimately determines what will happen in a criminal proceeding. It is the prosecutor who establishes the actual charges the defendant must respond to; it is the prosecutor who accepts or rejects a plea bargain and decides whether a case will go to trial.

Given the gravity of the tasks performed by the criminal courts, we should not be surprised that court operations are surrounded by controversy. Our courts function in an adversary setting and are subjected to intense and conflicting pressures. The need to protect individual rights often appears to collide with society's legitimate demand for protection. The volume of litigation has increased considerably over the past ten years, and persons accused of crimes have an increased number of rights. The result is delay in the court process and crowded dockets which judges must eventually clear while providing both the substance and appearance of justice. Because many citizens are suspicious of the courts, there is an unwillingness to invest the needed financial allocations in this aspect of the criminal justice system. Courts have enjoyed autonomy for many years. They have been ignored, and in their isolation have developed a host of problems which defy simple solutions. In the following section a number of these problems have been addressed.

Although the criminal justice system is supposed to consider each case on its own merits, this becomes less likely as the burden on the system increases. In "Maintaining the Myth of Individualized Justice," John Rosecrance illustrates how the sentencing recommendations of probation officers are based on a few relatively fixed criteria, but are written to provide the illusion that recommendations are based on a careful consideration of the individual characteristics of the offender. This again illustrates the system's continuing tension between bureaucratic efficiency and justice.

In "Fighting Crime in a Crumbling System," Steven Brill takes the reader on a discouraging journey through the day-to-day operation of the criminal court, and shows that it is neither efficient nor just. His study dramatically illustrates how court delays occur and how they undercut the idea of swift and certain justice. Whether a case is handled promptly and fairly is too often a matter of chance. His work illustrates what is meant by the phrase "justice delayed is justice denied."

In "The Practice of Law as a Con Game," Abraham Blumberg focuses on the role of the defense attorney. Blumberg contends that the image of an aggressive defense attorney fighting for the protection of his or her client's rights is a myth. The defense attorney is very much a part of the informal court organization. As a result, he or she tends to be cooperative with the prosecutor. By contributing to the negotiated plea both parties benefit—the defense attorney receives a fee for very little work and the prosecutor avoids an expensive trial. The right to counsel established by the United States Supreme Court becomes meaningless as a result of these informal relationships.

Milton Heumann addresses a related issue in his article "Adapting to Plea Bargaining: Prosecutors." Plea bargaining is central to the operation of our criminal courts. It is the final plea bargain agreed upon by the prosecutor and the defense attorney that will determine the sentence, a fact often ignored by those who focus solely on the judiciary in studying the sentencing process. By providing excerpts of conversations between prosecutors and other court personnel, Heumann gives a first-person account of the realities of plea bargaining and the politics and conflicts which are a part of the bargaining process. The distinction between prosecutor and judge becomes blurred as the prosecutor comes to expect that he or she will exercise sentencing powers.

In "Guilty Until Proved Innocent," Ronald Huff and his associates examine a fascinating, but seldom discussed problem, the wrongful conviction of innocent people. They estimate how often this might occur and show how it is possible, even in a system where accused individuals have a large number of rights and procedural safeguards.

9

Maintaining the Myth of Individualized Justice: Probation Presentence Reports

John Rosecrance

The Justice Department estimates that over one million probation presentence reports are submitted annually to criminal courts in the United States (Allen and Simonsen 1986: 111). The role of probation officers in the presentence process traditionally has been considered important. After examining criminal courts in the United States, a panel of investigators concluded: ''Probation officers are attached to most modern felony courts; presentence reports containing their recommendations are commonly provided and these recommendations are usually followed'' (Blumstein, Martin, and Holt 1983). Judges view presentence reports as an integral part of sentencing, calling them ''the best guide to intelligent sentencing'' (Murrah 1963: 67) and ''one of the most important developments in criminal law during the 20th century'' (Hogarth 1971: 246).

Researchers agree that a strong correlation exists between probation recommendations (contained in presentence reports) and judicial sentencing. In a seminal study of judicial decision making, Carter and Wilkins (1967) found 95 percent agreement between probation recommendation and sentence disposition when the officer recommended probation and 88 percent agreement when the officer opposed probation.

Although there is no controversy about the correlation between probation recommendation and judicial outcome, scholars disagree as to the actual

John Rosecrance. ''Maintaining the Myth of Individualized Justice: Probation Presentence Reports.'' *Justice Quarterly*. 5(2): 235-256. Reprinted with permission of the Academy of Criminal Justice Sciences.

influence of probation officers in the sentencing process. That is, there is no consensus regarding the importance of the presentence investigator in influencing sentencing outcomes. On the one hand, Myers (1979: 538) contends that the "important role played by probation officer recommendation argues for greater theoretical and empirical attention to these officers." Walsh (1985: 363) concludes that "judges lean heavily on the professional advice of probation." On the other hand, Kingsnorth and Rizzo (1979) report that probation recommendations have been supplanted by plea bargaining and that the probation officer is "largely superfluous." Hagan, Hewitt, and Alwin (1979), after reporting a direct correlation between recommendation and sentence, contend that the "influence of the probation officer in the presentence process is subordinate to that of the prosecutor" and that probation involvement is "often ceremonial."

My research builds on the latter perspective, and suggests that probation presentence reports do not influence judicial sentencing significantly but serve to maintain the myth that criminal courts dispense individualized justice. On the basis of an analysis of probation practices in California, I will demonstrate that the presentence report, long considered an instrument for the promotion of individualized sentencing by the court, actually deemphasizes individual characteristics and affirms the primacy of instant offense and prior criminal record as sentencing determinants. The present study was concerned with probation in California; whether its findings can be applied to other jurisdictions is not known. California's probation system is the nation's largest, however (Petersilia, Turner, Kahan, and Peterson 1985), and the experiences of that system could prove instructive to other jurisdictions.

In many California counties (as in other jurisdictions throughout the United States) crowded court calendars, determinate sentencing guidelines, and increasingly conservative philosophies have made it difficult for judges to consider individual offenders' characteristics thoroughly. Thus judges, working in tandem with district attorneys, emphasize the legal variables of offense and criminal record at sentencing (see, for example, Forer 1980; Lotz and Hewitt 1977; Tinker, Quiring, and Pimentel 1985). Probation officers function as employees of the court; generally they respond to judicial cues and emphasize similar variables in their presentence investigations. The probation officers' relationship to the court is ancillary; their status in relation to judges and other attorneys is subordinate. This does not mean that probation officers are completely passive; individual styles and personal philosophies influence their reports. Idiosyncratic approaches, however, usually are reserved for a few special cases. The vast majority of "normal" (Sudnow 1965) cases are handled in a manner that follows relatively uniform patterns.

Hughes's (1958) work provides a useful perspective for understanding the relationship between probation officers' status and their presentence duties. According to Hughes, occupational duties within institutions often serve to maintain symbiotic status relationships as those in higher-status positions pass on lesser duties to subordinates. Other researchers (Blumberg 1967; Neubauer 1974; Rosecrance 1985) have demonstrated that although judges may give lip service to the significance of presentence investigations, they remain suspicious of the probation officers' lack of legal training and the hearsay nature of the reports. Walker (1985) maintains that in highly visible cases judges tend to disregard the probation reports entirely. Thus the judiciary, by delegating the collection of routine information to probation officers, reaffirms its authority and legitimacy. In this context, the responsibility for compiling presentence reports can be considered a "dirty work" assignment (Hagan 1975) that is devalued by the judiciary. Judges expect probation officers to submit noncontroversial reports that provide a facade of information, accompanied by bottom-line recommendations that do not deviate significantly from a consideration of offense and prior record. The research findings in this paper will show how probation officers work to achieve this goal.

In view of the large number of presentence reports submitted, it is surprising that so little information about the presentence investigation process is available. The factors used in arriving at a sentencing recommendation, the decision to include certain information, and the methods used in collecting data have not been described. The world of presentence investigators has not been explored by social science researchers. We lack research about the officers who prepare presentence reports, and hardly understand how they think and feel about those reports. The organizational dynamics and the status positions that influence presentence investigators have not been identified prominently (see, for example, Shover 1979). In this article I intend to place probation officers' actions within a framework that will increase the existing knowledge of the presentence process. My research is informed by 15 years of experience as a probation officer, during which time I submitted hundreds of presentence reports.

Although numerous studies of probation practices have been conducted, an ethnographic perspective rarely has been included in this body of research, particularly in regard to research dealing with presentence investigations. Although questionnaire techniques (Katz 1982), survey data (Hagan et al. 1979), and decision-making experiments (Carter 1967) have provided some information about presentence reports, qualitative data, which often are available only through an insider's perspective,[1] are notably lacking. The subtle strategies and informal practices used routinely in preparing presentence reports often are hidden from outside researchers.

The research findings emphasize the importance of *typing* in the compilation of public documents (presentence reports). In this paper "typing" refers to "the process by which one person (the agent) arrives at a private definition of another (the target)" (Prus 1975: 81). A related activity, *designating*, occurs when "the typing agent reveals his attributions of the target to others" (Prus and Stratten 1976: 48). In the case of presentence investigations, private typings become designations when they are made part of an official court report. I will show that presentence recommendations are developed through a typing process in which individual offenders are subsumed into general dispositional categories. This process is influenced largely by probation officers' perceptions of factors that judicial figures consider appropriate; probation officers are aware that the ultimate purpose of their reports is to please the court. These perceptions are based on prior experience and are reinforced through judicial feedback.

Methods

The major sources of data used in this study were drawn from interviews with probation officers. Prior experience facilitated my ability to interpret the data. Interviews were conducted in two three-week periods during 1984 and 1985 in two medium-sized California counties. Both jurisdictions were governed by state determinate sentencing policies; in each, the district attorney's office remained active during sentencing and generally offered specific recommendations. I did not conduct a random sample but tried instead to interview all those who compiled adult presentence reports. In the two counties in question, officers who compiled presentence reports did not supervise defendants.[2]

Not all presentence writers agreed to talk with me; they cited busy schedules, lack of interest, or fear that I was a spy for the administration. Even so, I was able to interview 37 presentence investigators, approximately 75 percent of the total number of such employees in the two counties.[3] The officers interviewed included eight women and 29 men with a median age of 38.5 years, whose probation experience ranged from one year to 27 years. Their educational background generally included a bachelor's degree in a liberal arts subject (four had degrees in criminal justice, one in social work). Typically the officers regarded probation work as a "job" rather than a profession. With only a few exceptions, they did not read professional journals or attend probation association conventions.

The respondents generally were supportive of my research, and frequently commented that probation work had never been described adequately. My status as a former probation officer enhanced the interview process greatly. Because I could identify with their experiences, officers were candid, and I was able to collect qualitative data that reflected accurately the participants' perspectives. During the interviews I attempted to discover how probation officers conducted their presentence investigations. I wanted to know when a sentencing recommendation was decided, to ascertain which variables influenced a sentencing recommendation decision, and to learn how probation officers defined their role in the sentencing process.

Although the interviews were informal, I asked each of the probation officers the following questions:

1. What steps do you take in compiling a presentence report?
2. What is the first thing you do upon receiving a referral?
3. What do you learn from interviews with the defendant?
4. Which part of the process (in your opinion) is the most important?
5. Who reads your reports?
6. Which part of the report do the judges feel is most important?
7. How do your reports influence the judge?
8. What feedback do you get from the judge, the district attorney, the defense attorney, the defendant, your supervisor?

In addition to interviewing probation officers, I questioned six probation supervisors and seven judges on their views about how presentence reports were conducted.

The procedure I used to analyze the collected data was similar to the grounded theory method advocated by Glaser and Strauss (1967). This method seeks to develop analyses that are generated from the data themselves (Blumer 1979). Thus in the beginning of the study I maintained a flexible and unstructured approach. This flexibility was particularly important because I wanted to ensure that my years in the field had not left me with a preconceived conceptual model and that my research was not an attempt to justify conclusions already reached. By facing the issue of possible subjectivity at each stage of the investigation, I let the data lead me rather than the other way around. As the data accumulated and as theories and propositions emerged, they were modified and compared, and in turn formed the groundwork for further data collection. Initially, for example, I attempted to frame the presentence process in the context of factors related to the individual officer (reporting style, experience, or criminal justice philosophy). I could not discern a regular pattern, however, so I analyzed other factors.

Findings

In the great majority of presentence investigations, the variables of present offense and prior criminal record determine the probation officer's final sentencing recommendation. The influence of these variables is so dominant that other considerations have minimal influence on probation recommendations. The chief rationale for this approach is ''That's the way the judges want it.'' There are other styles of investigation; some officers attempt to consider factors in the defendant's social history, to reserve sentencing judgment until their investigation is complete, or to interject personal opinions. Elsewhere (Rosecrance 1987), I have developed a typology of presentence investigators which describes individual styles; these types include self-explanatory categories such as hard-liners, bleeding-heart liberals, and team players as well as mossbacks (those who are merely putting in their time) and mavericks (those who strive continually for independence).

All types of probation officers, however, seek to develop credibility with the court. Such reputation building is similar to that reported by McCleary (1978) in his study of parole officers. In order to develop rapport with the court, probation officers must submit reports that facilitate a smooth work flow. Probation officers assume that in the great majority of cases they can accomplish this goal by emphasizing offense and criminal record. Once the officers have established reputations as "producers," they have "earned" the right to some degree of discretion in their reporting. One investigation officer described this process succinctly: "When you've paid your dues, you're allowed some slack." Such discretion, however, is limited to a minority of cases, and in these "deviant" cases probation officers frequently allow social variables to influence their recommendation. In one report an experienced officer recommended probation for a convicted felon with a long prior record because the defendant's father agreed to pay for an intensive drug treatment program. In another case a probation officer decided that a first-time shoplifter had a "very bad attitude" and therefore recommended a stiff jail sentence rather than probation. Although these variations from normal procedure are interesting and important, they should not detract from our examination of an investigation process that is used in most cases.

On the basis of the research data, I found that the following patterns occur with sufficient regularity to be considered "typical." After considering offense and criminal record, probation officers place defendants into categories that represent the eventual court recommendation. This typing process occurs early in the course of presentence inquiry; the balance of the investigation is used to reaffirm the private typings that later will become official designations. In order to clarify the decision-making processes used by probation officers I will delineate the three stages in a presentence investigation: 1) typing the defendant, 2) gathering further information, and 3) filing the report.

Typing the Defendant

A presentence investigation is initiated when the court orders the probation department to prepare a report on a criminal defendant. Usually the initial court referral contains such information as police reports, charges against the defendant, court proceedings, plea-bargaining agreements (if any), offenses in which the defendant has pleaded or has been found guilty, and the defendant's prior criminal record. Probation officers regard such information as relatively unambiguous[4] and as part of the "official" record. The comment of a presentence investigator reflects the probation officer's perspective on the court referral:

> I consider the information in the court referral hard data. It tells me what I need to know about a case, without a lot of bullshit. I mean the guy has pled guilty to a certain offense—he can't get out of that. He has such and such a prior record—there's no changing that. So much of the stuff we put in these reports is subjective and open to interpretation. It's good to have some solid information.

Armed with information in the court referral, probation officers begin to type the defendants assigned for presentence investigation. Defendants are classified into general types based on possible sentence recommendations; a probation officer's statement indicates that this process begins early in a presentence investigation.

> Bottom line; it's the sentence recommendation that's important. That's what the judges and everybody wants to see. I start thinking about the recommendation as soon as I pick up the court referral. Why wait? The basic facts aren't going to change. Oh, I know some POs will tell you they weigh all the facts before coming up with a recommendation. But that's propaganda—we all start thinking recommendation right from the get-go.

At this stage in the investigation the factors known to probation officers are mainly legally relevant variables. The defendant's unique characteristics and special circumstances generally are unknown at this time. Although probation officers may know the offender's age, sex, and race, the relationship of these variables to the case is not yet apparent.

These initial typings are private definitions (Prus 1975) based on the officer's experience and knowledge of the court system. On occasion, officers discuss the case informally with their colleagues or supervisors when they are not sure of a particular typing. Until the report is complete, their typing remains a private designation. In most cases the probation officers type defendants by considering the known and relatively irrefutable variables of offense and prior record. Probation officers are convinced that judges and district attorneys are most concerned with that part of their reports. I heard the following comment (or versions thereof) on many occasions: "Judges read the offense section, glance at the prior record, and then flip to the back and see what we recommend." Officers indicated that during informal discussions with judges it was made clear that offense and prior record are the determinants of sentencing in most cases. In some instances judges consider extralegal variables, but the officers indicated that this occurs only in "unusual" cases with "special" circumstances. One such case involved a probation grant for a woman who killed her husband after she had been a victim of spouse battering.

Probation investigators are in regular contact with district attorneys, and frequently discuss their investigations with them. In addition, district attorneys seem to have no compunction about calling the probation administration to complain about what they consider an inappropriate recommendation. Investigators agreed unanimously that district attorneys typically dismiss a defendant's social history as "immaterial" and want probation officers to stick to the legal facts.

Using offense and prior record as criteria, probation officers place defendants into dispositional (based on recommendation) types. In describing these types[5] I have retained the terms used by probation officers themselves in the typing process. The following typology is community (rather than researcher) designated (Emerson 1983; Spradley 1970): (1) deal case, (2) diversion case, (3) joint case, (4) probation case with some jail time, (5) straight probation case. Within each of these dispositional types, probation officers designate the severity of punishment by labeling the case either lightweight or heavy-duty.

A designation of "lightweight" means that the defendant will be accorded some measure of leniency because the offense was minor, because the offender had no prior criminal record, or because the criminal activity (regardless of the penal code violation) was relatively innocuous. Heavy-duty cases receive more severe penalties because the offense, the offender, or the circumstances of the offense are deemed particularly serious. Diversion and straight probation types generally are considered lightweight, while the majority of joint cases are considered heavy-duty. Cases involving personal violence invariably are designated as heavy-duty. Most misdemeanor cases in which the defendant has no prior criminal record or a relatively minor record are termed lightweight. If the defendant has an extensive criminal record, however, even misdemeanor cases can call for stiff penalties; therefore such cases are considered heavy-duty. Certain felony cases can be regarded as lightweight if there was no violence, if the victim's loss was minimal, or if the defendant had no prior convictions. On occasion, even an offense like armed robbery can be considered lightweight. The following example (taken from an actual report) is one such instance: a first-time offender with a simulated gun held up a Seven-Eleven store and then returned to the scene, gave back the money, and asked the store employees to call the police.

The typings are general recommendations; specifics such as terms and conditions of probation or diversion and length of incarceration are worked out later in the investigation. The following discussion will clarify some of the criteria for arriving at a typing.

Deal cases involve situations in which a plea bargain exists. In California, many plea bargains specify specific sentencing stipulations; probation officers rarely recommend dispositions contrary to those stipulated in plea-bargaining agreements. Although probation officers allegedly are free to recommend a sentence different from that contained in the plea bargain, they have learned that such an action is unrealistic (and often counter-productive to their own interests) because judges inevitably uphold the primacy of sentence agreements. The following observation represents the probation officers' view of plea-bargaining deals:

> It's stupid to try and bust a deal. What's the percentage? Who needs the hassle? The judge always honors the deal—after all, he was part of it. Everyone, including the defendant, has already agreed. It's all nice and neat, all wrapped up. We are supposed to rubber-stamp the package—and we do. Everyone is better off that way.

Diversion cases typically involve relatively minor offenses committed by those with no prior record, and are considered "a snap" by probation officers. In most cases, those referred for diversion have been screened already by the district attorney's office; the probation investigator merely agrees that they are eligible and therefore should be granted diversionary relief (and eventual dismissal of charges). In rare instances when there has been an oversight and the defendant is ineligible (because of prior criminal convictions), the probation officer informs the court, and criminal proceedings are resumed. Either situation involves minimal decision making by probation officers about what disposition to recommend. Presentence investigators approach diversion cases in a perfunctory, almost mechanical manner.

The last three typings generally refer to cases in which the sentencing recommendations are ambiguous and some decision making is required of probation officers. These types represent the major consequences of criminal sentencing: incarceration and/or probation. Those categorized as joint (prison) cases are denied probation; instead the investigator recommends an appropriate prison sentence. In certain instances the nature of the offense (e.g., rape, murder, or arson) renders defendants legally ineligible for probation. In other situations, the defendants' prior record (especially felony convictions) makes it impossible to grant probation (see, e.g., Neubauer 1974: 240). In many cases the length of prison sentences has been set by legal statute and can be increased or decreased only marginally (depending on the aggravating or mitigating circumstances of the case).

In California, the majority of defendants sentenced to prison receive a middle term (between minimum and maximum); the length of time varies with the offense. Those cases that fall outside the middle term usually do so for reasons related to the offense (e.g., using a weapon) or to the criminal record (prior felony convictions or, conversely, no prior criminal record). Those typed originally as joint cases are treated differently from other probation applicants: concerns with rehabilitation or with the defendant's life situation are no longer relevant, and proper punishment becomes the focal point of inquiry. This perspective was described as follows by a probation officer respondent: "Once I know so-and-so is a heavy-duty joint case I don't think in terms of rehabilitation or social planning. It becomes a matter of how long to salt the sucker away, and that's covered by the code."

For those who are typed as probation cases, the issue for the investigator becomes whether to recommend some time in jail as a condition of probation. This decision is made with reference to whether the case is lightweight or heavy-duty. Straight probation usually is reserved for those convicted of relatively innocuous offenses or for those without a prior criminal record (first-timers). Some probation officers admitted candidly that all things being equal, middle-class defendants are more likely than other social classes to receive straight probation. The split sentence (probation and jail time) has become popular and is a consideration in most misdemeanor and felony cases, especially when the defendant has a prior criminal record. In addition, there is a feeling that drug offenders should receive a jail sentence as part of probation to deter them from future drug use.

Once a probation officer has decided that "some jail time is in order," the ultimate recommendation includes that condition. Although the actual amount of time frequently is determined late in the case, the probation officer's opinion that a jail sentence should be imposed remains constant. The following comment typifies the sentiments of probation officers whom I have observed and also illustrates the imprecision of recommending a period of time in custody:

> It's not hard to figure out who needs some jail. The referral sheet can tell you that. What's hard to know is exactly how much time. Ninety days or six months—who knows what's fair? We put down some number but it is usually an arbitrary figure. No one has come up with a chart that correlates rehabilitation with jail time.

Compiling Further Information

Once an initial typing has been completed, the next investigative stage involves collecting further information about the defendant. During this stage most of the data to be collected consists of extralegal considerations. The defendant is interviewed and his or her social history is delineated. Probation officers frequently contact collateral sources such as school officials, victims, doctors, counselors, and relatives to learn more about the defendant's individual circumstances. This aspect of the presentence investigation involves considerable time and effort on the part of probation officers. Such information is gathered primarily to legitimate earlier probation officer typings or to satisfy judicial requirements; recommendations seldom are changed during this stage. A similar pattern was described by a presentence investigator:

> Interviewing these defendants and working up a social history takes time. In most cases it's really unnecessary since I've already decided what I am going to do. We all know that a recommendation is governed by the offense and prior record. All the rest is just stuffing to fill out the court report, to make the judge look like he's got all the facts.

Presentence interviews with defendants (a required part of the investigation) frequently are routine interactions that were described by a probation officer as "anticlimactic." These interviews invariably are conducted in settings familiar to probation officers, such as jail interviewing rooms or probation department offices. Because the participants lack trust in each other, discussions rarely are candid and open. Probation officers are afraid of being conned or manipulated because they assume that defendants "will say anything to save themselves." Defendants are trying to present themselves in a favorable light and are wary of divulging any information that might be used against them.

It is assumed implicitly in the interview process that probation officers act as interrogators and defendants as respondents. Because presentence investigators select the questions, they control the course of the interview and elicit the kind of responses that serve to substantiate their original defendant typings. A probationer described his presentence interview to me as follows:

> I knew that the P.O. wanted me to say. She had me pegged as a nice middle-class kid who had fallen in with a bad crowd. So that's how I came off. I was contrite, a real boy scout who had learned his lesson. What an acting job! I figured if I didn't act up I'd get probation.

A probation officer related how she conducted presentence interviews:

> I'm always in charge during the interviews. I know what questions to ask in order to fill out my report. The defendants respond just about the way I expect them to. They hardly ever surprise me.

On occasion, prospective probationers refuse to go along with structured presentence interviews. Some offenders either attempt to control the interview or are openly hostile to probation officers. Defendants who try to dominate interviews often can be dissuaded by reminders such as "I don't think you really appreciate the seriousness of your situation" or "I'm the one who asks the questions here." Some defendants, however, show blatant disrespect for the court process by flaunting a disregard for possible sanctions.

Most probation officers have interviewed some defendants who simply don't seem to care what happens to them. A defendant once informed an investigation officer: "I don't give a fuck what you motherfuckers try and do to me. I'm going to do what I fuckin' well please. Take your probation and stick it."

Another defendant told her probation officer: "I'm going to shoot up every chance I get, I need my fix more than I need probation." Probation officers categorize belligerent defendants and those unwilling to "play the probation game" as dangerous or irrational (see, e.g., McCleary 1978). Frequently in these situations the investigator's initial typing is no longer valid, and probation either will be denied or will be structured stringently. Most interviews, however, proceed in a predictable manner as probation officers collect information that will be included in the section of the report termed "defendant's statement."

Although some defendants submit written comments, most of their statements actually are formulated by the probation officer. In a sociological sense, the defendant's statement can be considered an "account" (Scott and Lyman 1968). While conducting presentence interviews, probation officers typically attempt to shape the defendant's account to fit their own preconceived typing. Many probation officers believe that the defendant's attitude toward the offense and toward the future prospects for leading a law-abiding life are the most important parts of the statement. In most presentence investigations the probation investigator identifies and interprets the defendant's subjective attitudes and then incorporates them into the report. Using this procedure, probation officers look for and can report attitudes that "logically fit" with their final sentencing recommendation (see, for example, Davis 1983).

Defendants who have been typed as prison cases typically are portrayed as holding socially unacceptable attitudes about their criminal actions and unrealistic or negative attitudes about future prospects for living an upright life. Conversely, those who have been typed as probation material are described as having acceptable attitudes, such as contriteness about the present offense and optimism about their ability to lead a crime-free life. The structuring of accounts about defendant attitudes was described by a presentence investigator in the following manner:

> When POs talk about the defendant's attitude we really mean how that attitude relates to the case. Naturally I'm not going to write about what a wonderful attitude the guy has—how sincere he seems—and then recommend sending him to the joint. That wouldn't make sense. The judges want consistency. If a guy has a shitty attitude but is going to get probation anyway, there's no percentage in playing up his attitude problem.

In most cases the presentence interview is the only contact between the investigating officer and the defendant. The brevity of this contact and the lack of post-report interaction foster a legalistic perspective. Investigators are concerned mainly with "getting the case through court" rather than with special problems related to supervising probationers on a long-term basis. One-time-only interviews rarely allow probation officers to become emotionally involved with their cases; the personal and individual aspects of the defendant's personality generally are not manifested during a half-hour presentence interview. For many probation officers the emotional distance from offenders is one of the benefits of working in presentence units. Such an opinion was expressed by an investigation officer: "I really like the one-shot-only part of this job. I don't have time to get caught up with the clients. I can deal with facts and not worry about individual personalities."

The probation officer has wide discretion in the type of collateral information that is collected from sources other than the defendant or the official record. Although a defendant's social history must be sketched in the presentence report, the supplementation of that history is left to individual investigators. There are few established guidelines for the investigating officer to follow, except that the psychiatric or psychological reports should be submitted when there is compelling evidence that the offender is mentally disturbed. Informal guidelines, however, specify that in misdemeanor cases reports should be shorter and more concise than in felony cases. The officers indicated that reports for municipal court (all misdemeanor cases) should range from four to six pages in length, while superior court reports (felony cases) were expected to be six to nine pages long. In controversial cases (to which only the most experienced officers are assigned) presentence reports are expected to be longer and to include considerable social data. Reports in these cases have been as long as 30 pages.

Although probation officers learn what general types of information to include through experience and feedback from judges and supervisors, they are allowed considerable leeway in deciding exactly what to put in their reports (outside of the offense and prior record sections). Because investigators decide what collateral sources are germane to the case, they tend to include information that will reflect favorably on their sentencing recommendation. In this context the observation of one probation officer is understandable: "I pick from the mass of possible sources just which ones to put in the report. Do you think I'm going to pick people who make my recommendation look weak? No way!"

Filing the Report

The final stage in the investigation includes dictating the report, having it approved by a probation supervisor, and appearing in court. All three of these activities serve to reinforce the importance of prior record and offense in sentencing recommendations. At the time of dictation, probation officers determine what to include in the report and how to phrase their remarks. For the first time in the investigation, they receive formal feedback from official sources. Presentence reports are read by three groups important to the probation officers: probation supervisors, district attorneys, and judges. Probation officers recognize that for varying reasons, all these groups emphasize the legally relevant variables of offense and prior criminal record when considering an appropriate sentencing recommendation.[6] Such considerations reaffirm the probation officer's initial private typing.

A probation investigator described this process:

> After I've talked to the defendants I think maybe some of them deserve to get special consideration. But when I remember who's going to look at the reports. My supervisor, the DA, the judge; they don't care about all the personal details. When all is said and done, what's really important to them is the offense and the defendant's prior record. I know that stuff from the start. It makes me wonder why we have to jack ourselves around to do long reports.

Probation officers assume that their credibility as presentence investigators will be enhanced if their sentencing recommendations meet with the approval of probation supervisors, district attorneys, and judges. On the other hand, officers whose recommendations are consistently "out of line" are subject to censure or transfer, or they find themselves engaged in "running battles" (Shover 1974: 357) with court officials. During the last stage of the investigation probation officers must consider how to ensure that their reports will go through court without "undue personal hassle." Most investigation officers have learned that presentence recommendations based on a consideration of prior record and offense can achieve that goal.

Although occupational self-interest is an important component in deciding how to conduct a presentence investigation, other factors also are involved. Many probation officers agree with the idea of using legally relevant variables as determinants of recommendations. These officers embrace the retributive value of this concept and see it as an equitable method for framing their investigation. Other officers reported that probation officers' discretion had been "short-circuited" by determinate sentencing guidelines and that they were reduced to "merely going through the motions" in conducting their investigations. Still other officers view the use of legal variables to structure recommendations as an acceptable bureaucratic shortcut to compensate partially for large case assignments. One probation officer stated, "If the department wants us to keep pumping out presentence reports we can't consider social factors—we just don't have time." Although probation officers are influenced by various dynamics, there seems little doubt that in California, the social history which once was considered the "heart and soul" of presentence probation reports (Reckless 1967: 673) has been largely devalued.

Summary and Conclusions

In this study I provide a description and an analysis of the processes used by probation investigators in preparing presentence reports. The research findings based on interview data indicate that probation officers tend to deemphasize individual defendants' characteristics and that their probation recommendations are not influenced directly by factors such as sex, age, race, socioeconomic status, or work record. Instead, probation officers emphasize the variables of instant offense and prior criminal record. The finding that offense and prior record are the main considerations of probation officers with regard to sentence recommendations agrees with a substantial body of research (Bankston 1983; Carter and Wilkins 1967; Dawson 1969; Lotz and Hewitt 1977; Robinson, Carter, and Wahl 1969; Wallace 1974; Walsh 1985).

My particular contribution has been to supply the ethnographic observations and the data that explain this phenomenon. I have identified the process whereby offense and prior record come to occupy the central role in decision making by probation officers. This identification underscores the significance of private typings in determining official designations. An analysis of probation practices suggests that the function of the presentence investigation is more ceremonial then instrumental (Hagan 1985).

I show that early in the investigation probation officers, using offense and prior record as guidelines, classify defendants into types; when the typing process is complete, probation officers essentially have decided on the sentence recommendation that will be recorded later in their official designation. The subsequent course of investigations is determined largely by this initial private typing. Further data collection is influenced by a sentence recommendation that already has been firmly established. This finding answers affirmatively the research question posed by Carter (1967: 211):

> Do probation officers, after "deciding" on a recommendation early in
> the presentence investigation, seek further information which justifies
> the decision, rather than information which might lead to modification
> or rejection of that recommendation?

The type of information and observation contained in the final presentence report is generated to support the original recommendation decision. Probation officers do not regard defendant typings as tentative hypotheses to be disproved through inquiry but rather as firm conclusions to be justified in the body of the report.

Although the presentence interview has been considered an important part of the investigation (Spencer 1983), I demonstrate that it does not significantly alter probation officers' perceptions. In most cases probation officers dominate presentence interviews; interaction between the participants is guarded. The nature of interviews between defendants and probation officers is important in itself; further research is needed to identify the dynamics that prevail in these interactions.

Attitudes attributed to defendants often are structured by probation officers to reaffirm the recommendation already formulated. The defendant's social

history, long considered an integral part of the presentence report, in reality
has little bearing on sentencing considerations. In most cases the presentence
is no longer a vehicle for social inquiry but rather a typing process which
considers mainly the defendant's prior criminal record and the seriousness
of the criminal offense. Private attorneys in growing numbers have become
disenchanted with the quality of probation investigations and have
commissioned presentence probation reports privately (Rodgers, Gitchoff,
and Paur 1984). At present, however, such a practice is generally available
only for wealthy defendants.

The presentence process that I have described is used in the great majority
of cases; it is the "normal" procedure. Even so, probation officers are not
entirely passive actors in this process. On occasion they will give serious
consideration to social variables in arriving at a sentencing recommendation.
In special circumstances officers will allow individual defendants'
characteristics to influence their report. In addition, probation officers who
have developed credibility with the court are allowed some discretion in
compiling presentence reports. This discretion is not unlimited, however; it
is based on a prior record of producing reports that meet the court's approval,
and is contingent on continuing to do so. A presentence writer said, "You
can only afford to go to bat for defendants in a few select cases; if you try
to do it too much, you get a reputation as being 'out of step.'"

This research raises the issue of probation officers' autonomy. Although
I depict presentence investigators as having limited autonomy, other researchers
(Hagan 1975; Myers 1979; Walsh 1985) contend that probation officers have
considerable leeway in recommendation. This contradictory evidence can be
explained in large part by the type of sentencing structure, the professionalism
of probation workers, and the role of the district attorney at sentencing. Walsh's
study (1985), for example, which views probation officers as important actors
in the presentence process, was conducted in a jurisdiction with indeterminate
sentencing, where the probation officers demonstrated a high degree of
professionalism and the prosecutors "rarely made sentencing
recommendations." A very different situation existed in the California counties
that I studied: determinate sentencing was enforced, probation officers were
not organized professionally, and the district attorneys routinely made specific
court recommendations. It seems apparent that probation officers' autonomy
must be considered with reference to judicial jurisdiction.

In view of the primacy of offense and prior record in sentencing
considerations, the efficacy of current presentence investigation practices is
doubtful. It seems ineffective and wasteful to continue to collect a mass of
social data of uncertain relevance. Yet an analysis of courtroom culture suggests
that the presentence investigation helps maintain judicial mythology as well
as probation officer legitimacy. Although judges generally do not have the
time or the inclination to consider individual variables thoroughly, the

performance of a presentence investigation perpetuates the myth of individualized sentences. Including a presentence report in the court file gives the appearance of individualization without influencing sentencing practices significantly.

Even in a state like California, where determinate sentencing allegedly has replaced individualized justice, the judicial system feels obligated to maintain the appearance of individualization. After observing the court system in California for several years I am convinced that a major reason for maintaining such a practice is to make it easier for criminal defendants to accept their sentences. The presentence report allows defendants to feel that their case at least has received a considered decision. One judge admitted candidly that the "real purpose" of the presentence investigation was to convince defendants that they were not getting "the fast shuffle." He observed further that if defendants were sentenced without such investigations, many would complain and would file "endless appeals" over what seems to them a hasty sentencing decision. Even though judges typically consider only offense and prior record in a sentencing decision, they want defendants to believe that their cases are being judged individually. The presentence investigation allows this assumption to be maintained. In addition, some judges use the probation officer's report as an excuse for a particular type of sentence. In some instances they deny responsibility for the sentence, implying that their "hands were tied" by the recommendation. Thus judges are taken "off the hook" for meting out an unpopular sentence. Further research is needed to substantiate the significance of these latent functions of the presentence investigation.

The presentence report is a major component in the legitimacy of the probation movement; several factors support the probation officers' stake in maintaining their role in these investigations. Historically, probation has been wedded to the concept of individualized treatment. In theory, the presentence report is suited ideally to reporting on defendants' individual circumstances. From a historical perspective (Rothman 1980) this ideal has always been more symbolic than substantive, but if the legitimacy of the presentence report is questioned, so then is the entire purpose of probation.

Regardless of its usefulness (or lack of usefulness), it is doubtful that probation officials would consider the diminution or abolition of presentence reports. The number of probation workers assigned to presentence investigations is substantial, and their numbers represent an obvious source of bureaucratic power. Conducting presentence investigations allows probation officers to remain visible with the court and the public. The media often report on controversial probation cases, and presentence writers generally have more contact and more association with judges than do others in the probation department.

As ancillary court workers, probation officers are assigned the dirty work of collecting largely irrelevant data on offenders (Hagan 1975; Hughes 1958).

Investigation officers have learned that emphasizing offense and prior record in their reports will enhance relationships with judges and district attorneys, as well as improving their occupational standing within probation departments. Thus the presentence investigation serves to maintain the court's claim of individualized concern while preserving the probation officer's role, although a subordinate role, in the court system.[7]

The myth of individualization serves various functions, but it also raises serious questions. In an era of severe budget restrictions (Schumacher 1985) should scarce resources be allocated to compiling predictable presentence reports of dubious value? If social variables are considered only in a few cases, should courts continue routinely to require presentence reports in all felony matters (as is the practice in California)? In summary, we should address the issue of whether the criminal justice system can afford the ceremony of a probation presentence investigation.

References Cited

Allen, Harry E. and Clifford E. Simonsen. 1986. *Corrections in America*. New York: Macmillan.

Bankston, William B. 1983. "Legal and Extralegal Offender Traits and Decision-Making in the Criminal Justice System." *Sociological Spectrum*, 3: 1-18.

Blumberg, Abraham. 1967. *Criminal Justice*. Chicago: Quadrangle.

Blumer, Martin. 1979. "Concepts in the Analysis of Qualitative Data." *Sociological Review*, 27: 651-677.

Blumstein, Alfred J., S. Martin and N. Holt. 1983. *Research on Sentencing: The Search for Reform*. Washington, DC: National Academy Press.

Carter, Robert M. 1967. "The Presentence Report and the Decision-Making Process." *Journal of Research in Crime and Delinquency*, 4: 203-211.

Carter, Robert M. and Leslie T. Wilkins. 1967. "Some Factors in Sentencing Policy." *Journal of Criminal Law, Criminology, and Police Science*, 58: 503-514.

Clear, Todd and George Cole. 1986. *American Corrections*. Monterey, CA: Brooks/Cole.

Davis, James R. 1983. "Academic and Practical Aspects of Probation: A Comparison." *Federal Probation*, 47: 7-10.

Dawson, Robert. 1969. *Sentencing*. Boston: Little, Brown.

Emerson, Robert M. 1983 (reissued 1988). "Ethnography and Understanding Members' Worlds." In Robert M. Emerson (ed.), *Contemporary Field Research: A Collection of Readings*. Prospect Heights, IL: Waveland Press.

Forer, Lois G. 1980. *Criminals and Victims*. New York: Norton.

Glaser, Barney and Anselm Strauss. 1967. *The Discovery of Grounded Theory*. Chicago: Aldine.

Goldsborough, E. and E. Burbank. 1968. "The Probation Officer and His Personality." In Charles L. Newman (ed.), *Sourcebook on Probation, Parole, and Pardons*. Springfield, IL: Charles C Thomas, pp. 104-112.

Hagan, John. 1975. "The Social and Legal Construction of Criminal Justice: A Study of the Presentence Process." *Social Problems*, 22: 620-637.

———. 1977. "Criminal Justice in Rural and Urban Communities: A Study of the Bureaucratization of Justice." *Social Forces*, 55: 597-612.

———. 1985. *Modern Criminology: Crime, Criminal Behavior, and its Control*. New York: McGraw-Hill.

Hagan, John, John Hewitt and Duane Alwin. 1979. "Ceremonial Justice: Crime and Punishment in a Loosely Coupled System." *Social Forces*, 58: 506-525.

Hogarth, John. 1971. *Sentencing as a Human Process*. Toronto: University of Toronto Press.

Hughes, Everett C. 1958. *Men and Their Work*. New York: Free Press.

Katz, Janet. 1982. "The Attitudes and Decisions of Probation Officers." *Criminal Justice and Behavior*, 9: 455-475.

Kingsnorth, Rodney and Louis Rizzo. 1979. "Decision-Making in the Criminal Courts: Continuities and discontinuities." *Criminology*, 17: 3-14.

Lotz, Ray and John Hewitt. 1977. "The Influence of Legally Irrelevant Factors on Felony Sentencing." *Sociological Inquiry*, 47: 39-48.

Marquart, James W. 1986. "Outsiders as Insiders: Participant Observation in the Role of a Prison Guard." *Justice Quarterly*, 3: 15-32.

McCleary, Richard. 1978. *Dangerous Men*. Beverly Hills, CA: Sage.

McCleary, Richard, Barbara Nienstadt and James Erven. 1982. "Uniform Crime Reports as Organizational Outcomes: Three Time Series Experiments." *Social Problems*, 29: 361-373.

McHugh, John J. 1973. "Some Comments on Natural Conflict between Counsel and Probation Officer." *American Journal of Corrections*, 3: 15-32.

Michalowski, Raymond J. 1985. *Order, Law and Crime*. New York: Random House.

Murrah, A. 1963. "Prison or Probation?" In B. Kay and C. Veddar (eds.), *Probation and Parole*. Springfield, IL: Charles C Thomas, pp. 63-78.

Myers, Martha A. 1979. "Offended Parties and Official Reactions: Victims and the Sentencing of Criminal Defendants." *Sociological Quarterly*, 20: 529-546.

Neubauer, David. 1974. *Criminal Justice in Middle America*. Morristown, NJ: General Learning.

Petersilia, Joan, Susan Turner, James Kahan and Joyce Peterson. 1985. "Executive Summary of Rand's Study, Granting Felons Probation." *Crime and Delinquency*, 31: 379-392.

Prus, Robert. 1975. "Labeling Theory: A Statement on Typing." *Sociological Focus*, 8: 79-96.

Prus, Robert and John Stratten. 1976. "Factors in the Decision-Making of North Carolina Probation Officers." *Federal Probation*, 40: 48-53.

Reckless, Walter C. 1967. *The Crime Problem*. New York: Appleton.

Robinson, James, Robert Carter and A. Wahl. 1969. *The San Francisco Project*. Berkeley: University of California School of Criminology.

Rodgers, T.A., G.T. Gitchoff and I. Paur. 1984. "The Privately Commissioned Presentence Report." In Robert M. Carter, Daniel Glaser, and Leslie T. Wilkins (eds.), *Probation, Parole, and Community Corrections*. New York: Wiley, pp. 21-30.

Rosecrance, John. 1985. "The Probation Officers' Search for Credibility: Ball Park Recommendations." *Crime and Delinquency*, 31: 539-554.

———. 1987. "A Typology of Presentence Probation Investigators." *International Journal of Offender Therapy and Comparative Criminology*, 31: 163-177.

Rothman, David. 1980. *Conscience and Convenience: The Asylum and its Alternatives in Progressive America*. Boston: Little, Brown.

Schumacher, Michael A. 1985. "Implementation of a Client Classification and Case Management System: A Practitioner's View." *Crime and Delinquency*, 31: 445-455.

Scott, Marvin and Stanford Lyman. 1968. "Accounts." *American Sociological Review*, 33: 46-62.

Shover, Neal. 1974. "Experts and Diagnosis in Correctional Agencies." *Crime and Delinquency*, 20: 347-358.

———. 1979. *A Sociology of American Corrections*. Homewood, IL: Dorsey.

Spencer, Jack W. 1983. "Accounts, Attitudes and Solutions: Probation Officer-Defendant Negotiations of Subjective Orientations." *Social Problems*, 30: 570-581.

Spradley, Joseph P. 1970. *You Owe Yourself a Drunk: An Ethnography of Urban Nomads*. Boston: Little, Brown.

Sudnow, David. 1965. "Normal Crimes: Sociological Features of the Penal Code." *Social Problems*, 12: 255-276.

Tinker, John N., John Quiring and Yvonne Pimentel. 1985. "Ethnic Bias in California Courts: A Case Study of Chicano and Anglo Felony Defendants." *Sociological Inquiry*, 55: 83-96.

Walker, Samuel. 1985. *Sense and Nonsense About Crime*. Monterey, CA: Brooks/Cole.

Wallace, John. 1974. "Probation Administration." In Daniel Glaser (ed.), *Handbook of Criminology*. Chicago: Rand-McNally, pp. 940-970.

Walsh, Anthony. 1985. "The Role of the Probation Officer in the Sentencing Process." *Criminal Justice and Behavior*, 12: 289-303.

Notes

[1] For a full discussion of the insider-outsider perspective in criminal justice see Marquart (1986).

[2] In a few jurisdictions, officers who prepare investigations also supervise the defendants after probation has been granted, but, this procedure is becoming less prevalent in contemporary probation (Clear and Cole 1986). It is possible that extralegal variables play a significant role in the supervision process, but this paper is concerned specifically with presentence investigations.

[3] There was no exact way to determine whether the 25 percent of the officers I was unable to interview conducted their presentence investigations significantly differently from those I interviewed. Personal observation, however, and the comments of the officers I interviewed (with whom I discussed this issue) indicated that those who refused used similar methods in processing their presentence reports.

[4] On occasion police reports are written vaguely and are subject to various interpretations; rap sheets are not always clear, especially when some of the final dispositions have not been recorded.

[5] I did not include terminal misdemeanor dispositions, in which probation is denied in favor of fines or jail sentences, in this typology. Such dispositions are comparatively rare and relatively insignificant.

[6] Although defense attorneys also read the presentence reports, their reactions generally do not affect the probation officers' occupational standing (McHugh 1973; Rosecrance 1985).

[7] I did not discuss the role of presentence reports in the prison system. Traditionally, probation reports were part of an inmate's jacket or file and were used as a basis for classification and treatment. The position of probation officers was legitimated further by the fact that prison officials also used the presentence report. I would suggest, however, that the advent of prison overcrowding and the accompanying security concerns have rendered presentence reports relatively meaningless. This contention needs to be substantiated before presentence reports are abandoned completely.

10

Fighting Crime in a Crumbling System

Steven Brill

He picked them up in his yellow cab at about ten to three on a Sunday morning in October as they came out of a nightclub in the Chelsea section of Manhattan.

They were white, so it seemed safe enough, he'd later explain.

They were well-dressed; he'd later remember their designer leather jackets. They were even friendly; like him, they seemed in their thirties and joked pleasantly with him in their Russian-accented English about finding girls in the clubs.

They told him to pull over. He stopped the meter. Then one of them reached across the front seat, turned off the ignition, and yoked him around the neck with his bulky left forearm. "You know what this is," he whispered.

The other burly Russian drew a gun. A gold, shiny, fat nine-millimeter semiautomatic. The cabbie, who says he used to be an art dealer until he lost his business a year ago and has an eye for detail, says he can still see the gold metal barrel of the gun "when I close my eyes."

He begged for his life. "Please, please, please. I'll give you anything you want, all I have," he cried, yanking fives and tens and singles from the various pockets where he hid his money.

"More, more, more," the one with the gun yelled in his thick accent.

Soon there was $267 scattered on the cabbie's lap and front seat.

He turned out his pockets, then offered them his change, which they refused.

"More, more," repeated the gunman, waving the nine-millimeter. The cabbie begged again. He had a 2-year-old daughter whom he wanted to see in the morning, he cried.

Steven Brill is the President and Editor in Chief of *The American Lawyer*. This article is reprinted with permission from the July/August 1989 issue of *The American Lawyer*. Copyright 1991 *The American Lawyer*.

They made him spread across the front seat, face down. "I was sure this was the end of my life," he remembers. "I closed my eyes."

They told him he'd be dead if he looked up, but that if he waited three minutes, they wouldn't shoot him and they'd even throw his keys back.

They jumped out and into a waiting getaway car. He stayed down for five minutes before he peered over the dashboard.

They hadn't thrown back the keys.

Four days later, he was out again in the yellow cab, cruising the same neighborhood, determined to find the men who had threatened, he says, "to take me from my daughter." He was certain, he says, that he had figured out that "their M.O. was to hang around that nightclub waiting for a cabbie."

Sure enough, he spotted them. He drove some more and found a group of cops in a van that is part of a special team assigned to this neighborhood because of problems stemming from the nightclubs. He explained excitedly about the robbery four nights before and demanded they chase the suspects. The cops said they'd follow him in his cab. Flash your lights if you see them, they said.

The cab and the van circled the block once. The cabbie didn't spot his Russian robbers.

The cops told him to go home. They'd look without him, they promised. As he was driving away, he saw his Russians and hit the lights. The cops poured out of the van. The cabbie and the cops say that one of the two soon-to-be-defendants reached for the nine-millimeter tucked in his belt.

On television you'd now have one, maybe two, dead perpetrators and a snappy half-hour episode of *Police Story*. Here you have two very much alive defendants (a cop grabbed the guy's gun), and eight months' worth of justice, urban American-style.

Which means not much justice at all.

What you have instead is waiting. Delay. Laziness. Resignation. Judges, court officers, lawyers reading paperbacks, doing crossword puzzles, scanning the sports pages, exchanging jokes, planning lunch, and generally shooting the shit—there's just no other way to describe it—while the American criminal justice system, at least in this city, grinds to a halt.

But what you also have are people like Manhattan assistant district attorney Elizabeth Karas—who don't seem to understand about the futility of it all. Who care. Who navigate their way through the system, ignoring the indignities and the numbness and the debris around them and do their bit to redeem the rule of law.

Karas, a 32-year-old from a farm town in Western Massachusetts, seems to be a holdout in a system that has captured, beaten down, and bureaucratized almost everyone else. Spend a day with Beth Karas and you realize that restoring the rule of law for that cabdriver isn't about liberals or conservatives—Karas and the cabdriver consider themselves liberals—but about changing the mind-set of the system. It has to become a place where people are brought to justice, not a numbing, grimy bureaucracy where cases are processed.

And what gets ground down most by the processing of justice is, in fact, the sense that justice is what's being delivered. It's not so much that the sentences meted out in the plea bargaining that is at the center of the process are too lenient, though they are, as it is that almost everyone, except the victims and an oddball judge or two and some unhardened defense lawyers and prosecutors like Karas, seem numb to it all.

Spend time with Beth Karas and her 40 or 50 case files—walk with her into the deadened, shooting-the-shit courtrooms—and you want to scream. You want to remind people of the crisis we keep hearing about. You want to remind people that something important is supposed to be going on here.

It is Thursday morning, April 27, and Karas is on the phone explaining to the cabdriver why his case—which she calls "my Russians case—is going to be delayed for the ninth time. "Oh, you got robbed again?" she asks. "Another gun? Why didn't you report it? You really should.

"He didn't think he could ID this guy," she explains to me. ("This one was just another indistinguishable black face," the driver later tells me. "He could be anyone. There's no point in reporting it.")

She tells the cabbie to stay near the phone, that maybe the case will come on for the afternoon.

Meantime, one of the cops who made the arrest waits in the hall. He'll wait there all day, costing the city one cop on the street and about $25 an hour. But there will be no case. The two defense lawyers and one of the defendants (both are out on $3,500 bail) won't show up.

Karas is spending the day on the second floor of the Manhattan criminal courts building in what's called the Early Case Assessment Bureau, or ECAB. Of the 396 assistant district attorneys in Manhattan District Attorney Robert Morgenthau's office, some 300 are assigned to the trial division, which means they handle cases from arraignment through a plea bargain or verdict. (The others handle appeals or work in special units.) Of these 300, 200, including Karas, handle basic felonies. They pick up new cases by working once every 12 days in ECAB (either on an 8 A.M. to 4 P.M. shift or a 4 P.M. to 12 A.M. shift), where they meet with police who have just made arrests, go over their arrest reports, and process felony complaints that may lead to grand jury indictments.

ECAB, then, is the beginning of the pipeline for the 40 to 50 cases apiece that Karas and the other ADAs will typically be handling at any one time. As a relatively mid-level ADA (she's been there for about three years since graduating from Fordham law school), Karas now gets a mix of serious and not-so-serious crimes.

Such is the general lack of confidence in the court scheduling system that Karas has been assigned to ECAB today even though her Russians case is scheduled to go to trial at 9:30 that morning. Were it to go to trial, she'd be replaced in ECAB by another ADA.

But of course, it won't go to trial, despite the face that she stayed up the night before preparing her opening and her direct examinations, and despite the presence of her lead-off police witness and the standby readiness of her cabbie and five more cops.

Karas's first case in ECAB seems like a yawner. A man was arrested just after midnight in a locker room at *The New York Times* building, after he was allegedly seen by a security guard looking through the lockers of *Times* deliverymen. The arresting officer is a 24-year veteran who stares at Karas's legs whenever she gets up, and who talks so much like Archie Bunker that it's not a cliche to describe him as such. He's vague on the details, despite a self-proclaimed "photogenic mind."

He's also tired, he says, slurping a cup of coffee; he's been waiting since about 2 A.M., earning overtime since his shift ended.

Like all but three of the defendants whose cases Karas will be working on today and during the next two weeks when I will be tracking her, this one is nonwhite. He's a 33-year-old black man.

The purpose of ECAB is for Karas to assess the case, to see if it's worth prosecuting and for what charges. She's skeptical of this one. As she gets the cop to talk more, it turns out that the suspect has worked as a *Times* deliveryman on and off, though he wasn't working that night. It also turns out that no one has reported anything missing from a locker and that the cop didn't get the name of the right person at the *Times* who could tell him, or Karas, this morning if anyone subsequently reported a theft. So the burglary charge will probably have to go. At best, this will be a trespass.

But Karas presses on. "I'll write it up as a burglary because I want to see his sheet," she tells the cop, meaning that she wants to see the defendant's "rap sheet," or arrest and conviction record.

"I had a trespass at Columbia [University] a few months ago," she explains, "[and] it looked like nothing, until I noticed one of the other ADAs had the same guy on a burglary, which he said was a weak case that he was happy to unload on me. Then we got his sheet and saw he had a bunch of trespasses and a burglary." Karas and another ADA have since indicted that defendant, she says, "on four burglaries of dorms up there, with solid cases. So let's see what comes up here."

Nearly half the time in ECAB the ADAs don't yet have the arrest and conviction records back on defendants because, says Karas, "the computer system . . . bogs down."

"Did you *Miranda* him?" Karas asks the cop.

Oh yeah, right off of my card."

"When?"

"At the [police] precinct."

"Did you ask him anything before that?"

"Just if he was working that night at the paper, and he said he wasn't."

Which, of course, makes that admission not admissible.

Karas, who has been writing feverishly on a form (that she will ultimately have to turn over to the defense), now reads back a synopsis of the circumstances surrounding the arrest and the alleged crime.

"That's it in a nutshell, my dear," the cop replies, winking at me.

"This case won't be much," says Karas after the cop leaves. "He had to make the arrest because the security guards caught the guy and said they'd seen him looking in lockers, but there's no proof of anything stolen and the guards' descriptions of what happened are sketchy; it's not clear they could really see the guy, just that he was in there when he wasn't authorized to be there."

Within a week, Karas will have determined that although the defendant has a long police record she still cannot make much of this case. So, she will be about to reduce it to a trespass, which is a misdemeanor, and let the defendant off with no jail time. Except that the defendant, released on his own recognizance, will never return to court, and a bench warrant will be issued for him.

It's now 9:30 and Karas calls the clerk in state supreme court justice Robert Haft's court to find out about her Russians case. There's no answer.

"This is incredible," she sputters. "There's not even anyone there yet, and my trial's supposed to start."

Ten minutes later, she gets an answer. The clerk tells her that the lawyers and defendants haven't shown up, and that one of the two lawyers has called and said he won't be able to be there until the afternoon.

"This is ludicrous," she mutters.

Since the arrest of the Russians on October 6, the case has been called in court nine times, and rarely has anything gone according to schedule.

On October 28 only one of the two defendants could be arraigned, because the city's Correction Department did not deliver the alleged gunwielder to court. (Both were being held in jail, until they made bail in January.)

On November 16 one of the two defense lawyers failed to show up for motions for pre-trial hearings. Justice Haft adjourned the case until December 14. "I have a busy calendar," Haft says, explaining the near-month delay, "and my guess is that between my calendar and the lawyers' calendars this is the best we could do." (A *Manhattan Lawyer* random survey of all the judges in criminal sections of the state supreme court in Manhattan on May 9, 1989, found that Justice Haft started court at 9:55 A.M. on May 9 and left at 3:45 P.M.; Haft asserts that he generally runs court "from about 10:00 to 4:30," and works in chambers before and after each session.)

On December 14 Haft ruled that the grand jury minutes had been sufficient to establish the indictment. (Defense lawyers routinely make a fruitless motion questioning the indictment on those grounds.) But he adjourned the case until January 11, 1989, to give Karas time to respond to other defense motions having to do with the arrest, the cabbie's identification of the suspects, and the search and confiscation of the gun.

All of these motions are "boilerplate," Karas contends, asserting that "there is nothing in this case at all controversial about the arrest, the ID, or the gun." Asked about that, Jeffrey Granat, a Mineola, New York, solo practitioner who represents the alleged gunman, says, "You always like to file these motions just to see what's going on. You'd be committing malpractice not to. If you don't file these kinds of motions within forty-five days, you lose your right to, and that would be malpractice. . . . Besides," he adds, "you do try to slow things down."

Indeed, in most cases these motions, though thoroughly justified by any lawyer wanting to lodge a competent defense, are nothing more than the dance that precedes the plea bargain. "A lot of our deals," says Karas, "don't get made until the hearings are held and even until the defendants and their lawyers see us picking a jury; then they want to deal. They figure if they delay it, some of our evidence will go bad—maybe the witness will disappear or something—or something else will happen. But that's no reason," she adds, "for a judge to hold it up a month or two."

By January 11 Karas had filed her response. In court that day, Haft granted the defense motion to hold a hearing on the pre-trial motions that Karas had responded to in writing. He set the hearing for February 1. Meantime, the defendants were able to post their $3,500 bail.

By January Karas had established that the defendant who had not had the gun but had allegedly yoked the cabdriver had a prior conviction for attempted possession of a weapon in 1984. Attempted possession is one of the clumsier plea bargain pleas (one pictures someone lunging for a gun); it means, in this case, that he'd been caught with a loaded gun but had pled down to the attempt charge, which is the lowest-level felony on the books. His sentence: a $250 fine and five years' probation.

However, that conviction could now hurt him. For, as Karas points out, a second felony conviction would make him a predicate felon, which, under a state law requiring all repeat felons to serve at least a year and a half in prison for even the lowest-level felony, would mandate a higher sentence on the cab robbery case.

Thus, by January, Karas was prepared to offer the defendant with the felony record a plea that would get him a four-to-eight-year sentence, meaning he would have to serve a minimum of four years before he could be paroled. She was prepared to offer three to nine years to the defendant who allegedly had had the gun.

If they didn't accept these plea bargains and instead went to trial, the first defendant's maximum sentence could be twelve-and-a-half to twenty-five years; the second defendant's could be eight-and-a-third to twenty-five years. Karas could not guarantee the lower sentences she was proposing; sentencing was technically up to the judge. But judges customarily go along with these negotiated deals.

So by January Karas was already talking plea bargains to the defense lawyers, and it was clear, she says, that "they didn't want to go to trial."

On February 1 the alleged gunman didn't show up. His lawyer announced that he was being held in New Jersey on warrants for burglary, car theft, receiving stolen property, and possession of heroin. Karas had not known about the New Jersey arrests because, incredibly, the computer system that New York uses to check criminal records does not tie into the national computer bank that would allow it to access other states' criminal records. "You could have a guy wanted for murder in North Carolina or convicted five times in Connecticut and not know it," Karas says. "I asked this guy if he'd ever been arrested before and, of course, he said no."

Karas also found out that the gun he had had when arrested, which the cabbie says was the same gun that had been pointed at him, had been traced by the police to a burglary in Virginia. "The prints the cops had in Virginia weren't good," Karas says. "So I couldn't connect him to that."

On February 1 Justice Haft told Karas to work with New Jersey prosecutors on producing the alleged gunman, and he adjourned the case until March 2.

On March 2 the alleged gunman, having made bail in New Jersey, showed up. But his co-defendant, also out on bail, didn't appear in the morning. His lawyer, Queens solo practitioner Alan Kudisch, was there in the morning but was not there in the afternoon because, he says, "I had a sentencing hearing in Queens." The alleged gunman's lawyer, Granat, didn't appear all day because, he says, "I had other business." He declined to be more specific.

"I try to get the lawyers to come to court," says Haft. "But they're busy, too, you know. I think these guys had other trials. . . . When you have a case with two defendants and two defense lawyers," he adds, "it's almost impossible to get them there.

Did he ever consider sanctions for them?

"Well, as far as I know," he answers, "they called the court the day they were supposed to be here and said they couldn't come because they had trials."

Haft acknowledges that by not calling until after they were supposed to be in court at 9:30—in fact, according to the judge's clerk and law secretary the two defense lawyers typically called in the late morning or afternoon if at all; and according to Karas, they sometimes didn't call at all—they had caused Karas's police witnesses to waste a day. But, says Haft, "that's a matter of courtesy between counsel. I have nothing to do with that."

"It may be that they didn't call in a few times," Haft concedes. "But what can you do? Everyone is so busy."

Haft, who has been a judge for 18 years, says he has "never felt that any case was so severe that I should impose sanctions on a lawyer for not appearing."

Karas doubts that the two lawyers were on trial all those days. "Their only goal," she asserts, "is to string this out. They just don't want this case to come to trial. Who knows, maybe the Russians owe them money. . . . A couple of times, I even tried to ask them where they were on trial, but got nothing."

Court rules require lawyers to submit affidavits when they can't make a date because of another trial, stating the name of the competing case and where it is being tried. Haft says he didn't require the affidavits (actually, he has no discretion not to require them) because "if a lawyer is a member of the bar, I think I can assume he's telling the truth."

As for why a warrant wasn't issued for the missing defendant's arrest, Haft said first that he thought he had issued warrants, then that "if the lawyers don't show, that's probably why their clients didn't show.

So on March 2 Haft adjourned the case until March 15 for the pre-trial hearings.

On March 15 the alleged gunman didn't show up but the lawyers did. No warrant was issued. The case was adjourned for April 5.

On April 5 both defense lawyers didn't show up. Granat sent a message that he had another trial, according to Karas's case notes. Kudisch says he "doesn't know" if he was there that day, but that "it wouldn't matter, since the other lawyer wasn't there."

April 13 neither defense lawyer showed up but their clients did, though one appeared late in the afternoon. Both lawyers sent word that they were on trial. Justice Haft adjourned the case until today, April 27.

It is now 9:45 on April 27, and Karas picks up another ECAB file and calls the arresting cop's name into a microphone, hoping to fetch him from the police waiting room across from Karas's ECAB cubicle. (The waiting room is so filthy and overcrowded that one has to wonder who got the better of the deal, the arrestee or the arrester.)

"It's a wolfpack case," she explains, using a term that's old hat to her but that had become part of the language of New York only a week before, when a woman jogging in Central Park one evening had been attacked and raped by a roaming group of teenage thugs, called a wolfpack in police parlance.

A young cop who has answered Karas's page sits opposite her and explains that he had arrested his suspect for the beating and attempted robbery of a night security guard who'd been attacked by a group of "six or seven black kids." The gang had piled out of a van and went after their prey at about four in the morning a week before at Park Avenue and 49th Street. The guard, who was unarmed and worked at a law firm, had been held at gunpoint and beaten.

But a cabdriver had seen the attack and followed the van long enough to get a license plate number.

"So we put a bulletin out for the van," the cop explains, "and over the weekend the cops in Elmira, upstate [New York], pick it up. Unbelievable.

"Turns out this kid's [the alleged driver of the van] father has a business driving relatives of prisoners up from New York to the prison in Elmira. The van is set up like a bus. . . . So the cops up there see all these blacks and Puerto Ricans—that's who the families are—riding around in a van in this rural area and they check it out, and the license plate comes up that it's wanted on a robbery. So all kinds of cops and sheriffs close in on it with shotguns, and these poor bastards in the van, including the driver, who's the kid's father, spend all night in the lockup until they call us, and we tell them we're looking for a kid. . . .

"They tell us the driver is an older man. So we talk to him on the phone, find out he's got a kid who uses the van, and tell them to let him go as long as he promises to bring his son in. . . . You see, we couldn't go up there and arrest him because the captain wouldn't give us the expense money. I say, 'Captain, what if this guy knocks off a gas station on his way home?' But he won't let us go. Can you imagine that? We've got to get this guy to promise to come back to New York and bring in his son.

"Anyway, he brings the kid in with his mother, and the mother faints when we put the cuffs on the kid. She's carrying a Bible with her; these are a good family. The kid has no record until then. But here he's completely screwed up his father's business and all. . . . And you know what, when he gets bailed out, he turns to the old man and says, 'Dad, I need some money to get home.' The father tells him to get lost. I'd have crippled him."

The suspect arrested today, the one whose case Karas now has, is the van owner's son's friend. His name had been mentioned during the van owner's son's arrest.

"[The van owner's son] told us the whole story about how he and his friends got drunk, took the van, and went riding around," the cop explains. "First they went to Forty-Second Street to those machines that take pictures and pumped money into the machines to have pictures taken of themselves with their guns.

"That's right, they take pictures of themselves with their illegal pieces; they get some kind of charge out of it.

"Then, he says, they drove around some more, and that when he was driving, some of his friends, but not him of course, jumped out and might have robbed a guy—but it wasn't him. But he did mention this other guy's name, so we picked him up last night.''

This defendant, too, claimed to have no record, but the cop explains that he's just learned that two days after this alleged robbery this defendant had been arrested for the gunpoint theft of a Jaguar. ''He pointed a gun at a guy, got in, and drove off. But he got stopped a few minutes later,'' the cop explains. ''In one week he became a two-time loser. Must have just started on crack or something.''

The wolfpack robbery victim had now picked this defendant out in what's called a photo array—a group of mug shots of similar-looking young blacks.

Karas writes up the case then calls Haft's court again, only to find that there's still no sign of the Russian defendants or their lawyers.

A month later, the wolfpack case will still be in the early plea bargaining stages.

Karas then takes the information on two drug cases. One involves a young man and woman who were arrested by two undercover cops when they were found allegedly smoking crack in a rental van parked in the rental company's Lower East Side parking lot. Karas says the case is unlikely to stick because it's not clear that the cops actually saw them smoking the crack and it's not certain that the residue in the crack pipe, which was all that was left when the cops reached the defendants after seeing them light up, will test out in the laboratory.

The male defendant has a long drug arrest record that includes three convictions, none of them felonies, but no prison time. His girlfriend has no apparent record, though she has given as her address a drug clinic near where the truck was parked.

A month later the case will be reduced from a drug possession and burglary (entering a commercial vehicle) to a misdemeanor of attempted drug possession. Both defendants will have been given probation.

In the second drug case, a uniformed cop allegedly saw the defendant dispensing vials of crack on 42nd Street at about six that morning. ''These people just have no fear anymore,'' says the cop, a large, athletic type who's slurping coffee to stay awake and looks about 18 years old. ''He's standing there with a vial in one hand and ten others in a plastic bag. Then we found ten more in his pocket. . . . They were ten-dollar vials, you know, two hits or two chunks each.

''He told us they were for him, that he wasn't selling,'' the cop continues, ''that that's what he uses in a day. Then he gets mad at us when we call him a crackhead at the precinct.

''The guy's a career criminal,'' the cop adds.

This is not the cop's assessment of the man's character. The computer has already spit out his record, and at age 29 he's got nine arrests, including three for burglary and four for drugs, and two convictions—but a total of only about two years' prison time. Now, Karas says, "there's enough drugs here to give him some tough time."

"Did you voucher [log in as evidence] the plastic bag?" Karas asks the cop.

"No, just the vials he had."

"Next time voucher it. The defense lawyer will try to make something of it. He'll say you made it up. . . . These days it's hard enough to be a cop in this town and get a jury or judge to believe you. You shouldn't give them any chances to slip you up."

Two months later the case will be awaiting the usual pretrial hearings because the defense lawyer and his client have refused a two-and-a-half-to-five-year plea bargain suggested by the judge. (Karas had wanted a higher sentence.)

"He's out now," says Karas, so he's in no hurry. "The judge told him he won't go below three-and-a-half-to-seven if he didn't take [this] offer. But they're waiting. And I'll probably give in, and so will the judge." (Although judges are not supposed to get involved in plea bargaining, many do. Again, they have the ultimate say on sentences; the ADA can only recommend a sentence to a judge.)

At about 11:30 Karas takes the elevator to Justice Haft's courtroom to find out firsthand about her Russians case. She is by now so accustomed to the elevators in the criminal courts building at 100 Centre Street that she doesn't realize that she's waited about eight minutes until I point it out. Her patience, or oblivious tolerance, seems metaphorical.

Haft's court is a large, 40-foot-ceilinged empty room with long-since-cracked leather chairs for the jurors, a relic of the majesty of the process that once was.

The only people there are four uniformed, armed court officers, all reading newspapers, and a clerk, who cheerfully tells Karas to forget it when she says she's there and ready for trial. "No one's showing up today," he says with a chuckle.

In fact, one of the defendants, the one who allegedly had the gun, is sitting in the back, but his lawyer and his co-defendant are nowhere to be found.

When the clerk sees Karas's frown, he adds, matter-of-factly, that one of the lawyers has phoned in to say he's got a trial today in Queens, and won't be there until late in the afternoon. (Why he hasn't given that news to the defendant who was nice enough to drop by is anyone's guess.)

Just then, the second defendant arrives. The clerk tells them to go out for lunch.

Although Karas will return, as instructed by the clerk, at 4 P.M., they won't come back from lunch until 5:05, whereupon Karas will ask the judge if she can make a record of the fact that she is there and ready but the opposing lawyers aren't. The judge will tell her he'd like to oblige her but that the court reporter has gone home because it is after 5 P.M.

When Karas gets back to the ECAB cubicle at about noon, she's got another wolfpack case, this one involving a 17-year-old defendant (with one prior robbery arrest and one drug arrest but no convictions) who, with his friends, allegedly robbed and beat a man on Madison Avenue and 130th Street in Harlem at about 4 A.M. (The victim hailed a police car, which caught up with the alleged attackers.)

It turns out that the defendant is also a defendant in a wolfpack case that Karas got in ECAB earlier in April. In that case the defendant had allegedly beaten a man who worked at an all-night delicatessen at the same location after having smashed the window of the deli's door.

When I rejoin Karas the next morning, April 28, she's in her office (a ten-by-twenty piece of linoleum that she shares with another ADA on the sixth floor of the criminal courts building) interviewing two witnesses to that earlier wolfpack case involving this defendant.

One witness is the victim, the man who works in the deli. The other is the deli's owner. They are cousins, and both are immigrants from Yemen.

The owner explains that the defendant "always comes in and takes things. A bottle of soda, some chips, and he says to me, 'I'm not going to pay for this, and I don't give a f——— what you do about it.'

"But I don't call the cops," he explains, "because these guys are tough. He's very big"—at age 17, he's listed as 6 feet 1 inch and 200 pounds on the arrest report—"and I see his guns all the time."

"When do you see his gun?" Karas asks.

"Well, I don't want to say anything more about it, but he sells crack in the building next door, him and his friends, and they always have guns. If he knows I tell you this, he will come and shoot me."

Karas notes that the defendant's drug dealing would explain why he was carrying a paging beeper when he was arrested; running a drug business is usually the reason 17-year-old high school dropouts need to stay in touch, she explains.

"Do the police know he sells crack?" she asks.

"Yeah. They come by in the morning and board up the hole where he passes it out from, but he and his friends fix it the same day.

"But," he continues, "I don't make trouble. I let him take what he wants. But this time he started to smash my door for no reason. So my cousin goes outside to tell him to stop. That's when he beat my cousin."

While Karas questions the cousin about the beating, the deli owner explains to me that he used to work in a grocery store for his other cousin in another rough neighborhood in Brooklyn, but that a few months ago he had bought this store for $40,000 in cash.

"The owner told me it was safe, a good neighborhood," he says. "He lied. . . . We have to keep the store open twenty-four hours, because if we leave it, everything will be gone when we come back. . . . At night I sell through a window with bars. . . . So my cousin and I and another brother work there and live in the apartment on the second floor. . . . Now, I think we will move. But do you know anyone who would buy a store like this?"

He fidgets, looking at his watch. "Can we go?" he asks Karas. "We have to get back to the store."

"Soon."

"Will we have to come back?"

"Just once, to go to the grand jury, next week," she says, explaining too quickly and too technically about the grand jury being 23 people who will decide to indict. "Then, you won't have to come back again, unless he doesn't accept a plea. Then you'll have a trial."

"Will we see him there?"

"Well, you will, but that's only if he doesn't accept a plea."

Of course, there's always the chance the cousins will see the suspect at their store; he was released on his own recognizance (that is, without bail) in their case, because it was originally listed on the police report only as criminal mischief (the smashing of the gate), rather than an assault. And he's made his $3,000 bail on the new assault and robbery case that Karas picked up in ECAB the afternoon before.

As they leave, Karas promises that she'll call over the weekend to remind them of the details of their grand jury appearance the following Monday, and reminds them to "wear better clothes and no hats" that day.

One of them, apparently thinking the government is the government, turns as he's leaving, pulls a crumpled document out of his pocket, and asks Karas for help with a social security problem. She patiently gets the number and address of a local social security office for him.

"The guy who owns the store is [five years] younger than me and has three children and a wife back in the Middle East that he wants to bring over here after he makes his fortune," Karas says after they leave. "It's sad. He's got no chance up there on Madison Avenue.

A month later, the deli owner will tell me that he's worried about testifying and that the defendant has been to see him to offer to pay for his broken door, an offer he has refused, because Karas, who calls him regularly, has urged him not to take the money. "But I want to take the money," he tells me. "Who else will pay for my door? And I won't go down to testify [at a trial] if he's going to be there. . . . What can I do if he comes after me? Call the police? They already know about him, and look what they do."

Meanwhile, Karas will have presented both of this defendant's cases to the grand jury and gotten indictments.

By early June Karas will be ready to offer the defendant a plea with a sentence of two-to-six years that will probably cover not only these two cases but a robbery case he has pending in the Bronx (assuming the prosecutor there agrees) stemming from a December arrest.

Why only two years? "Because," Karas explains, "the witnesses aren't that tight for the robberies. Who knows why [the robbery victim] really was out on the street that late? And in the case of the Arabs it was only an assault, not a robbery. . . . And they could go back to Yemen for six months, and where would I be?

"Besides, he's a seventeen-year-old with no felony convictions," she adds, "and no judge is going to give him the maximum for robbery two"—second degree robbery, which is five-to-fifteen years. "On the scale of things, two-to-six or even one-and-a-half-to-four-and-a-half is what this rates."

Later that morning, April 28, Karas brushes past a woman cop reading a magazine who's been parked outside her office for more than an hour, on overtime, waiting for Karas to get a secretary to type an affidavit that she can sign. Karas takes the 10:40 elevator back up to Haft's courtroom to see if she can get her Russians case going.

A murder defendant in a different case is sitting at the defense table, without his lawyer, who is late; Haft is to begin jury selection for the man's trial. The court officers are finishing the sports pages; the judge is on the clerk's phone making lunch plans.

When the clerk sees Karas, he whispers to the judge, then tells Karas that the lawyers still haven't arrived. One of the two defendants (the one who allegedly wielded the gun) is there again.

Karas takes a seat, and we wait for about a half hour. Then, the courtroom fills with prospective jurors for the murder case. Haft gives them a little speech about the civic duty they are about to perform, then tells them to take an early lunch break because he has other business to transact.

Karas predicts that Granat, the lawyer for the defendant who allegedly had the gun, will want to plea bargain today. "He's told me his guy wants to serve time in New York, not New Jersey," she explains, "and he's about to go in in New Jersey. If he's sentenced there first, he'll do his time there."

What's so good about serving time in New York?

"Well, I wondered about that, too," she answers, "but I asked around the office and found out that these Russians have kind of a network in the prisons in New York. There are now a lot of Russian immigrants involved in crime," she adds. "So he probably figures he'll be safer here."

Karas spots Kudisch, the lawyer for the guy who hadn't had the gun. They walk out of the courtroom together.

What are you offering?" asks Kudisch. "I think my guy's ready."

"He's a predicate [felon]," says Karas, referring to his prior conviction. "And this is a bad case. So I want a plea to the top count." (This means she will not accept a plea to a count one count lower than the charge, which, under a state law intended to limit plea bargaining, is the limit to any ADA's bargaining leeway in cases such as this.)

"What sentence?"

"I'll recommend four-to-eight. He did something really bad here.

"He's got to allocute [admit to the crimes] and testify against the other guy, if I need him," she adds, as they walk through the crowded hall past another defense lawyer explaining to a scowling, tall, thin black who looks to be in his teens that "your problem is that you're a career criminal under the law."

"You really want him to testify?" Kudisch asks incredulously. "You should have your head examined if you want this guy to take a witness stand. No way he's credible about anything."

"What do you want to do?"

"I'll recommend it to him, if he shows."

"I'm going for a warrant if he doesn't show."

Another half hour passes, before Granat, the alleged gunman's lawyer, strolls down the hall.

"I've been tied up," he explains to Karas, as if explaining why he's late for a dental appointment. "Where are we?"

Karas offers him three-to-nine, and also the opportunity for the defendant to serve his time in New York instead of New Jersey where he has the other charges pending. Granat rolls his eyes. "Let's go talk to the judge," he says.

The three lawyers and the one defendant approach the bench, but there's no judge.

Haft comes back in at about 12:30, but one defendant is still missing. Haft announces that "we'll wait a short time." Meanwhile, he goes over the proposed plea bargains with the two defense lawyers and Karas, who at 5 feet 2 inches has to mount a step of sorts and stretch to converse with the judge at the bench.

One court officer points out the view of her legs to another.

Finally, at 12:55, our alleged gunman strolls in, showing no sign that he knows he's late, let alone that he regrets it. His lawyer chats briefly with him. Then the three lawyers approach the bench again.

Haft tells Karas, according to her subsequent account, that he wants her to take two-and-a-half-to-seven-and-a-half years for the alleged gunman in order to close that deal. But now he is also insisting that the men begin to serve their time immediately, rather than come back at some later date for sentencing.

Their lawyers huddle with them, approach the bench with Karas, exchange whispers, then step back.

They've refused the deal, Karas explains to me, "because they don't want to go in today. But the judge is pissed."

Haft announces that because the defendants have repeatedly missed court dates he is now revoking their bail. What he seems most upset about is that they haven't taken his plea bargain.

The defendants seem dumbfounded; they obviously hadn't realized, nor had their lawyers, that by refusing the bargain of the day they'd be put in jail to await their trial (or a new bargaining session).

The court officers lead them away, as Haft sets May 3 (five days from now) for hearings and trial.

On May 3 Karas, who by then will have found out that the accused gunman had been arrested for new alleged crimes in New Jersey (heroin possession and passing phony $20 bills) in March while out on bail, will be ready for trial once again. She'll have again studied her case the night before and have one of her cops there all day, with the other cops and cabbie standing by their phones ready to get the word to come testify. But one of the lawyers won't show up. The case will be adjourned until May 18.

On May 18 Karas will be ready once again with a cop. But both lawyers won't show. Haft will adjourn the case to May 24.

On May 24 Karas will be ready once again with a cop. But both lawyers won't show and neither will either defendant. Haft will adjourn the case to June 7.

The two lawyers, Kudisch and Granat, maintain that they had trials, or in Granat's words, "other business," on all of the days that they missed in this case. Kudisch supplied case names and courtrooms for the days in question; Granat refused.

Granat counted himself as present on two days when he'd shown up in the afternoon for 9:30 calls, explaining "the 9:30 time is a fiction, and it's especially a fiction if" — as happened on April 28 in this case — "your client is locked up, because corrections almost never delivers prisoners on time in the morning." That assessment is echoed by numerous judges, prosecutors, and defense lawyers interviewed for this article. Spokeswoman Ruby Ryles of the city's Department of Correction, which delivers 1,700-1,800 prisoners a day to courtrooms, says that inmates are delivered on time 90 percent of the time, an estimate that everyone else I spoke with laughs at.

"Look," adds Granat, "I'm a solo practitioner practicing out of Long Island, New York, and there are days when I am supposed to be in six courtrooms in six different places around the city at 9:30 in the morning. At my rates, I can't take just one case at a time. So what am I supposed to do?

"Besides, in this case," Granat continues, "I knew my co-counsel wasn't going to be there, because he had a trial, so why should I show?"

Why hadn't he called Karas in advance, so as not to waste the police witnesses' time? "If she's so worried about that, why can't she call me?" he explains. ("That's hardly my burden," says Karas.)

The solution for all the delays and adjournments, Granat explains, sounding a bit like a drunk who wants the bartender to stop serving him, "is for a judge to set a time and a date and mean it, and sanction prosecutors and lawyers who don't show up."

Granat's co-counsel, Kudisch, who also handles cases throughout the city that are scheduled simultaneously, says that he or his secretary "always call the judge's clerk or secretary the day before if I can't be there."

Haft's clerk, Kenneth Kaplan, says, "These two lawyers never called me the day before. Maybe he called the judge's secretary."

Haft's secretary, Laura Held, says that she "believes almost certainly" that neither Granat or Kudisch "ever called until the late morning or afternoon of the day they were supposed to be here. And sometimes they never called, I think. . . . We were all quite annoyed."

On June 7 both lawyers will show up but the judge will ask, for the first time, that the court find a Russian interpreter. The clerk will report that that will take at least until the afternoon. Karas, who says she remembers that the defendants spoke good English when she interviewed them, will show up at 2 P.M., only to be told that Haft is conducting a trial and that there are no other judges available that afternoon for the hearing and trial on this case. The case is adjourned until 9:30 on July 5, which is the first day Karas will be back from a vacation.

Despite Karas's protests, Haft has set another of Karas's cases for hearings and trial for 9:30 on July 5, which means that at least some witnesses, including police officers in one of the two cases, will be wasting their time.

This is not at all unusual. Most judges set most of their cases for 9:30 rather than stagger them, and they typically schedule more than one case. Thus, Karas, despite her protests to each judge involved, has four trials or hearings in three different courtrooms scheduled for 9:30 on July 5, plus six other motions or sentencings scheduled in other courts at that hour of that day.

The generous explanation for this absurd scheduling is that the judges know that most people won't show up most of the time and, therefore, figure that they'll hit it lucky if they have five or ten chances to get a case going. Also, one or more cases could be plea bargained just before a trial is to start, leaving the judge and his courtroom free to take on another one.

The cynical explanation is that judges are too dumb or too lazy to do otherwise, or that they just don't care about keeping lawyers waiting, or giving lawyers the comfort of knowing that they needn't really show up because some other case can replace theirs.

Haft says he routinely schedules everything for 9:30 because "who knows who's going to show or who's going to decide to cut a deal? Maybe if I had a computer we could do it differently. . . . And on a day like July 5," he adds, "which is after a holiday weekend, I really put a lot of cases on because it's not likely too many people will be here."

"If the defense doesn't show up, the judge can't convict the guy and put him away," Karas complains. "But if we don't show up, the judge can dismiss our case or make us look bad with our bosses. So, we have to show up or send someone else from the office."

"I love this job, because I believe in my cases and I get to handle them on my own," Karas declares later over lunch. "I spent two years as a paralegal at Arnold & Porter before law school and did some fun things—they did some work on Nicaragua that I was involved in—and I have a lot of friends now at big firms who like it. But I couldn't see doing that. Here I get to do my own cases, and the cases really count."

According to Karas and her boss, trial division chief John Fried, her independence on individual cases is tempered only by the law that limits plea bargains in serious cases to a discount of one count off the indicted charge, and by office practice that all drafts of indictments are routinely reviewed by a supervisor and that she check any dicey plea bargain or trial questions with her supervisor or with Fried.

But does Karas accomplish anything by putting a violent robber in prison for a year or two or three after she's jumped through all the procedural hoops? "Well, I hope I do. It takes them off the street, and the next time, they'll get even more," she says. "Sure, I wish the sentences were longer; they should be, but that's not my job."

Isn't she frustrated by the trials that are always on the verge but never happen?

"Sure, but I do get some," she answers, her eyes brightening. "I tried nineteen misdemeanor cases, including eleven jury trials in my first two years, and loved it." (Karas says she has won "more than half.")

"When you have to assemble all the witnesses and evidence, it's like being a director of a movie. And when it's all unfolding, when you're making it unfold, the rush of adrenalin is amazing. It's a blast, especially when you believe in your cases."

Karas has now tried two felonies since becoming more senior. She's lost both of them. "The first was a police misconduct case, a low-grade felony, which we had to try," she maintains. "I was devastated to lose it, but if you can believe it, a half hour later my second trial began. The judge was a tough judge, one of the few who doesn't like delays, and he made me go right into it. . . . It was an attempted robbery of a South American [student] at Times Square. . . . I got him to come back for the trial; I'm real good at keeping on top of my witnesses, staying in touch with them, and it worked. . . . My problem was that my victim was twice the size of the defendant, and the jury just didn't believe he'd been threatened. . . . Sometimes I think Manhattan juries want proof beyond all possible doubt, not beyond a reasonable doubt. . . . I was crushed by the two losses, but everyone in the office told me to forget it. It's hard, though.

"You burn out here," Karas continues. "It's a wonderful job, but you can't do it for more than five years. You make a commitment to stay for three years, and I don't think you can do it for much more than two years after that. You get too frustrated by all the delays."

A week later, on May 4, Karas is in her office preparing three policemen for a hearing on an arrest they made in October. It was on a Sunday afternoon, three days after two policemen had been shot and killed by drug dealers in two separate incidents the same night. This time, the cops received a radio dispatch that someone had called the 911 emergency number to report that a man with a gun was walking on 115th Street between Park and Lexington avenues, which is a known drug activity location, according to Karas and subsequent police testimony. The caller said the man was wearing a gray jacket and blue jeans.

Three cops, one Italian, the other two Puerto Rican, are telling Karas about the arrest. The Italian and one of the Puerto Ricans got the radio call while on patrol in a squad car on 106th Street and Park Avenue. They drove over to 115th Street, turned down the block, and saw the defendant walking up the street on the left side of the block.

"When the guy saw us, he turned around and walked the other way," the cop explains.

"No, that's inadmissible. You can't testify to what he saw," Karas interrupts. "Just tell what you saw."

"Okay. As we turned down the block, he was looking our way; then he turned and walked the other way."

"Good."

"So we kept after him, and pulled up alongside him. I got out from the driver's side and my partner got out from the other side. . . . I approached him from the back, and my partner approached him from the front, just as the other guys in the unmarked car were coming up the street from the other direction."

"Isn't it a one-way street?"

"They were driving the wrong way. . . . So he turned again, and I saw him reach for something in his waistband in his back."

"He probably was reaching for the gun to ditch it, not shoot it out with a group of cops," Karas later explains. "But with two cops shot a few days before, who knows? The cops at least had a right to be scared."

After seizing the gun, their subsequent search yielded several hundred empty tiny glassine bags, commonly used for dispensing drugs, a plastic bag full of marijuana, another bag with five eighths of an ounce of cocaine, and a scale used for weighing drugs. And he'd been wearing a second holster.

Now the cops faced a hearing about whether their arrest and subsequent search had been made with probable cause.

It would seem that Karas's tape recording of the 911 tape, which she carried today in her pocketbook, along with evidence that the defendant had indeed been wearing a gray jacket and jeans and had been walking up 115th Street, constitutes enough cause for the police to have stopped him and, therefore, to have patted him down to make sure he had no gun, and, therefore, to have arrested him and searched him once they found the gun.

But that doesn't prevent defense counsel — nor should it — from raising all kinds of issues and testing the bona fides of all the circumstances related to the search and the evidence.

It's now 9:45 on May 4, but Karas has called the court and found that Justice Richard Andrias isn't there yet.

At 10 Karas and the three cops decide to go to court anyway.

Andrias's court, like Haft's, is a dusty relic of its once-majestic self. At the front bench in the spectator's gallery a Legal Aid Society lawyer waiting for another case reads a romance paperback. Six court officers are sitting around the prosecution table exchanging jokes. One cracks that the state's chief judge — Court of Appeals Judge Sol Wachtler, who has been making headlines asking for more funds to solve the criminal justice crisis by building new courtrooms and hiring more judges — looks like The Fonz. Two other court officers are talking baseball.

The court reporter, tieless and jacketless, is reading a newspaper.

Someone jokes about the two men, ages 71 and 78, who'd been arrested the night before on gambling and assault charges. "Whatta they gonna get," a court officer smirks, "three-to-life?"

What would this place be like with cameras in the courtroom in place and on all the time, I ask myself as I watch the hijinks. Things would change in a hurry if the taxpayers could see this.

The clerk acknowledges Karas, whose seriousness makes her seem like the chaperone at a frat party. She takes a seat, and thumbs through her defendant's rap sheet, which runs two-and-a-half pages and recounts five arrests — for petit larceny, possession of stolen property, drug possession, fare-beating on the subway, and another petit larceny. For the first larceny, the record shows, inexplicably, that he failed to appear after making bail but that nothing happened after that. For the stolen property case, the drug case, and the second petit larceny case he was given a total of six months in jail and five years' probation. He received a fine for the fare beat.

The case file also says that he'd been able to post $1,500 in cash bail in this case.

According to the file, the defendant had been arrested on October 23 and indicted on November 4. He hadn't been arraigned until December 9,

KVCC KALAMAZOO VALLEY COMMUNITY COLLEGE LIBRARY

apparently because the correction department had not delivered him for an earlier date from prison. (He hadn't made bail until January.) At a conference on December 14, defense lawyer Michael Pineiro of the Legal Aid Society of New York asked for a hearing on the arrest and the admissibility of the resulting evidence.

Did Pineiro really believe that the stop and subsequent search had been illegal? "It's my job to make sure that it was legal," he explains, adding: "The police probably had enough cause to go up and question him. But did they have enough to pat him down? The cases go all over the lot on this. . . . The police just can't stop everyone in the community and pat them down. On the other hand, in a situation like this, some judges will say that they don't have to wait until they see the glint of a gun. . . . It's a balancing. And it depends on the judge's view of the police officer's credibility. . . . Remember, these guys are trained at the [police] academy in search and seizure law, so they know what to say after the fact."

"A lawyer who didn't make motions in a case like this would be guilty of malpractice," says Legal Aid Society criminal defense division chief Robert Baum, responding to my description of the case. "You have to make sure they really had a reason to stop him. You want to check out that 911 tape. . . . You want to make sure they really had cause to pat him down. It seems also that they . . . searched him immediately [which they would not have had probable cause to do], instead of patting him down first."

On December 14 Andrias adjourned the case to allow the two sides to submit papers on the search and evidence issues.

Karas says that at this point, she offered Pineiro a plea which would result in a three-to-six-year sentence, but he turned it down. (Pineiro confirms the offer but says he told Karas he'd consider it and never formally turned it down. "My client, however, was determined to have a hearing on the search," he adds.)

On January 25 Andrias adjourned the case until February 8 to allow Pineiro to submit more papers by March 17. A hearing was then scheduled for March 21.

On March 21 Karas was on trial, and Andrias adjourned the case until March 31, despite a note Karas says she had sent to the judge saying she'd be away that day.

The March 31 date was postponed to April 18, but on April 18 the defendant, now out on bail, failed to show up. Andrias ordered a warrant issued for his arrest, but he was not arrested, which is no surprise since 150 police in New York are in charge of enforcing more than two hundred thousand such warrants each year. The hearing was rescheduled for May 2.

On May 2 Andrias failed to show up for work, telling the lawyers the next time he saw them that he'd had to go to a funeral.

Now it is May 4, and the hearing is to begin.

Except that it doesn't begin. At 10:55, after Karas had been waiting almost an hour, defense lawyer Pineiro arrives.

"Oh, everybody's here," the clerk exclaims, getting up to go get the judge.

As the judge walks in, robeless, the clerk looks up again and realizes that the defendant hasn't yet arrived. "Looks like they can't find the defendant," he tells Andrias.

Unbothered, Andrias engages in some banter with the clerk, then goes to make a phone call.

Karas is obviously angry. "I've got so much to do," she mutters. The three cops, who are waiting outside in the hall, peek in occasionally.

It is now 11:15.

As I sit there watching the operators of our criminal justice system passing the time like retirees at a country filling station, I devise a plan to spot-check the productivity of the entire system. I will pull all of our reporters and editors from *The American Lawyer* and *Manhattan Lawyer*, and even some from our sister paper in New Jersey, into this building one day and sit one reporter or editor in each courtroom—all 45 of them—for the full working day to clock how long each court is in session conducting business.

The result, published in *Manhattan Lawyer* on May 30, would be that on average each court was in session on May 9 for four hours and 27 minutes, with Andrias's court running four hours and seven minutes. The rest of the day in this and most courtrooms—there were notable exceptions of courtrooms run by judges who know how to run things—would be given over to missing lawyers, missing defendants, missing witnesses, and missing jurors, all unsupervised by docile judges.

Andrias would begin court at 9:57 the day of the spot-check, take a one-hour-and-41-minute lunch break, and adjourn court at 3:45. He would later tell me that he regularly gets to court at about 8 A.M. and works in chambers, and typically leaves "sometime after five thirty," though on occasion he has worked until 8 P.M. or later, and that on the day of the *Manhattan Lawyer* survey he worked until after 5 P.M. on a special court task force. He would also report that he writes about "three to six opinions a month" that vary from "one to thirty pages." The problem with the system, he would explain, is that "you have a small pool of lawyers who are overloaded, and I'm not the kind of ego who feels he should impose sanctions on a lawyer because he can't be here because he has other pressing business. I was once a lawyer too, you know.

"Sure, I schedule lots of things at the same time," Andrias would add. "But that's because you have to be flexible and be ready to go when all the lawyers get here."

At 11:20 on May 4 Andrias tells the clerk to call another case. A Puerto Rican woman is brought in from the lockup and sentenced by the judge to a year in prison for what seems (from what can be discerned from the prosecutor's and clerk's muffled tones) to be some kind of crime involving stolen credit cards. "Counsel has been vociferous in your defense and been quite an effective advocate; I now wish you good luck," Andrias lectures the young, bewildered woman, oblivious to the obvious fact that she can't understand words like counsel and vociferous.

It is now 11:40. Andrias announces that he's ready for Karas's case. But Pineiro has now disappeared, and his client still isn't here.

At 11:45 Pineiro appears with his client. Pineiro approaches the bench with Karas and they talk to the judge for about a minute. Then the first cop is called.

Karas, her words tightly clipped, her presentation unflashy but confident, takes him through a recap of his career, eliciting his experience; he's been involved in "sixty to seventy drug arrests" in the last six months, he says, explaining that since November he's been moved off regular patrol to a special drug unit in the same precinct. Then, Karas has him describe the arrest.

When it's his turn, Pineiro asks the judge "for a minute or two." Then he begins by having the cop answer almost exactly the same questions that Karas had asked him about the circumstances of the arrest. His one new question: "About how many blocks' drive was it from 106th on Park Avenue to 115th?"

Pineiro then asks if the dispatcher had described the race or age of the man in the gray jacket and bluejeans, as if that mattered—as if the cop couldn't have stopped everyone with a gray jacket and blue jeans on that particular street once he'd gotten the call.

Though the questioning is pointless, Karas seems nervous. "He's got a witness outside—that woman we saw before," she whispers, referring to a fidgety young Hispanic woman we had seen waiting in the back of the courtroom.

Karas suspects that the witness is the defendant's girlfriend and that she's probably the one who made the 911 call. "Only now," says Karas, "they've made up after having some kind of fight and she's gonna say he was walking with her or something."

As the questioning continues it becomes increasingly clear—and increasingly annoying to the cop in the dock justifying the good faith of his arrest—that Justice Andrias isn't listening to it all. He can be heard discussing lunch plans with his clerk, then whispering about another case. At least three times he asks the cop (who later tells Karas how upset he felt about being ignored) to repeat something; one time Andrias even says, "I wasn't listening." Of course, this pre-trial, pre-jury hearing is solely for the judge's ear.

("I was taking careful notes, twenty-six pages' worth," Andrias later recalls, noting that he rarely gets a transcript of the proceedings. "And I might have asked him to repeat something because my notes weren't clear, or because I was distracted momentarily.")

After about a half hour, Pineiro finishes his cross-examination, and Karas puts another cop on the stand. After his cross-examination of that cop and a lunch recess, Pineiro calls the mystery witness.

She says that while out walking her dog she saw the arrest and that there had been "fifty people" on the street at the time. (The cops had said there was no one on the street, let alone anyone with a gray jacket and jeans.)

Karas begins her cross-examination at about 3:30. Yes, the defendant is a friend of hers, but she hasn't spoken to him since April, she swears, until the other day when he'd asked her to testify.

At about 4 P.M., Andrias adjourns the hearing until the following Monday, May 8, so he can hear another case.

"All in all, that wasn't a bad day," Andrias says in a later interview. "I booked four cases for trial that day, which is what I usually try to do, and sentenced two of them after pleas [actually it was one defendant sentenced on two pleas], held the hearing with Miss Karas, and held that other hearing, which I took a plea on the next morning after I dictated a decision [on that hearing] from the bench. . . . Sure, there was some chaos, but you have that when you're a judge and under siege with sixty-five or seventy-five cases to handle. But what we got done that day is not half-bad by our standards. . . . I'm not defensive about that day at all; it's fairly illustrative and fairly good. . . . There's a limit within which even the most efficient judge can operate."

As their hearing ends, Pineiro takes Karas aside and asks, according to Karas's later account, if she's still offering a three-to-six deal. She says no, that now that he's seen her case and put her through all this trouble, she wants four-to-eight. Pineiro, according to Karas, says he'll think about it. (Pineiro confirms this account but stresses that he had not gotten his client to agree to any plea at that point.)

Karas tries to reach the defendant's former common law wife the next day to find out about his relationship with the witness, but she is unable to find her.

On May 8 Karas has all six arresting police officers in Andrias's court (the cops from the patrol car and two unmarked cars), but the defendant doesn't show up at all and the witness doesn't arrive until 4:55. At about 5 P.M. Andrias adjourns the case until May 10.

On May 10 the hearing, called for the morning, doesn't begin until 3 P.M., again because the defendant and his witness, who arrive together, don't appear until then.

On cross-examination, Karas establishes that the woman is unemployed, on welfare, and enrolled in a drug clinic. "I was trying to show Andrias that she was doing it to get drugs from [the defendant]," she later explains.

She also gets the woman to admit that her friend had been wearing a gray jacket and jeans and that he'd had a gun that the cops had patted down. "That proves the cops didn't make it up," Karas later asserts.

Nonetheless Andrias sets an oral argument for May 12, which takes place on schedule, after which he promises a decision by June 5.

After the May 10 hearing Pineiro, according to Karas and Pineiro, again asked Karas if she'd go back to the three-to-six offer. She refused.

"Why should I do that?" she later explains to me. "The guy's put me through all this trouble; he's had all these cops here all these days, and his client's a walking drug factory—and he had a loaded gun. Forget it. I'm ready for trial. All these guys want to do is delay, delay, delay. Well, they pay a price for trying that."

On June 5 Andrias's clerk will tell Karas that he still hasn't decided on the arrest and the resulting evidence. So that case, too, will be put off for decision or trial (assuming he decides the obvious, that the case should go forward) on July 5—which is when Karas has the Russians case and another case scheduled for Justice Haft's courtroom.

When I next see Karas, in late May, she's still regularly calling her cabbie witness and the two men from Yemen, telling them to keep the faith. She's been to the Immigration and Naturalization Service and discovered, in reading through one of the Russians' recent immigration filings, that he's lied about whether he's been arrested. "I can get him deported," she explains, "except that they tell me we don't deport people to the Soviet Union. . . . So after he gets out of prison, we can put him in an INS detention center. Not bad."

She is also working that day on a robbery case involving a man with a long criminal record who had accosted and robbed two women window shoppers one evening and been caught after a Good Samaritan had chased him down and held him at bay until the police came.

"It's a relief from all the drug cases we've all been getting," she notes, referring to New York's crack crisis and the recent arrest crackdowns that have clogged the courts. "Yesterday, five of the seven files I worked on were drug cases, which is a little discouraging. But this [robbery] case is great. . . . Right after the victims picked him out in the lineup, he said he had started hearing voices and is now pleading insanity. That ought to be fun, an insanity defense."

Could she ever be the lawyer on the other side, lodging a defense like that, or any other defense for that matter?

"No, and I've thought about that a lot," she says, eager to explain. "After this I don't want to be a defense lawyer. . . . I don't think of myself as prosecution-oriented or conservative"—Karas has told me she voted for Dukakis, supports the exclusionary rule, and is still "squeamish" about the death penalty—"but with all I see here, I just wouldn't want to do that. . . .

"I only make thirty-four thousand dollars a year now [her salary was raised to $39,000 on July 1], and pay seven hundred dollars a month in rent and [several hundred dollars] for student loans, so I'd like more money. But I don't want to do corporate law either. . . . I'll probably do public service law or government work of some kind. And get married and have some babies, too, I hope.

"No, I've thought a lot about it, and defense work isn't for me. . . . There are a lot of defense lawyers around here whom I respect, but by and large defense lawyers here play a game. It's called delay. The more you delay your cases, the weaker they get for the prosecution. And I don't believe that's what lawyers are for."

"It is arguable that stringing out a case is better for us," concedes the Legal Aid Society's Baum. "But we have an obligation to make all the motions we feel are necessary to establish that the evidence is admissible and that our clients' rights are protected. It's not the motions that take so long," Baum adds persuasively, "it's that the judges take three weeks or a month between every event in the process—and that is not our fault."

Karas's more cynical view of defense work is formed in the main by her assessment that "one hundred percent of the people I see are guilty of something and usually what we're charging them with. . . . In twenty or thirty percent of the cases, we may have to change the charges at ECAB, but after that the cases are real. Let's face it, there may be all kinds of root causes for their crimes—and I believe that, and I think we have to do something about it— but these people are guilty.

"I'd have never believed when I was a college liberal"—at Mount Holyoke in Western Massachusetts, near where she grew up in South Deerfield— "that I'd hear myself saying this, but what the cops do is a noble thing," she adds. "Sure, they sometimes embellish and tell us they saw bulges that they didn't see when they pick up guns, but by and large they do great work that they don't get enough credit for with juries. They really do risk their lives going after very guilty people. I guess that sounds pretty conservative but it's not, because you have to consider my victims."

Indeed, if Karas's defendants are mostly nonwhite and poor, so too are her victims. And to watch Karas work in Haft's or Andrias's courtroom is to understand that crime is no longer a liberal or conservative issue. If, as urban politicians like to say, there is no liberal or conservative way to pick up the garbage, there is also no liberal or conservative way to make the courts run better than at a pace of four hours and 27 minutes a day. Of Karas's three favorite judges, two are conservative and one is a flaming liberal. What they have in common is that they work hard to schedule things and discipline lawyers so that the crisis out there on the streets is translated at least into some sense of urgency at the bench—some sense of purpose that gives those who get caught the idea that they're going to be dealt with quickly and sternly.

But the change has to go further than that. New York and other cities are now so riddled with crime that a sense of futility has set in, a capitulation to fear that is eating away at us — and especially at the poor and near-poor (Karas's grocer Yemenites or the cabbie) among us who are most victimized by crime.

The police claim to have solved just 24 percent of the 86,000 (ten an hour) reported robberies in New York last year; 10 percent of the 128,000 (15 an hour) burglaries; and 7 percent of the 110,000 (12 an hour) larcenies. And those percentages of cases solved are drastically overstated because they include thousands of cases that by their nature get "solved" automatically because they involve people who know each other and crimes that really aren't what their labels make them seem. (For example, a man who breaks up with his girlfriend but then comes back to retrieve his stereo is guilty of a burglary if she's not there and a robbery if she is there and he pushes her aside.) Also, crime experts know that as many as half the serious crimes committed may go unreported because the victims, like the cabbie after his second hold-up, sense the futility of it all.

Nor is New York an anomaly. New York is hardly the only place where stores now sell "No Radio" signs for people to hang in their car windows to ward off the radio thieves who almost never get caught. (Is there any better testament to the middle class's capitulation to crime?) New York is hardly the only city where kids growing up in the ghettos can see almost as much violence outside their window as they see on television.

So when we're lucky enough to catch criminals, and then lucky enough to get over all the hurdles of our undeniably necessary and valuable safeguards, such as *Miranda* and the exclusionary rule, to convict them, we have to deal with them more harshly. In all 40 cases that involved violence or the threat of violence that Karas was working on during the times we spoke, none seemed likely to result in a prison sentence of more than four years, and almost all seemed destined to yield a year or two. Indeed, I discovered a kind of unwritten rule of thumb that a first violent offense will get a year on average and a second one may get two to three years. And everyone, including Karas, seems so used to — or resigned to — what this outsider-liberal finds to be this undue leniency that they seem to accept it.

Similarly, drug cases, which almost always involve people associated with some violent crime sooner or later, almost never yield a prison sentence the first time around.

The penal law has to be changed to acknowledge the crisis and the simple reality that what we have now just doesn't work. We have to put people away for five or six years for their first violent crime, which means that the minimums and maximums would have to go much higher than they are now so that Karas's plea bargains would yield those results.

And we ought to make the second violent offense with a deadly weapon punishable by a minimum of ten years. This would raise the odds for those who now know they have little chance of being caught, and, more importantly, warehouse them longer when they are caught. For the simple fact is that warehousing is important because, as Karas puts it, "I almost never see a defendant who's over twenty-five who doesn't already have a record."

This would be unfair to some convicts capable of rehabilitation. It's also unfair to kill soldiers during a war who are simply taking orders from their leaders. But we do it because we have to do it.

Again, it's not simply New York's penal law that needs to be overhauled, in fact, New York's sentencing provisions—which, among other things, mandate at least a year and a half in prison for even the lowest-level second felony offender and work up from there—are relatively severe.

The common reaction to suggestions to toughen sentences and eliminate the incentives for plea bargaining is that this would bog down the system in hundreds of trials. But the system is already bogged down in thousands of pseudo pre-trials. We shouldn't worry all that much about whether tougher sentences will cut down on plea bargaining and force more cases to trial. One thing is clear from the way Karas spends her day, not to mention the way her plea-bargained cases now drag on for six to nine months, thereby robbing plea bargaining of its one virtue, swift punishment: It's that trials, which usually last a day or two in common criminal cases, wouldn't add that much to the length of the process, and would add some dignity to it.

As for the drug cases, we ought to force each illegal possession and small-sale first offender to go into a treatment program—and make sure we spend billions to provide programs for everyone in need. But we also ought to lower the boom on them the second time around, sending them to long terms in special prisons, which, would, of course, cost still more money.

But none of the punishment schemes will work if we don't make the system work, and here we have to start acting like we really do have a crisis, indeed, like we are in a war. On the streets there may be a war, but in the courtrooms where the Beth Karases of the world try to fight the war, it's paperback books and sports pages and jokes and, at best, five o'clock good-byes.

The result of all the chaos and delays is a mentality that assumes plea bargaining, that assumes that sentences meted out by judges will fall at the lower end of the spectrum that is within their discretion (even Karas assumes and accepts it), and, in general, assumes that no aspect of bringing people to justice will be swift, dignified, or otherwise consistent with the notion that the defendant has to be dealt with sternly and with credibility.

When we were at war, we operated our munitions factories overtime. We have to do the same with the courts—and run them with competent managers and accountable, competent judges. We should ask court officers, judges, ADAs, and Legal Aid lawyers to work ten hours a day at the same wage.

(Most of the ADAs and many of the Legal Aid lawyers seem to put in those hours already.)

Moreover, we should draft prosperous lawyers into the war, the kind who now don't ever step their wing tips into Beth Karas's stalled elevators.

If we really do have an urban crisis in law enforcement, why shouldn't we require all lawyers coming out of law school to help solve that crisis? We could require them to work — at salaries even lower than Karas's — two or three years in either a Legal Aid office or an assistant district attorney's office in a city in the state where they want to practice. (Perhaps we could give them the option of working for Legal Aid offices on the civil side, too.) The manpower from these public service criminal justice internships (which would be akin to the below-wage, forced training, and work that doctors provide as interns) could be used to operate the courts on extended schedules.

Besides, putting so many of the best and brightest into these systems would do wonders to force changes in the dumb, lazy system we now have. Today, the poor worry every day about crime on their doorsteps (so much so that fighting crime ought to be viewed as part of the liberals' agenda). But the middle and upper classes worry about crime only when they read a headline story of some middle- or upper-class white being a victim (which are typically the only headline stories about crime). They never really have to deal with the system, except in the unlikely event that they are victims themselves and a suspect is caught. But if thousands of heavy-hitting future corporate lawyers were exposed to this brazenly ridiculous system for two or three years, it would have to change.

One can quibble, or even laugh at, any of these ideas, because some of the details are missing or impractical, or even because they're bad at their core. But my real point is that we have to think differently, and radically, about what we're doing about crime. And we have to commit enormous resources to doing something about it.

And, of course, the last but most important place where we have to put those resources has to do with the state of our underclass. Crime is committed mostly by poor people; and, although it's not nice to talk about it this way, in this country's cities most of our poor people are non-white, and they commit most of the crimes. (Such is our collective state of sensitivity about this that I couldn't get our *Manhattan Lawyer* editors to print that all but a handful of the hundreds of defendants our reporters saw in those 45 courtrooms that day in May were black or Hispanic.)

Yes, for the sake of our own preservation and especially for the sake of the poor and minorities for whom every night in America is now like a night in Beirut, we need to spend billions to put the system on a war footing that will deal much more toughly with criminals over the short term. But if we don't also spend billions to do something over the longer term about a burgeoning nonwhite underclass, in which for a minority (indeed, a surprisingly tiny minority given the state of the options available to them) crime is sometimes the only opportunity and criminals the only role models, we may do a better job of warehousing criminals, but we'll lose the war because there will always be replacements.

What we need overall, then, is a different mind-set about crime, one that acts on the reality that there really is a crisis that is eating away at us every bit as much as a terrorist guerrilla attack beginning at sundown every night would eat away at us. For amid all the public rhetoric about that crisis there is anything but a crisis atmosphere among those who operate the system now.

This is not to say that there are villains in this story. Anyone who's part of the system will read this article and say that I've picked unfairly on the judges, on some of the lawyers, and on the others singled out; and in the sense that there's nothing evil or especially bad about these people they'll be right. But no one will quibble with the facts; they'll just say that I don't "understand" all the problems of the system.

The problem, though, is that all those who run the system and who work in the system—and even the reporters, including our own from *Manhattan Lawyer*, who cover it—"understand" too well. They "understand" it so well that they accept the absurdity, the lunacy, of it all.

Sure, the players are probably worn down by the futility of it all. And it could be argued that any organization this big with this many cases—154,000 felony arrests were processed in New York in 1988 and arrests are up in Manhattan 24 percent so far this year—is destined to become a gray, linoleum, dull-witted, numb-sensed, gallows-humor bureaucracy.

So perhaps the reason that victims like the cabbie-robbery victim feel so frustrated about the system is that for them the arrest and the prospect of a prosecution is a special, rejuvenating event after the horror of the crime— while for everyone else involved (except maybe the as-yet unjaded, like Karas) there's a numbing, bureaucratic routine to it all.

As the cabbie puts it, "I was euphoric after the arrest, because I thought I had really gotten these guys and put them away for a good long time. But then I realized that no one, except maybe Beth, really gave a shit about the case."

We can't let that continue.

The people who run these urban justice systems—mayors, governors, chief judges, prosecutors, defense lawyers—should stop "understanding" the problem and start screaming from the rooftops that we can't let this go on, that we need more resources, more taxes, hard-nosed management, better people, and, above all, a new mind-set to achieve criminal justice.

We can't continue to operate our law enforcement system like a third-rate motor vehicles bureau. We can't continue to process cases rather than redeem the rule of law.

We can't continue to burn out the Beth Karases after five years.

Their work is too important, and they're too good at it.

We have to decide instead to give them a place—a system, a penal code, judges, defense lawyers, colleagues—that they want to work in forever.

11

The Practice of Law as a Con Game

Abraham S. Blumberg

A recurring theme in the growing dialogue between sociology and law has been the great need for a joint effort of the two disciplines to illuminate urgent social and legal issues. Having uttered fervent public pronouncements in this vein, however, the respective practitioners often go their separate ways. Academic spokesmen for the legal profession are somewhat critical of sociologists of law because of what they perceive as the sociologist's preoccupation with the application of theory and methodology to the examination of legal phenomena, without regard to the solution of legal problems. Further, it is felt that "contemporary writing in the sociology of law...betrays the existence of painfully unsophisticated notions about the day-to-day operations of courts, legislatures and law offices."[1] Regardless of the merit of such criticism, scant attention—apart from explorations of the legal profession itself—has been given to the sociological examination of legal institutions, or their supporting ideological assumptions. Thus, for example, very little sociological effort is expended to ascertain the validity and viability of important court decisions, which may rest on wholly erroneous assumptions about the contextual realities of social structure. A particular decision may rest upon a legally impeccable rationale; at the same time it may be rendered nugatory

Blumberg, Abraham, "The Practice of Law as a Confidence Game," *Law and Society Review*. (June, 1967), pp. 15-39.

or self-defeating by contingencies imposed by aspects of social reality of which the lawmakers are themselves unaware.

Within this context, I wish to question the impact of three recent landmark decisions of the United States Supreme Court; each hailed as destined to effect profound changes in the future of criminal law administration and enforcement in America. The first of these, *Gideon vs. Wainwright,* 372 U.S. 335 (1963) required states and localities henceforth to furnish counsel in the case of indigent persons charged with a felony.[2] The Gideon ruling left several major issues unsettled, among them the vital question: What is the precise point in time at which a suspect is entitled to counsel?[3] The answer came relatively quickly in *Escobedo v. Illinois*, 378 U.S. 478 (1964), which has aroused a storm of controversy. Danny Escobedo confessed to the murder of his brother-in-law after the police had refused to permit retained counsel to see him, although his lawyer was present in the station house and asked to confer with his client. In a 5-4 decision, the court asserted that counsel must be permitted when the process of police investigative effort shifts from merely investigatory to that of accusatory: "when its focus is on the accused and its purpose is to elicit a confession — our adversary system begins to operate, and, under the circumstances here, the accused must be permitted to consult with his lawyer."

As a consequence, Escobedo's confession was rendered inadmissible. The decision triggered a national debate among police, district attorneys, judges, lawyers, and other law enforcement officials, which continues unabated, as to the value and propriety of confessions in criminal cases.[4] On June 13, 1966, the Supreme Court in a 5-4 decision underscored the principle enunciated in *Escobedo* in the case of *Miranda v. Arizona.*[5] Police interrogation of any suspect in custody, without his consent, unless a defense attorney is present, is prohibited by the self-incrimination provision of the Fifth Amendment. Regardless of the relative merit of the various shades of opinion about the role of counsel in criminal cases, the issues generated thereby will be in part resolved as additional cases move toward decision in the Supreme Court in the near future. They are of peripheral interest and not of immediate concern in this paper. However, the *Gideon, Escobedo,* and *Miranda* cases pose interesting questions. In all three decisions, the Supreme Court reiterates the traditional legal conception of a defense lawyer based on the ideological perception of a criminal case as an *adversary, combative* proceeding, in which counsel for the defense assiduously musters all the admittedly limited resources at his command to *defend* the accused.[6] The fundamental question remains to be answered: Does the Supreme Court's conception of the role of counsel in a criminal case square with social reality?

The task of this paper is to furnish some preliminary evidence toward the illumination of that question. Little empirical understanding of the function of defense counsel exists; only some ideologically oriented generalizations and commitments. This paper is based upon observations made by the writer during many years of legal practice in the criminal courts of a large metropolitan area. No claim is made as to its methodological rigor, although it does reflect a conscious and sustained effort for participant observations.

Court Structure Defines Role of Defense Lawyer

The overwhelming majority of convictions in criminal cases (usually over 90 per cent) are not the product of a combative, trial-by-jury process at all, but instead merely involve the sentencing of the individual after a nego-tiated, bargained-for plea of guilty has been entered.[7] Although more recently the overzealous role of police and prosecutors in producing pretrial confessions and admissions has achieved a good deal of notoriety, scant attention has been paid to the organizational structure and personnel of the criminal court itself. Indeed, the extremely high conviction rate produced without the features of an adversary trial in our courts would tend to suggest that the "trial" becomes a perfunctory reiteration and validation of the pretrial interrogation and investigation.[8]

The institutional setting of the court defines a role for the defense counsel in a criminal case radically different from the one traditionally depicted.[9] Sociologists and others have focused their attention on the deprivations and social disabilities of such variables as race, ethnicity, and social class as being the source of an accused person's defeat in a criminal court. Largely overlooked is the variable of the court organization itself, which possesses a thrust, purpose, and direction of its own. It is grounded in pragmatic values, bureaucratic priorities, and administrative instruments. These exalt maximum production and the particularistic career designs of organizational incumbents, whose ocupational and career commitments tend to generate a set of priorities. These priorities exert a higher claim than the stated ideological goals of "due process of law," and are often inconsistent with them.

Organizational goals and discipline impose a set of demands and conditions of practice on the respective professions in the criminal court, to which they respond by abandoning their ideological and professional commitments to the accused client, in the service of these higher claims of the court organization. All court personnel, including the accused's own lawyer, tend to be coopted to become agent-mediators[10] who help the accused redefine his situation and restructure his perceptions concomitant with a plea of guilty.

Of all the occupational roles in the court the only private individual who is officially recognized as having a special status and concomitant obligations is the lawyer. His legal status is that of "an officer of the court" and he is held to a standard of ethical performance and duty to his client as well as to the court. This obligation is thought to be far higher than that expected of ordinary individuals occupying the various occupational statuses in the court community. However, lawyers, whether privately retained or of the legal-aid, public defender variety, have close and continuing relations with the prosecuting office and the court itself through discreet relations with the judges via their law secretaries of "confidential" assistants. Indeed, lines of communication, influence and contact with those offices, as well as with the Office of the Clerk of the court, Probation Division, and with the press, are essential to present and prospective requirements of criminal law practice. Similarly, the subtle involvement of the press and other mass media in the court's organizational network is not readily discernible to the casual observer. Accused persons come and go in the court system schema, but the structure and its occupational incumbents remain to carry on their respective career, occupational and organizational enterprises. The individual stridencies, tensions, and conflicts a given accused person's case may present to all the participants are overcome, because the formal and informal relations of all the groups in the court setting require it. The probability of continued future relations and interactions must be preserved at all costs.

This is particularly true of the "lawyer regulars" i.e., those defense lawyers, who by virtue of their continuous appearances in behalf of defendants, tend to represent the bulk of a criminal court's non-indigent case workload, and those lawyers who are not "regulars," who appear almost casually in behalf of an occasional client. Some of the "lawyer regulars" are highly visible as one moves about the major urban centers of the nation, their offices line the back streets of the courthouses, at times sharing space with bondsmen. Their political "visibility" in terms of local club house ties, reaching into the judge's chambers and prosecutor's office, are also deemed essential to successful practitioners. Previous research has indicated that the "lawyer regulars" make no effort to conceal their dependence upon police, bondsmen, jail personnel. Nor do they conceal the necessity for maintaining intimate relations with all levels of personnel in the court setting as a means of obtaining, maintaining, and building their practice. These informal relations are the *sine qua non* not only of retaining a practice, but also in the negotiation of pleas and sentences.[11]

The client, then, is a secondary figure in the court system as in certain other bureaucratic settings.[12] He becomes a means to other ends of the organization's incumbents. He may present doubts, contingencies, and pressures which challenge existing informal arrangements or disrupt them; but these tend to be resolved in favor of the continuance of the organization and its relations as before. There is a greater community of interest among all the principal organizational structures and their incumbents than exists elsewhere in other settings. The accused's lawyer has far greater professional, economic, intellectual and other ties to the various elements of the court system than he does to his own client. In short, the court is a closed community.

This is more than just the case of the usual "secrets" of bureaucracy which are fanatically defended from an outside view. Even all elements of the press are zealously determined to report on that which will not offend the board of judges, the prosecutor, probation, legal-aid, or other officials, in return for privileges and courtesies granted in the past and to be granted in the future. Rather than any view of the matter in terms of some variation of a "conspiracy" hypothesis, the simple explanation is one of an ongoing system handling delicate tensions, managing the trauma produced by law enforcement and administration, and requiring almost pathological distrust of "outsiders" bordering on group paranoia.

The hostile attitude toward "outsiders" is in large measure engendered by a defensiveness itself produced by the inherent deficiencies of assembly line justice, so characteristic of our major criminal courts. Intolerably large caseloads of defendants which must be disposed of in an organizational context of limited resources and personnel, potentially subject the participants in the court community to harsh scrutiny from appellate courts, and other public and private sources of condemnation. As a consequence, an almost irreconcilable conflict is posed in terms of intense pressures to process large numbers of cases on the one hand, and the stringent ideological and legal requirements of "due process of law," on he other hand. A rather tenuous resolution of the dilemma has emerged in the shape of a large variety of bureaucratically ordained and controlled "work crimes," short cuts, deviations, and outright rule violations adopted as court practice in order to meet production norms. Fearfully anticipating criticism on ethical as well as legal grounds, all the significant participants in the court's social structure are bound into an organized system of complicity. This consists of a work arrangement in which the patterned, covert, informal breaches, and evasions of "due process" are institutionalized, but are nevertheless denied to exist.

These institutionalized evasions will be found to occur to some degree, in all criminal courts. Their nature, scope and complexity are largely determined by the size of the court, and the character of the community in which it is located, e.g., whether it is a large, urban institution, or a relatively small rural county court. In addition, idiosyncratic, local conditions may contribute to a unique flavor in the character and quality of the criminal law's administration in a particular community. However, in most instances a variety of stratagems are employed — some subtle, some crude, in effectively disposing of what are often too large caseloads. A wide variety of coercive devices are employed against an accused-client, couched in a depersonalized, instrumental, bureaucratic version of due process of law, and which are in reality a perfunctory obeisance to the ideology of due process. These include some very explicit pressures which are exerted in some measure by all court personnel, including judges, to plead guilty and avoid trial. In many instances the sanction of a potentially harsh sentence is utilized as the visible alternative to pleading guilty, in the case of recalcitrants. Probation and psychiatric reports are "tailored" to organizational needs, or are at least responsive to the court organization's requirements for the refurbishment of a defendant's social biography, consonant with his new status. A resourceful judge can, through his subtle domination of the proceedings, impose his will on the final outcome of a trial. Stenographers and clerks, in their function as record keepers, are on occasion pressed into service in support of a judicial need to "rewrite" the record of a courtroom event. Bail practices are usually employed for purposes other than simply assuring a defendant's presence on the date of a hearing in connection with his case. Too often, the discretionary power as to bail is part of the arsenal of weapons available to collapse the resistance of an accused person. The foregoing is a most cursory examination of some of the more prominent "short cuts" available to any court organization. There are numerous other procedural strategies constituting due process deviations, which tend to become the work style artifacts of a court's personnel. Thus, only court "regulars" who are "bound in" are really accepted; others are treated routinely and in almost a coldly correct manner.

The defense attorneys, therefore, whether of the legal-aid, public defender variety, or privately retained, although operating in terms of pressures specific to their respective role and organizational obligations, ultimately are concerned with strategies which tend to lead to a plea. It is the rational, impersonal elements involving economies of time, labor, expense and a superior commitment of the defense counsel to these rationalistic values of maximum production[13] of court organization that prevail, in his relationship with a client. The lawyer "regulars" are frequently former staff members of the prosecutor's office and utilize the prestige, know-how and contacts of their former affiliation as part of their stock in trade. Close and continuing relations between the lawyer "regular" and his former colleagues in the prosecutor's office generally overshadow the relationship between the regular and his client. The continuing colleagueship of supposedly adversary counsel rests on real professional and organizational needs of a *quid pro quo*, which goes behind the limits of an accommodation or *modus vivendi* one might ordinarily expect under the circumstances of an otherwise seemingly adversary relationship. Indeed, the adversary features which are manifest are for the most part muted and exist even in their attenuated form largely for external consumption. The principals, lawyer and assistant district attorney, rely upon one another's cooperation for their continued professional existence, and so the bargaining between them tends usually to be "reasonable" rather than fierce.

Fee Collection and Fixing

The real key to understanding the role of defense counsel in a criminal case is to be found in the area of the fixing of the fee to be charged and its collection. The problem of fixing and collecting the fee tends to influence to a significant degree the criminal court process itself, and not just the relationship of the lawyer and his client. In essence, a lawyer-client "confidence game" is played. A true confidence game is unlike the case of the emperor's new clothes wherein that monarch's nakedness was a result of inordinate gullibility and credulity. In a genuine confidence game, the perpetrator manipulates the basic dishonesty of his partner, the victim or mark, toward his own (the confidence operator's) ends. Thus, "the victim of a con scheme must have some larceny in his heart."[14]

Legal service lends itself particularly well to confidence games. Usually, a plumber will be able to demonstrate empirically that he has performed a service by clearing up the stuffed drain, repairing the leaky faucet or pipe—and therefore merits his fee. He has rendered, when summoned, a visible, tangible boon for his client in return for the requested fee. A physician, who has not performed some visible surgery or otherwise engaged in some readily discernible procedure in connection with a patient, may be deemed by the patient to have "done nothing" for him. As a consequence, medical practitioners may simply prescribe or administer by injection a placebo to overcome a patient's potential reluctance or dissatisfaction in paying a requested fee, "for nothing."

In the practice of law there is a special problem in this regard, no matter what the level of the practitioner or his place in the hierarchy of prestige. Much legal work is intangible either because it is simply a few words of advice, some preventive action, a telephone call, negotiation of some kind, a form filled out and filed, a hurried conference with another attorney or an official of a government agency, a letter or opinion written, or a countless variety of seemingly innocuous, and even prosaic procedures and actions. These are the basic activities, apart from any possible court appearance, of almost all lawyers, at all levels of practice. Much of the activity is not in the nature of the exercise of the traditional, precise professional skills of attorney such as library research and oral argument in connection with appellate briefs, court motions, trial work, drafting of opinions, memoranda, contracts, and other complex documents and agreements. Instead, much legal activity, whether it is at the lowest or highest "white shoe" law firm levels, is of the brokerage, agent, sales representative, lobbyist type of activity, in which the lawyer acts for someone else in pursuing the latter's interests and designs. The service is intangible.[15]

The large scale law firm may not speak as openly of the "contacts," their "fixing' abilities, as does the lower level lawyer. They trade instead upon a facade of thick carpeting, walnut panelling, genteel low pressure, and superficialities of traditional legal professionalism. There are occasions when even the large firm is on the defensive in connection with the fees they charge because the services rendered or results obtained do not appear to merit the fee asked.[16] Therefore, there is a recurrent problem in the legal profession in fixing the amount of fee, and in justifying the basis for the requested fee.

Although the fee at times amounts to what the traffic and the conscience of the lawyer will bear, one further observation must be made with regard to the size of the fee and its collection. The defendant in a criminal case and the material gain he may have acquired during the course of his illicit activities are soon parted. Not infrequently the ill gotten fruits of the various modes of larceny are sequestered by a defense lawyer in payment of his fee. Inexorably, the amount of the fee is a function of the dollar value of the crime committed, and is frequently set with meticulous precision at a sum which bears an uncanny relationship to that of the net proceeds of the particular offense involved. On occasion, defendants have been known to commit additional offenses while at liberty on bail, in order to secure the requisite funds with which to meet their obligations for payment of legal fees. Defense lawyers condition even the most obtuse clients to recognize that there is a firm interconnection between fee payment and the zealous exercise of professional expertise, secret knowledge, and organizational "connections" in their behalf. Lawyers, therefore, seek to keep their clients in a proper state of tension, and to arouse in them the precise edge of anxiety which is calculated to encourage prompt fee payment. Consequently, the client attitude in the relationship between defense counsel and an accused is in many instances a precarious admixture of hostility, mistrust, dependence, and sycophancy. By keeping his client's anxieties aroused to the proper pitch, and establishing a seemingly causal relationship between a requested fee and the accused's ultimate extrication from his onerous difficulties, the lawyer will have established the necessary preliminary groundwork to assure a minimum of haggling over the fee and its eventual payment.

In varying degrees, as a consequence, all law practice involves a manipulation of the client and a stage management of the lawyer-client relationship so that at least an *appearance* of help and service will be forthcoming. This is accomplished in a variety of ways, often exercised in combination with each other. At the outset, the lawyer-professional employs with suitable varition a measure of sales-puff which may range from an air of unbounding self-confidence, adequacy, and dominion over events, to that of complete arrogance. This will be supplemented by the affectation of a studied, faultless mode of personal attire. In the larger firms, the furnishings and office trappings will serve as the backdrop to help in impression management and client intimidation. In all firms, solo or large scale, an access to secret knowledge, and to the seats of power and influence is inferred, or presumed to a varying degree as the basic vendible commodity of the practicitioncrs.

The lack of visible end product offers a special complication in the course of the professional life of the criminal court lawyer with respect to his fee and in his relations with his client. The plain fact is that an accused in a criminal case always "loses" even when he has been exonerated by an acquittal, discharge, or dismissal of his case. The hostility of an accused which follows as a consequence of his arrest, incarceration, possible loss of job, expense and other traumas connected with his case is directed, by means of displacement, toward his lawyer. It is in this sense that it may be said that a criminal lawyer never really "wins" a case. The really satisfied client is rare, since in the very nature of the situation even an accused's vindication leaves him with some degree of dissatisfaction and hostility. It is this state of affairs that makes for a lawyer-client relationship in the criminal court which tends to be a somewhat exaggerated version of the usual lawyer-client confidence game.

At the outset, because there are great risks of nonpayment of the fee, due to the impecuniousness of his clients, and the fact that a man who is sentenced to jail may be a singularly unappreciative client, the criminal lawyer collects his fee *in advance*. Often, because the lawyer and the accused both have questionable designs of their own upon each other, the confidence game can be played. The criminal lawyer must serve three major functions, or stated another way, he must solve three problems. First, he must arrange for his fee; second, he must prepare and then, if necessary, "cool out" his client in case of defeat[17] (a highly likely contingency); third, he must satisfy the court organization that he has performed adequately in the process of negotiating the plea, so as to preclude the possibility of any sort of embarrassing incident which may serve to invite "outside" scrutiny.

In assuring the attainment of one of his primary objectives, his fee, the criminal lawyer will very often enter into negotiations with the accused's kin, including collateral relatives. In many instances, the accused himself is unable to pay any sort of fee or anything more than a token fee. It then becomes important to involve as many of the accused's kin as possible in the situation. This is especially so if the attorney hopes to collect a significant part of a proposed substantial fee. It is not uncommon for several relatives to contribute toward the fee. The larger the group, the greater the possibility that the lawyer will collect a sizable fee by getting contributions from each.

A fee for a felony case which ultimately results in a plea, rather than a trail, may ordinarily range anywhere from $500 to $1,500. Should the case go to trial, the fee will be proportionately larger, depending upon the length of the trial. But the larger the fee the lawyer wishes to exact, the more impressive his performance must be, in terms of his stage managed image as a personage of great influence and power in the court organization. Court personnel are keenly aware of the extent to which a lawyer's stock in trade involves the precarious stage management of an image which goes beyond the usual professional flamboyance, and for this reason alone the lawyer is "bound in" to the authority system of the court's organizational discipline. Therefore, to some extent, court personnel will aid the lawyer in the creation and maintenance of.that impression. There is a tacit commitment to the lawyer by the court organization, apart from formal etiquette, to aid him in this. Such augmentation of the lawyer's stage managed image as this affords, is the partial basis for the *quid pro quo* which exists between the lawyer and the court organization. It tends to serve as the continuing basis for the higher loyalty of the lawyer to the organization; his relationship with his client, in contrast is transient, ephemeral and often superficial.

Defense Lawyer as Double Agent

The lawyer has often been accused of stirring up unnecessary litigation, especially in the field of negligence. He is said to acquire a vested interest in a cause of action or claim which was initially his client's. The strong incentive of possible fee motivates the lawyer to promote litigation which would otherwise never have developed. However, the criminal lawyer develops a vested interest of an entirely different nature in his client's case: to limit its scope and duration rather than do battle. Only in this way can a case be "profitable." Thus, he enlists the aid of relatives not only to assure payment of his fee, but he will also rely on these persons to help him in his agent-mediator role of convincing the accused to plead guilty, and ultimately to help in "cooling out" the accused if necessary.

It is at this point that an accused-defendant may experience his first sense of "betrayal." While he had perhaps perceived the police and prosecutor to be adversaries, or possibly even the judge, the accused is wholly unprepared for his counsel's role performance as an agent-mediator. In the same vein, it is even less likely to occur to an accused that members of his own family or other kin may become agents, albeit at the behest and urging of other agents or mediators, acting on the principle that they are in reality helping an accused negotiate the best possible plea arrangement under the circumstances. Usually, it will be the lawyer who will activate next of kin in this role, his ostensible motive being to arrange for his fee. But soon latent and unstated motives will assert themselves, with entreaties by counsel to the accused's next of kin, to appeal to the accused to "help himself" by pleading. *Gemeinschaft* sentiments are to this extent exploited by a defense lawyer (or even at times by a district attorney) to achieve specific secular ends, that is, of concluding a particular matter with all possible dispatch.

The fee is often collected in stages, each installment usually payable prior to a necessary court appearance required during the course of an accused's career journey. At each stage, in his interviews and communications with the accused, or in addition, with members of his family, if they are helping with the fee payment, the lawyer employs an air of professional confidence and "inside-dopesterism" in order to assuage anxieties on all sides. He makes the necessary bland assurances, and in effect manipulates his client, who is usually willing to do and say the things, true or not, which will help his attorney extricate him. Since the dimensions of what he is essentially selling, organizational influence and expertise, are not technically and precisely measurable, the lawyer can make extravagant claims of influence and secret knowledge with impunity. Thus, lawyers frequently claim to have inside knowledge in connection with information in the hands of the D.A., police, probation officials or to have access to these functionaries. Factually, they often do, and need only to exaggerate the nature of their relationships with them to obtain the desired effective impression upon the client. But, as in the genuine confidence game, the victim who has participated is loath to do anything which will upset the lesser plea which his lawyer has "conned" him into accepting.[18]

In effect, in his role as double agent, the criminal lawyer performs an extremely vital and delicate mission for the court organization and the accused. Both principals are anxious to terminate the litigation with a minimum of expense and damage to each other. There is no other personage or role incumbent in the total court structure more strategically located, who by training and in terms of his own requirements, is more ideally suited to do so than the lawyer. In recognition of this, judges will cooperate with attorneys in many important ways. For example, they will adjourn the case of an accused in jail awaiting plea or sentence if the attorney requests such action. While explicitly this may be done for some innocuous and seemingly valid reason, the tacit purpose is that pressure is being applied by the attorney for the collection of his fee, which he knows will probably not be forthcoming if the case is concluded. Judges are aware of this tactic on the part of lawyers, who, by requesting an adjournment, keep an accused incarcerated awhile longer as a not too subtle method of dunning a client for payment. However, the judges will go along with this, on the ground that important ends are being served. Oftcn, the only end served is to protect a lawyer's fee.

The judge will help an accused's lawyer in still another way. He will lend the official aura of his office and courtroom so that a lawyer can stage manage an impression of an "all out" performance for the accused in justification of his fee. The judge and other court personnel will serve as a backdrop for a scene charged with dramatic fire, in which the accused's lawyer makes a stirring appeal in his behalf. With a show of restrained passion, the lawyer will intone the virtues of the accused and recite the social deprivations which have reduced him to his present state. The speech varies somewhat, depending on whether the accused has been convicted after trial or has pleaded guilty. In the main, however, the incongruity, superficiality, and ritualistic character of the total performance is underscored by a visibly impassive, almost bored reaction on the part of the judge and other members of the court retinue.

Afterward, there is a hearty exchange of pleasantries between the lawyer and district attorney, wholly out of context in terms of the supposed adversary nature of the preceding events. The fiery passion in defense of his client is gone, and the lawyers for both sides resume their offstage relations, chatting amiably and perhaps including the judge in their restrained banter. No other aspect of their visible conduct so effectively serves to put even a casual observer on notice, that these individuals have claims upon each other. These seemingly innocuous actions are indicative of continuing organizational and informal relations, which, in their intricacy and depth, range far beyond any priorities or claims a particular defendant my have.[19]

Criminal law practice is a unique form of private law practice since it really only appears to be private practice.[20] Actually it is bureaucratic practice, because of the legal practitioner's enmeshment in the authority, discipline, and perspectives of the court organization. Private practice, supposedly, in a professional sense, involves the maintenance of an organized, disciplined body of knowledge and learning; the individual practitioners are imbued with a spirit of autonomy and service, the earning of a livelihood being incidental. In the sense that the lawyer in the criminal court serves as a double agent, serving higher organizational rather than professional ends, he may be deemed to be engaged in bureaucratic rather than private practice. To some extent the lawyer-client "confidence game," in addition to its other functions, serves to conceal this fact.

The Client's Perception

The "cop-out" ceremony, in which the court process culminates, is not only invaluable for redefining the accused's perspectives of himself, but also in reiterating publicly in a formally structured ritual the accused person's guilt for the benefit of significant "others" who are observing. The accused not only is made to assert publicly his guilt of a specific crime, but also a complete recital of its details. He is further made to indicate that he is entering his plea of guilty freely, willingly, and voluntarily, and that he is not doing so because of any promises or in consideration of any commitments that may have been made to him by anyone. This last is intended as a blanket statement to shield the participants from any possible charges of "coercion" or undue influence that may have been exerted in violation of due process requirements. Its function is to preclude any later review by an appellate court on these grounds, and also to obviate any second thoughts an accused may develop in connection with his plea.

However, for the accused, the conception of self as a guilty person is in large measure a temporary role adaptation. His career socialization as an accused, if it is successful, eventuates in his acceptance and redefinition of himself as a guilty person.[21] However, the transformation is ephemeral, in that he will, in private, quickly reassert his innocence. Of importance is that he accept his defeat, publicly proclaim it, and find some measure of pacification in it.[22] Almost immediately after his plea, a defendant will generally be interviewed by a representative of the probation division in connection with a presentence report which is to be prepared. The very first question to be asked of him by the probation officer is: "Are you guilty of the crime to which you pleaded?" This is by way of double affirmation of the defendant's guilt. Should the defendant now begin to make bold assertions of his innocence, despite his plea of guilty, he will be asked to withdraw his plea and stand trial on the original charges. Such a threatened possibility is, in most instances, sufficient to cause an accused to let the plea stand and to request the probation officer to overlook his exclamations of innocence. Table I that follows is a breakdown of the categorized responses of a random sample of male defendants in Metropolitan Court[23] during 1962, 1963, and 1964 in connection with their statements during presentence probation interviews following their plea of guilty.

It would be well to observe at the outset, that of the 724 defendants who pleaded guilty before trial, only 43 (5.94 per cent) of the total group had confessed prior to their indictment. Thus, the ultimate judicial process was predicated upon evidence independent of any confession of the accused.[24]

As the data indicate, only a relatively small number (95) out of the total number of defendants actually will even admit their guilt, following the "cop-out" ceremony. However, even though they have affirmed their guilt, many of these defendants felt that they should have been able to negotiate a more favorable plea. The largest aggregate of defendants (373) were those who reasserted their "innocence" following their public profession of guilt during the "cop-out" ceremony. These defendants employed differential degrees of fervor, solemnity and credibility, ranging from really mild, wavering assertions of innocence which were embroidered with a variety of stock explanations and rationalizations, to those of an adamant, "framed" nature. Thus, the "Innocent" group, for the most part, were largely concerned with underscoring for their probation interviewer their essential "goodness" and "worthiness," despite their formal plea of guilty. Assertion of his innocence at the post-plea stage, resurrects a more respectable and acceptable self concept for the accused defendant who has pleaded guilty. A recital of the structural exigencies which precipitated his plea of guilt, serves to embellish a newly proffered claim of innocence, which many

Table I

Defendant Responses as to Guilt or Innocence after Pleading Guilty

N = 724   Years — 1962, 1963, 1964

Nature of Response		N of Defendants
Innocent (Manipulated)	"The lawyer or judge, police or D.A. 'conned me'"	86
Innocent (Pragmatic)	"Wanted to get it over with" "You can't beat the system" "They have you over a barrel when you have a record"	147
Innocent (Advice of counsel)	"Followed my lawyer's advice"	92
Innocent (Defiant)	"Framed" — "Betrayed by 'Complainant,' 'Police,' 'Squealers,' 'Lawyer,' 'Friends,' 'Wife,' 'Girlfriend'"	33
Innocent (Adverse social data)	Blames probation officer or psychiatrist for "Bad Report," in cases where there was pre-pleading investigation	15
Guilty	"But I should have gotten a better deal" Blames Lawyer, D.A., Police, Judge	74
Guilty	Won't say anything further	21
Fatalistic (Doesn't press his "Innocence," won't admit "Guilt")	"I did it for convenience" "My lawyer told me it was only thing I could do" "I did it because it was the best way out"	248
No Response		8
Total		724

defendants mistakenly feel will stand them in good stead at the time of sentence, or ultimately with probation or parole authorities.

Relatively few (33) maintained their innocence in terms of having been "framed" by some person or agent-mediator, although a larger number (86) indicated that they had been manipulated or "conned" by an agent-mediator to plead guilty, but as indicated, their assertions of innocence were relatively mild.

A rather substantial group (147) preferred to stress the pragmatic aspects of their plea of guilty. They would only perfunctorily assert their innocence and would in general refer to some adverse aspect of their situation which they believed tended to negatively affect their bargaining leverage, including in some instances a prior criminal record.

One group of defendants (92), while maintaining their innocence, simply employed some variation of a theme of following "the advice of counsel" as a covering response, to explain their guilty plea in the light of their new affirmation of innocence.

The largest single group of defendants (248) were basically fatalistic. They often verbalized weak suggestions of their innocence in rather halting terms, wholly without conviction. By the same token, they would not admit guilt readily and were generally evasive as to guilt or innocence, preferring to stress aspects of their stoic submission in their decision to plead. This sizable group of defendants appeared to perceive the total court process as being caught up in a monstrous organizational apparatus, in which the defendant role expectancies were not clearly defined. Reluctant to offend anyone in authority, fearful that clear-cut statements on their part as to their guilt or innocence would be negatively construed, they adopted a stance of passivity, resignation and acceptance. Interestingly, they would in most instances invoke their lawyer as being the one who crystallized the available alternatives for them, and who was therefore the critical element in their decision-making process.

In order to determine which agent-mediator was most influential in altering the accused's perspectives as to his decision of plead or go to trial (regardless of the proposed basis of the plea), the same sample of defendants were asked to indicate the person who first suggested to them that they plead guilty. They were also asked to indicate which of the persons or officials who made such suggestion, was most influential in affecting their final decision to plead.

The following table indicates the breakdown of the responses to the two questions:

It is popularly assumed that the police, through forced confessions, and the district attorney, employing still other pressures, are most instrumental in the inducement of an accused to plead guilty.[25] As Table II indicates, it is actually the defendant's own counsel who is most effective in this role.

Further, this phenomenon tends to reinforce the extremely rational nature of criminal law administration, for an organization could not rely upon the sort of idosyncratic measures employed by the police to induce confessions and maintain its efficiency, high production and overall rational-legal character. The defense counsel becomes the ideal agent-mediator since, as "officer of the court" and confidant of the accused and his kin, he lives astride both worlds and can serve the ends of the two as well as his own.[26]

Table II
Role of Agent-mediators in Defendant's Guilty Plea

Person or Official	First Suggested Plea of Guilty	Influenced the Accused Most in His Final Decision to Plead
Judge	4	26
District attorney	67	116
Defense counsel	407	411
Probation officer	14	3
Psychiatrist	8	1
Wife	34	120
Friends and kin	21	14
Police	14	4
Fellow inmates	119	14
Others	28	5
No response	8	10
Total	724	724

While an accused's wife, for example, may be influential in making him more amenable to a plea, her agent-mediator role has, nevertheless, usually been sparked and initiated by defense counsel. Further, although a number of first suggestions of a plea came from an accused's fellow jail inmates, he tended to rely largely on his counsel as an ultimate source of influence in his final decision. The defense counsel, being a crucial figure in the total organizational scheme in constituting a new set of perspectives for the accused, the same sample of defendants were asked to indicate at which stage of their contact with counsel was the suggestion of a plea made. There are three basic kinds of defense counsel available in Metropolitan Court: Legal-aid, privately retained counsel, and counsel assigned by the court (but may eventually be privately retained by the accused).

The overwhelming majority of accused persons, regardless of type of counsel, related a specific incident which indicated an urging or suggestion, either during the course of the first or second contact, that they plead guilty to a lesser charge if this could be arranged. Of all the agent-mediators, it is the lawyer who is most effective in manipulating an accused's perspectives, notwithstanding pressures that may have been previously applied by police, district attorney, judge or any of the agent-mediators that may have been activated by them. Legal-aid and assigned counsel would apparently be more likely to suggest a possible plea at the point of initial interview as response to pressures of time. In the case of the assigned counsel, the strong possibility that there is no fee involved, may be an added impetus to such a suggestion at the first contact.

In addition, there is some further evidence in Table III of the perfunctory, ministerial character of the system in Metropolitan Court and similar criminal courts. There is little real effort to individualize, and the lawyer's role as agent-mediator may be seen as unique in that he is in effect a double agent. Although, as "officer of the court" he mediates between the court organization and the defendant, his roles with respect to each are rent by conflicts of interest. Too often these must be resolved in favor of the organization which provides him with the means for his professional existence. Consequently, in order to reduce the strains and conflicts imposed in what is ultimately an overdemanding role obligation for him, the lawyer engages in the lawyer-client "confidence game" so as to structure more favorably an otherwise onerous role system.[27]

Table III

Stage at Which Counsel Suggested Accused to Plead

N = 724

	Counsel Type							
Contact	*Privately Retained*		*Legal-aid*		*Assigned*		*Total*	
	N	*%*	*N*	*%*	*N*	*%*	*N*	*%*
First	66	35	237	49	28	60	331	46
Second	83	44	142	29	8	17	233	32
Third	29	15	63	13	4	9	96	13
Fourth or more	12	6	31	7	5	11	48	7
No response	0	0	14	3	2	4	16	2
Total	190	100	487	101*	47	101*	724	100

Conclusion

Recent decisions of the Supreme Court, in the area of criminal law administration and defendant's rights, fail to take into account three crucial aspects of social structure which may tend to render the more libertarian rules as nugatory. The decisions overlook (1) the nature of courts as formal organization; (2) the relationship that the lawyer-regular *actually* has with the court organization; and (3) the character of the lawyer-client relationship in the criminal court (the routine relationships, not those unusual ones that are described in "heroic" terms in novels, movies, and TV).

Courts, like many other modern large-scale organizations possess a monstrous appetite for the cooptation of entire professional groups as well as individuals.[28] Almost all those who come within the ambit of organizational authority, find that their definitions, perceptions and values have been refurbished, largely in terms favorable to the particular organization and its goals. As a result, recent Supreme Court decisions may have a long range effect which is radically different from that intended or anticipated. The more libertarian rules will tend to produce the rather ironic end result of augmenting the *existing* organizational arrangements, enriching court organizations with more personnel and elaborate structure, which in turn will maximize organizational goals of "efficiency" and production. Thus, many defendants will find that courts will possess an even more sophisticated apparatus for processing them toward a guilty plea!

Notes

[1] H.W. Jones, *A View From the Bridge,* Law and Society: Supplement to Summer, 1965 Issue of Social Problems 42 (1965). See G. Geis, *Sociology, Criminology, and Criminal Law,* 7 Social Problems 40-47 (1959); N.S. Timasheff, *Growth and Scope of Sociology of Law,* in *Modern Sociological Theory in Continuity and Change* 424-49 (H. Becker & A. Boskoff, eds. 1957), for further evaluation of the strained relations between sociology and law.

[2] This decision represented the climax of a line of cases which had begun to chip away at the notion that the Sixth Amendment of the Constitution (right to assistance of counsel) applied only to the federal government, and could not be held to run against the states through the Fourteenth Amendment. An exhaustive historical analysis of the Fourteenth Amendment and the Bill of Rights will be found in C. Fairman, *Does the Fourteenth Amendment Incorporate the Bill of Rights? The Original Understanding,* 2 Stan. L. Rev. 5-139 (1949). Since the Gideon decision, there is already evidence that its effect will ultimately extend to indigent persons charged with misdemeanors — and perhaps ultimately even traffic cases and other minor offenses. For a popular account of this important development in connection with the right to assistance of counsel, see A. Lewis, *Gideon's Trumpet* (1964). For a scholarly histor-

ical analysis of the right to counsel see W.M. Beaney, *The Right to Counsel in American Courts* (1955). For a more recent comprehensive review and discussion of the right to counsel and its development, see Note, *Counsel at Interrogation*, 73 Yale L.J. 1000-57 (1964).

With the passage of the Criminal Justice Act of 1964, indigent accused persons in the federal courts will be defended by federally paid legal counsel. For a general discussion of the nature and extent of public and private legal aid in the United States prior to the Gideon case, see E.A. Brownell, *Legal Aid in the United States* (1961); also R.B. von Mehren, et al., *Equal Justice for the Accused* (1959).

[3] In the case of federal defendants the issue is clear. In *Mallory v. United States,* 354 U.S. 449 (1957), the Supreme Court unequivocally indicated that a person under federal arrest must be taken "without any unnecessary delay "before a U.S. commissioner where he will receive information as to his rights to remain silent and to assistance of counsel which will be furnished, in the event he is indigent, under the Criminal Justice Act of 1964. For a most interesting and richly documented work in connection with the general area of the Bill of Rights, see C.R. Sowle, *Police Power and Individual Freedom* (1962).

[4] See N.Y. Times, No.v 20, 1965, p. 1, for Justice Nathan R. Sobel's statement to the effect that based on his study of 1,000 indictments in Brooklyn, N.Y. from February-April, 1965, fewer than 10% involved confessions. Sobel's detailed analysis will be found in six articles which appeared in the New York Law Journal, beginning November 15, 1965, through November 21, 1965, titled *The Exclusionary Rules in the Law of Confessions: A Legal Perspective — A Practical Perspective*. Most law enforcement officials believe that the majority of convictions in criminal cases are based upon confessions obtained by police. For example, the District Attorney of New York County (a jurisdiction which has the largest volume of cases in the United States), Frank S. Hogan, reports that confessions are crucial and indicates "if a suspect is entitled to have a lawyer during preliminary questioning...any lawyer worth his fee will tell him to keep his mouth shut," N.Y. Times, Dec. 2, 1965, p. 1. Concise discussions of the issue are to be found in D. Robinson, Jr. *Massiah, Escobedo and Rationales for the Exclusion of Confessions,* 56 J. Crim. L.C. & P.S. 412-31 (1965); D.C. Dowling, *Escobedo and Beyond: The Need for a Fourteenth Amendment Code of Criminal Procedure*, 56 J. Crim. L.C. & P.S. 143-57 (1965).

[5] *Miranda v. Arizona,* 384 U.S. 436 (1966).

[6] Even under optimal circumstances a criminal case is a very much one-sided affair, the parties to the "contest" being decidedly unequal in strength and resources. See A.S. Goldstein, *The State and the Accused: Balance of Advantage in Criminal Procedure*, 69 Yale L.J. 1149-99 (1960).

[7] F.J. Davis et al., *Society and the Law: New Meanings for an Old Profession* 301 (1962); L. Orfield, *Criminal Procedure from Arrest to Appeal* 297 (1947).

D.J. Newman, *Pleading Guilty for Considerations: A Study of Bargain Justice,* 46 J. Crim. L.C. & P.S. 780-90 (1954). Newman's data covered only one year, 1954, in a midwestern community, however, it is in general confirmed by my own data drawn from a far more populous area, and from what is one of the major criminal courts in the country, for a period of fifteen years from 1950 to 1964 inclusive. The English experience tends also to confirm American data, see N.Walker, *Crime and Punishment in Britain: An Analysis of the Penal System* (1965). See also D.J. Newman, *Conviction: The Determination of Guilt or Innocence Without Trial* (1966), for a comprehensive legalistic study of the guilty plea sponsored by the American Bar Foundation. The criminal court as a social system, an analysis of "bargaining" and its functions in the criminal court's organizational structure, are examined in my forthcoming book, *The Criminal Court: A Sociological Perspective,* to be published by Quadrangle Books, Chicago.

[8] G. Feifer, *Justice in Moscow* (1965). The Soviet trial has been termed "an appeal from the pretrial investigation" and Feifer notes that the Soviet "trial" is simply a recapitulation of

the data collected by the pretrial investigator. The notions of a trial being a "tabula rasa" and presumptions of innocence are wholly alien to Soviet notions of justice. "...the closer the investigation resembels the finished script, the better...." *Id.* at 86.

[9]For a concise statement of the constitutional and economic aspects of the right to legal assistance, see M.G. Paulsen, *Equal Justice for the Poor Man* (1964); for a brief traditional description of the legal profession see P.A. Freund, *The Legal Profession,* Daedalus 689-700 (1963).

[10]I use the concept in the general sense that Erving Goffman employed it in his *Asylums: Essays on the Social Situation of Mental Patients and Other Inmates* (1961).

[11]A.L. Wood, *Informal Relations in the Practice of Criminal Law,* 62 Am. J. Soc. 48-55 (1956); J.E. Carlin, *Lawyers on Their Own* 105-109 (1962); R. Goldfarb, *Ransom — A Critique of the American Bail System* 114-15 (1965). Relatively recent data as to recruitment to the legal profession, and variables involved in the type of practice engaged in, will be found in J. Ladinsky, *Careers of Lawyers, Law Practice, and Legal Institutions,* 28 Am. Soc. Rev. 47-54 (1963). See also S. Warkov & J. Zelan, *Lawyers in the Making* (1965).

[12]There is a real question to be raised as to whether in certain organizational settings, a complete reversal of the bureaucratic-ideal has not occurred. That is, it would seem, in some instances the organization appears to exist to serve the needs of its various occupational incumbents, rather than its clients. A. Etzioni, *Modern Organizations* 94-104 (1964).

[13]Three relatively recent items reported in the New York Times, tend to underscore this point as it has manifested itself in one of the major criminal courts. In one instance the Bronx County Bar Association condemned "mass assembly-line justice," which "was rushing defendants into pleas of guilty and into convictions, in violation of their legal rights." N.Y. Times, March 10, 1965, p. 51. Another item, appearing somewhat later that year reports a judge criticizing his own court system (the New York Criminal Court), that "pressure to set statistical records in disposing of cases had hurt the administration of justice." N.Y. Times, Nov. 4, 1965, p. 49. A third, and most unusual recent public discussion in the press was a statement by a leading New York appellate judge decrying "instant justice" which is employed to reduce court calendar congestion "converting our courthouses into counting houses..., as in most big cities where the volume of business tends to overpower court facilities." N.Y. Times, Feb. 5, 1966, p. 58.

[14]R.L. Gasser, *The Confidence Game,* 27 Fed. Prob. 47 (1963).

[15]C.W. Mills, *White Collar* 121-29 (1951); J.E. Carlin, *supra,* note 11.

[16]E.O. Smigel, *The Wall Street Lawyer* (New York: The Free Press of Glencoe, 1964), p. 309.

[17]Talcott Parsons indicates that the social role and function of the lawyer can be therapeutic, helping his client psychologically in giving him necessary emotional support at critical times. The lawyer is also said to be acting as an agent of social control in the counseling of his client and in the influencing of his course of conduct. See T. Parsons, *Essays in Sociological Theory,* 382 et seq. (1954); E. Goffman, *On Cooling the Mark Out; Some Aspects of Adaptations to Failure,* in *Human Behavior and Social Processes* 482-505 (A. Rose ed., 1962). Goffman's "cooling out" analysis is especially relevant in the lawyer-accused client relationship.

[18]The question has never been raised as to whether "bargain justice," "copping a plea," or justice by negotiations is a constitutional process. Although it has become the most central aspect of the process of criminal law administration, it has received virtually no close scrutiny by the appellate courts. As a consequence, it is relatively free of legal control and supervision. But, apart from any questions of the legality of bargaining, in terms of the pressures and devices that are employed which tend to violate due process of law, there remain ethical and practical questions. The system of bargain-counter justice is like the proverbial iceberg, much of its danger is concealed in secret negotiations and its least alarming feature, the final plea, being the one presented to public view. See A.S. Trebach, *The Rationing of Justice* 74-

94 (1964); Note, *Guilty Plea Bargaining: Compromises by Prosecutors to Secure Guilty Pleas,* 112 U. Pa. L. Rev. 865-95 (1964).

[19]For a conventional summary statement of some of the inevitable conflicting loyalties encountered in the practice of law, see E.E. Cheatham, *Cases and Materials on the Legal Profession* 70-79 (2d ed., 1955).

[20]Some lawyers at either end of the continuum of law practice appear to have grave doubts as to whether it is indeed a profession at all. J.E. Carlin, *op. cit., supra,* note 11, at 192; E.O. Smigel, *supra,* note 16 at 304-305. Increasingly, it is perceived as a business with widespread evasion of the Canons of Ethics, duplicity and chicanery being practiced in an effort to get and keep business. The poet, Carl Sandburg, epitomized this notion in the following vignette: "Have you a criminal lawyer in this burg?" "We think so but we haven't been able to prove it on him." C. Sandburg, *The People, Yes* 154 (1936).

Thus, while there is considerable amount of dishonesty present in law practice involving fee splitting, thefts from clients, influence peddling, fixing, questionable use of favors and gifts to obtain business or influence others, this sort of activity is most often attributed to the "solo," private practice lawyer. See A.L. Wood, *Professional Ethics Among Criminal Lawyers,* Social Problems (1959). However, to some degree, large scale "downtown" elite firms also engage in these dubious activities. The difference is that the latter firms enjoy a good deal of immunity from these harsh charges because of their institutional and organizational advantages, in terms of near monopoly over more desirable types of practice, as well as exerting great influence in the political, economic and professional realms of power.

[21]This does not mean that most of those who plead guilty are innocent of any crime. Indeed, in many instances those who have been able to negotiate a lesser plea, have done so willingly and eagerly. The system of justice-by-negotiation, without trial, probably tends to better serve the interests and requirements of guilty persons, who are thereby presented with formal alternatives of "half a loaf," in terms of, at worst, possibilities of a lesser plea and a concomitant shorter sentence as compensation for their acquiescence and participation. Having observed the prescriptive etiquette in compliance with the defendant role expectancies in this setting, he is rewarded. An innocent person, on the other hand, is confronted with the same set of role prescriptions, structures and legal alternatives, and in any event, for him this mode of justice is often an ineluctable bind.

[22]Any communicative network between persons whereby the public identity of an actor is transformed into something looked on as lower in the local scheme of social types will be called a 'status degradation ceremony.'" H. Garfinkel, *Conditions of Successful Degradation Ceremonies,* 61 Am. J. Soc. 420-24 (1956). But contrary to the conception of the "cop out" as a "status degradation ceremony," is the fact that it is in reality a charade, during the course of which an accused must project an appropriate and acceptable amount of guilt, penitence and remorse. Having adequately feigned the role of the "guilty person," his hearers will engage in the fantasy that he is contrite, and thereby merits a lesser plea. It is one of the essential functions of the criminal lawyer that he coach and direct his accused-client in that role performance. Thus, what is actually involved is not a "degradation" process at all, but is instead, a highly structured system of exchange cloaked in the rituals of legalism and public professions of guilt and repentance.

[23]The name is of course fictitious. However, the actual court which served as the universe from which the data were drawn, is one of the largest criminal courts in the United States, dealing with felonies only. Female defendants in the years 1950 through 1964 constituted from 7-10% of the totals for each year.

[24]My own data in this connection would appear to support Sobel's conclusion (see note 4 *supra*), and appears to be at variance with the prevalent view, which stresses the importance of confessions in law enforcement and prosecution. All the persons in my sample were originally charged with felonies ranging from homicide to forgery; in most instances the

original felony charges were reduced to misdemeanors by way of a negotiated lesser plea. The vast range of crime categories which are available, facilitates the patterned court process of plea reduction to a lesser offense, which is also usually a socially less opprobrious crime. For an illustration of this feature of the bargaining process in a court utilizing a public defender office, see D. Sudnow, *Normal Crimes: Sociological Features of the Penal Code in a Public Defender Office,* 12 Social Problems 255-76 (1964).

[25]Failures, shortcomings and oppressive features of our system of criminal justice have been attributed to a variety of sources including "lawless" police, overzealous district attorneys, "hanging" juries, corruption and political connivance, incompetent judges, inadequacy or lack of counsel, and poverty or other social disabilties of the defendant. See A. Barth, *Law Enforcement versus the Law* (1963), for a journalist's account embodying this point of view; J.H. Skolnick, *Justice without Trial: Law Enforcement in Democratic Society* (1966), for a sociologist's study of the role of the police in criminal law administration. For a somewhat more detailed, albeit legalistic and somewhat technical discussion of American police procedures, see W.R. LaFave, *Arrest: The Decision to Take a Suspect into Custody* (1965).

[26]Aspects of the lawyer's ambivalences with regard to the expectancies of the various groups who have claims upon him, are discussed in H.J. O'Gorman, *The Ambivalence of Lawyers,* paper presented at the Eastern Sociological Association meetings, April 10, 1965.

[27]W.J. Goode, *A Theory of Role Strain,* 25 Am. Soc. Rev. 483-96 (1960); J.D. Snok, *Role Strain in Diversified Role Sets,* 71 Am. J. Soc. 363-72 (1966).

[28]Some of the resources which have become an integral part of our courts, e.g., psychiatry, social work and probation, were originally intended as part of an ameliorative, therapeutic effort to individualize offenders. However, there is some evidence that a quite different result obtains, than the one originally intended. The ameliorative instruments have been coopted by the court in order to more "efficiently" deal with a court's caseload, often to the legal disadvantage of an accused person. See F.A. Allen, *The Borderland of Criminal Justice* (1964); T.S. Szasz, *Law, Liberty and Psychiatry* (1963) and also Szasz's most recent, *Psychiatric Justice* (1965); L. Diana, "The Rights of Juvenile Delinquents: An Appraisal of Juvenile Court Procedures," 47 *J. Crim. L. C. & P.S.* 561-69 (1957).

12

Adapting to Plea Bargaining: Prosecutors

Milton Heumann

The new prosecutor shares many of the general expectations that his counterpart for the defense brings to the court. He expects factually and legally disputable issues, and the preliminary hearings and trials associated with these. If his expectations differ at all from the naive "Perry Mason" orientation, it is only to the extent that he anticipates greater success than the hapless Hamilton Burger of Perry Mason fame.

The new prosecutor's views about plea bargaining parallel those of the defense attorney. He views plea bargaining as an expedient employed in crowded urban courts by harried and/or poorly motivated prosecutors. He views the trial as "what the system is really about," and plea bargaining as a necessary evil dictated by case volume. The following exchange with a newly appointed prosecutor is illustrative.

> Q: Let's say they removed the effects of case pressure, provided you with more manpower. You wouldn't have that many cases....
> A: Then everybody should go to trial.
> Q: Everybody should go to trial?
> A: Yeah.
> Q: Why?
> A: Because supposedly if they're guilty they'll be found guilty. If they're not guilty they'll be found not guilty. That's the fairest way...judged by a group of your peers, supposedly.

Reprinted from *Plea Bargaining* by Milton Heumann by permission of The University of Chicago Press and the author. © 1978 by the University of Chicago Press.

Q: So you think that plea bargaining is a necessary evil?
A: Yeah.
Q: Would justice be better served if all cases went to trial?
A: That's the way it's supposed to be set up. Sure. Why wouldn't it?
Q: Would prosecutors be more satisfied?
A: Probably.
Q: If cases went to trial?
A: Sure.
Q: Why?
A: Because they could talk in front of twelve people and act like a lawyer. Right. Play the role.

It should be emphasized that these expectations and preferences of the new prosecutor are founded on the minimal law school preparation discussed earlier. The newcomers simply do not know very much about the criminal justice system.

Unlike defense attorneys, however, the new prosecutor is likely to receive some form of structured assistance when he begins his job. The chief prosecutor or chief state's attorney may provide this aid, if the prosecutor's office is staffed by a number of prosecutors or state's attorneys — that is, if the newcomer is not the only assistant prosecutor — it is more common for the chief prosecutor to assign to one or more of his experienced assistants the responsibility for helping the newcomer adjust. Since the newcomer's actions reflect on the office as a whole, it is not surprising that this effort is made.

The assistance the newcomer receives can be described as a form of structured observation. For roughly two weeks, he accompanies an experienced prosecutor to court and to plea bargaining sessions and observes him in action. The proximity of the veteran prosecutor — and his designation as the newcomer's mentor — facilitate communication between the two. The experienced prosecutor can readily explain or justify his actions, and the newcomer can ask any and all relevant questions. Certainly, this is a more structured form of assistance than defense attorneys receive.

However, new prosecutors still feel confused and overwhelmed during this initial period. Notwithstanding the assistance they receive, they are disoriented by the multitude of tasks performed by the prosecutor and by the environment in which he operations. This is particularly true in the circuit court, where the seemingly endless shuffling of files, the parade of defendants before the court and around the courtroom, the hurried, early morning plea bargaining sessions all come as a surprise to the new prosecutor.

Q: What were your initial impressions of the court during this "orientation period?"
A: The first time I came down here was a Monday morning at the

arraignments. Let's face it, the majority of people here, you don't expect courts to be as crowded as they are. You don't expect thirty to thirty-five people to come out of the cell block who have been arrested over the weekend. It was...you sit in court the first few days, you didn't realize the court was run like this. All you see, you see Perry Mason on TV, or pictures of the Supreme Court, or you see six judges up there in a spotless courtroom, everyone well dressed, well manicured, and you come to court and find people coming in their everyday clothes, coming up drunk, some are high on drugs, it's...it's an experience to say the least.

Q: Could you describe your first days when you came down here? What are your recollections? Anything strike you as strange?

A: Just the volume of business and all the stuff the prosecutor had to do. For the first week or two, I went to court with guys who had been here. Just sat there and watched. What struck me was the amount of things he [the prosecutor] has to do in the courtroom. The prosecutor runs the courtroom. Although the judge is theoretically in charge, we're standing there plea bargaining and calling the cases at the same time and chewing gum and telling people to quiet down and setting bonds, and that's what amazed me. I never thought I would learn all the terms. What bothered me also was the paperwork. Not the Supreme Court decisions, not the *mens rea* or any of this other stuff, but the amount of junk that's in those files that you have to know. We never heard about this crap in law school.

As suggested in the second excerpt, the new prosecutor is also surprised by the relative insignificance of the judge. He observes that the prosecutor assumes — through plea bargaining — responsibility for the disposition of many cases. Contrary to his expectations of being an adversary in a dispute moderated by the judge, he finds that often the prosecutor performs the judge's function.

It is precisely this responsibility for resolving disputes that is most vexing to the new superior court state's attorney. Unlike his circuit court counterpart, he does not generally find hurried conferences, crowded courts, and so on. But he observes that, as in the circuit court, the state's attorney negotiates cases, and in the superior court far more serious issues and periods of incarceration are involved in these negotiations. For the novice state's attorney, the notion that he will in short order be responsible for resolving these disputes is particularly disturbing.

Q: What were your initial impressions of your job here [as a state's attorney]?

A: Well, I was frightened of the increased responsibility. I knew the stakes were high here....I didn't really know what to expect, and I would say it took me a good deal of time to adapt here.

Q: Adapt in which way?

A: To the higher responsibilities. Here you're dealing with felonies, serious felonies all the way up to homicides, and I had never been involved in that particular type of situation.... I didn't believe that I was prepared to handle the type of job that I'd been hired to do. I looked around me and I saw the serious charges, the types of cases, and the experienced defense counsel on the one hand and the inexperience on my part on the other, and I was, well....

Q: Did you study up on your own?

A: No more than.... Before I came over here I had done some research and made a few notes, et cetera, about the procedures. I think I was prepared from the book end of things to take the job, but, again, it was the practical aspects that you're not taught in law school and that you can only learn from experience that I didn't have, and that's what I was apprehensive about.

These first weeks in the court, then, serve to familiarize the newcomer with the general patterns of case resolution. He is not immediately thrust into the court but is able to spend some time simply observing the way matters are handled. The result, though, is to increase his anxiety. The confusion of the circuit court and the responsibilities of a state's attorney in the superior court were not anticipated. The newcomer expects to be able to prepare cases leisurely and to rely on the skills learned in law school. Yet he finds that his colleagues seem to have neither the time nor the inclination to operate in this fashion. As the informal period of orientation draws to a close, the newcomer has a better perspective on the way the system operates, but still is on very uneasy footing about how to proceed when the responsibility for the case is his alone. In short, he is somewhat disoriented by his orientation.

The Prosecutor on His Own:
Initial Firmness and Resistance to Plea Bargaining

Within a few weeks after starting his job, the prosecutor and the state's attorney are expected to handle cases on their own. Experienced personnel are still available for advice, and the newcomer is told that he can turn to them with his problems. But the cases are now the newcomer's, and, with one exception, he is under no obligation to ask anyone for anything.

The new prosecutor is confronted by a stream of defense attorneys asking for a particular plea bargain in a case. If the prosecutor agrees, his decision is irreversible. It would be a violation of all the unwritten folkways of the criminal court for either a defense attorney or a prosecutor to break his word. On the other hand, if the prosecutor does not plea bargain, offers nothing in exchange for a plea, he at least does not commit himself to an outcome that may eventually prove to be a poor decision on his part. However, a refusal to plea bargain also places him "out of step" with his colleagues and with the general expectation of experienced defense attorneys.

Like the new attorney, the new prosecutor is in no hurry to dispose of the case. He is (1) inclined toward an adversary resolution of the case through formal hearings and trial, (2) disinclined to plea bargain in general, and (3) unsure about what constitutes an appropriate plea bargain for a particular case. Yet he is faced with demands by defense attorneys to resolve the case through plea bargaining. The new defense attorney has the luxury of postponing his decision for any given case. He can seek the advice of others before committing himself to a particular plea bargain in a particular case. For the new prosecutor, this is more difficult, since he is immediately faced with the demands of a number of attorneys in a number of different cases.

When the new prosecutor begins to handle his own cases, then, he lacks confidence about how to proceed in his dealings with defense attorneys. He often masks his insecurity in this period with an outward air of firmness. He is convinced that he must appear confident and tough, lest experienced attorneys think they can take advantage of him.

Q: What happened during your first few days of handling cases on your own?

A: Well, as a prosecutor, first of all, people try to cater to you because they want you to do favors for them. If you let a lawyer run all over you, you are dead. I had criminal the first day, on a Monday, and I'm in there [in the room where cases are negotiated], and a guy comes in, and I was talking to some lawyer on his file, and he's just standing there. Then I was talking to a second guy, and he was about fourth or fifth. So he looked at me and says: "When the hell you going to get to me?" So I says: "You wait your fucking turn. I'll get to you when I'm ready. If you don't like it, get out." It's sad that you have to swear at people, but it's the only language they understand — especially lawyers. Lawyers are the most obstinate, arrogant, belligerent bastards you will ever meet. Believe me. They come into this court — first of all — and we are really the asshole of the judicial system [circuit court], and they come in here and don't really have any respect for you. They'll come in here and be nice to you, because they feel you'll given them a *nolle.* That's all. Lawyers do not respect this court. I don't know if I can blame them or not blame them. You can come in here and see the facilities here; you see how things are handled; you see how it's like a zoo pushing people in and out.... When they do come here, lawyers have two approaches. One, they try to soft soap you and kiss your ass if you give them a *nolle.* Two, they'll come in here and try to ride roughshod over you and try to push you to a corner. Like that lawyer that first day. I had to swear at him and show him I wasn't going to take that shit, and that's that. The problem of dealing with lawyers is that you can't let them bullshit you. So, when I first started out I tried to be.... It's like the new kid on the block. He comes to a new neighborhood, and you've got to prove yourself. If you're a patsy, you're going to live with that as long as you're in court. If you let a couple of lawyers run over you, word will get around to go to _____, he's a pushover. Before you know it, they're running all over you. So you have to draw a line so they will respect you.

At first I was very tough because I didn't know what I was doing. In other words, you have to be very wary. These guys, some of them, have been practicing in this court for forty years. And they'll take you to the cleaners. You have to be pretty damn careful.

The new prosecutor couples this outward show of firmness toward attorneys with a fairly rigid plea bargaining posture. His reluctance to offer incentives to the defendant for a plea or to reward the defendant who chooses to plead is, at this point in the prosecutor's career, as much a function of his lack of confidence as it is a reflection of his antipathy toward plea bargaining. During this very early stage he is simply afraid to make concessions. Experienced court personnel are well aware that new prosecutors adopt this rigid stance.

Q: Have you noticed any differences between new prosecutors and prosecutors that have been around awhile?
A: Oh, yes. First of all, a new prosecutor is more likely to be less flexible in changing charges. He's afraid. He's cautious. He doesn't know his business. He doesn't know the liars. He can't tell when he's lying or exaggerating. He doesn't know all the ramifications. He doesn't know how tough it is sometimes to prove the case to juries. He hasn't got the experience, so that more likely than not he will be less flexible. He is also more easily fooled. [circuit court judge]

I can only answer that question in a general way. It does seem to me that the old workhorses [experienced prosecutors] are more flexible than the young stallions. [superior court judge]
Q: You were saying about the kids, the new prosecutors, the new state's attorneys. Are they kind of more hard-assed?
A: They tend to be more nervous. They tend to have a less well-defined idea of what they can do and what they can't do without being criticized. So, to the extent that they are more nervous, they tend to be more hard-assed. [private criminal attorney]
Q: What about new prosecutors? Do they differ significantly from prosecutors who have been around awhile?
A: Initially a new prosecutor is going to be reluctant to *nolle,* reluctant to give too good a deal because he is scared. He is afraid of being taken advantage of. And if you are talking about the circuit court, they've got the problem that they can't even talk it over with anybody. They've got a hundred fifty cases or whatever, and they make an offer or don't make an offer, that's it. Maybe at the end of the day they may get a chance to talk it over and say: "Gee, did I do

> the right thing?'' The defense attorney, when the offer is made, has
> the opportunity to talk to somebody plus his client before making a
> decision. So I think it takes the prosecutor a longer time to come
> around and work under the system. [legal aid attorney]

It is not difficult to understand why the new prosecutor is reluctant to plea
bargain and why he appears rigid to court veterans. Set aside for the
moment the prosecutor's personal preference for an adversary resolution
and consider only the nature of the demands being made on him.
Experienced attorneys want charges dropped, sentence recommendations,
and *nolles*. They approach him with the standard argument about the
wonderful personal traits of the defendant, the minor nature of the crime,
the futility of incarceration, and so on. When the new prosecutor picks up
the file, he finds that the defendant probably has an extensive prior criminal
record and, often, that he has committed a crime that does not sound minor
at all. Under the statute for the crime involved, it is likely that the defendant
faces a substantial period of incarceration, yet in almost all circuit court
cases and in many superior court cases, the attorneys are talking about a no-
time disposition. What to the new prosecutor frequently seems like a serious
matter is treated as a relatively inconsequential offense by defense
attorneys. And, because the newcomer views the matter as serious, his
resolve to remain firm—or, conversely, his insecurity about reducing
charges—is reinforced.

Illustrations of this propensity for the new prosecutor or state's attorney
to be ''outraged'' by the facts of the case, and to be disinclined to offer
''sweet'' deals, are plentiful. The following comments by two circuit court
prosecutors and a superior court state's attorney, respectively, illustrate the
extent to which the newcomer's appraisal of a case differed from that of the
defense attorney and from that of his own colleagues.

> Q: You used to go to _____ [chief prosecutor] for help on early
> cases. Were his recommendations out of line with what you thought
> should be done with the case?
> A: Let's say a guy came in with a serious crime...a crime that I thought
> was serious at one time, anyway. Take fighting on _____ Avenue
> [a depressed area of Arborville]. He got twenty-five stitches in the
> head and is charged with aggravated assault. One guy got twenty-
> five stitches, the other fifteen. And the attorneys would want me to
> reduce it. I'd go and talk to _____ [chief prosecutor]. He'd say:
> ''They both are drunk, and both got head wounds. Let them plead
> to breach of peace, and the judge will give them a money fine.''
> Things like that I didn't feel right about doing, since, to me, right
> out of law school, middle class, you figure twenty-five stitches in
> the head, Jesus Christ.
> Q: How did you learn what a case was worth?
> A: What do you mean, what it's worth?

Q: In terms of plea bargaining. What the going rate....

A: From the prosecutors and defense attorneys who would look at me dumbfounded when I would tell them that I would not reduce this charge. And then they would go running to my boss and he'd say, "Well, it's up to him." Some would even go running to the judge, screaming. One guy claimed surprise when I intended to go to trial for assault in second, which is a Class D felony. Two counts of that and two misdemeanor counts. It was set for jury trial. His witnesses were there. His experience in this court, he said, having handled two or three hundred cases, was that none has ever gone to trial. So he claimed surprise the day of trial. He just couldn't believe it.

Q: Were you in any way out of step with the way things were done here when you first began handling cases on your own?

A: In one respect I was. I evaluated a case by what I felt a proper recommendation should be, and my recommendations were almost always in terms of longer time. I found that the other guys in the office were breaking things down more than I expected. As a citizen, I couldn't be too complacent about an old lady getting knocked down, stuff like that. I thought more time should be recommended. I might think five to ten, six to twelve, while the other guys felt that three to seven was enough.

Implicit in these remarks are the seeds of an explanation for a prosecutor's gradually becoming more willing to plea bargain. One can hypothesize that as his experience with handling cases increases, he will feel less outraged by the crime, and thus will be more willing to work out a negotiated settlement. One assistant state's attorney likened his change in attitude to that of a nurse in an emergency room.

It's like nurses in emergency rooms. You get so used to armed robbery that you treat it as routine, not as morally upsetting. In the emergency room, the biggest emergency is treated as routine. And it's happening to me. The nature of the offense doesn't cause the reaction in me that it would cause in the average citizen. Maybe this is a good thing; maybe it isn't.

Though there is merit in this argument—prosecutors do become accustomed to crime—it is hardly a sufficient explanation of prosecutorial adaptation to plea bargaining. Other factors, often far more subtle, must be considered if we are to understand how and why the novice prosecutor becomes a seasoned plea bargainer.

Learning about Plea Bargaining

In the preceding sections I have portrayed the new prosecutor as being predisposed toward an adversary resolution of a case, uncertain about his responsibilities, rigid in his relations with defense attorneys, reluctant to drop charges and to plea bargain in cases that he considers serious, and anxious to try out the skills he learned in law school. This characterization of the newcomer contrasts sharply with that of the veteran prosecutor portrayed earlier. The veteran prosecutor was described as taking an active role in plea bargaining—urging, cajoling, and threatening the defense atorney to share in the benefits of a negotiated disposition. How is the veteran prosecutor to be reconciled with the new prosecutor of the preceding section?

The answer lies in what the prosecutor learns and is taught about plea bargaining. His education, like the defense attorney's, is not structured and systematic. Instead, he works his way through cases, testing the adversary and plea bargaining approaches. He learns piecemeal the costs and benefits of these approaches, and only over a period of time does he develop an appreciation for the relative benefits of a negotiated disposition.

Rather than proceed with a sequential discussion of the newcomer's experience, I think it more profitable at this point to distill from his experiences those central concerns that best explain his adaptation to the plea bargaining system. Some of the "flavor" of the adaptation process is sacrificed by proceeding in this fashion, but, in terms of clarity of presentation, I think it is a justifiable sacrifice. Thus, I will discuss separately the considerations that move the prosecutor in the plea bargaining direction, and later tie these together into an overall perspective on prosecutorial adaptation.

The Defendant's Factual and Legal Guilt

Prosecutors and state's attorneys learn their roles primarily entail the processing of factually guilty defendants. Contrary to their expectations that problems of establishing factual guilt would be central to their job, they find that in most cases the evidence in the file is sufficient to conclude (and prove) that the defendant is factually guilty. For those cases where there is a substantial question as to factual guilt, the prosecutor has the power—and is inclined to exercise it—to *nolle* or dismiss the case. If he himself does not believe the defendant to be factually guilty, it is part of his formal responsibilities to filter the case out. But, of the cases that remain after the initial screening, the prosecutor believes the majority of defendants to be factually guilty.

Furthermore, he finds that defense attorneys only infrequently contest the prosecutor's own conclusion that the defendant is guilty. In their initial approach to the prosecutor they may raise the possibility that the defendant is factually innocent, but in most subsequent discussions their advances focus on disposition and not on the problem of factual guilt. Thus, from the prosecutor's own reading of the file (after screening) and from the comments of his "adversary," he learns that he begins with the upper hand; more often than not, the factual guilt of the defendant is not really disputable.

Q: Are most of the defendants who come to this court guilty?

A: Yeah, or else we wouldn't have charged them. You know, that's something that people don't understand. Basically the people that are brought here are believed very definitely to be guilty or we wouldn't go on with the prosecution. We would *nolle* the case, and, you know, that is something, when people say, "Well, do you really believe...." Yeah. I do. I really do, and if I didn't and we can clear them, then we *nolle* it, there's no question about it.

But most cases are good, solid cases, and in most of them the defendant is guilty. We have them cold-cocked. And they plead guilty because they are guilty...a guy might have been caught in a package store with bottles. Now, he wasn't there to warm his hands. The defendant may try some excuse, but they are guilty and they know they are guilty. And we'll give them a break when they plead guilty. I don't think we should throw away the key on the guy just because we got him cold-cocked. We've got good cases, we give them what we think the case is worth from our point of view, allowing the defendant's mitigating circumstances to enter.

Q: The fact that you're willing to offer a pretty good bargain in negotiations might lead a person to plead guilty even if he had a chance to beat it at trial. But if he was found guilty at the trial he might not get the same result?

A: That's possible. I mean, only the accused person knows whether or not he's committed the crime, and.... It's an amazing thing, where, on any number of occasions, you will sit down to negotiate with an accused's attorney...and you know [he will say]: "No, no, he's not guilty, he wants his trial." But then if he develops a weakness in the case, or points out a weakness to you, and then you come back and say: "Well, we'll take a suspended sentence and probation," suddenly he says, "Yes, I'm guilty." So it leads you to conclude that, well, all these people who are proclaiming innocence are really not innocent. They're just looking for the right disposition. Now, from my point of view, the ideal situation might be if the person is not guilty, that he pleads not guilty, and we'll give him his trial and let the jury decide. But most people who are in court don't want a trial. I'm not the person who seeks them out and says, "I will drop this charge" or "I will reduce this charge, I will reduce the amount of time you have to do." They come to us, so, you know, the conclusion I think is there that any reasonable person could draw, that these people are guilty, that they are just looking for the best disposition possible. Very few people ask for a speedy trial.

In addition to learning of the factual culpability of most defendants, the prosecutor also learns that defendants would be hard-pressed to raise legal challenges to the state's case. As was discussed earlier, most cases are simply barren of any contestable legal issue, and nothing in the prosecutor's file or the defense attorney's arguments leads the prosecutor to conclude otherwise.

The new prosecutor or state's attorney, then, learns that in most cases the problem of establishing the defendant's factual and legal guilt, is nonexistent. Typically, he begins with a very solid case, and, contrary to his expectations, he finds that few issues are in need of resolution at an adversary hearing or trial. The defendant's guilt is not generally problematic; it is conceded by the defense attorney. What remains problematic is the sentence the defendant will receive.

Distinguishing Among the Guilty Defendants

Formally, the prosecutor has some powers that bear directly on sentence. He has the option to reduce or eliminate charges leveled against the defendant; the responsibility for the indictment is his, and his alone. Thus, if he *nolles* some of the charges against the defendant, he can reduce the maximum exposure the defendant faces or insure that the defendant is sentenced only on a misdemeanor (if he *nolles* a felony), and so forth. Beyond these actions on charges, the formal powers of the prosecutor cease. The judge is responsible for sentencing. He is supposed to decide the conditions of probation, the length of incarceration, and so on. Notwithstanding this formal dichotomy of responsibility, prosecutors find that defense attorneys approach them about both charge and sentence reduction.

Since charge reduction bears on sentence reduction, it is only a small step for defense attorneys to inquire specifically about sentences; and, because there is often an interdependence between charge and sentence, prosecutors are compelled at least to listen to the attorney's arguments. Thus, the prosecutor finds attorneys parading before him asking for charge and sentence reduction, and, in a sense, he is obligated to hear them out.

It is one thing to say that prosecutors and state's attorneys must listen to defense attorneys' requests about disposition and another to say that they must cooperate with these attorneys. As already indicated, new prosecutors feel acutely uneasy about charge and sentence reduction. They have neither the confidence nor the inclination to usurp what they view as primarily the judge's responsibility. Furthermore, one would think that their resolve not to become involved in this area would be strengthened by their learning that most defendants are factually and legally guilty. Why should they discuss dispositions in cases in which they "hold all the cards?"

This query presupposes that prosecutors continue to conceive of themselves as adversaries, whose exclusive task is to establish the defendant's guilt or innocence. But what happens is that as prosecutors gain greater experience handling cases, they gradually develop certain standards for evaluating cases, standards that bear not just on the defendant's guilt or innocence, but, more importantly, on the disposition of the defendant's case. These standards better explain prosecutorial behavior in negotiating dispositions than does the simple notion of establishing guilt or innocence.

Specifically prosecutors come to distinguish between serious and non-serious cases, and between cases in which they are looking for time and cases in which they are not looking for time. These standards or distinctions evolve after the prosecutor has processed a substantial number of factually and legally guilty defendants. They provide a means of sorting the raw material—the guilty defendants. Indeed, one can argue that the adversary component of the prosecutor's job is shifted from establishing guilt or innocence to determining the seriousness of the defendant's guilt and whether he should receive time. The guilt of the defendant is assumed, but the problem of disposition remains to be informally argued.

Prosecutors and state's attorneys draw sharp distinctions between serious and nonserious cases. In both instances, they assume the defendant guilty, but they are looking for different types of dispositions, dependent upon their classification of the case. If it is a nonserious matter, they are amenable to defense requests for a small fine in the circuit court, some short, suspended sentence, or some brief period of probation; similarly, in a nonserious superior court matter the state's attorney is willing to work out a combination suspended sentence and probation. The central concern with these nonserious cases is to dispose of them quickly. If the defense attorney requests some sort of no-time disposition that is dependent upon either a prosecutorial reduction of charges or a sentence recommendation, the prosecutor and state's attorney are likely to agree. They have no incentive to refuse the attorney's request, since the attorney's desire comports with what they are "looking for." The case is simply not worth the effort to press for greater penalty.

On the other hand, if the case is serious, the prosecutor and state's attorney are likely to be looking for time. The serious case cannot be quickly disposed of by a no-time alternative. These are cases in which we would expect more involved and lengthy plea bargaining negotiations.

Whether the case is viewed as serious or nonserious depends on factors other than the formal charges the defendant faces. For example, these non-formal considerations might include the degree of harm done the victim, the amount of violence employed by the defendant, the defendant's prior record, the characteristics of the victim and defendant, the defendant's motive; all are somewhat independent of formal charge, and yet all weigh heavily in the prosecutor's judgment of the seriousness of the case. Defendants facing the same formal charges, then, may find that prosecutors sort their cases into different categories. Two defendants charged with robbery with violence may find that in one instance the state's attorney is willing to reduce the charge and recommend probation, while in the second case he is looking for a substantial period of incarceration. In the former case, the defendant may have simply brushed against the victim (still technically robbery with violence), whereas in the second, he may have dealt the victim a severe blow. Or possibly, the first defendant was a junkie supporting his habit, whereas the second was operating on the profit motive. These are, of course, imperfect illustrations, but the point is that the determination as to whether a case is serious or not serious only partially reflects the charges against the defendant. Often the determination is based on a standard that develops with experience in the court, and operates, for the most part, independently of formal statutory penalties.

The following excerpts convey a sense of the serious/nonserious dichotomy and also support the argument that charge does not necessarily indicate seriousness.

Q: How did you learn what cases were worth?

A: You mean sentences.

Q: Yeah.

A: Well, that's a hit-or-miss kind of an experience. You take a first offender; any first offender in a nonviolent crime certainly is not going to jail for a nonviolent crime. And a second offender, well, it depends again on the type of crime, and maybe there should be some supervision, some probation. And a third time, you say, well now this is a guy who maybe you should treat a little more strictly. Now, a violent crime, I would treat differently. How did I learn to? I learned because there were a few other guys around with experience, and I got experience, and they had good judgments, workable approaches, and you pick it up like that. In other words, you watch others, you talk to others, you handle a lot of cases yourself.

Q: Does anybody, the public, put pressure on you to be tougher?

A: Not really.

Q: Wouldn't these sentences be pretty difficult for the public to understand?

A: Yeah, somewhat...Sure, we are pretty easy on a lot of these cases except that.... We are tough on mugging and crimes by violence. Say an old lady is grabbed by a kid and knocked to the ground and her pocketbook taken as she is waiting for the bus. We'd be as tough as anybody on that one, whether you call it a breach of peace or a robbery. We'd be very tough. And in this case there would be a good likelihood of the first offender going to jail, whatever the charge we give him. The name of the charge isn't important. We'd had the facts regardless.

Q: So you think you have changed? You give away more than you used to?

A: I don't give away more. I think that I have reached the point
where.... When I started I was trying to be too fair, if you want to
say that, you know, to see that justice was done, and I was severe.
But, you know, like _____ [head prosecutor] says, you need to
look for justice tempered with mercy, you know, substantial justice,
and that's what I do now. When I was new, a guy cut [knifed] someone he had to go to jail. But now I look for substantial justice — if
two guys have been drinking and one guy got cut, I'm not giving
anything away, but a fine, that's enough there.

Q: But you are easier now? I mean, you could look for time?

A: Look, if I get a guy that I feel belongs in jail, I try to sentence bargain and get him in jail. We had this one guy, _____. He was
charged with breach of peace. We knew he had been selling drugs
but we couldn't prove anything. He hits this girl in _____'s
parking lot [large department store], and tried to take her purse. She
screams and he runs. This was a real son-of-a-bitch, been pimping
for his own wife. On breach of peace I wanted the full year, and
eventually got nine months. Cases like that I won't give an inch on.
And the lawyer first wanted him to plead to suspended sentence and
a money fine. I said this guy is a goddamned animal. Anybody who
lets his wife screw and then gets proceeds from it, and deals in
drugs... well, if you can catch the bastard on it, he belongs behind
bars.

• • •

The second standard used by prosecutors and state's attorneys in processing
factually and legally guilty defendants is the time/no-time distinction.
There is an obvious relationship between the serious/nonserious standard
and this one: in the serious case time is generally the goal; whereas in the
nonserious case, a no-time disposition is satisfactory to the prosecutor. But
this simple relationship does not always hold, and it is important for us to
consider the exceptions.

In some serious cases, the prosecutor or state's attorney may not be
looking for time. Generally, these are cases in which the prosecutor has a
problem establishing either a factual or legal guilt of the defendant, and
thus is willing to settle for a plea to the charge and offer a recommendation
of a suspended sentence. The logic is simple: the prosecutor feels the
defendant is guilty of the offense but fears that if he insists on time, the
defense attorney will go to trial and uncover the factual or legal defects of
the state's case. Thus, the prosecutor "sweetens the deal" to extract a guilty
plea and to decrease the likelihood that the attorney will gamble on
complete vindication.

Of the prosecutors I interviewed, a handful expressed disenchantment
with plea bargaining. They felt that their associates were being too lenient,
giving away too much in return for the defendant's plea. They argued that
the prosecutor's office should stay firm and go to trial if necessary in order
to obtain higher senences. They were personally inclined to act this way:

they "didn't like plea bargaining." But when pushed a bit, it became clear that their antipathy to plea bargaining was not without its exceptions. In the serious case with factual or legal defects they felt very strongly that plea bargaining was appropriate. The sentiments of such an "opponent" to plea bargaining are presented below.

Q: So you are saying that you only like some kinds of plea bargaining?
A: I like to negotiate cases where I have a problem with the case. I know the guy is guilty, but I have some legal problem, or unavailability of a witness that the defendant doesn't know about that will make it difficult for us to put the case on. I would have trouble with the case. Then it is in my interest to bargain; even in serious cases with these problems, it is in the best interests of the state to get the guy to plead, even if it's to a felony with suspended sentence.
Q: If there was no plea bargaining, then the state would lose out?
A: Yes, in cases like these. These would be cases that without plea bargaining we would have trouble convicting the defendant. But this has nothing to do with the defendant's guilt or innocence. Yet we might have to let him go. It is just to plea bargain in cases like this. It is fair to get the plea from the defendant, since he is guilty. Now, there is another situation; whereas in the first situation, I have no philosophical problems with plea bargaining. We may have a weak case factually. Maybe the case depends on one witness, and I have talked to the witness and realized how the witness would appear in court. Maybe the witness would be a flop when he testifies. If I feel the defendant is guilty, but the witness is really bad, then I know that we won't win the case at trial, that we won't win a big concession in plea bargaining. So I will evaluate the case, and I will be predisposed to talking about a more lenient disposition.

• • •

The other unexpected cross between the standards—nonserious case/looking for time—occurs in several types of situations. First, there is the case in which the defendant has a long history of nonserious offenses, and it is felt that a short period of incarceration will "teach him a lesson," or at least indicate that there are limits beyond which prosecutors cannot be pushed. Second, there is the situation where the prosecutor holds the defense attorney in disdain and is determined to teach the attorney a lesson. Thus, though the defendant's offense is nonserious, the prosecutor would generally be amenable to a no-time disposition, the prosecutor chooses to hold firm. It is precisely in these borderline cases that the prosecutor can be most successful in exercising sanctions against the uncooperative defense attorney. The formal penalties associated with the charges against the defendant give him ample sentencing range, and by refusing to agree to a no-time disposition, the costs to the defense attorney become great. The attorney is not able to meet his client's demands for no time, and yet he must be leery about trial, given the even greater exposure the defendant faces. These borderline decisions by prosecutors, then, are fertile grounds for exploring sanctions against defense attorneys. It is here that we can expect the cooperative defense attorneys to benefit most, and the recalcitrant defense attorney to suffer the most. Relatedly, one can also expect prosecutors to be looking for time in nonserious offenses in which the defendant or his counsel insists on raising motions and going to trial. These adversary activities may be just enough to tip the prosecutor into looking for time.

In addition to its relationship to the serious/nonserious standard, the time/no-time standard bears on prosecutorial plea bargaining behavior in another way. As prosecutors gain experience in the plea bargaining system, they tend to stress "certainty of time" rather than "amount of time." This is to say that they become less concerned about extracting maximum penalties from defendants and more concerned with insuring that in cases in which they are looking for time, the defendant actually receives some time. Obviously, there are limits to the prosecutor's largesse — in a serious case thirty days will not be considered sufficient time. But prosecutors are willing to consider periods of incarceration substantially shorter than the maximum sentence allowable for a particular crime. In return, though, prosecutors want a guarantee of sorts that the defendant will receive time. They want to decrease the likelihood that the defendant, by some means or other, will obtain a suspended sentence. Thus, they will "take" a fixed amont of time if the defendant agrees not to try to "pitch" for a lower sentence, or if the defendant pleads to a charge in which all participants know some time will be meted out by the judge. In the latter instance, the attorney may be free to "pitch," but court personnel know his effort is more a charade for the defendant than a realistic effort to obtain a no-time disposition. The following excerpts illustrate prosecutorial willingness to trade off years of time for certainty of time.

> I don't believe in giving away things. In fact _____ [a public defender] approached me; there's this kid _____, he has two robberies, one first degree, on second, and three minor cases. Now, this kid I made out an affidavit myself for tampering with a witness. This kid is just n.g. _____ came to me and said, "We'll plead out, two to five." He'll go to state's prison. I agreed to that — both these offenses are bindovers. These kids belong in jail. I'd rather take two to five here than bind them over to superior court and take a chance on what will happen there. At least my two to five will be a year and three-quarters in state's prison. The thing is, if I want to get a guy in jail for a year, I'll plea bargain with him, and I'll take six months if I can get it, because the guy belongs in jail, and if I can get him to jail for six months why should I fool around with that case, and maybe get a year if I am lucky? If I can put a guy away for six months I might be cheated out of six months, but at least the guy is doing six months in jail.

What is a proper time? It never bothers me if we could have gotten seven years and instead we got five. In this case, there was no violence; minor stuff was stolen. We got time out of him. That is the important thing.

A: It makes no difference to me really if a man does five to ten or four to eight. The important thing is he's off the street, not a menace to society for a period of time, and the year or two less is not going to make that great a difference. If you do get time, I think it's... you know, many prosecutors I know feel this way. They have achieved confinement, that's what they're here for.

Q: Let's take another example. Yesterday an attorney walked in here when I was present on that gambling case. He asked you if it could be settled without time?

A: And I said no. That ended the discussion.

Q: What will he do now?

A: He'll file certain motions that he really doesn't have to file. All the facts of our case were spelled out; he knows as much about our cases as he'll ever know. So his motions will just delay things. There'll come a point, though, when he'll have to face trial; and he'll come in to speak with us, and ask if we still have the same position. We'll have the same position. We'll still be looking for one to three. His record goes back to 1923, he's served two or three terms for narcotics, and he's been fined five times for gambling. So we'd be looking for one to three and a fine. Even though he's in his sixties, he's been a criminal all his life, since 1923....

Q: But if the attorney pushes and says, "Now look. He's an old guy. He's sixty-two years old, how about six months?"

A: I might be inclined to accept it because, again, confinement would be involved. I think our ends would be met. It would show his compadres that there's no longer any immunity for gambling, that there is confinement involved. So the end result would be achieved.

Justice Holmes, who is supposed to be the big sage in American jurisprudence, said it isn't the extent of the punishment but the certainty of it. This is my basic philosophy. If the guy faces twelve years in state's prison, I'm satisfied if on a plea of guilty he'll go to state's prison for two or three years.

The experienced prosecutor, then, looks beyond the defendant's guilt when evaluating a case. He learns — from a reading of the file and from the defense attorney's entreaties — that most defendants are factually and legally guilty and that he generally holds the upper hand. As he gains experience in processing these cases, he gradually begins to draw distinctions within this pool of guilty defendants. Some of the cases appear not to be serious, and the prosecutor becomes willing to go along with the defense attorney's request for no-time dispositions. The cases simply do not warrant a firmer prosecutorial posture. In serious cases, when he feels time is in order, he often finds defense attorneys in agreement on the need for some incarceration.

In a sense, the prosecutor redefines his professional goals. He learns that the statutes fail to distinguish adequately among guilty defendants, that they "sweep too broadly," and give short shrift to the specific facts of the offense, to the defendant's prior record, to the degree of contributory culpability of the victim, and so on. Possessing more information about the defendant than the judge does, the prosecutor — probably unconsciously — comes to believe that it is his professional responsibility to develop standards that distinguish among defendants and lead to "equitable" dispositions. Over time, the prosecutor comes to feel that if he does not develop these standards, if he does not make these professional judgments, no one else will.

The prosecutor seems almost to drift into plea bargaining. When he begins his job he observes that his colleagues plea bargain routinely and quickly finds that defense attorneys expect him to do the same. Independent of any rewards, sanctions, or pressures, he learns the strengths of his cases, and learns to distinguish the serious from the nonserious ones. After an initial period of reluctance to plea bargain at all (he is fearful of being taken advantage of by defense attorneys), the prosecutor finds that he is engaged almost unwittingly in daily decisions concerning the disposition of cases. His obligation to consider alternative charges paves the way for the defense attorney's advances; it is only a small jump to move to sentence discussions. And as he plea bargains more and more cases, the serious/nonserious and time/no-time standards begin to hold sway in his judgments. He feels confident about the disposition he is looking for, and if a satisfactory plea bargain in line with his goals can be negotiated, he comes to feel that there is little point to following a more formal adversary process.

$$• • •$$

Case Pressure and Potential Backlog

Though they may do so during the first few weeks, the newcomer's peers and superiors do not generally pressure him to move cases because of volume. Instead, he is thrust in the fray largely on his own and is allowed to work out his own style of case disposition. Contrary to the "conspiratorial perspective" of the adaptation process, he is not coerced to cooperate in processing "onerously large case loads."

The newcomer's plea bargaining behavior is conditioned by his reactions to particular cases he handles or learns about and not by caseload problems of the office. The chief prosecutor within the jurisdiction may worry about his court's volume and the speed with which cases are disposed, but he does not generally interfere with his assistant's decision about how to proceed in a case. The newcomer is left to learn about plea bargaining on his own, and for the reason already discussed, he learns and is taught the value of negotiating many of his cases. The absence of a direct relationship between prosecutor plea bargaining and case pressure is suggested in the following remarks.

Q: Is it case pressure that leads you to negotiate?

A: I don't believe it's the case pressure at all. In every court, whether there are five cases or one hundred cases, we should try to settle it. It's good for both sides. If I were a public defender I'd try to settle all the cases for my guilty clients. By negotiating you are bound to do better. Now take this case. [He reviewed the facts of a case in which an elderly man was charged with raping a seven-year-old girl. The defendant claimed he could not remember what happened, that he was drunk, and that, though the girl might have been in the bed with him, he did not think he raped her.] I think I gave the defense attorney a fair deal. The relatives say she was raped, but the doctors couldn't conclusively establish that. I offered him a plea to a lesser charge, one dealing with advances toward minors, but excluding the sex act. If he takes it, he'll be able to walk away with time served [the defendant had not posted bail and had spent several months in jail]. It's the defendant's option though. He can go through trial if he wants, but if he makes that choice, the kid and her relatives will have to be dragged through the agonies of trial also. Then I would be disposed to look for a higher sentence for the defendant. So I think my offer is fair, and the offer has nothing to do with the volume of this court. It's the way I think the case — all things considered — should be resolved.

Q: You say the docket wasn't as crowded in 1966, and yet there was plea bargaining. If I had begun this interview by saying why is there plea bargaining here....

A: I couldn't use the reason there's plea bargaining because there are a lot of cases. That's not so; that's not so at all. If we had only ten cases down for tomorrow and an attorney walked in and wanted to discuss a case with me, I'd sit down and discuss it with him. In effect, that's plea bargaining. Whether it's for the charge or for an agreed recommendation or reduction of the charge or what have you, it's still plea bargaining. It's part of the process that has been going on for quite a long time.

Q: And you say it's not because of the crowded docket, but if I gave you a list of reasons for why there was plea bargaining and asked you to pick the most important....

A: I never really thought about the.... You talk about the necessity for plea bargaining, and you say, well, it's necessary, and one of the reasons is because we have a crowded docket, but even if we didn't we still would plea bargain.

Q: Why?

A: Well, it has been working throughout the years, and the way I look at it, it's beneficial to the defendant, it's beneficial to the court, and not just in saving time but in avoiding police officers coming to

court, witnesses being subpoenaed in, and usually things can be discussed between prosecutors and defense counsel which won't be
said in the open court and on the record. There are many times that
the defense counsel will speak confidentially with the prosecutor
about his client or about the facts or about the complainant or a
number of things. So I don't know if I can justify plea bargaining
other than by speaking of the necessity of plea bargaining. If there
were only ten cases down for one day, it still would be something
that would be done.

Maybe in places like New York they plea bargain because of case pressure. I don't know. But here it is different. We dispose of cases on the
basis of what is fair to both sides. You can get a fair settlement by plea
bargaining. If you don't try to settle a case quickly, it gets stale. In New
York the volume probably is so bad that it becomes a matter of "getting
rid of cases." In Connecticut, we have some pretty big dockets in some
cities, but in other areas — here, for example — we don't have that kind
of pressure. Sure, I feel some pressure, but you can't say that we negotiate our cases out to clear the docket. And you probably can't say that
even about the big cities in Connecticut either.

Prosecutors, then, do not view their propensity to plea bargain as a direct
outcome of case pressure. Instead, they speak of "mutually satisfactory
outcomes," "fair dispositions," "reducing police overcharging," and so
on. We need not here evaluate their claims in detail; what is important is
that collectively their arguments militate against according case pressure the
"top billing" it so often receives in the literature.

Another way to conceptualize the relationship between case pressure and
plea bargaining is to introduce the notion of a "potential backlog." Some
prosecutors maintain that if fewer cases were plea bargained, or if plea
bargaining were eliminated, a backlog of cases to be disposed of would
quickly clog their calendars. A potential backlog, then, lurks as a possibility
in every jurisdiction. Even in a low volume jurisdiction, one complex trial
could back up cases for weeks, or even months. If all those delayed cases
also had to be tried, the prosecutor feels he would face two not so enviable
options. He could become further backlogged by trying as many of them as
was feasible, or he could reduce his backlog by outright dismissal of cases.
The following comments are typical of the potential backlog argument.

Q: Some people have suggested that plea bargaining not be allowed in
   the court. All cases would go to trial before a judge or jury and. . . .
A: Something like that would double, triple, and quadruple the backlog. Reduce that 90 percent of people pleading guilty, and even if
   you were to try a bare minimum of those cases, you quadruple your
   backlog. It's feasible.

Well, right now we don't have a backlog. But if we were to try even

> 10 percent of our cases, take them to a jury, we'd be so backed up that we couldn't even move. We'd be very much in the position of ...some traffic director in New York once said that there will come a time that there will be one car too many coming into New York and nobody will be able to move. Well, we can get ourselves into that kind of situation if we are going to go ahead and refuse to plea bargain even in the serious cases.

Though a potential backlog is an ever-present possibility, it should be stressed that most prosecutors develop this argument more as a prediction as to the outcome of a rule decreasing or eliminating plea bargaining than as an explanation for why they engage in plea bargaining. If plea bargaining were eliminated, a backlog would develop; but awareness of this outcome does not explain why they plea bargain.

Furthermore, prosecutors tend to view the very notion of eliminating plea bargaining as a fake issue, a straw-man proposition. It is simply inconceivable to them that plea bargaining could or would be eliminated. They maintain that no court system could try all of its cases, even if huge increases in personnel levels were made; trials consume more time than any realistic increase in personnel levels could manage. They were willing to speculate on the outcome of a rule proscribing plea bargaining, but the argument based on court backlog that they evoked was not a salient consideration in understanding their day-in, day-out plea bargaining behavior.

It is, of course, impossible to refute with complete certainty an argument that prosecutors plea bargain because failure to do so would cause a backlog of unmanageable proportions to develop. However, the interviews indicate other more compelling ways to conceptualize prosecutorial adaptation to plea bargaining, and these do not depend on a potential backlog that always can be conjured up. Though the backlog may loom as a consequence of a failure to plea bargain, it—like its case-pressure cousin—is neither a necessary nor sufficient explanatory vehicle for understanding the core aspects of prosecutorial plea bargaining behavior.

A Perspective on Prosecutorial Adaptation

Perhaps the most important outcome of the prosecutor's adaptation is that he evidences a major shift in his own presumption about how to proceed with a case. As a newcomer, he feels it to be his responsibility to establish the defendant's guilt at trial, and he sees no need to justify a decision to go to trial. However, as he processes more and more cases, as he drifts into plea bargaining, and as he is taught the risks associated with trials, his own assumption about how to proceed with a case changes. He approaches every case with plea bargaining in mind, that is, he presumes that the case will be plea bargained. If it is a "nonserious" matter, he expects it to be quickly resolved; if it is "serious" he generally expects to negotiate time as part of the disposition. In both instances, he anticipates that the case will eventually be resolved by a negotiated disposition and not by a trial. When a plea bargain does not materialize, and the case goes to trial, the prosecutor feels compelled to justify his failure to reach an accord. He no longer is content to simply assert that it is the role of the prosecutor to establish the defendant's guilt at trial. This adversary component of the prosecutor's role has been replaced by a self-imposed burden to justify why he chose to go to trial, particularly if a certain conviction — and, for serious cases, a period of incarceration — could have been obtained by means of a negotiated disposition.

Relatedly, the prosecutor grows accustomed to the power he exercises in these plea bargaining negotiations. As a newcomer, he argued that his job was to be an advocate for the state and that it was the judge's responsibility to sentence defendants. But, having in fact "sentenced" most of the defendants whose files he plea bargained, the distinction between prosecutor and judge becomes blurred in his own mind. Though he did not set out to usurp judicial prerogatives — indeed, he resisted efforts to engage him in the plea bargaining process — he gradually comes to expect that he will exercise sentencing powers. There is no fixed point in time when he makes a calculated choice to become adjudicator as well as adversary. In a sense, it simply "happens"; the more cases he resolves (either by charge reduction or sentence recommendations), the greater the likelihood that he will lose sight of the distinction between the roles of judge and prosecutor.

13

Guilty Until Proved Innocent: Wrongful Conviction and Public Policy

*C. Ronald Huff
Arye Rattner
Edward Sagarin*

The prisons are filled with convicts who claim that they were "framed" or "railroaded." Others who have already "done time" claim that they were erroneously convicted and imprisoned. Still others have pleaded guilty only to go free on probation or with suspended sentences. Some of these men and women have firm adherents who believe in their denials of guilt: family, friends, counsel, the general public—even victims—who uphold the contention that they, the convicted, are themselves the victims of a miscarriage of justice. If there is some reasonable doubt as to their guilt (that is, if they have been convicted although the evidence does not demon-

*This article is dedicated to the memory of our coauthor, colleague, and close friend, Ed Sagarin, who passed away on June 10, 1986. Ed's scholarly contributions were enormous, and this article reflects two of the concerns for which he will best be remembered: human rights and disvalued people.

Ed was a constant source of intellectual stimulation and encouragement to many younger criminologists. We were fortunate to be among them, and we shall miss him greatly.*

C. Ronald Huff, Arye Rattner, and Edward Sagarin, "Guilty Until Proved Innocent: Wrongful Conviction and Public Policy," *Crime and Delinquency*, Vol. 34, *No. 4* (October, 1986), pp. 518-44. Copyright © 1986 by Sage Publications, Inc. Reprinted by permission of Sage Publications, Inc.

strate guilt beyond a reasonable doubt), then the verdict of guilt was wrong, and it can be said to be a *wrongful conviction,* from a strictly legal point of view. However, so long as guiltlessness has itself not been established, one cannot categorize such individuals as convicted innocents.

Our definition of *wrongful conviction* includes only those cases in which a person is convicted of a felony but later is found to be innocent beyond a reasonable doubt, generally due to a confession by the actual offender, evidence that had been available but was not sufficiently used at the time of conviction, new evidence that was not previously available, and other factors.

We are, in short, focusing our attention on convicted innocents. Few of these cases become *causes célèbres,* for the convicted are generally unknown, often penniless and friendless, persons who are punished for crimes that they did not commit. In seeking to further our understanding of such miscarriages of justice, we shall address three major questions: (1) How frequent is wrongful conviction? (2) What are the major causes of error in such cases? and (3) What policy implications may be derived from this study?

How Big is the Problem?

This is perhaps the most frequently asked question, and it is a query for which there is no definitive answer. Just as we have no precise method of measuring the universe of criminal behavior, we cannot quantify the universe of wrongful convictions because only the most highly publicized cases ever come to the public's attention.

Most of those who have addressed the problem of wrongful conviction have come away convinced that it is not a rare phenomenon. Radin (1964:9) cites an estimate by a highly respected judge (whom he does not name), who opined that there might be as many as 14,000 cases of false conviction in the United States in a given year. At the time this estimate was made, it would have represented a 5% error!

Reported estimates of the frequency of wrongful conviction range from very few cases each year up to 20% of all convictions. Given such a considerable variance in estimates, we decided to conduct a survey, using a "panel of judges" (some of whom really were judges!).

Our sample consisted of (1) the universe of attorneys general in the United States and its territories and (2) an Ohio sample, which included all presiding judges of common pleas courts; all county prosecutors; all county public defenders; all county sheriffs; and the chiefs of police of Ohio's seven major cities (Columbus, Cleveland, Cincinnati, Toledo, Akron, Dayton, and Youngstown).

Comments volunteered by our respondents suggested the controversial nature of research on wrongful conviction. One judge wrote that after having served as a visiting judge in all of Ohio's major cities, "I have a strong suspicion that each year in Ohio, at least one or two dozen persons are convicted of crimes of which they are innocent." On the other hand, another respondent, an Ohio State alumnus, was so upset by our study that he seemed ready to return his football tickets:

> I am deeply disappointed that my old university is even remotely involved in this type of venture. Aren't there more pressing topics in this world that your efforts can be funneled to?

Nearly three-fourths of those who provided estimates agreed that wrongful conviction comprises less than 1% of all felony convictions in the United States. Another 20% of our estimates were in the 1%-5% range.

Thus if these apparently conservative estimates are reasonable, we could be facing an interesting dilemma: A high-volume criminal justice system, even if 99.5% accurate, could still generate nearly 6,000 erroneous convictions (for index crimes alone) each year.

Therefore, although there is no known method of determining exactly how many wrongful convictions occur each year, our literature review, our survey, our own primary database of nearly 500 wrongful conviction cases, and our analysis of the dynamics of wrongful conviction cause us to feel relatively confident in this conservative estimate of less than 1%. In other words, for every 200 persons convicted of felonies in the United States, we (and the great majority of our survey respondents) believe that 1 or 2 of them may well be innocent. The frequency of error may well be much higher in cases involving less serious felonies and misdemeanors.

How Does It Happen?

How can an innocent defendant be convicted? What would possibly induce an innocent person to plead guilty? What goes wrong with a criminal justice system that has created an elaborate system of safeguards to protect suspects' and defendants' rights?

In seeking to answer these questions, we have developed a large database, currently consisting of nearly 500 cases (and growing almost daily) of wrongful felony conviction, the great majority having occurred in the United States. This database is the product of our ongoing review of published literature, newspapers, and legal documents from around the country, as well as cases identified through our survey. Our analysis of these cases has enabled us to identify the major factors responsible for the conviction of innocent defendants. Our data suggest that, in general, more than one of these factors is involved in a case of wrongful conviction; in other words, it appears to us that the most likely scenario for wrongful conviction is when the system breaks down in more than one way.

Eyewitness Error

We believe that the single most important factor leading to wrongful conviction in the United States and England (Brandon and Davies, 1973) is eyewitness misidentification. Nearly 60% of the cases in our database involve such errors.

Sometimes these eyewitnesses have no doubt whatsoever about the accuracy of their testimony; in other cases, they had either slight or lingering questions in their own minds, but nevertheless felt sufficiently confident that they were willing to testify against a defendant.

Item: Lenell Geter, a young black engineer employed in the Dallas area, is at work one day when a fast food restaurant is robbed 50 miles away. A white woman tells of Geter's "suspicious" habit of reading and feeding ducks in the park near her home. Several witnesses to the crime identify Geter from photographs, even though their previous descriptions of the robber bore little resemblance to Geter. Geter's coworkers testify that he was at work when the robbery occurred. There is no physical evidence linking Geter to the crime. Nonetheless, Geter is convicted and sentenced to life in prison. Following intense national publicity, including a feature story on CBS's *60 minutes*, Geter is finally released *(New York Times,* 1984: March 28).

Item: Steven Titus and his girlfriend have just left a restaurant, where they were celebrating her twenty-first birthday. While driving, they are stopped by police, who ask if Steven minds their taking his photograph. He agrees, joking that it is a good chance to be photographed with his girlfriend. The next day, a 17-year-old rape victim finds herself staring at Titus's picture in a "photo lineup." Saying, "This one is the closest; it has to be the one," she identifies Titus as the man who raped her on a secluded road near the Seattle-Tacoma airport. Titus is convicted and nearly goes to prison before his innocence is established—not through the efforts of the police or the prosecutor, but through his own efforts and the investigative reporting of Paul Henderson of the *Seattle Times.* Henderson wins a Pulitzer Prize; Titus is still trying to put his life back together (*Seattle Times,* 1982; *Los Angeles Times,* 1983, January 4:9).

Many of the cases we have identified involve errors by victims of robbery and rape, where the victim was close to the offender and was able to get a look at him—but under conditions of extreme stress. As Loftus (1979), Buckhout (1974), and Brigham and Barkowitz (1978) have shown in their published research, such stress can significantly affect perception and memory and should give us cause to question the realiability of such eye-witness testimony.

Although jurors attach great significance to eyewitness testimony, experts and judges increasingly share the view of Judge Lumbard of the Second Circuit, who observed:

> Centuries of experience in the administration of criminal justice have shown that convictions based solely on testimony that identifies a defen-dant previously unknown to the witness is highly suspect. Of the various kinds of evidence it is the least reliable, especially where unsupported by corroborating evidence [*Jackson v. Fogg,* 1978].

Despite the steps taken by the Supreme Court to establish safeguards against eyewitness misidentification, such errors continue to surface. In 1982, a Texas prisoner, Howard Mosley of Galveston, who had been convicted in a stabbing death and sentenced to a life term, was exonerated after new evidence indicated that the crime had been committed by a man who also admitted killing eleven others (*Houston Chronicle,* 1982). In a highly publicized Ohio case where great weight was placed on eyewitness identification by the victims of rape, William Jackson spent nearly five years in prison for two rapes he did not commit. He was released from prison after a grand jury indicted a Columbus physician (also named Jackson, but unrelated) on 36 counts of rape and 46 counts of aggravated burglary (*Columbus Citizen-Journal,* 1982: September 25; *New York Times,* 1982: September 24). These two cases also illustrate that the wrongly accused may or may not physically resemble the actual offender. Although fully a foot taller than Watts (the actual offender), Mosley was nevertheless identified and a jury was convinced of his guilt beyond a reasonable doubt. By contrast, in the Ohio case, both men bore the same last name; both were black; and both had trimmed Afro haircuts, similar facial shapes and mustaches, and were approximately the same height.

Accounts of eyewitness error are myriad, and sometimes bizarre. In one incredible case, Jeffrey Streeter was convicted without even having been arrested! Streeter had been sitting outside a courtroom and was asked by a defense attorney if he would sit next to him as a way of testing the credibility of the eyewitnesses. The defense attorney failed to inform the judge of the switch. Despite the fact that the real defendant was also in the courtroom at the time, three eyewitnesses pointed to the startled Streeter, who was seated next to the defense attorney. Streeter was convicted and sentenced to a year in jail for beating up an old man. He spent the night in jail before being released on his own recognizance. His conviction was subsequently reversed (*Atlanta Constitution,* 1980).

In another case, Robert Duncan, president of the Missouri Association of Criminal Defense Lawyers, was representing a Mexican-American defendant who had been arrested after being identified by a woman who was raped by "an Italian-looking man." When a second suspect was brought in, she identified him, too, as the guilty offender. She reportedly told authorities, "I'm getting tired of coming down here to identify this man." According to defense attorney Duncan, "The second guy didn't look anything at all like my client" (*U.S. News & World Report,* 1984:46).

Errors and/or Unprofessional Conduct by Police and Prosecutors

> Far too many cases come from the states to the Supreme Court present-
> ing dismal pictures of official lawlessness, of illegal searches and
> seizures, illegal detentions attended by prolonged interrogation and
> coerced admissions of guilt, of the denial of counsel, and downright
> brutality [Brennan, 1961:20-21].

Our survey respondents ranked police and prosecutorial errors, respectively, as the second and third most frequent contributing causes, and this rank order is justified, based on the cases in our own database. A common scenario in this type of error is the overzealous officer and/or prosecutor. Convinced of the suspect's or defendant's guilt, there is a temptation to buttress the case by prompting witnesses, suggesting what may have occurred at the time of the crime, concealing or fabricating evidence, or even committing perjury in court to "get their man."

Such unprofessional behavior is often well-intentioned, motivated by a sincere desire to strengthen the case against a suspect or defendant they "just know" is guilty. Given the view that police and prosecutors are part of that "thin line" that is civilized society's last hope for protection against the forces of evil, it is tempting for a police officer to twist the facts just enough to insure that the "twelve rocks in a box" (the jury) won't fail to convict the defendant. Likewise, crusading prosecutors who are bent on seeking convictions, rather than justice, often fail to advise defense attorneys of exculpatory evidence.

Item: A prosecutor brings as evidence a pair of men's undershorts found a mile from the crime scene. Alleging that these shorts belong to the accused and are heavily stained with blood that is the same type as the victim's, the prosecutor calls a chemist who verifies these "facts." The defense requests, and is denied, an opportunity to examine the shorts. Despite the defendant's denial that the shorts (the only link in a chain of circumstantial evidence) are his, the jury convicts him. The convicted prisoner subsequently petitions the Supreme Court for habeas corpus. A microanalyst appears for the petitioner and testifies that the shorts were indeed stained—with paint! The prosecutor later admits having known that the stains were paint—a fact that was unknown to the defense *(Miller v. Pate,* 1967).

Item: An innocent man, George Reissfelder, is convicted of first degree murder and armed robbery and is sentenced to life imprisonment with no possibility of parole. He spends 16 years in prison, despite the fact that his codefendant testified that Reissfelder was not his partner. Five policemen, an FBI agent, and a probation officer later submit statements indicating that authorities conducting the original investigation knew that Reissfelder was not Sullivan's partner in the robbery (*Atlanta Constitution,* 1983).

Item: In May, 1980, Juan Venegas, along with Lawrence Reyes, is convicted of murdering a 65 year-old man. Despite the fact that Reyes confesses to the murder, Venegas spends 2½ years in prison in California before being released and winning a civil award of $1 million *(San Francisco Chronicle,* 1980). Evidence presented at the civil trial shows that the police intimidated witnesses to perjure themselves and orchestrated a "frameup" of Mr. Venegas (Granelli, 1980).

Plea Bargaining

Many innocent defendants were convicted after "willingly" pleading guilty via the plea bargaining process. For most people, this may be the most puzzling of all such cases; after all, why would a perfectly innocent person plead guilty? This is one of the least publicized dynamics of wrongful conviction. Typically, the innocent defendant protests his innocence to counsel (and because many guilty defendants also claim innocence, counsel may regard such claims with cynicism) and to others, but not to the judge (at least not in open court), who must approve the plea bargain.

As for the question of why an innocent person would plead guilty, a social psychological experiment using role playing casts some light on the issue. Gregory (1978) found that innocent "defendants" were more likely to accept a plea bargain when they faced a number of charges or when the probable severity of punishment was great. For this reason, we are particularly concerned about the possible effect of resuming executions in the United States. With so much to lose, who among us would not plead guilty if he thought that by doing so, he could save his own life and, perhaps, eventually go free when the error is discovered?

Item: In Richmond, Virginia, Harry Siegler awaits the verdict of a jury who has heard the prosecution's case against him. Siegler, charged with first degree murder, fears that the jury will find him guilty and sentence him to death by electrocution. Minutes before the jury returns, Siegler desperately changes his plea to guilty. Meanwhile, the jury had already voted to find him not guilty (*Columbus Dispatch,* 1982: September 26).

In cases of less serious charges, a defendant who is unable to make bail and is offered, in exchange for a plea of guilt, immediate release with nothing more consequential than a minor criminal record (typically in a community where such records are not uncommon and not highly stigmatizing), cannot easily resist the lure of a guilty plea. That one will be found not guilty, although the defendant knows himself to be guiltless, is not at all certain. Alibis are difficult to establish; eyewitnesses can swear that they are confident in their identification of the defendant (even though they are often wrong); an assigned lawyer may not have the time or other resources for a good investigation; or an attorney unconvinced of his client's innocence may not proceed with enthusiasm, thus compromising the entire concept of the adversarial process.

In the subculture of the courts, the defense attorney, like the prosecutor, feels pressure to play the game of speedy disposal of cases (Rosett and Cressey, 1976; Heumann, 1978). Unwilling to bargain in one case, he is offered little opportunity to bargain in another where he desires to do so. If his client has a criminal record, he informs him of the difficulty in placing him on the stand.

Guilty pleas are usually accompanied by a ritualistic colloquy between the judge and the accused, in which the judge may subtly compel the defendant to confess to his guilt. Insofar as there has been a "bargain," the judge does not wish to clutter the record with the suspicion that an innocent person was compelled to plead guilty. Actually, it adds little to the record, in that the distinction between a plea of guilty and an admission of guilt is not one that is carefully drawn, although such a distinction becomes clear when the not guilty plea is contrasted with a denial of guilt.

Community Pressure for a Conviction

In a period of high crime and great public outcry against criminals, and a period when group pressures are felt in the courtroom, conviction rates may be higher. Pressure by whites has sometimes resulted in verdicts against blacks where there was at least reasonable doubt; blacks and other minority groups have sometimes tried to exert pressure in cases where whites were being tried for crimes against minorities, particularly when the alleged crimes appeared to be racially motivated. Certainly there has been pressure by women's groups (feminist and other) in some rape cases.

Pressure from the public, sometimes intensified by newspaper coverage, can be an expression of democratic participation in the criminal justice process. It can sometimes make the system more responsive to the social needs, values, and feelings of large numbers of residents. It can serve as watchdog, lest corruption and malfeasance in the system go unmentioned. It may thus result in prosecution of a case that warrants pursuit, but that might otherwise be dropped because of the standing and influence of the accused and his family, or in an appropriate finding of not guilty when the spotlight is on the court.

Public pressure, then, is a two-edged sword. It may be democratic pressure for social and criminal justice, or it may simply reflect public vengeance and fears, easily manipulated by demagogues who are ready and willing to oblige.

Inadequacy of Counsel

Since at least 1932 (*Powell v. Alabama*), inadequacy of counsel has been a basis for appealing conviction in criminal cases. The basic rationale of such an appeal is that the original defense counsel, for whatever reasons, did not adequately represent his client's interests in the case. Such appeals are not easy to win, despite the fact that many attorneys are inadequately prepared for trial work. Collegial relationships within the legal profession, though pitting lawyer against lawyer as adversaries, stop short of promoting the idea of attacking colleagues for mishandling a case (just as doctors are not eager to testify against other doctors). Lawyers assigned anew, or on appeal, are not eager to pursue this line for a reversal, preferring to characterize as "new evidence" that which had formerly been overlooked, for example.

Such cases as appear in the literature and in our database do not generally show a defense attorney in league with prosecutors or working against the interests of a client. Rather, the counsel for the defense is more likely to have been inexperienced, harried, overworked, with few or no investigative resources. Sometimes the defense counsel is unreceptive to a client's wishes because of a belief in the defendant's guilt and in the futility, even self-destructiveness, of pursuing the line of defense suggested by the accused.

Defense attorney errors include failure to make discovery motions or to pursue them vigorously, using poor judgment in placing a defendant on the stand, allowing a defendant to take a polygraph exam (especially in the absence of the defense attorney), and failure to challenge vigorously contentions made by the prosecution in court (Finer, 1973).

False Accusations

Item: Nathaniel Carter is arrested for murder in the stabbing death of Clarice Herndon. Carter's chief accuser is his estranged wife, who says she watched helplessly as Carter attacked her foster mother with a knife, inflicting 23 stab wounds. Carter is sentenced to a prison term of 25 years to life. After he serves 2 years in prison, his former wife admits that she, in fact, killed her foster mother. The police state that the cuts on Mrs. Carter's hands at the time of the crime made them believe she had also been attacked by her former husband. She seemed to be the perfect witness *(New York Times,* 1984).

False accusations fall into two categories: those in which a crime did occur and someone is deliberately and falsely accused (sometimes, in fact, by the perpetrator, as in the Carter case above), and others in which no crime ever occurred. There are several cases of men who have served prison terms for "murders" that never took place, only to have the putative "victim" turn up, alive and well.

Knowledge of Criminal Record

The old adage, "where there's smoke, there's fire," seems alive and well in the minds of the public and some criminal justice personnel. Where the accused has a history of prior arrest (not necessarily even conviction), many would more readily believe current accusations. This becomes a factor in wrongful conviction insofar as the police and other criminal justice personnel are likely to believe the worst about such suspects and perhaps ignore other leads. Also, the accused's past criminal record may be made known when the defendant voluntarily takes the stand or may be brought out through the questioning of other defense witnesses. It is sometimes common knowledge in the community that the accused has "a record." Where any of these factors is present, it makes the task of confining the verdict to the current facts more difficult. If one is conceived of as evil, there is no loss, it is reasoned, and there may even be social good, in punishment.

Other Factors

Other factors that are either less prevalent or about which less is known include judicial errors, bias, or neglect of duty; errors (generally, though not always unintentional) made by criminalists, medical examiners, and forensic science experts; errors in criminal recordkeeping and computerized information systems; voluntary and deliberate false confessions; and the mental incompetency of the accused.

Implications for Public Policy

It is not within the realm of possibility to prevent all wrongful convictions. A system of law that never caught an innocent person in its web would probably be so narrow that it would catch few of the guilty, as well.

Moreover, our research has established the existence of an important systemic phenomenon that has significant implications for the production of false convictions. We call this phenomenon the *ratification of error*. That is, the criminal justice system, starting with the police investigation of an alleged crime and culminating in the appellate courts, tends to ratify errors made at lower levels in the system. The further a case progresses in the system, the less chance there is that an error will be discovered and corrected, unless it involves a basic issue of constitutional rights and due process.

Recall the case of Nathaniel Carter, who was falsely convicted of stabbing his ex-wife's foster mother. A *New York Times* (1984) analysis of police reports, court records, and more than 100 interviews reveals a succession of serious errors, neglect, and incompetence that collectively led to Mr. Carter's wrongful conviction:

(1) An officer and another witness saw a man in bloody clothes running from the murder scene—a man whose description did not match Mr. Carter's. But in violation of prescribed practices, their accounts were never passed on to the prosecutors or the defense attorney, and the incident remains unexplained.

(2) A prosecutor lied at the trial, leading the jury to believe that Mr. Carter had admitted he was at the crime scene on the day of the murder.

(3) The District Attorney's staff never questioned Mrs. Carter's story, despite her background of violence. Instead, shortly after receiving the case, she was granted immunity from prosecution.

(4) The defense attorney failed to contact many of the witnesses who saw Mr. Carter far from the scene of the murder. Of at least ten such witnesses, only two were called to testify.

As one observer commented, "This was a breakdown of major proportions in the justice system.... It is a justice system so overworked that it has grown cynical to the possibility of a man's innocence." Mr. Carter characterized his experience more succinctly: "I was railroaded" *(New York Times,* 1984).

Compensation

Item: A 20-year-old man is wrongfully convicted of rape and robbery and spends nearly 2 years in prison before another man confesses to these crimes. While in prison, the innocent man is treated as a rapist by other prisoners. Following his release from prison, he is still unable to function sexually due to the psychological humiliation he experienced concerning his sexuality. The case is now in civil litigation (Anonymous Interview, 1983).

Item: 34-year-old Charles Daniels, though innocent, is convicted of sexually attacking a 2-year-old boy and attempting to murder him by hurling him from a rooftop. Despite alibi witnesses, Daniels is convicted and sentenced to 6-18 years in prison. While in prison, he is treated as any child sex molester might be treated: he is beaten, scalded with boiling water and, due to threats against his life, kept in virtual solitary confinement for 4 years before being exonerated. In an out-of-court settlement, he is awarded $600,000. Mr. Daniels says of his experience in prison, "Going through what I did is almost as bad as being executed for a crime you didn't commit. Because the other prisoners thought I had raped a child I knew I could be killed at any moment while I was in prison" *(New York Times,* 1985).

How much financial compensation are such experiences worth? Occasionally, one hears of a seemingly large award, such as that in the Daniels case (above); the $1 million award won by Isidore Zimmerman, who spent 24 years in prison, including 9 months on death row, and came within 2 hours of being executed for a murder he never committed (Wise, 1983), or the $1 million awarded to Juan Venegas, whose ordeal we discussed earlier (Granelli, 1980). However, our study reveals that in the great majority of cases where, as a result of wrongful conviction, innocent persons have lost their families, opportunities to pursue careers, and have been humiliated, little or no compensation has been provided for such suffering. As Rosen (1976) noted, "The United States has lagged far behind many nations in its failure to compensate the innocent victims of erroneous criminal accusations."

In most states, in order to compensate a citizen who was convicted but innocent, a special bill must be introduced and passed by the state legislature. Such bills generally empower the state claims court to set the amount of the award, and claims courts tend to apply very conservative criteria, such as "lost wages" and legal expenses. Given the economic status of most wrongfully convicted persons, the use of criteria such as "lost wages" cannot begin to approximate the "value" of time spent in prison as a result of false conviction.

Only a handful of states (California, Wisconsin, Illinois, New York, and Tennessee) have established special funds for compensating the victims of wrongful conviction. Even in these states, however, the awards are generally small and, in some cases, the statutorily prescribed ceilings on such awards amount to $5,000 or less per year of imprisonment (American Bar Association, 1984). The other option, of course, is through civil litigation. But one attorney, whose client was awarded only $5,800 by the Wisconsin Claims Board after serving 14 months in prison for an armed robbery he didn't commit, commented:

> You're talking about an expensive proposition. My client certainly doesn't have the money to pursue a civil suit. Most of these cases aren't like Geter. They're not getting the publicity. These are small cases in comparison and these people have to take what they can get. Sometimes they don't get anything [American Bar Association, 1984].

States should acknowledge their responsibility to provide fair compensation for innocent citizens who are wrongfully convicted, or at least for those who are wrongfully incarcerated. As Ohio's Tenth District Court of Appeals recently proclaimed in reversing a "grossly inadequate" Court of Claims award that "shocked the conscience" of the appellate court:

> No society has developed a perfect system of criminal justice in which no person is ever treated unfairly. The American system of justice has developed a myriad of safeguards to prevent the type of miscarriage to which the claimant herein was subjected, but it, too, has its imperfections. Fortunately, cases in which courts have unlawfully or erroneously taken a person's freedom by finding him or her guilty of a crime which he or she did not commit are infrequent. But, when such a case is identified, the legislature and the legal system have a responsibility to admit the mistake and diligently attempt to make the person as whole as is possible where the person has been deprived of his freedom and forced to live with criminals. Indeed the legal system is capable of creating few errors that have a greater impact upon an individual than to incarcerate him when he has committed no crime [*Leonard O'Neil v. State of Ohio,* 1984].

We are aware that many people regard wrongful convictions as the inevitable errors of a criminal justice system that is our social defense against crime—that such errors are indications of the essential strength of the system (social defense) and that in a time of high crime rates, an effort to reduce the incidence of such errors would result in so few convictions that the system could not tolerate the large numbers of guilty going free. Contrary to this belief, we suggest that the opposite effect may be at work. That is, the knowledge of false convictions, through the rather frequent newspaper and media accounts of such cases, may instill in the minds of many jurors and other citizens doubts as to the guilt of large numbers of accused, as well as those found guilty. Thus these "false positives" may be (or could become) a force working to reduce the rate of conviction for those whose guilt seems to be apparent beyond a reasonable doubt. A reduction in the number of wrongful convictions, then, could have important positive effects by increasing public respect for the criminal justice system and, perhaps, increasing the rate of conviction for those who are truly guilty—not to mention the most positive outcome of all, protecting the innocent.

Finally, wrongful conviction is not really an issue that should separate "liberals" from "conservatives." It does not require a fervent devotion to due process rights to comprehend that for every case of wrongful conviction, the real criminal may still be at large, free to victimize others.

References Cited

American Bar Association, (1984) "Innocents in jail." Amer. Bar Assn. J. 70 (June): 34-35.

Atlanta Constitution, (1980) "Court stand-in is convicted of crime he didn't commit." July 17: 12A.

Atlanta Constitution, (1983) "16 years in jail, case dismissed." Aug. 31: 1A.

Brandon, R., and C. Davies, (1973) Wrongful Imprisonment: Mistaken Convictions and their Consequences. London: Allen and Unwin.

Brennan, W.J., (1961) "The bill of rights and the states." Santa Barbara, CA: Center for the Study of Democratic Institutions.

Brigham, J.C., and P. Barkowitz, (1978) "Do they all look alike? The effects of race, sex, experience, and attitudes on the ability to recognize faces." J. Applied Psychology 8: 306-18.

Buckhout, R., (1974) "Eyewitness testimony." Scientific Amer. 231: 23-33.

Finer, J.J., (1973) "Ineffective assistance of counsel." Cornell Law Rev. 58: 1077-1120.

Granelli, J.S., (1980) "Trials—and errors." National Law J. December 15: 1.

Gregory, W.L., et al., (1978) "Social psychology of plea bargaining—applications, methodology, and theory." J. of Personality and Social Psychology 36: 1521-30.

Heumann, M., (1978) Plea Bargaining: The Experiences of Prosecutors, Judges, and Defense Attorneys. Chicago: Univ. of Chicago Press.

Houston Chronicle, (1982) "Monday finally comes for weekend killer." August 15.

Loftus, E.F., (1979) Eyewitness Testimony. Cambridge, MA: Harvard Univ. Press.

New York Times, (1984) "How errors convicted the wrong man." March 15: B1.

New York Times, (1985) "Man wrongfully imprisoned by New York to get $600,000." March 18.: 1.

Radin, E.D., (1964) The Innocents. New York: William Morrow.

Rosen, S.K., (1976) "Compensating the innocent accused." Ohio State Law J. 37: 705-28.

Rosett, A., and D.R. Cressey, (1976) Justice by Consent: Plea Bargains in the American Courthouse. Philadelphia: Lippincott.

San Francisco Chronicle, (1980) "Innocent prisoner gets $1 million." September 4: 38.

Seattle Times, (1982) Special reprint of P. Henderson's Pulitzer Prize-winning reports.

U.S. News & World Report, (1984) "When nightmare of false arrest comes true." December 17: 45-47.

Section IV

Change Without Progress: Corrections

Corrections is in need of reforms which are unlikely to occur. Many of the problems facing corrections can be attributed to philosophical and operational conflicts. There is a lack of consensus regarding the purpose of punishment. On the one hand, there are those who hold the retributive position and contend that we are right and proper in our desires to seek revenge for wrongs suffered and that those who commit those wrongs must be severely punished. On the other hand, there are those who support a utilitarian position and contend that the purpose of punishment is to prevent antisocial behavior. Punishment, according to this position, should be assessed with the goal of influencing the future behavior of the offender. Millions of dollars are invested annually in a large variety of rehabilitation and treatment programs. Many of these programs have proven to be of questionable value, and some are not appreciated by the participating offenders.

Because there is little agreement regarding the purpose of punishment, individuals and groups argue and debate in the legislative process as a part of an effort to make certain that their particular perspective is reflected in criminal codes. As a result, we find corrections riding the pendulum movements of the political process, and many aspects of corrections are perceived as confused and purposeless.

Public attitudes toward corrections are inconsistent. Many Americans believe that persons convicted of crimes should spend longer periods of time incarcerated in prison. At the same time, the public is also likely to agree with the contention that prisons do not rehabilitate and that a person may be more dangerous *after* incarceration in one of our overpopulated, violent prisons. We seem to want a continued reliance on the kinds of punishment mechanisms we have used in the past even though we readily acknowledge they have not worked.

While there are a number of topics and issues in the field of corrections, this section focuses on incarceration, inmate subcultures, parole, and community based corrections. Incarceration in a maximum security prison is a terribly degrading experience. Overpopulated and understaffed, a number of prisons have become unmanageable as inmate gangs control major aspects of institutional life. Narcotics traffic flourishes in many prisons and homosexual rape is a common occurrence as the weak succumb to the strong in this human jungle. Few of us have any conception of the levels of violence that occur behind prison walls. While prison riots have called public attention to the degrading and dehumanizing experience of incarceration, there is an abundance of public apathy that overwhelms any short-term concern. In the process of incarceration, we heap deprivation upon the inmate, failing to realize that ninety-eight percent of those incarcerated will be released to society in the future, many after being incarcerated only two to five years. We cannot constantly and continually expose these persons to violent behavior without their internalizing violent attitudes and the predisposition for violence. Simply stated, violence begets violence.

In "The Pains of Imprisonment," Gresham Sykes demonstrates the forms of pain caused by imprisonment. It is not simply that inmates are restricted in their movements, but that imprisonment also cuts important ties to the outside world.

In "A Critical Look at the Idea of Boot Camp as Correctional Reform," Merry Morash and Lila Rucker examine a trend toward institutions modeled after harsh and degrading military boot camps of the past. Ironically, this strategy was tried in the past with little luck, and the military itself is moving away from this model because it too often does more harm that good. It is also noted that such approaches glorify and officially sanction machismo and a reliance on brute force, which often is what led to the incarceration in the first place.

While much has been written about the moral and practical issues surrounding the death penalty, surprisingly little work has focused on the execution process. Robert Johnson's "This Man Has Expired," presents a stark firsthand account of how a modern death team operates and the process by which the offender is psychologically "dead" well before the execution.

"Inside America's Toughest Prison" uses one of the most secure prisons in Texas to illustrate the current problems of running a prison and the conflicting expectations of the prison's role in society. It also demonstrates that while prison reform may solve some problems, it often creates new problems which are difficult to anticipate in advance.

Finally, ''Removing Children from Adult Jails, A Guide to Action,'' using a number of research and case studies, addresses a problem long ignored by the juvenile justice system. The article examines a number of myths about children in jails and the extent to which throwaway children are housed in facilities that are inhumane.

14

The Pains of Imprisonment

Gresham Sykes

The Deprivation of Liberty

Of all the painful conditions imposed on the inmates of the New Jersey
State Prison, none is more immediately obvious than the loss of liberty. The
prisoner must live in a world shrunk to thirteen and a half acres and within
this restricted area his freedom of movement is further confined by a strict
system of passes, the military formations in moving from one point within
the institution to another, and the demand that he remain in his cell until
given permission to do otherwise. In short, the prisoner's loss of liberty is a
double one — first, by confinement to the institution and second, by
confinement within the institution.

The mere fact that the individuals's movements are restricted, however, is
far less serious than the fact that imprisonment means that the inmate is cut
off from family, relatives, and friends, not in the self-isolation of the hermit
or the misanthrope, but in the involuntary seclusion of the outlaw. It is true
that visiting and mailing privileges partially relieve the prisoner's
isolation — if he can find someone to visit him or write to him and who will
be approved as a visitor or correspondent by the prison officials. Many
inmates, however, have found their links with persons in the free

Gresham M. Sykes, *The Society of a Maximum Security Prison.* Copyright © 1958 by
Princeton University Press. "The Pains of Imprisonment," pp. 65-78, reprinted with permission of Princeton University Press.

community weakening as the months and years pass by. This may explain in part the fact that an examination of the visiting records of a random sample of the inmate population, covering approximately a one-year period, indicated that 41 percent of the prisoners in the New Jersey State Prison have received no visits from the outside world.

It is not difficult to see this isolation as painfully depriving or frustrating in terms of lost emotional relationships, of loneliness and boredom. But what makes this pain of imprisonment bite most deeply is the fact that the confinement of the criminal represents a deliberate, moral rejection of the criminal by the free community. Indeed, as Reckless has pointed out, it is the moral condemnation of the criminal — however it may be symbolized — that converts hurt into punishment, i.e. the just consequence of committing an offense, and it is this condemnation that confronts the inmate by the fact of his seclusion.

Now it is sometimes claimed that many criminals are so alienated from conforming society and so identified with a criminal subculture that the moral condemnation, rejection, or disapproval of legitimate society does not touch them; they are, it is said, indifferent to the penal sanctions of the free community, at least as far as the moral stigma of being defined as a criminal is concerned. Possibly this is true for a small number of offenders such as the professional thief described by Sutherland[1] or the psychopathic personality delineated by William and Joan McCord.[2] For the great majority of criminals in prison, however, the evidence suggests that neither alienation from the ranks of the law-abiding nor involvement in a system of criminal value is sufficient to eliminate the threat to the prisoner's ego posed by society's rejection.[3] The signs pointing to the prisoner's degradation are many — the anonymity of a uniform and a number rather than a name, the shaven head,[4] the insistence on gestures of respect and subordination when addressing officials, and so on. The prisoner is never allowed to forget that, by committing a crime, he has foregone his claim to the status of a full-fledged, *trusted* member of society. The status lost by the prisoner is, in fact, similar to what Marshall has called the status of citizenship — that basic acceptance of the individual as a functioning member of the society in which he lives.[5] It is true that in the past the imprisoned criminal literally suffered civil death and that although the doctrines of attainder and corruption of blood were largely abandoned in the 18th and 19th Centuries, the inmate is still stripped of many of his civil rights such as the right to vote, to hold office, to sue in court, and so on.[6] But as important as the loss of these civil rights may be, the loss of that more diffuse status which defines the individual as someone to be trusted or as morally acceptable is the loss which hurts most.

In short, the wall which seals off the criminal, the contaminated man, is a constant threat to the prisoner's self-conception and the threat is continually repeated in the many daily reminders that he must be kept apart from "decent" men. Somehow this rejection or degradation by the free community must be warded off, turned aside, rendered harmless. Somehow the imprisoned criminal must find a device for rejecting his rejectors, if he is to endure psychologically.[7]

The Deprivation of Goods and Services

There are admittedly many problems in attempting to compare the standard of living existing in the free community and the standard of living which is supposed to be the lot of the inmate in prison. How, for example, do we interpret the fact that a covering for the floor of a cell usually consists of a scrap from a discarded blanket and that even this possession is forbidden by the prison authorities? What meaning do we attach to the fact that no inmate owns a common piece of furniture, such as a chair, but only a home-made stool? What is the value of a suit of clothing which is also a convict's uniform with a stripe and a stencilled number? The answers are far from simple although there are a number of prison officials who will argue that some inmates are better off in prison, in strictly material terms, than they could ever hope to be in the rough-and-tumble economic life of the free community. Possibly this is so, but at least it has never been claimed by the inmates that the goods and services provided the prisoner are equal to or better than the goods and services which the prisoner could obtain if he were left to his own devices outside the walls. The average inmate finds himself in a harshly Spartan environment which he defines as painfully depriving.

Now it is true that the prisoner's basic material needs are met—in the sense that he does not go hungry, cold, or wet. He receives adequate medical care and he has the opportunity for exercise. But a standard of living constructed in terms of so many calories per day, so many hours of recreation, so many cubic yards of space per individual, and so on, misses the central point when we are discussing the individual's feeling of deprivation, however useful it may be in setting minimum levels of consumption for the maintenance of health. A standard of living can be hopelessly inadequate, from the individual's viewpoint, because it bores him to death or fails to provide those subtle symbolic overtones which we invest in the world of possessions. And this is the core of the prisoner's problem in the area of goods and services. He wants—or needs, if you will—not just the so-called necessities of life but also the amenities: cigarettes and liquor as well as calories, interesting foods as well as sheer bulk, individual clothing as well as adequate clothing, individual furnishings for his living quarters as well as shelter, privacy as well as space. The "rightfulness" of the prisoner's feeling of deprivation can be questioned. And the objective reality of the prisoner's deprivation—in the sense that he has actually suffered a fall from his economic position in the free community—can be viewed with skepticism, as we have indicated above. But these criticisms are irrelevant to the significant issue, namely that legitimately or illegitimately, rationally or irrationally, the inmate population defines its present material impoverishment as a painful loss.

Now in modern Western culture, material possessions are so large a part of the individual's conception of himself that to be stripped of them is to be attacked at the deepest layers of personality. This is particularly true when poverty cannot be excused as a blind stroke of fate or a universal calamity. Poverty due to one's own mistakes or misdeeds represents an indictment against one's basic value or personal worth and there are few men who can philosophically bear the want caused by their own actions. It is true some prisoners in the New Jersey State Prison attempt to interpret their low position in the scale of goods and services as an effort by the State to exploit them economically. Thus, in the eyes of some inmates, the prisoner is poor not because of an offense which he has committed in the past but because the State is a tyrant which uses its captive criminals as slave labor under the hypocritical guise of reformation. Penology, it is said, is a racket. Their poverty, then, is not punishment as we have used the word before, i.e., it is just consequence of criminal behavior; rather, it is an unjust hurt or pain inflicted without legitimate cause. This attitude, however, does not appear to be particularly widespread in the inmate population and the great majority of prisoners must face their privation without the aid of the wronged man's sense of injustice. Furthermore, more prisoners are unable to fortify themselves in their low level of material existence by seeing it as a means to some high or worthy end. They are unable to attach any significant meaning to their need to make it more bearable, such as present pleasures foregone for pleasures in the future, self-sacrifice in the interests of the community, or material asceticism for the purpose of spiritual salvation.

The inmate, then, sees himself as having been made poor by reason of his own acts and without the rationale of compensating benefits. The failure is *his* failure in a world where control and possession of the material environment are commonly taken as sure indicators of a man's worth. It is true that our society, as materialistic as it may be, does not rely exclusively on goods and services as a criterion of an individual's value; and, as we shall see shortly, the inmate population defends itself by stressing alternative or supplementary measures of merit. But impoverishment remains as one of the most bitter attacks on the individual's self-image that our society has to offer and the prisoner cannot ignore the implications of his straitened circumstances.[8] Whatever the discomforts and irritations of the prisoner's Spartan existence may be, he must carry the additional burden of social definitions which equate his material deprivation with personal inadequacy.

The Deprivation of Heterosexual Relationships

Unlike the prisoner in many Latin-American countries, the inmate of the maximum security prison in New Jersey does not enjoy the privilege of so-called conjugal visits. And in those brief times when the prisoner is allowed to see his wife, mistress, or "female friend," the woman must sit on one side of a plate glass window and the prisoner on the other, communicating by means of a phone under the scrutiny of a guard. If the inmate, then, is rejected and impoverished by the facts of his imprisonment, he is also figuratively castrated by his involuntary celibacy.

Now a number of writers have suggested that men in prison undergo a reduction of the sexual drive and that the sexual frustrations of prisoners are therefore less than they might appear to be at first glance. The reports of reduced sexual interest have, however, been largely confined to accounts of men imprisoned in concentration camps or similar extreme situations where starvation, torture, and physical exhaustion have reduced life to a simple struggle for survival or left the captive sunk in apathy. But in the American prison these factors are not at work to any significant extent and Lindner has noted that the prisoner's access to mass media, pornography circulated among inmates, and similar stimuli serve to keep alive the prisoner's sexual impulses.[9] The same thought is expressed more crudely by the inmates of the New Jersey State Prison in a variety of obscene expressions and it is clear that the lack of heterosexual intercourse is a frustrating experience for the imprisoned criminal and that it is a frustration which weights heavily and painfully on his mind during his prolonged confinement. There are, of course, some "habitual" homosexuals in the prison — men who were homosexuals before their arrival and who continue their particular form of deviant behavior within the all-male society of the custodial institution. For these inmates, perhaps, the deprivation of heterosexual intercourse cannot be counted as one of the pains of imprisonment. They are few in number, however, and are only too apt to be victimized or raped by aggressive prisoners who have turned to homosexuality as a temporary means of relieving their frustration.

Yet as important as frustration in the sexual sphere may be in physiological terms, the psychological problems created by the lack of heterosexual relationships can be even more serious. A society composed exclusively of men tends to generate anxieties in its members concerning their masculinity regardless of whether or not they are coerced, bribed, or seduced into an overt homosexual liaison. Latent homosexual tendencies may be activated in the individual without being translated into open behavior and yet still arouse strong guilt feelings at either the conscious or unconscious level. In the tense atmosphere of the prison with its known perversions, its importunities of admitted homosexuals, and its constant references to the problems of sexual frustration by guards and inmates alike, there are few prisoners who can escape the fact that an essential component of a man's self conception—his status of male—is called into question. And if an inmate has in fact engaged in homosexual behavior within the walls, not as a continuation of an habitual pattern but as a rare act of sexual deviance under the intolerable pressure of mounting physical desire, the psychological onslaughts on his ego image will be particularly acute.[10]

In addition to these problems stemming from sexual frustration per se, the deprivation of heterosexual relationships carries with it another threat to the prisoner's image of himself—more diffuse, perhaps, and more difficult to state precisely and yet no less disturbing. The inmate is shut off from the world of women which by its very polarity gives the male world much of its meaning. Like most men, the inmate must search for his identity not simply within himself but also in the picture of himself which he finds reflected in the eyes of others; and since a significant half of his audience is denied him, the inmate's self image is in danger of becoming half complete, fractured, a monochrome without the hues of reality. The prisoner's looking-glass self, in short—to use Cooley's fine phrase—is only that portion of the prisoner's personality which is recognized or appreciated by men and this partial identity is made hazy by the lack of contrast.

The Deprivation of Autonomy

We have noted before that the inmate suffers from what we have called a loss of autonomy in that he is subjected to a vast body of rules and commands which are designed to control his behavior in minute detail. To the casual observer, however, it might seem that the many areas of life in which self-determination is withheld, such as the language used in a letter, the hours of sleeping and eating, or the route to work, are relatively unimportant. Perhaps, it might be argued, as in the case of material deprivation, that the inmate in prison is not much worse off than the individual in the free community who is regulated in a great many aspects of his life by the iron fist of custom. It could even be argued, as some writers have done, that for a number of imprisoned criminals, the extensive control of the custodians provides a welcome escape from freedom and that the prison officials thus supply an external Super-Ego which serves to reduce the anxieties arising from an awareness of deviant impulses. But from the viewpoint of the inmate population, it is precisely the triviality of much of the officials' control which often proves to be most galling. Regulation by a bureaucratic staff is felt far differently than regulation by custom. And even though a few prisoners do welcome the strict regime of the custodians as a means of checking their own aberrant behavior which they would like to curb but cannot, most prisoners look on the matter in a different light. Most prisoners, in fact, express an intense hostility against their far-reaching dependence on the decisions of their captors and the restricted ability to make choices must be included among the pains of imprisonment along with restrictions of physical liberty, the possession of goods and services, and heterosexual relationships.

Now the loss of autonomy experienced by the inmates of the prison does not represent a grant of power freely given by the ruled to the rulers for a limited and specific end. Rather, it is total and it is imposed — and for these reasons it is less endurable. The nominal objectives of the custodians are not, in general, the objectives of the prisoners.[11] Yet regardless of whether or not the inmate population shares some aims with the custodial bureaucracy, the many regulations and orders of the New Jersey State Prison's official regime often arouse the prisoner's hostility because they don't "make sense" from the prisoner's point of view. Indeed, the incomprehensible order or rule is a basic feature of life in prison. Inmates, for example, are forbidden to take food from the messhall to their cells. Some prisoners see this as a move designed to promote cleanliness; others are convinced that the regulation is for the purpose of preventing inmates from obtaining anything that might be used in the *sub rosa* system of barter. Most, however, simply see the measure as another irritating, pointless gesture of authoritarianism. Similary, prisoners are denied parole but are left in ignorance of the reasons for the decision. Prisoners are informed that the delivery of mail will be delayed — but they are not told why.

Now some of the inmate population's ignorance might be described as "accidental"; it arises from what we can call the principle of bureaucratic indifference, i.e. events which seem important or vital to those at the bottom of the heap are viewed with an increasing lack of concern with each step upward. The rules, the commands, the decisions which flow down to those who are controlled are not accompanied by explanations on the grounds that it is "impractical" or "too much trouble." Some of the inmate population's ignorance, however, is deliberately fostered by the prison officials in that explanations are often withheld as a matter of calculated policy. Providing explanations carries an implication that those who are ruled have a right to know — and this in turn suggests that if the explanations are not satisfactory, the rule or order will be changed. But this is in direct contradiction to the theoretical power relationship of the inmates and the prison officials. Imprisoned criminals are individuals who are being punished by society and they must be brought to their knees. If the inmate population maintains the right to argue with its captors, it takes on the appearance of an enemy nation with its own sovereignty; and in so doing it raises disturbing questions about the nature of the offender's deviance. The criminal is no longer simply a man who has broken the law; he has become a part of a group with an alternative viewpoint and thus attacks the validity of the law itself. The custodians' refusal to give reasons for many aspects of their regime can be seen in part as an attempt to avoid such an intolerable situation.

The indignation aroused by the "bargaining inmate" or the necessity of justifying the custodial regime is particularly evident during a riot when prisoners have the "impudence" to present a list of demands. In discussing the disturbances at the New Jersey State Prison in the Spring of 1952, for example, a newspaper editorial angrily noted that "the storm, like a nightmarish April Fool's dream, has passed, leaving in its wake a partially wrecked State Prison as a debasing monument to the ignominious rage of desperate men."

The important point, however, is that the frustration of the prisoner's ability to make choices and the frequent refusals to provide an explanation for the regulations and commands descending from the bureaucratic staff involve a profound threat to the prisoner's self image because they reduce the prisoner to the weak, helpless, dependent status of childhood. As Bettelheim has tellingly noted in his comments on the concentration camp, men under guard stand in constant danger of losing their identification with the normal definition of an adult and the imprisoned criminal finds his picture of himself as a self-determining individual being destroyed by the regime of the custodians.[12] It is possible that this psychological attack is particularly painful in American culture because of the deep-lying insecurities produced by the delays, the conditionality and the uneven progress so often observed in the granting of adulthood. It is also possible that the criminal is frequently an individual who has experienced great difficulty in adjusting himself to figures of authority and who finds the many restraints of prison life particularly threatening in so far as earlier struggles over the establishment of self are reactivated in a more virulent form. But without asserting that Americans in general or criminals in particular are notably ill-equipped to deal with the problems posed by the deprivation of autonomy, the helpless or dependent status of the prisoner clearly represents a serious threat to the prisoner's self image as a fully accredited member of adult society. And of the many threats which may confront the individual, either in or out of prison, there are few better calculated to arouse acute anxieties than the attempt to reimpose the subservience of youth. Public humiliation, enforced respect and deference, the finality of authoritarian decisions, the demands for a specified course of conduct because, in the judgment of another, it is in the individual's best interest — all are features of childhood's helplessness in the face of a superior adult world. Such things may be both irksome and disturbing for a child, especially if the child envisions himself as having outgrown such servitude. But for the adult who has escaped such helplessness with the passage of years, to be thrust back into childhood's helplessness is even more painful, and the inmate of the prison must somehow find a means of coping with the issue.

The Deprivation of Security

However strange it may appear that society has chosen to reduce the criminality of the offender by forcing him to associate with more than a thousand other criminals for years on end, there is one meaning of this involuntary union which is obvious — the individual prisoner is thrown into prolonged intimacy with other men who in many cases have a long history of violent, aggressive behavior. It is a situation which can prove to be anxiety-provoking even for the hardened recidivist and it is in this light that we can understand the comment of an inmate of the New Jersey State Prison who said, "The worst thing about prison is you have to live with other prisoners."

The fact that the imprisoned criminal sometimes views his fellow prisoners as "vicious" or "dangerous" may seem a trifle unreasonable. Other inmates, after all, are men like himself, bearing the legal stigma of conviction. But even if the individual prisoner believes that he himself is not the sort of person who is likely to attack or exploit weaker and less resourceful fellow captives, he is apt to view others with more suspicion. And if he himself is prepared to commit crimes while in prison, he is likely to feel that many others will be at least equally ready.... Regardless of the patterns of mutual aid and support which may flourish in the inmate population, there are a sufficient number of outlaws within this group of outlaws to deprive the average prisoner of that sense of security which comes from living among men who can be reasonably expected to abide by the rules of society. While it is true that every prisoner does not live in constant fear of being robbed or beaten, the constant companionship of thieves, rapists, murderers, and aggressive homosexuals is far from reassuring.

An important aspect of this disturbingly problematical world is the fact that the inmate is acutely aware that sooner or later he will be "tested" — that someone will "push" him to see how far they can go and that he must be prepared to fight for the safety of his person and his possessions. If he should fail, he will thereafter be an object of contempt, constantly in danger of being attacked by other inmates who view him as an obvious victim, as a man who cannot or will not defend his rights. And yet if he succeeds, he may well become a target for the prisoner who wishes to prove himself, who seeks to enhance his own prestige by defeating the man with a reputation for toughness. Thus both success and failure in defending one's self against the aggressions of fellow captives may serve to provoke fresh attacks and no man stands assured of the future.[13]

The prisoner's loss of security arouses acute anxiety, in short, not just because violent acts of aggression and exploitation occur but also because behavior constantly calls into question the individual's ability to cope with it, in terms of his own inner resources, his courage, his "nerve." Can he stand up and take it? Will he prove to be tough enough? These uncertainties constitute an ego threat for the individual forced to live in prolonged intimacy with criminals, regardless of the nature or extent of his own criminality; and we can catch a glimpse of this tense and fearful existence in the comment of one prisoner who said, "It takes a pretty good man to be able to stand on an equal plane with a guy that's in for rape, with a guy that's in for murder, with a man who's well respected in the institution because he's a real tough cookie...." His expectations concerning the conforming behavior of others destroyed, unable and unwilling to rely on the officials for protection, uncertain of whether or not today's joke will be tomorrow's bitter insult, the prison inmate can never feel safe. And at a deeper level lies the anxiety about his reactions to this unstable world, for then his manhood will be evaluated in the public view.

Notes

[1]Cf. Edwin H. Sutherland, *The Professional Thief,* Chicago: The University of Chicago Press, 1937.

[2]Cf. William and Joan McCord, *Psychopathy and Delinquency,* New York: Grune and Stratton, 1956.

[3]For an excellent discussion of the symbolic overtones of imprisonment, see Walter C. Reckless, *The Crime Problem,* New York: Appleton-Century-Crofts, Inc., 1955, pp. 428-429.

[4]Western culture has long placed a peculiar emphasis on shaving the head as a symbol of degradation, ranging from the enraged treatment of collaborators in occupied Europe to the more measured barbering of recruits in the Armed Forces. In the latter case, as in the prison, the nominal purpose has been cleanliness and neatness, but for the person who is shaved the meaning is somewhat different. In the New Jersey State Prison, the prisoner is clipped to the skull on arrival but not thereafter.

[5]See T.H. Marshall. *Citizenship and Social Class,* Cambridge, England: The Cambridge University Press, 1950.

[6]Paul W. Tappan, "The Legal Rights of Prisoners," *The Annals of the American Academy of Political and Social Science,* Vol. 293, May 1954, pp. 99-111.

[7]See Lloyd W. McCorkle and Richard R. Korn, "Resocialization Within Walls." *Ibid.,* pp. 88-98.

[8]Komarovsky's discussion of the psychological implications of unemployment is particularly apposite here, despite the markedly different context, for she notes that economic failure

provokes acute anxiety as humiliation cuts away at the individual's conception of his manhood. He feels useless, undeserving of respect, disorganized, adrift in a society where economic status is a major anchoring point. Cf. Mirra Komarovsky's, *The Unemployed Man and His Family,* New York: The Dryden Press, 1940, pp. 74-77.

[9]See Robert M. Lindner, "Sex in Prison," *Complex,* Vol. 6, Fall 1951, pp. 5-20.

[10]Estimates of the proportion of inmates who engage in homosexuality during their confinement in the prison are apt to vary. In the New Jersey State Prison, however, Wing Guards and Shop Guards examined a random sample of inmates who were well known to them from prolonged observation and identified 35 per cent of the men as individuals believed to have engaged in homosexual acts. The judgments of these officials were substantially in agreement with the judgments of a prisoner who possessed an apparently well-founded reputation as an aggressive homosexual deeply involved in patterns of sexual deviance within the institution and who had been convicted of sodomy. But the validity of these judgments remains largely unknown and we present the following conclusions, based on a variety of sources, as provisional at best: First, a fairly large proportion of prisoners engage in homosexual behavior during their period of confinement. Second, for many of those prisoners who do engage in homosexual behavior, their sexual deviance is rare or sporadic rather than chronic. And third, as we have indicated before, much of the homosexuality which does occur in prison is not part of a life pattern existing before and after confinement; rather, it is a response to the peculiar rigors of imprisonment.

[11]The nominal objectives of the officials tend to be compromised as they are translated into the actual routines of day-to-day life. The modus vivendi reached by guards and their prisoners is oriented toward certain goals which are in fact shared by captors and captives. In this limited sense, the control of the prison officials is partly concurred in by the inmates as well as imposed on them from above. In discussing the pains of imprisonment our attention is focused on the frustrations or threats posed by confinement rather than the devices which meet these frustrations or threats and render them tolerable. Our interest here is in the vectors of the person's social system — if we may use an analogy from the physical sciences — rather than the resultant.

[12]Cf. Bruno Bettelheim, "Individual and Mass Behavior in Extreme Situations," in *Readings in Social Psychology,* edited by T.M. Newcomb and E.L. Hartley, New York: Henry Holt and Company, 1947.

[13]As the Warden of the New Jersey State Prison has pointed out, the arrival of an obviously tough professional hoodlum creates a serious problem for the recognized "bad man" in a cellblock who is expected to challenge the newcomer immediately.

15

A Critical Look at the Idea of Boot Camp as a Correctional Reform

Merry Morash
Lila Rucker

Introduction: The Boot Camp Idea

In several states, correctional boot camps have been used as an alternative to prison in order to deal with the problem of prison overcrowding and public demands for severe treatment (Parent, 1988). Correctional boot camps are styled after the military model for basic training, and, similar to basic training, the participants are primarily young males. However, the "recruits" are offenders, though usually nonviolent and first-time ones (Parent, 1988). Boot camps vary in their purpose, but even when they are instituted primarily to reduce overcrowding, the implicit assumption is that their programs are of equal or greater deterrent or rehabilitative value than a longer prison sentence.

By the end of 1988, boot camps were operating in one county (Orleans Parish, Louisiana) and in eight states (Georgia, Oklahoma, Mississippi, Louisiana, South Carolina, New York, Florida, and Michigan), they were planned in three states (North Carolina, Kansas, and New Hampshire), and they were being considered in at least nine other states (Parent, 1988). The model was also being considered for a large number of youthful Detroit offenders. And in the summer of 1989, the boot camp model was put forth

Merry Morash and Lila Rucker, "A Critical Look at the Idea of Boot Camp as a Correctional Reform," *Crime and Delinquency*, Vol. 36, No. 2 (April 1990), pp. 204-222. Copyright © 1990 by Sage Publications, Inc.

by the House Crime Subcommittee chairman as a potential national strategy for treating drug abusers (Gannett News Service, 1989).

The National Institute of Justice is supporting evaluations of correctional boot camp programs, and other evaluations without federal support are also underway. Such formal evaluations will no doubt provide invaluable evidence of the effect of the programs on participants and, in some cases, on the correctional system (e.g., the resulting diversion of offenders from more restrictive environments). The purpose of this article is to provide another type of assessment, specifically, a critical analysis of the history and assumptions underlying the use of a military model in a correctional setting.

The popular image of military boot camp stresses strict and even cruel discipline, hard work, and authoritarian decision making and control by a drill sergeant. It should be noted that this image does not necessarily conform to either current practices in the U.S. military or to all adaptations of boot camp in correctional settings. However, in a survey of existing correctional boot camp programs, Parent (1988) found commonality in the use of strict discipline, physical training, drill and ceremony, military bearing and courtesy, physical labor, and summary punishment for minor misconduct. Some programs have combined selected elements of the military boot camp model with more traditional forms of rehabilitation. In Oklahoma, for example, the paramilitary structure, including the use of regimentation, has been only one aspect of an otherwise "helping, supportive environment" that is considered by the administration to be a prerequisite if "change is to last or have any carry over" (Kaiser, 1988). In Michigan, the major emphasis has been on developing the "work ethic" by utilizing various motivational tactics (e.g., chants), strong discipline, and rehabilitation (Hengish, 1988). All participants work from 8:00 AM to 3:30 PM daily; evenings involve educational and therapeutic programs. When more traditional methods of rehabilitation are included, a consideration of the boot camp idea is more complex, requiring an analysis of both the costs and benefits of mixing the imagery or the reality of a boot camp approach with other measures.

Regardless of the actual degree to which a militaristic, basic training model has been emphasized, the press has taken this emphasis as primary and usually has portrayed it in a positive light. Numerous stories have been printed under titles such as "Boot Camp—In Prison: An Experiment Worth Watching" (Raspberry, 1987, p. H21), "New York Tests a Boot Camp for Inmates" (Martin, 1988), "'Squeeze You Like a Grape': In Georgia, A Prison Boot Camp Sets Kids Straight" (*Life*, 1988), and "Some Young US Offenders Go To 'Boot Camp'—Others Are Put in Adult Jails" (Sitomer, 1987, p. 1). The text similarly has reflected a positive evaluation of the approach. For example, Raspberry (1987) wrote of the Louisiana boot camp that "[t]he idea [is] to turn a score of lawbreakers into disciplined, authority-respecting men." He quoted the warden: "[W]e're giving an inmate a chance to get out of prison in 90 days instead of seven years. But you're making him work for it. . . . We keep them busy from the time they wake up until they fall asleep with chores that include such sillinesses as cleaning latrines with a toothbrush." The warden concluded that the approach "teaches them self-discipline and self-control, something many of these men have never had" (Raspberry, 1987). Similarly, Martin (1988, p. 15) wrote about the New York program:

> Days are 16 hours long, and two-mile runs and calisthenics on cold asphalt are daily staples. Work is chopping down trees or worse. The discipline recalls Parris Island. . . . those who err may be given what is genteelly termed 'a learning experience,' something like carrying large logs around with them everywhere they go or, perhaps, wearing baby bottles around their necks.

Life's (1988, p. 82) coverage of the Georgia program included the following statement by one of the sergeants: "[Here] being scared is the point. You have to hit a mule between the eyes with a two-by-four to get his attention . . . and that's exactly what we're doing with this Program."

The journalistic accounts of boot camps in corrections have celebrated a popular image of a relatively dehumanizing experience that is marked by hard, often meaningless, physical labor. The inmate has been portrayed as deficient, requiring something akin to being beaten over the head in order to become "a man."

The imagery of the people that we send to boot camp as deserving of dehumanizing treatment is in itself troubling, but even more so in light of the fact that the inmates are disproportionately minorities and underclass members. The boot camp idea also raises the disturbing question: Why would a method that has been developed to prepare people to go into war, and as a tool to manage legal violence, be considered as having such potential in deterring or rehabilitating offenders? Wamsley (1972, p. 401) concluded from a review of officers' manuals and prior research that military basic training is designed to promote fundamental values of military subculture, including

> (1) acceptance of all-pervasive hierarchy and deference patterns; (2) extreme emphasis on dress, bearing, and grooming; (3) specialized vocabulary; (4) emphasis on honor, integrity, and professional responsibility; (5) emphasis on brotherhood; (6) fighter spirit marked by aggressive enthusiasm; and (7) special reverence for history and traditions.

In another summary of the values stressed in military basic training, Merryfinch (1981, p. 9) identified "a commitment to organized violence as the most effective way to resolve conflicts, a glorification of 'hard' emotions (aggression, hatred, brutality) and a strict channeling of 'soft' emotions (compassion, love, suffering). . . ." Clearly, many of the objectives of military basic training are not shared by the policymakers who promote correctional boot camps.

What is even more striking is that none of them make sense as a means to promote either rehabilitation or deterrence, and the emphasis on unquestioned obedience to authority and aggression is inconsistent with prosocial behavior.

What Has Been Tried and What Works in Corrections?

The correctional boot camp model has been touted as a new idea. However, militarism, the use of hard labor, and efforts to frighten offenders—most recently surfacing in the "Scared Straight" programs—have a long history in prison settings. We will focus first on militarism. In 1821, John Cray, the deputy keeper of the newly constructed Auburn Prison, moved away from the use of solitary confinement when suicides and mental breakdowns increased. As an alternative, he instituted a military regime to maintain order in overcrowded prisons (McKelvey, 1977, p. 14). The regime, which was based in part on his experiences as a Canadian army officer, required downcast eyes, lockstep marching, no talking or other communication among prisoners, and constant activity under close supervision (McKelvey, 1977). The issue for Cray and his contemporaries was the prevention of crime "through fear of punishment; the reformation of offenders being of minor consideration" (Lewis, 1983, p. 26).

Neither Cray's attempts nor those of his Pennsylvania cohorts, however, achieved either deterrence or reform (Cole, 1986, p. 497). During the Progressive Era, there was a shift away from the sole emphasis on punishment. At Elmira Reformatory, Zebulon Brockway added a new twist to Cray's militaristic regulations, certain of which (lockstep marching and rules of silence) had fallen into disrepute because they were now seen as debasing, humiliating, and destructive of initiative (Cole, 1986, p. 497). By 1896, the industrial reformatory at Elmira had ". . . well coordinated discipline which centered around the grading and marking system, an honest application of the indeterminate sentence, trade and academic schools, military organization and calisthenic exercises" (McKelvey, 1977, p. 137). Similar to many of the contemporary boot camps, at Elmira the philosophy was to combine both rehabilitation approaches and work with military discipline and physical activity to, among other things, improve self-esteem. However, the legacy of Brockway's Elmira Reformatory was not a move toward rehabilitation (Johnson, 1987, p. 41). Instead, the militaristic atmosphere set the stage for abusive punishment, and the contradiction between military discipline and rehabilitation was apparent (Pisciotta, 1983, pp. 620-21).

Some might counter the argument that the militaristic approach opens the door for abusive punishment by pointing out that in contemporary correctional settings, physical punishment and harm are eliminated. However, as Johnson

(1987, p. 48; see also Christie, 1981) noted, nonphysical abuse can be viewed as a "civilized" substitute. Also, in some cases physical abuse is a matter of definition, as is seen in the accounts of dropouts from one contemporary boot camp. They reported being treated like "scum," working 18-hour days, being refused permission to use the bathroom, being provoked to aggression by drill instructors, being forced to push a bar of soap along the floor with their noses, and being forced to participate in an exercise called "air raids" in which trainees run and dive face down, landing on their chests with arms stretched out to their sides (Bellew, 1988, p. 10). At least in some settings, the military model has provided a legitimization of severe punishment. It has opened the door for psychological and even physical abuse that would be rejected as cruel and unusual punishment in other correctional settings.

Turning now to work in correctional settings, its persistent use has been supported by its congruence with alternative objectives, including punishment, incapacitation, rehabilitation, and control inside the institution (Lejins, 1970, pp. 309-10). However, the form of work at a particular time has not been influenced just by ideals and objectives, but by basic economic forces (Rusche and Kirchheimer, 1939). For example, in order to protect private enterprise, the treadmill was used to occupy offenders following prohibitions against the use of prison labor (Morse, 1973, p. 33; see also Morash and Anderson, 1978). Also, in the nineteenth century, a major purpose of imprisonment was to teach the regular work habits demanded by employers (Rusche and Kirchheimer, 1939; Melossi and Pavarini, 1981). In contemporary discussions of correctional boot camp programs, work has been justified as both punitive and rehabilitative, as both exemplifying the harsh result of breaking the law and teaching the "work ethic." However, the economic constraints imposed by limited budgeting for rehabilitation efforts and the shrinking number of jobs for unskilled workers have shaped the form of work. Thus, hard physical labor, which has no transfer to the contemporary job market, has been the choice in correctional boot camps.

Further criticism of the form of work used in the boot camp settings rests on empirical research. The literature on work programs in general has not supported the conclusion that they produce a decrease in recidivism (Taggart, 1972; Fogel, 1975, pp. 114-16; Lipton, Martinson, and Wilks, 1975). Especially pertinent to the present analysis, in a recent article Maguire, Flanagan, and Thornberry (1988) showed that labor in a correctional institution was unrelated to recidivism after prisoner differences were taken into account. The exception was work programs that actually provided employment (e.g., Jeffrey and Woolpert, 1974; Rudoff and Esselstyn, 1973). Based on an extensive review of the literature, Gendreau and Ross (1987, p. 380; see also Walter and Mills, 1980) further specified the characteristics of correctional work programs that were related to lower recidivism: "Work programs must enhance practical skills, develop interpersonal skills, minimize prisonization, and ensure that work is not punishment alone." Clearly, the evaluation literature contradicts the idea that hard, often meaningless, labor in the boot camp setting has some positive effect.

Moreover, although negative attitudes and lack of the work ethic might be one influence on the choice of economic crime instead of a job, structural arguments have provided alternative explanations. For example, Wilson (1987) documented that low-skilled minorities have been hardest hit by deindustrialization of the national labor force and changes in the geographic location of industries. The labor surplus in low-technology fields, and the strength of general social and psychological factors thought to cause criminal behavior, have been found to counteract most offender work programs (Maguire et al., 1988, p. 16). In a supporting ethnography, Sullivan (1983) showed that the slightly greater availability of jobs in white, working-class neighborhoods explained residents' lesser criminality; in black, lower class neighborhoods where there were no work opportunities, males in their late teens used robbery as a regular source of income. Altering men's attitudes toward work does nothing to combat these structural deficiencies.

The "Scared Straight" programs, a contemporary version of correctional efforts intended to deter offenders through fright, also are not supported by empirical research. In a San Quentin program of this type, older adolescent participants were arrested less often but for more serious crimes than a comparison group (Lewis, 1983). An evaluation of a similar New Jersey program showed that participants were more seriously delinquent than a control group (Finckenauer, 1982). On the surface, an evaluation of a "tough" detention regime in British detention centers suggests that though there were no increases in recidivism, there also were no decreases (Thornton et al., 1984). However, although the British detention center programs incorporated such "military" approaches as strict discipline, drill, and parades, a primary focus was on staff being personally helpful to the youth. Also, humiliating and punitive staff reactions were prohibited by general guidelines. Thus, the British detention center model departed markedly from many of the U.S. models. In general, then, the program elements of militarism, hard labor, and fear engendered by severe conditions do not hold much promise, and they appear to set the stage for abuse of authority.

Military Boot Camps

The idea of boot camp as applied in correctional settings is often a simplification and exaggeration of an outdated system of military training that has been examined and rejected as unsatisfactory by many experts and scholars and by the military establishment itself. The difficulties that the military has discovered with the traditional boot camp model, and the resulting implications for reforms, could be instructive to people in search of positive correctional measures.

A number of difficulties with what will be referred to as the "traditional" military boot camp approach that is now mimicked in correctional settings were uncovered by a task force appointed in the 1970s (Raupp, 1978; Faris, 1975). The first difficulty with the traditional boot camp approach involved inconsistent philosophies, policies, and procedures. Ten years after the task force report was published, a follow-up study provided further insight into the problem of inconsistency and the related patterns of unreasonable leadership and contrived stressful situations. The study documented the "severe effects" of lack of predictability in such areas as standards for cleanliness and how cadence was called (Marlowe et al., 1988, p. 10). According to the study, "predictability and reasonableness contribute to trainee self-esteem, sense of being valued by the unit and commitment to the organization." Further, "when authority is arbitrarily imposed, or when leaders lead strictly by virtue of their power or authority, the result is often anger and disrespect" (Marlowe et al., 1988, pp. 11-12). Also, "dysfunctional stress [which results when work is irrelevant or contrived], heightens tensions, shortens tempers, and increases the probability of abuse while generally degrading the effectiveness of training" (Raupp, 1978, p. 99). By contrast, "functional" stress is legitimate and work-related, resulting from such instances as "the mental and physical stress of a tactical road march (Raupp, 1978, p. 98)."

The second difficulty that the task force identified with traditional boot camp training was a widespread "we-versus-they" attitude and the related view that trainees were deserving of degrading treatment (Raupp, 1978, p. 9). The we-versus-they attitude was manifested by different behavioral and/or dress standards for trainees and for other personnel. Specifically, trainees were given "skin-head" haircuts and were prohibited from swearing and shouting, and physical training was used as punishment.

Aside from the investigative reports sponsored by the military, empirical studies of the effects of military boot camps, the effects of physical training (which is a major component of many correctional boot camp programs), and learning in general have provided relevant findings. Empirical evidence regarding the psychological impact of traditional military basic training on young recruits between the ages of 18 and 22 has demonstrated that "there was no increase in scores on ego-strength, or any other evidence of beneficial psychological effects accruing from basic training" (Ekman, Friesen, and Lutzker, 1962, p. 103). Administration of the MMPI to recruits revealed that "the change in the shape of the [MMPI] profiles suggests that aggressive, impulsive, and energetic features became slightly more prominent" (Ekman et al., 1962, p. 103). The authors concluded that the changes on the subscales imply that more callous attitudes, a tendency to ignore the needs of others, and feelings of self-importance increase slightly during basic training. The recruits appear less prone to examine their own responsibility for conflicts, and more ready to react aggressively. (Ekman et al., 1962, p. 104)

The importance of this finding is heightened by the conclusion of Gendreau, Grant, and Leipciger (1979, p. 71) that components of self-esteem that were good predictors of recidivism include the very same characteristics, namely, "self-centered, exploitive of others, easily led, and anxious to please." Sonkin and Walker (1985; see also Walker, 1983; Eisenberg and Micklow, 1979) also speculated that basic training in the military can result in the transfer of violent solutions to family settings. Eisenberg and Micklow (1979, p. 50) therefore proposed that military basic training be modified to include classes on "communication skills, stress reduction, and anger management." Although correctional boot camps do not provide training in the use of weapons or physical assault, they promote an aggressive model of leadership and a conflict-dominated style of interaction that could exacerbate tendencies toward aggression.

In another empirical study of military basic training, Wamsley (1972) contrasted the effects of Air Force Aviation Cadet Pre-Flight Training School with Air Force Officer's Training School. The Cadet School employed harsh techniques—including such activities as head shaving, marching miles in stiff shoes, and impromptu exercises as physical punishment—to inculcate basic values and eliminate the "unfit." After one week, 33% of recruits left. Wamsley (1972, p. 401) wrote that "Those with low capacities for anxiety, insufficient self-esteem to withstand and discredit abuse, inability to control or suppress anger, or those with latent neuroses or psychoses literally 'cracked' under the stress, and attempted suicides and psychiatric referrals were not uncommon." The purpose of constant exhortations to "get eager, mister" or "get proud, Raunch" was to promote an aggressive fighter spirit, and the "common misery and despair created a bond" among the trainees.

Increased aggression and a bond among inmates are not desired outcomes of correctional boot camps, so again the efficacy of using the military boot camp model is in question. Moreover, it is unlikely that the offenders in correctional boot camps are more mentally healthy than Air Force recruits. What is the effect of using such techniques when there is no escape valve through dropping out of the program? And, if only the best-adjusted stay, what is accomplished by the program? The contrast of the Cadet School with the Officer's Training School, which did not use humiliation and severe physical conditions and punishment, provides convincing evidence of the ineffectiveness of such an approach to training people. Wamsley (1972, p. 418) concluded that there was a "lack of a clear utility for Pre-Flight's intense socialization'' and that the ''socialization process was brutally expensive in human terms and produced exaggerated forms of behavior which were not clearly related to effective task accomplishments.''

Additional research has shown that positive improvements in self-esteem result from physical training primarily when the environment is supportive. For example, Hilyer and Mitchell (1979, p. 430) demonstrated that college students with low self-concepts who received physical fitness training in a helpful, facilitative, supportive environment demonstrated an increase in self-concept scores. The improvement was two and one-half times as great as that of low-concept peers who received physical fitness training and no support.

Also contradicting the negatively oriented training strategy that is characteristic of the old-style military boot camp model, virtually no empirically supported criminological theories have suggested that aggressive and unpredictable reactions by authority figures encourage prosocial behavior. The opposite has been promulgated by most learning theorists. For instance, Satir (1973, p. 13) concluded that learning happens only when a person feels valued and is valued, when he or she feels like a connected part of the human race (see also Rogers, 1975, p. 6). Feelings of self-worth can only flourish in an atmosphere in which individual differences are appreciated and mistakes are tolerated; communication is direct, clear, specific, and honest; rules are flexible, human, appropriate, and subject to change; and links to society are open (Satir, 1972, p. 4-6). Finally, there has been considerable theory and research showing that antisocial behavior is increased when authority figures provide aggressive models for behavior (e.g., Bandura, 1973, pp. 252-53). Research in the sociology of sport has provided further evidence that physical training under the direction of an authoritarian trainer increases aggression (Coakley, 1986).

There is no systematic evidence of the degree to which the problems in traditional-style military boot camps are manifested in correctional settings, but there is evidence that they do occur. The introductory descriptions of the correctional boot camp model clearly reveal a tendency for some of the ''drill sergeants'' to use negative leadership. Telephone interviews with representatives of nine correctional boot camps show a tendency to focus on ''tearing down the individuals and then building them back up.'' Reflective of this philosophy are negative strategies alluded to earlier, such as the utilization of debasing ''welcoming speeches,'' the ''chair position,'' and ''learning experiences'' that require men to wear baby bottles around their necks or to carry tree limbs with them all day.

Correctional boot camps also provide settings conducive to high levels of unpredictability and contrived stress. In one program (Bellew, 1988, p. 5), dropouts, current trainees, and parolees who had completed the program all reported that ''differences between DI [drill instructor] styles made it tough to avoid trouble. Trainees' beds may be made to satisfy DI 'A,' but at shift change, if DI 'B' doesn't approve of that particular style, trainees are punished.'' As further illustration, another inmate reported that on the first day of participation in the boot camp, he was told that he had quit and could not participate. When the inmate sat down for the rest of the day, he was reportedly "kicked out for sitting down," and his having left the program was listed as voluntary. The inmate reported that he had tried to participate but that the drill instructor kept telling him that he had quit. The interviewer reported that at the time of the interview, the offender was "still confused as to what actually had happened that day" (Bellew, 1988, p. 10).

It is true that, as proponents of correctional boot camps claim, many military recruits feel that their survival of basic training is evidence of maturity and a major achievement in their lives (Gottlieb, 1980, pp. 166-67). However, the sense of achievement is linked to the notion that the experience is the first step in preparing them for the unique role of a soldier. Moreover, military boot camp is intended as just a prelude to acquaint the recruits with their new environment, in which they will take more control of their lives (Rabinowitz, 1982, p. 1084). It is not obvious that the boot camp experience alone, including elements of capricious and dehumanizing treatment, would be seen in such a positive light by inmate participants.

Clearly, the view that boot camp is just the first step in a socialization process has not been carried over into the correctional setting. While nearly all programs reported either regular or intensive probation or parole periods following release (Parent, 1988), none of the postrelease programs have had the capability to provide the continuous and multifaceted support network inherent in being a member of the military "family" or process. Postrelease programs are not designed to provide either the tightly knit structure or the guaranteed work that characterize military life.

It could be argued that the purpose of correctional boot camp is not to bind soldiers to their leaders or to develop group solidarity. Thus, the failure of the outmoded military boot camp model to achieve these results may not be a serious concern. Even if we accept this argument, the research on military basic training raises serious questions about the potential for undesirable outcomes, including increased aggression.

Stereotypes of Masculinity and Correctional Measures

The very idea of using physically and verbally aggressive tactics in an effort to "train" people to act in a prosocial manner is fraught with contradiction. The idea rests on the assumption that forceful control is to be valued. The other unstated assumption is that alternative methods for promoting prosocial behavior, such as the development of empathy or a stake in conformity (e.g., through employment), are not equally valued. Feminist theorists (Eichler, 1980; Bernard, 1975) have noted the societywide valuation of the stereotypically masculine characteristics of forcefulness and aggression and of the related devaluation of the stereotypically feminine characteristics of empathy and cooperative group behavior. Heidensohn (1987, p. 25) specifically wrote that programs like boot camp have been "designed to reinforce conventional male behaviour" and that they range from "quasi-militaristic short, sharp shocks to adventure training."

There is little doubt that the military is a male-dominated institution (*Defense*, 1987) and that there is a military ideology that rejects both women and stereotypically female characteristics (Yuval-Davis, 1985; Yudkin, 1982; Larwood, Glasser, and McDonald, 1980; Stiehm, 1981, p. 57, 1989, p. 226; Enloe, 1983). As Enloe (1983, p. 7; see also Ruddick, 1983; O'Brien, 1979) wrote, there is a common assumption that "the military . . . is a *male* preserve, run by men and for men according to masculine ideas and relying solely on *man* power." In some military settings, terms such as "little girl," "woman," and "wife" have been routinely used to negatively label a trainee who is viewed as having failed in some way (Eisenhart, 1975; Stiehm, 1982, p. 371). Traditional marching chants have included degrading comments about women, and sexist terms for women and their body parts have been common in military settings (Ruddick, 1983, p. 231). Stiehm (1981, p. 257) concluded from her research that even after the mandated inclusion of women in the U.S. Military Academy, considerable derogatory name calling and ridicule of women were common. The implication is that to fail is to be female, or, conversely, to succeed is to be aggressive, dominant, and therefore unquestionably "male."

One might argue that name calling is not used in correctional settings. Given the military background of many correctional staff involved in the reforms and the popular image of boot camp experiences, the degree to which such an antiwoman attitude exists is an important empirical question. Aside from overt rejection of women and femaleness, the boot camp model, with its emphasis on unquestioned anthority and aggressive interactions and its deemphasis on group cooperation and empathy, promotes a limited image of the "true man."

It is not surprising that few have questioned the distorted image of masculinity embodied in the idea of boot camp, for this imagery is implicit in the assumptions of many criminological theories (Naffine, 1987), and it is shared by many offenders. Focusing on criminologists, Naffine (1987) showed how several major theories have presented male offenders' aggression and assertiveness in a positive light while they have devalued characteristics associated with women. To be more specific, major theories have accepted the stereotypical characteristics of men as normal and have presented women as dependent, noncompetitive, and passive. Naffine's (1987, p. 126) analysis revealed the "curious result of extolling the virtues of the male, as a good criminal, and treating conforming women as if they were the socially deviant group.'' This result has been echoed in the use of a military model that similarly extols the virtues that are often associated with both masculinity and aggression in our society.

Writing about images of masculinity among economically marginalized men, who are overrepresented in the offender population, Messerschmidt (1986, p. 59) built on the notion that in our society ''both masculinity and power are linked with aggression/violence while femininity and powerlessness are linked with nonviolence'' (also see Schwendinger and Schwendinger, 1985, p. 161). He went on to note that as a result of the unavailability of jobs that are not degrading, powerless men seek out alternative avenues through which to exercise their masculinity. Other supports of criminality include an orientation toward ''exploitative individualism,'' as opposed to any caring ties to group members, and male bonding, which is the ritual rejection of ''weakness'' associated with femininity. This rejection is demonstrated through activities like gang fights. Again, there is a parallel with the stereotype of masculinity embodied in the boot camp model. Specifically, Eisenhart (1975) has described military training's emphasis on self-sufficiency and the avoidance of attachment to others.

The irony in emphasizing an aggressive model of masculinity in a correctional setting is that these very characteristics may explain criminality. Theorists working in the area of crime causation have focused on both the identification with male stereotypical traits and roles, which are consistent with illegal behavior (Oakley, 1972, p. 72; see also Tolson, 1977), and the frustration that males feel when they cannot achieve these stereotypes because of low social status (Messerschmidt, 1986, pp. 59-68). The empirical support to link stereotypical masculinity with criminality has been inconsistent (Cullen, Golden, and Cullen, 1979; Norland, James, and Shover, 1978; Thornton and James, 1979; Loy and Norland, 1981). There is some evidence, however, that female stereotypical characteristics predict prosocial behavior (Morash, 1983; Gilligan, 1982; Hoffman, 1975; Eisenberg and Miller, 1987).

An additional irony is found in the inclusion of women in correctional boot camps. Holm (1982, p. 273) observed that in the military, ''women . . . suffered from role identification problems when put through military training programs designed traditionally 'to make men out of boys,''' programs that had ''more to do with the rites of manhood than the requirements of service jobs.'' There is serious doubt about the efficacy of placing women in a militaristic environment that emphasizes masculinity and aggressiveness and that in some cases rejects essentially prosocial images and related patterns of interaction associated with the stereotype of femininity.

Alternative Models in Corrections

Correctional policymakers and program staff are not alone in their application of the traditional boot camp model as an approach for training people outside of military settings. Looking again at news reports, we see that the boot camp type of training has been accepted in a variety of organizations as a means to increase the productivity, skill levels, efficiency, and effectiveness of participants. Such enterprises are as diverse as the Electronic Data Systems Corporation (Klausner, 1984, p. 17), the Nick Bollettieri Tennis Academy (Arias, 1986, p. 107), and Japan's Managers' Training School (Bueil, 1983). In keeping with the boot camp model, participants are made to endure humiliation so that a bond can develop with the teacher (Klausner, 1984, p. 17). There appear to be social forces supporting acceptance of the general idea that the boot camp model is appropriate as a method for promoting training and human development. In spite of the societal pressures to use such a model, our assessment has a number of negative implications for the application of boot camps in correctional settings.

The first implication is based on the research on boot camp and the development of human potential in a military setting. At certain times and in certain geographic locations, military personnel have been charged with training and employing populations that are not markedly dissimilar from the economically marginalized young men and women that populate the prisons. They also have been engaged in the imprisonment of people for the violation of criminal laws. A continued examination of their techniques and outcomes could provide further instruction. As a starting point, it might be noted that in the military, the version of boot camp used in correctional settings is not commonly viewed as an effective correctional measure. Furthermore, through *Project 10,000*, the military has been successful in integrating poorly educated recruits into their own workforce, though often in relatively low-skill positions that restricted transfer to the civilian workforce (Sticht et al., 1987). Contrary to critics' anticipation of disciplinary problems with poorly educated recruits, less than 5% of the participants failed to conform to military rules and regulations. The approach to integration involved traditional methods of literacy training coupled with individualized teaching geared to a specific job assignment. This approach is consistent with the findings that we have reviewed on effective work programs in correctional settings.

A second implication of our analysis of the idea of boot camp is that we need to reconsider correctional alternatives. Harris (1983, p. 166) wrote that the "development of a more humane, caring and benevolent society involves a continuing quest for higher standards of decency and good will and an ever decreasing resort to . . . degrading sanctions." For her, the continued and fundamental interdependence of self and other is primary, and she thinks in terms of "persuasion, nonviolent action, positive reinforcement, personal example, peer support and the provision of life-sustaining and life-enhancing services and opportunities" (Harris, 1983, p. 166). It is noteworthy that the rehabilitation models of corrections that many experts have publicly rejected reflect a deemphasis on the questionable stereotypes of "how to be a man" that are promoted by the boot camp model.

A third implication has to do with the evaluation of existing and planned boot camp programs. A number of potential, negative outcomes of a boot camp environment have been identified. One of these is increased aggression, including physical and nonphysical punishment, directed against offenders by prison staff. Also included are increased offender aggression, a devaluation of women and so-called "feminine traits" (e.g., sensitivity), and other negative effects of an unpredictable, authoritarian atmosphere. In addition to considering these effects directly, program evaluation should monitor the degree to which the environment is characterized by inconsistent standards and expectations, dysfunctional stress, a we-versus-they attitude, and negative leadership styles. Furthermore, because correctional boot camp programs mix the elements of a military model with less coercive methods of human change, it is important to design research that reveals the actual program elements that produce both desired and undesired program outcomes.

Our review and analysis suggest that even when the elements of the military boot camp model are mixed with traditional rehabilitative approaches, there can be negative outcomes. Thus, the boot camp model is unlikely to provide a panacea for the needs of rehabilitation or for the pressures arising from the problems of both prison overcrowding and public demands for severe punishment. Whether the point is to provide rehabilitation, to deter, or to divert people from prison, alternatives other than boot camp should be given careful consideration.

References Cited

Arias, Ron. 1986. "At Nick Bollettieri's Florida Boot Camp, Tennis Is Played Only One way, To Win." *People Weekly*, October 20: 107.

Bandura, Albert. 1973. *Aggression: A Social Learning Analysis*. Englewood Cliffs, NJ: Prentice-Hall.

Bellew, Deena C. 1988. *An Evaluation of IMPACT Using Intensive Interviews: The Inmate Perspective*. Unpublished manuscript. Baton Rouge: Louisiana State University.

Bernard, Jesse. 1975. *Women, Wives, Mothers: Values and Options*. Chicago: Aldine.

Bueil, Barbara. 1983. "Corporate Boot Camp in Japan." *Life*, September: 40.

Christie, Nils. 1981. *Limits to Pain*. Oxford: Mattin Robertson.

Coakley, Jay J. 1986. *Sport in Society: Issues and Controversies*. St. Louis, MO: Mosby.

Cole, George F. 1986. *The American System of Criminal Justice*. Monterey, CA: Brooks/Cole.

Cullen, Francis T., Kathryn M. Golden and John B. Cullen. 1979. "Sex and Delinquency: A Partial Test of the Masculinity Hypothesis." *Criminology*, 17: 301-310.

Defense. 1987. "Almanac: People in Active Duty." September/October: 32.

Eichler, Margrit. 1980. *The Double Standard: A Feminist Critique of Feminist Social Science*. New York: St. Martin's Press.

Eisenberg, Nancy and Paul A. Miller. 1987. "The Relation of Empathy to Prosocial and Related Behaviors." *Psychological Bulletin*, 101: 91-119.

Eisenberg, Sue E. and Patricia L. Micklow. 1979. "The Assaulted Wife: 'Catch 22' Revisited." *Women's Rights Law Reporter*, 3: 138-161.

Eisenhart, R. Wayne. 1975. "You Can't Hack It Little Girl: A Discussion of the Covert Psychological Agenda of Modern Combat Training." *Journal of Social Issues*, 31: 13-23.

Ekman, Paul, Wallace V. Friesen and Daniel R. Lutzker. 1962. "Psychological Reactions to Infantry Basic Training." *Journal of Consulting Psychology*, 26: 103-104.

Enloe, Cynthia. 1983. *Does Khaki Become You? The Militarization of Women's Lives*. Boston: South End.

Faris, John H. 1975. "The Impact of Basic Combat Training: The Role of the Drill Sergeant." Pp. 13-24 in *The Social Psychology of Military Service*, edited by E. Goldman and D.R. Segal. Beverly Hills, CA: Sage.

Finckenauer, James O. 1982. *Scared Straight and the Panacea Phenomenon*. Englewood Cliffs, NJ: Prentice-Hall.

Fogel, David. 1975. . . . *We Are the Living Proof* . . . Cincinnati: Anderson.

Gannett News Service. 1989. "Boot Camp Prisons." *Lansing State Journal*, 135 (June 19): 11.

Gendreau, Paul, Brian A. Grant and Mary Leipciger. 1979. "Self-Esteem, Incarceration, and Recidivism." *Criminal Justice and Behavior*, 6: 67-75.

Gendreau, Paul and Robert R. Ross. 1987. "Revivification of Rehabilitation: Evidence from the 1980s." *Justice Quarterly*, 4: 349-396.

Gilligan, Carol. 1982. *In a Different Voice*. Cambridge, MA: Harvard University Press.

Gottlieb, David. 1980. *Babes in Arms: Youth in the Army*. Beverly Hills, CA: Sage.

Harris, M. Kay. 1983. "Strategies, Values, and the Emerging Generation of Alternatives to Incarceration." *Review of Law and Social Change*, 12: 141-170.

Heidensohn, Francis. 1987. "Women and Crime: Questions for Criminology." Pp. 16-27 in *Gender, Crime and Justice*, edited by P. Carlen and A. Worral. Milton Keynes, England: Open University Press.

Hengish, Donald. 1988. Michigan Bureau of Correctional Facilities, Community Alternatives Program. Telephone interview, December 1.

Hilyer, James S., Jr. and William Mitchell. 1979. "Effects of Systematic Physical Fitness Training Combined with Counseling on the Self-Concept of College Students." *Journal of Counseling Psychology*, 26: 427-436.

Hoffman, Martin L. 1975. "Sex Differences in Moral Internalization and Values." *Journal of Personality and Social Psychology*, 32: 720-729.

Holm, Jeanne. 1982. *Women in the Military*. Novato, CA: Presidio.

Jeffrey, Ray and Stephen Woolpert. 1974. "Work Furlough as an Alternative to Incarceration: An Assessment of its Effects on Recidivism and Social Cost." *Journal of Criminal Law and Criminology*, 65: 404-415.

Johnson, Robert. 1987. *Hard Time*. Monterey, CA: Brooks/Cole.

Kaiser, Steven. 1988. Warden, Lexington Assessment and Reception Center, Lexington, Oklahoma. Telephone interview, November 16.

Klausner, Michael. 1984. "Perot's Boot Camp." *Wall Street Journal*, August 3: 17.

Larwood, Laurie, Eric Glasser and Robert McDonald. 1980. "Attitudes of Male and Female Cadets Toward Military Sex Integration." *Sex Roles*, 6: 381-390.

Lejins, Peter P. 1970. "Ideas Which Have Moved Corrections." *Proceedings of the One Hundredth Annual Congress of Corrections of the American Correctional Association*: 308-322.

Lewis, Roy V. 1983. "Scared Straight—California Style: Evaluation of the San Quentin Squire Program." *Criminal Justice and Behavior*, 10: 209-226.

Life. 1988. "'Squeeze You Like a Grape': In Georgia, A Prison Boot Camp Sets Kids Straight," July: 82.

Lipton, Douglas, Robert Martinson and Judith Wills. 1975. *The Effectiveness of Correctional Treatment*. New York: Praeger.

Loy, Pamela and Stephen Norland. 1981. "Gender Convergence and Delinquency." *Sociological Quarterly*, 22: 275-283.

Maguire, Kathleen E., Timothy J. Flanagan and Terence P. Thornberry. 1988. "Prison Labor and Recidivism." *Journal of Quantitative Criminology*, 4: 3-18.

Marlowe, David H., James A. Martin, Robert J. Schneider, Larry Ingraham, Mark A. Vaitkus and Paul Bartone. 1988. *A Look at Army Training Centers: The Human Dimensions of Leadership and Training*. Washington, DC: Department of Military Psychiatry, Walter Reed Army Institute of Research.

Martin, Douglas. 1988. "New York Tests a Boot Camp for Inmates." *New York Times*, March 4: 15.

McKelvey, Blake. 1977. *American Prisons: A History of Good Intentions*. Montclair, NJ: Patterson Smith.

Melossi, Dario and Massimo Pavarini. 1981. *The Prison and the Factory: Origins of the Penitentiary System*. London: Macmillan.

Merryfinch, Lesley. 1981. "Militarization/Civilization." Pp. 9-13 in *Loaded Questions: Women in the Military*, edited by W. Chapkis. Washington, DC: Transnational Institute.

Messerschmidt, James W. 1986. *Capitalism, Patriarchy, and Crime: Toward a Socialist Feminist Criminology*. Totowa, NJ: Rowman and Littlefield.

Morash, Merry. 1983. "An Explanation of Juvenile Delinquency: The Integration of Moral-Reasoning Theory and Sociological Knowledge." Pp. 385-410 in

Personality Theory, Moral Development, and Criminal Behavior, edited by W. S. Laufer and J. M. Day. Lexington, MA: Lexington Books.

Morash, Merry and Etta Anderson. 1978. "Liberal Thinking on Rehabilitation: A Work-Able Solution to Crime?" *Social Problems*, 25: 556-563.

Morse, Wayne. 1973. "The Attorney General's Survey of Release Procedures." Pp. 23-53 in *Penology: The Evolution of Corrections in America*, edited by G. C. Killinger and P. F. Cromwell, Jr. St. Paul, MN: West.

Naffine, Ngaire. 1987. *Female Crime: The Construction of Women in Criminology.* Sydney: Allen and Unwin.

Norland, Stephen, Jennifer James and Neal Shover. 1978. "Gender Role Expectations." *Sociology Quarterly*, 19: 545-554.

Oakley, Ann. 1972. *Sex, Gender and Society.* London: Temple Smith.

O'Brien, Tim. 1979. *If I Die in a Combat Zone, Box Me Up and Ship Me Home.* New York: Delacorte.

Parent, Dale. 1988. "Shock Incarceration Programs." Paper Presented at the American Correctional Association Winter Conference, Phoenix.

Pisciotta, Alexander W. 1983. "Scientific Reform: The New Penology at Elmira, 1876-1900." *Crime and Delinquency*, 29: 613-630.

Rabinowitz, Stanley. 1982. "Inauguration for Adulthood: The Military System as an Effective Integrator for Adult Adaptation: An Israel Air Force Base Perspective." *Psychological Reports*, 51: 1083-1086.

Raspberry, William. 1987. "Boot Camp—In Prison: An Experiment Worth Watching." *Washington Post*, March 21: Section H, p. 21.

Raupp, Edward R. 1978. *Toward Positive Leadership for Initial Entry Training. A Report by the Task Force on Initial Entry Training Leadership.* Fort Monroe, VA: United States Army Training and Doctrine Command.

Rogers, Carl R. 1975. "Empathic: An Unappreciated Way of Being." *Journal of the Counseling Psychologist*, 5: 2-10.

Ruddick, Sara. 1983. "Drafting Women: Pieces of a Puzzle." Pp. 214-243 in *Conscripts and Volunteers: Military Requirements, Social Justice and the All-Volunteer Force*, edited by R.K. Rullinwinder. Totowa, NJ: Rowman and Allenheld.

Rudoff, Alvin and T. C. Esselstyn. 1973. "Evaluating Work Furlough: A Follow-Up." *Federal Probation*, 37: 48-53.

Rusche, Georg and Otto Kirchheimer. 1939. *Punishment and Social Structure.* New York: Columbia University Press.

Satir, Virginia. 1972. *Peoplemaking.* Palo Alto, CA: Science and Behavior Books.

Schwendinger, Julia R. and Herman Schwendinger. 1985. *Adolescent Subcultures and Delinquency.* New York: Praeger.

Sitomer, Curtis J. 1987. "Some Young U.S. Offenders Go to 'Boot Camp'—Others are Put in Adult Jails." *Christian Science Monitor*, October 27: 1.

Sonkin, Daniel Jay, Del Martin and Leonard E. Aurbach Walker. 1985. *The Male Batterer: A Treatment Approach.* New York: Springer.

Sticht, Thomas G., William B. Armstrong, Daniel T. Hickey and John S. Caylor. 1987. *Cast-Off Youth Policy and Training Methods from the Military Experiences.* New York: Praeger.

Stiehm, Judith H. 1981. *Bring Me Men and Women: Mandated Change at the U.S. Air Force Academy*. Berkeley: University of California Press.

———. 1982. "The Protected, the Protector, the Defender." *Women's Studies International Forum*, 5: 367-376.

———. 1989. *Arms and the Enlisted Woman*. Philadelphia: Temple University Press.

Sullivan, Mercer. 1983. "Youth Crime: New York's Two Varieties." *New York Affairs: Crime and Criminal Justice*. New York: New York University Press.

Taggart, Robert, III. 1972. *The Prison of Unemployment*. Baltimore: Johns Hopkins University Press.

Thornton, David, Len Curran, David Grayson and Vernon Holloway. 1984. *Tougher Regimes in Detention Centres: Report of an Evaluation by the Young Offender Psychology Unit*. London: Her Majesty's Stationery Office.

Thornton, William E. and Jennifer James. 1979. "Masculinity and Delinquency Revisited." *British Journal of Criminology*, 19: 225-241.

Tolson, Andrew. 1977. The Limits of Masculinity: Male Identity and the Liberated Woman. New York: Harper & Row.

Walker, Lenore. 1983. "The Battered Woman Syndrome Study." Pp. 31-48 in *The Dark Side of Families: Current Family Violence Research*, edited by D. Finkelhor, R.J. Gelles, G. Hotaling and M. Straus. Beverly Hills, CA: Sage.

Walter, Timothy L. and Carolyn M. Mills. 1980. "A Behavioral-Employment Intervention Program for Reducing Juvenile Delinquency." Pp. 185-206 in *Effective Correctional Treatment*, edited by R.R. Ross and P. Gendreau. Toronto: Butterworths.

Wamsley, Gary L. 1972. "Contrasting Institutions of Air Force Socialization: Happenstance or Bellwether?" *American Journal of Sociology*, 78: 399-417.

Wilson, William Julius. 1987. *The Truly Disadvantaged: Inner City, the Underclass, and Public Policy*. Chicago: University of Chicago Press.

Yudkin, Marcia. 1982. "Reflections on Wolf's *Three Guineas*." *Women's Studies International Forum*, 5: 263-269.

Yuval-Davis, Nira. 1985. "Front and Rear: The Sexual Division of Labor in the Israeli Army." *Feminist Studies*, 11: 649-675.

16

Inside America's Toughest Prison

Daniel Pedersen
Daniel Shapiro
Ann McDaniel

The sun had just set when Keith Price stepped outside his captain's quarters, stared across 200 yards of Texas plains and saw that his prison was on fire. Beleaguered state officials had built tents in the southern yard to ease the overcrowding in the Eastham Unit's main house, and now 250 inmates were repaying the kindness. The ranking uniformed officer coming on duty that night in November 1981, Price expected that he would lead a troop of guards to quell the uprising; it was the kind of task he relished. "I liked action," Price says now. "I went to work waiting for it—almost hoping for it. Here I was, a captain, a middle-management person. There was no reason to wear combat boots every day, but I wore them."

In the yard, the flames spread. As inmates later told it, the riot flared when two inmate trusties kept "jugging"—harassing—six Hispanic prisoners. The shoving turned to blows, and the trusties, in an unusual loss of face, fled for the safety of the main prison building. Ornery under the best of circumstances, the inmates went on a rampage. Working with matches and paper kindling, they lit 20 tents, then built burning barricades out of mattresses piled onto trash cans. As smoke filled the yard, the men dancing around the flames had bought a moment of anarchy that they mistook for freedom.

Copyright © October 6, 1986, Newsweek, Inc. All rights reserved. Reprinted by permission.

Inside the prison, a general alarm sounded. Sixty officers, including Price, ran for the gymnasium to form a riot squad. While the guards milled about, testing the heft of their three-foot black batons, Price saw another group forming in the gym. About 150 inmate trusties, known in Texas prisons as building tenders, plus 150 of their aides and chums were also preparing to restore order. They were the inmates who really ran the asylum: the meanest characters the administration could co-opt into doing the state's bidding. While rocks smashed against the gym's barred windows, Sonny Evans, the boss tender, ordered *his* troops to tie white bandannas on their heads so they wouldn't be confused with the rioters. As they tore the ubiquitous white cloth made in the prison factory, the tenders *growled,* a kind of primal cry that frightened Price. "They're carrying trash-can lids, pipes, clubs, weight-lifting bars," he recalls. "The adrenaline's really flowing, flowing so much it's spooky."

While the fury grew, Price pleaded with warden Edward Turner to let the guards handle the riot and wait for reinforcements from other prisons. Turner refused. Price, whose adrenaline was also really flowing, took off his eyeglasses, pulled on his riot helmet and led the charge.

The guards aimed for the center of the yard, pushing through the barricades. With the agility of the football lineman he once was, Price moved ahead of his troops. Peering through the smoke, he saw the rioters fleeing toward one corner of the yard. And pursuing them were the building tenders. One of the tenders, who calls himself Tommy B., remembers what happened next: "We had clubs, bats, chains, knives, everything, and we formed what we called a 'whupping' line." The only way to the safety of the gym was down that gantlet, and the rioters, now edging toward panic, began running through. Inmate Ronnie Roland was inside the main building as the "whupped" staggered in. "Some of the guys you couldn't recognize, and a lot were unconscious. I wasn't sure if they was alive or dead." The inmates who could walk staggered back to the cell blocks; the others were carried inside to wait for ambulances.

After the screaming and the sirens stopped, Roland walked back to his cell, passing a day room where blood stained the floor. Bunch, a building tender, was ordering the others not to clean the mess. "Leave the blood on the floor, man, so those mother----s can see it," he insisted. And it was there the next morning when Roland walked past again. "The blood on the wall was still there, the blood on the floor was there, the rags were there. The only thing missing was the bodies."

In the silence, minds were changing. Price had missed most of the action at the gantlet, but he heard the thuds and the cries. "It's a miracle," he thought, "that nobody was killed." That was little comfort. He, and by extension the state apparatus, could pull on combat gear and threaten mayhem, but the bloodstains were evidence that they no longer had control of their turf. The old ways weren't working, and Keith Price said to himself, "I don't want to be a part of this anymore."

Price stayed on, as did Ronnie Roland and Tommy B. Although they didn't know it at the time, the Eastham riot had pushed the old order into its final days. A federal judge had ordered sweeping reforms, dismantling the building-tender system and forcing the state to finally police its own. But the change was slow and sloppy; vicious prison gangs seized power in the vacuum. Inmates turned on inmates. Between January 1984 and September 1985, 52 prisoners were fatally shivved and mangled throughout the 27-unit system; six died at Eastham. The killings ended only when the state resorted to a rudimentary control technique: locking the most dangerous inmates away in isolation, buying an uneasy peace in which inmates still watch their backs, and guards complain that they, too, feel like prisoners.

This is the story of the 14-year effort to change the nation's second largest prison system, and the unintended consequences of reform. It focuses on just one state pen, the Eastham Unit of the Texas Department of Corrections. It describes the intersecting lives of inmates, guards, administrators and lawyers; a federal judge hellbent on change and a stone-walling bureaucracy, jealous of its prerogatives and resistant to outside interference. It is, of necessity, filled with the particular horror of life on the inside, the volatile mix of brutal men and a brutal environment.

The story has lessons that extend far beyond Texas. For two decades dedicated, well-intentioned people have tried to transform America's prisons into respectable and relatively enlightened places by invoking the U.S. Constitution. Thirty-three states now operate their jails under the watchful eye of the federal bench. Testing the limits of reform has been expensive—costly in human life and to the public purse. Officials estimate Texas alone has spent $1 billion repairing its system, and the future promises only more demands on its oil-busted treasury. At $70,000 a cell, prisons are now a scarce resource. States have to learn to manage them—and husband their use. It's a dreadful conundrum: just as the nation has found that it cannot tolerate its fear of crime, it is also learning that it cannot afford to lock up all its criminals.

The Ham

As a place and a state of mind, Eastham is a symbol for America's prisons. Set on 13,000 acres in East Texas, it is literally at the end of the road—the two-lane State FM (Farm-to-Market) 230 peters out at the front gate. It's out of sight and, except when trouble flares, out of mind. Lifelong neighbors ignore it unless they're caught on a bar stool next to a guard.

Eastham is the end of the road for prisoners, too. Every prison system has a place reserved for the worst cases: in California it's San Quentin; in the federal prisons it's Marion, in Illinois. In Texas, other wardens ship discipline problems to "The Ham." And few inmates are rookies: 98 percent of the 2,500 inmates are recidivists 25 years and older.

Isolated and prickly, Eastham developed its own traditions. Old-timers still refer to "the Eastham way" of doing things: one part head knocking, one part line toeing and two parts hard laboring. Entering inmates know its rep. "If you were going to Eastham, you knew you were going to the bottom of the barrel," says inmate Roland. He rode out to the prison in chains, fresh from a stay in San Quentin for armed robbery and bound over for a new Texas sentence. On the bus, Roland said, "I'm thinking that I'm going to have a murder case on me in six months or end up dead. I had the butterflies — I'm not going to lie."

Roland's appearance, like Eastham's is deceptive. A sweet-faced young man from Lubbock, Texas, Roland spent his criminal career selling cocaine and pulling stickups with pearl-handled pistols. As he gazed out at Eastham, he didn't see the familiar, ominous walls that ring San Quentin and every prison that's ever been featured in a movie. Instead, he saw three-story brick building, surrounded by 10-foot-tall fences with razor-wire frosting. It looked most like a huge farm, albeit one run by a very paranoid owner, a spread that reminded Roland of nothing so much as the plantations he saw in the television series "Roots." Those shows filled him with dread of working as a field slave, yet when he got off the bus he thought he found something worse. A building major — a top guard — assigned him to work on the farm's hoe squad. Roland took umbrage.

"Whoe squad?" he asked in his broad Southern accent. "Man, I'm not no whoe."

No, but he learned to use one, turning the dirt and keeping up with the line of white-uniformed men stretched across a cotton patch. Because if he fell behind, he would have to face the inmate "strikers" who stood ready to "touch him up" with their fists or whatever else was handy.

For Roland, it was a new prison with a new code. In San Quentin, tough as it was, he had understood that "as long as you didn't snitch, steal or disrespect anybody, you didn't have to worry too much — unless it was gang-war time." But in Eastham he wouldn't be left alone to do his own time, because his debt to society was going to be collected by a heavyset white boy named Bunch, the building tender and boss of cell block R.

Even before he boarded the Eastham bus, Roland had been warned about the F and K cell blocks, where black prisoners walked gently and stayed clear of the day room that featured a black doll with a noose around its neck hanging from the television set. The R line was by comparison an equal-opportunity employer: Bunch used one white and two black inmates as assistants. On Roland's first day, the three ushered him into the washroom and began asking questions, a radical departure from the laissez-faire norms of Quentin.

"Where you from, man?"

"Lubbock."

"When do you meet the parole board?"

"2001."

With the preliminaries out of the way, they laid down the law: "We're gonna tell you once how this place works. Any squabbles, you bring them to us. You see anything going on that's not right, bring it to us." Not the guards, *us*. Eventually, Roland also learned why the inmate who controlled the gate to the cell block was banging it shut so often. One slam meant two inmates were fighting; two slams meant a guard was fighting an inmate. The alarms summoned reinforcements. But there was no signal if Bunch, the building tender, was administering a tuneup, Texas prison parlance for a beating. Bunch, it was thought, didn't need any help.

The Tender Trap

In the Texas prisons, architecture was destiny. The cell blocks were 110-foot-long fingers running off the central hallway. When the inmates weren't locked in, or out in the fields working, they could mingle outside their cells in a narrow corridor. But unlike other designs, there was no separate catwalk where guards could patrol safely and observe the entire area. So the guards tended to stay off the tiers, leaving the inmates to police their own ranks. The boss cons were the building tenders: ostensibly responsible for keeping the halls clean but in fact the administration's first line of defense. "It was control from within, with reinforcements," says Keith Price, who has, while working in the Texas prisons, earned his doctorate in criminal justice. "To put it in sociological terms, we co-opted a group of the subculture and, through that, we controlled behavior. We re-enforced it with a kick in the ass or a slap upside the head. That was pretty much the philosophy."

Seldom has there been a utilitarian philosopher quite like Jerry Ray Bolden. He was the tender on Eastham's infamous F line, a "bull tank" reserved for the most difficult inmates, about which Roland had been warned. Bolden was a prize bull, carefully trained for his role. Busted for auto theft at the age of 14, he was sent to a state youth reformatory, known to all as "a gladiator school." He graduated with honors, landing at Eastham in 1958 with a robbery conviction. Since then he's made the round trip twice more, the last time aborting a parole with an aggravated robbery. He is a fearsome character, his hard-muscled body covered with tattoos.

Those on his neck advertise his raison d'etre. One side sports a machine gun, the other a peace sign. "It means peace if you want it, f--- you if you don't," he says with a grin that never manages to reach his eyes.

Jerry Ray was the sort of fellow the prison administrators wanted on their side. Inmates under his charge had one choice: befriend Jerry Ray or fight him. Jerry Ray puts a different gloss on it: "If inmates were wrong, it was eye for an eye and they'd get the shit whipped out of them, see how they liked it... You can't control people who consider themselves gangsters by word of mouth. You let them know every day who's running the tank — whatever it took to convince them. You don't say, 'Would you please do this?' because they'd f--- your ass. You needed a certain amount of force, a certain amount of fear and a certain amount of respect."

Tenders kept order on their blocks, they turned their inmates out for work on time and they snitched to the building major about inmates who were plotting trouble or filing legal complaints. In return came privileges. They wore special clothes. Their cells were never locked. And the carried weapons; Jerry Ray kept a 4½-inch knife in his boot. These inmates had more authority than many guards. "Anytime we were beating someone on the run [cell block] and a guard would tell us to stop, we'd say, 'Shove it,' and 'If you don't like it, call the major'," says onetime tender Tommy B. "And we'd tell the major, 'You've got an idiot working down here who doesn't like us whupping these inmates,' and the next thing, the officer would be put on one of the outside towers." That may sound like inmate braggadocio, but sociologist James W. Marquart spent 19 months working as a guard in Eastham, and he confirms that officers were "reprimanded for messing with building tenders."

But who guards the guard's assistants? For a time in the 1960s that job belonged to Dr. George Beto, director of the state prison system. According to Princeton University Prof. John DiIulio Jr., who has studied Beto's reign, Beto provided hands-on, charismatic leadership. After starting each day reading the Bible in Greek translation, Beto would travel the state, visiting the various prison sites and signing off on the selection of every tender. "Walking George," as he was known, began as a reformer who emphasized work and education. But when he retired in 1972 to teach criminal justice at Sam Houston State University, Beto left a successor, W.J. Estelle, and a system that contained the seeds of its own destruction.

By March 1977, prison officials were losing control over their inmate allies. Building tenders had set up stores, selling food, garments and contraband. Some extorted sex from weaker inmates, others took full-time lovers known as punks. The prison now mirrored life on the streets, only inside the BT's had a license to steal. At Eastham, warden O.S. Savage picked Keith Price out of an administrative job, promoted him to captain and sent him to the cell blocks to restore order. "In the back of your mind you know these BT's are thugs and criminals, and you only trust 'em so far," says Price. But he couldn't make too many threats stick: the state needed the BT's, and both sides knew it.

Unable to change the system, Price became part of it. He didn't stop the beatings, he just tried to have them appropriately administered. Like the times he'd mention to a tender that an inmate "is getting pretty arrogant, knowing that when I put that word out all of a sudden he's gonna get in a fight and probably lose." Or the time he heard about a new prisoner who had injured a child. Says Price, "I let the word out that he was a real sorry human being and people took that to heart." After four months of fist-fights and harassment, the inmate was carried out of Eastham in a strait-jacket. "One of the problems with co-opting inmates," Price says with typical earnestness, "is that it's hard to draw the line between what's right and what's wrong."

The system couldn't reform itself. And conditions over which the prisons had no control were making matters worse. During the '70s the Eastham prison population grew from 1,416 to 2,938, forcing the triple-celling of some prisoners. The cadre of tenders kept pace, but there was no increase in guards. Still, most of the staff were content. Superficially, at least, the joint was orderly, the guards seldom endangered. And the BT's had no interest in changing; at last they had found a place worthy of them. As Tommy B. says, "I think back to whupping men for slamming dominoes too loud or for coming back from chow late, and I ask, 'Why did I do that?' The reason was power."

Justice, Texas Style

The inevitable challenge to the prison structure began sometime in 1970 when an otherwise undistinguished armed robber named David Ruiz found his way into the closet that served as Eastham's law library. There he drafted a 30-page handwritten petition that complained about the conditions of his imprisonment. It was his first writ, and Ruiz, foolhardy but proud, brought it to warden Billy McMillan to be notarized. But the warden, says Ruiz, refused to cooperate. "You know what he did?" Ruiz recalled 16 years later. "He said, 'I'm going to tell you what I think about inmates' rights...This.' And he tore it in half." Ruiz laughed at the memory. "So, I drafted another one."

Billy McMillan and Texas had underestimated the power of an idea whose time had come. A landmark U.S. Supreme Court decision in 1964 had given state prisoners the right to challenge state-prison practices in federal courts. That news slowly spread through the inmate grapevine, often stimulated by circuit-riding civil-rights lawyers looking for injustices to battle. The inmates involved—known to all as "writ writers"—were heirs to the traditional jailhouse lawyers; only these men weren't pleading their own innocence, they were intent on holding entire prison systems guilty of constitutional violations. By late 1971 George Beto found inmates like Ruiz sprinkled through his system; in a classic miscalculation, he ordered them all shipped to the Wynne prison where warden "Beartracks" McAdams had a reputation for bridling troublemakers. But unintentional-ly,, by lumping the men together, Beto created a jailhouse law firm. Synergy had come to the Texas prisons, and the result was a production line of petitions.

These complaints caught the eye of a U.S. district judge in eastern Texas named William Wayne Justice, who saw a pattern of the abuse emerging from the *pro se* filings. As events later proved, Justice was quite willing to apply his vision of constitutional standards to the prisons, once he had a case before him. That technical hurdle evaporated on June 29, 1972, when David Ruiz and other members of the Wynne hoe squad filed their fourth petition. Ruiz had not forgotten warden Billy McMillan: among his complaints, Ruiz challenged the conditions of his confinement at Eastham.

Using Ruiz as a foundation, Justice, the judge, constructed a lawsuit. He pulled seven other complaints from his files and consolidated them into a single action, one which touched every aspect of the prisons, from the reign of the building tenders to the amount of candlepower that lit each cell. Then Justice appointed a lawyer for the inmates, seeking out William Bennett Turner, a litigator from the NAACP Legal Defense Fund, Inc., whom he had met at a prisoners' rights conference in Dallas. Finally, Justice asked the U.S. Department of Justice to join with the inmates as a friend of the court.

This was extraordinary behavior for a judge. But Justice, a self-styled populist who identifies with the "politically powerless," had a long history of judging state and local governments and finding them wanting since Lyndon Johnson put him on the bench. He had ordered school desegregation in his hometown of Tyler. He had forced the state to reorganize its warehouses for the mentally retarded and its youth reformatories—the gladiator schools that turn out Jerry Ray Boldens. These decisions made him a target for abuse. He received obscene mail and phone calls. Local hairdressers turned his wife away. But the attacks seemed to fuel Justice's engines for reform. The son of a popular, emotive trial lawyer, Justice preferred the solitary life of the bench, coolly restraining his passions except in his opinions.

The Ruiz case began in 1972 but didn't come to trial until 1978. For six years the state tried to get a different judge to hear it. The pretrial marathon was one long mind game, as the state and Turner maneuvered for position. On the eve of the trial, Assistant Attorney General Edward Idar asked for a change of venue, to transfer the case from remote Tyler to Houston, a convenient location for the witnesses and lawyers and, incidentally, one outside Justice's district. To everyone's amazement, the judge granted the motion; Idar emerged triumphant. But Justice enjoyed the game, too: privately he had arranged with the federal court in Houston that he would accompany the transferred case.

The trial dragged on for 159 days as inmates told their horror stories and Idar cross-examined them in excruciating detail. In defense, the state denied all of the complaints—insisting, among other things, that the building tenders were no more than janitors—and argued that it ran an efficient, safe and cheap system. "Without being too Texan," TDC director Estelle said, "we think it's a unique organization."

On the bench, Justice had also concluded that it was unique. Early in the trial he had privately decided that the inmates were telling the truth about being abused. The issue for him then became how to force Texas to change its prisons. His friend Frank Johnson, a legendary federal judge in Alabama who also had ordered reforms in state prisons, advised him to treat the state like a mule "and hit it right between the eyes." So, 15 months later, Justice hit the TDC with a 188-page decision, declaring the prisons an affront to civilized society and ordering sweeping remedies that would lead, among other things, to less crowding, more guards, more medical care and the abandonment of the building-tender system. "When the legislature says that you're to be imprisoned, they don't also say that you are to be anally raped or subject to inferior medical care or have someone assaulting you on a day-to-day basis," he says. "The incarceration is punishment, the rest is punishment above what is authorized by law."

W.J. Estelle snorted that the opinion read like "a cheap dime-store novel." In Eastham, nothing changed, except that inmates were being moved into tents in the southern yard.

Cracking the Stone Wall

Call it the Alamo complex. At the headquarters of the Texas Department of Corrections, defiance was the order while Estelle appealed Justice's ruling. There would be no negotiations and no compliance: as Texans like to say, there was nothing broke that needed fixing.

Anticipating this reaction, Justice appointed a special master, Vincent Nathan, to begin enforcing his ruling. Nathan, a transplanted Texan who was teaching law at the University of Toledo, chose to first attack the building tenders whom Estelle insisted were mere glorified janitors. Nathan sent an investigator named David Arnold into the prisons, and he found that the BT's were just what the inmates had described: a brutal, light brigade of guard substitutes. With Arnold's report in hand, Justice decided to force the issue and set a hearing for March 1982.

TDC's lawyers fired back. They asked an appeals court to remove Nathan for "misconduct"—spreading dissension and refusing to turn in inmate informers who possessed weapons. And TDC assigned Steve Martin, a junior lawyer on the headquarters staff, to rebut Arnold's damning report. Martin was one of TDC's own. He had grown up in the panhandle of Texas, fascinated by prisons from the time he read about the notorious Caryl Chessman case in newspapers that he was supposed to be delivering. Martin had started in the TDC system as a guard, had gone to college in his off hours, had worked as a federal probation officer while going to law school and had returned to Texas hoping to make his career in corrections. Within two months he had re-established his local bona fides: part of a ballroom brawl in Huntsville, Martin smashed a beer mug into the face of another man. News of that incident spread reassurance through the prison headquarters: Martin might have earned his law degree, but he still had the sensibility of a good ole guard.

He hadn't lost his memory, either. Martin knew the building-tender system very well. As a novice guard "I learned how to run a cell block from the BT's," he says. "Actually, I learned how to let them run it." On his watch, he had witnessed violence and brutality—one tender had slammed a cell door on a disruptive inmate's head, dragged him to the infirmary and ordered another inmate to stitch the wound with no anesthesia. Handed an assignment to deny the BT's existence, Martin had only one private question: had the system changed?

Martin found that the system had only become worse. And he began hearing tales of the Eastham riot: the official reports were sanitized, but a few guards had told friends the story of the rampaging tenders. As a lawyer, Martin was in an impossible position: not only did his client seem prepared to lie, but the story was not credible.

Anxious and angry, Martin reported his finding to Lee Clyburn, a partner in a private law firm hired by the state. "I started saying, 'Hey, Lee, the system still exists. We're going to get killed in court'." Several times Clyburn interrupted Martin's story, muttering, "This can't be true, this can't be true." His own reputation was involved because a few days earlier he had filed court papers that had denied that the BT system existed.

Clyburn arranged a meeting in Austin with Attorney General Mark White. Preparing for a gubernatorial race, White had personally signed the court papers that attacked Nathan. At the meeting, Martin recalls that Clyburn said simply, "General, we think you should hear what Mr. Martin has discovered." At the back of the room, Martin shuddered. If he told the truth, Estelle might fire him; if he lied, he was postponing the inevitable.

"General," Martin recalls saying, "the TDC has a sophisticated building-tender system under which serious abuses occur frequently, maybe daily."

"You mean," asked White, "we're using inmates as guards?"

"You are," replied Martin, "probably since the first day the lawsuit was filed."

White was dumbfounded. "You mean," he asked, "they've been lying to me all these years?"

There was no immediate change in public posture: the state continued to denounce Justice and Nathan while Martin prepared for another trial his agency was sure to lose. But word of Martin's disclosures reached a couple of key state legislators and members of TDC's civilian board of overseers. Concerned about the mounting cost of the legal bills, now they knew they held a losing hand. Privately, they contacted Nathan and began suing for peace.

By Easter 1982, Nathan had mediated a deal between Texas and William Bennett Turner. In essence, the state agreed to obey Justice's order, pledging to end the reign of inmate rule. Building tenders are never mentioned by name, but the state agreed to install guards where the unmentionables formerly trod. As part of the deal, the state wasn't required to drop its appeal. Eventually a federal appeals court upheld most of the decision, except for Justice's ban on double-celling inmates. While the case was under way the U.S. Supreme Court had ruled that the Constitution does not include a one man, one cell guarantee.

The Warning

At Eastham, reports of the new order were greeted the old-fashioned way. After one inmate told some friends that they didn't have to obey the building tenders anymore, a gang of BT's jumped him. "There were four or five of us, and we beat him so bad with pipes that we knocked his teeth out and you could see his skull," says Tommy B., the building tender. "They [the wardens] put him in solitary for three days because they wanted his swelling to go down before they took him to court." When he recovered, prison officials ordered him to spend two more weeks in isolation—as punishment for fighting.

Meanwhile, in the front office, warden Edward Turner was required to appoint a compliance officer to supervise the court order. He chose Capt. Keith Price, one of his most reliable agents, who didn't do a very thorough job. The settlement called for treating the building tenders like other inmates, including locking them in their cells at night and taking away their weapons. "It was clear in the warden's mind that we just weren't going to do that," Price says. "Some of the paperwork things, that was fine to go ahead and do. But when it came to anything operational, like pinning shut cells, that just wasn't going to happen."

Price faced a personal crisis. His marriage was in trouble; his grad-school classes and regular prison duties left him with little spare time or passion for his family. "Eastham," he says, "was my heart and soul." The riot taught him that his control over the prison was illusory; his identity, his "maleness," as he called it, was utterly tied to his work, but now it seemed wilted. Only his ambition remained pure and unquenched. So he walked away. "I took the first opportunity to get out," he says, which happened to be an opening to head the TDC's operational-audits office, the internal-affairs squad. Price chuckles at the role reversal: "All of a sudden I was the guy comin' around saying, 'Hey, how come you all don't have the cells shut?'"

Inevitably, Price became the nemesis—and hated foe—of his former colleagues. Among other things, his office investigated misconduct charges against wardens and guards. In personal terms, the worst case for Price involved his friend Archie Maples. In September 1983 an Eastham inmate forged a signature on a commissary slip. Learning of the infraction, two assistant wardens, including Maples, took the inmate into an office, where he was slapped around. The inmate complained, but Maples was promoted to head warden at Eastham anyway.

Price and Maples were hunting buddies; Maples was Price's instructor in the local Masonic lodge. But Price supervised the investigation and approved a finding against Maples. He resigned as warden and took a $7,000 pay cut and a job in prison industry. "It bothered me that standard operating procedure suddenly became something that we were going to punish and that certain people were offered up as scapegoats," Price says without showing much lingering regret. "Some of the things I did had a high price, but they were morally right and good for the agency." Maples, who maintains his innocence and still works for TDC, says of his former friend: "We had some differences."

Under pressure, even Eastham began to change. By January 1983, 140 new guards were hired to replace 150 building tenders—an inadequate ratio since the officers left after eight-hour shifts while the BT's worked round the clock. Jerry Ray Bolden watched this transfer of power with disgust. "There are more bosses now, but so many are inexperienced and young," he says. "So many are scared, so many don't know how to stop certain situations. The inmates know there's no one there." More important, the new guards had no sources to keep them abreast of inmate developments. Nor did they patrol the blocks as intimately as the old building tenders.

The inmates' world shifted radically. "I didn't know about Ruiz until the BT's went to panickin'," says Ronnie Roland. "They were losing their jobs, getting reassigned or transferred. A lot were losing sleep. I'd never feel sorry for none of 'em." But the fluid situation called for adjustments. Roland had worked out a détente with his BT; by becoming a competitive boxer, he was free to train—and the BT's made money by wagering on him. Now in a Hobbesian environment, Roland took again to what the prisoners call "playing the fool." Roland explains: "A fool will say anything. 'If you hurt me, I'll kill ya while you eat'." Ronnie, the studied fool, was left alone.

The old order was tottering. By December 1983 Estelle had quit. Within one year, four assistant directors and five wardens resigned, and five others were removed. To put the state's big houses back in order, TDC's board of overseers hired Ray Procunier, the former chief of the California and Virginia prisons. Corrections commissioners are like baseball managers: they rotate among jobs, trying to stay ahead of an unfriendly governor or a riot.

Procunier named lawyer/whistle blower Steve Martin as his executive assistant. In any cultural revolution, the first job of the new leaders is re-education, and TDC was no exception. The prisons were moving from order imposed by a club to one run in a "bureaucratic-legal" manner. Volumes of rules replaced informal norms. The system was set adrift in paper, filing reports with teams of internal and external auditors. It was Martin's job to sell the new way to the guards. "This business that guards can't do anything to control inmates under the court order is a bunch of malarkey," he insists. "What they're really saying is that they don't want to take the trouble or don't know how to do it." Martin's message: don't beat the inmates, punish them. If they won't work, take away privileges. If they lash out, throw them in the hole—following the niceties of due process, of course.

There was a hidden cost to focusing so much official attention on the guards' practices. Gary Gomez, a second-generation officer at Eastham, neatly sums up the frustration: "It got to the point where we had to wonder who the criminal was, me or the guy who did the crime." Along with that resentment came fear and resignation. Sheldon Ekland-Olson, a University of Texas sociologist who has done extensive research on the Texas prisons, says that many guards grew "afraid of the inmates. A lot were unsure of what was required of them. They had families to feed; they just weren't eager to get involved."

With the tenders demoted, and the guards retreating, who was left in charge?

Both Gary Gomez and Judge Justice saw the problem coming. Back in the cell blocks, officers had to deal with inmates without the BT buffer. Like Price before him, Gomez experienced a prison epiphany: "All of a sudden we realized we didn't have control." Instead, "We had some liberal judge telling us how to run a penitentiary, and he's never worked inside a pen." True enough, but Justice had read a lot, and he knew the potential for prison explosions. A power vacuum in the prison, he warned during a 1982 hearing, "will remain unfilled only briefly... Predatory prisoners, disorganized or otherwise, will seize the opportunity to achieve control. As the experiences of other states have demonstrated, such power structures once they arise... defy... vigorous efforts aimed at their elimination."

There was one word missing from his remarks: Gangs. Usually organized along ethnic lines, gangs had become the scourge of many large prison systems, taking over entire institutions. Texas had no tradition of powerful gangs, and Justice worried that they were going to be an unintended consequence of his decision. In 1983 he hired two sociologists to measure the fuse. They too concluded that unless more guards were hired quickly, the system would become "very dangerous and unmanageable."

The fears were justified: is a disaster any worse because you see it coming?

A Time to Die

As best as anyone can tell, the first prison gang members drifted into the Texas system in the mid-'70s, transfers from California who brought their allegiances with them. Locally they became known as the Texas Syndicate (mostly Hispanic) and the Texas Aryan Brotherhood (all white). They organized drug rings to satisfy their own needs, but they were so insignificant a threat that the TDC intelligence unit didn't open a gang file until 1984.

At that point it seemed that any inmate with a letterhead and a friend could establish his own group. The syndicate built on its early foothold, competing for Hispanic loyalty with the Mexican Mafia. The Aryans divided turf with the Texas Mafia. Black inmates formed the Mandingo Warriors and the Brotherhood Self-Defense Family. The gangs were part adolescent peer group, part parody of mobster movies. Admission required ritual tattooing. Their constitutions demanded loyalty till death. They wrote business plans for jailhouse rackets. And, when threatened, they stabbed people.

Darrell Adams joined the Texas Mafia in October 1984 when he was 25 years old and had been a speed addict for 10 years. Sentenced for various burglary, assault and escape charges, Adams saw the gang as the chance of a lifetime. "I thought it might give me the opportunity to make something out of myself because I feel the only thing that's ever stopped me is money," he says. "I was looking for something to give me an edge, some money to start my own business. They also told me I might have to kill somebody."

For a time, Adams helped run the drug trade. The suppliers were visitors who brought the dope into Eastham. Some would flush a small wrapped package down the visitors' toilet and an ally in the prison sewer plant would retrieve it. Others could drop a packet along the road earmarked for a Texas Mafia member working in the fields. But the best drug mules were rogue guards, a fact of prison life that the administration concedes. "You bullshit a guard about how you're rolling in money, and if you could get someone to help it would be worth four, five hundred dollars. He laughs, but he's thinking that he can't buy his old lady a new dress, so he comes back," Adams explains. "You start off small, have him bring in sunglasses and pay him. Then comes whisky. Then you say, 'All you have to do is bring in a lid [of marijuana] a day.' You can always hold this over his head."

By December 1984, Adams was ready for mayhem. Together with three other gang members, Adams says they jumped inmate David Allen Robideaux in an unguarded day room. Robideaux's suspected offense: turning in a gang brother. His punishment: 28 stab wounds, 9 to the chest. The killers were careful, bringing a change of clothes because knife wounds spatter blood. But they were also brazen: when the deed was done, they covered the body with exercise mats, warned nearby inmates to keep their mouths shut and walked away.

That was the third Eastham murder in 1984, one of a record 25 throughout the system. Twenty-seven more were killed in 1985, again three in Eastham. There would have been more but the gangs couldn't stab straight; an additional 622 inmates survived knife wounds. As Adams says, "Hey, not everybody's a professional killer."

By 1985 the prison Zeitgeist had changed: from violence as an instrument of control it had moved to violence as a matter of course. Nor was it confined just to gang activities. The Texas Department of Corrections estimates that there were only 1,300 members in the entire system—most concentrated in a few places like Eastham—yet reported more than 80,000 incidents in '84 and '85. But the joints were crowded, and the inmates had a sense that thanks to the faceless Ruiz they were in the saddle. So they took it out on each other—and increasingly on the guards.

TDC headquarters was in a state of siege. Each death was dealt with as a separate incident, not as part of a systemic collapse. Ray Procunier kept pushing his staff to comply with the court orders. But while new classification rules were being drafted, the cell blocks had become killing grounds. The hand wringing was widespread. Judge Justice demanded more guards. William Bennett Turner wrote to friendly inmates asking them to cool down. Vince Nathan's staff couldn't find a handle on the problem. But all reassured themselves that stopping the killing was beyond their power.

And the state wouldn't act. Steve Martin says he urged the brass to order a massive lock-down, grabbing the suspicious characters and tossing them into isolation cells. But they hesitated, Martin says, because of a state law that required the parole board to begin releasing inmates when the prison population reached 95 percent of capacity. "The administration knew that the way to control [violence] was to segregate people," Martin says now with some bitterness. "Segregating more people meant a need for more single cells. And a need for more single cells meant a need for more early paroles in order to get those cells. And that was not politically popular.

Procunier quit in June 1985. Martin resigned to teach at the University of Texas. The violence remained.

The First Duty of Government

On Aug. 22, 1985, an inmate rushed into Arturo Aguilar's cell at Eastham just as the guards were cranking the doors open and stabbed him in the heart with a nine-inch butcher knife.

From Aug. 31 through Sept. 9, 1985, eight inmates were killed in Texas prisons.

Finally, the state moved. Headquarters ordered a general lock-down and confined 17,000 men to their cells. At Eastham, 1,121—about half the population—were locked in for two weeks while cells were searched and gang members identified. When the siege ended, 587 men had been sent into administrative segregation, Eastham's isolation area. Most will serve the rest of their sentences there. The lock-down was ordered by Procunier's former deputy and his successor, O. Lane McCotter, a retired Army colonel who combined Martin's instincts with Procunier's patience. Looking back, McCotter calls 1985 "the most frustrating time of my life because we couldn't stop the killing as quickly as we needed to. It took us from January to September to get the cells ready and train people in how to use them.

At last, a reform that all Texans could accept: keep the inmates from killing each other. It was not a radical notion; the first duty of government is protecting its citizens, even the ones incarcerated. But first principles can be casualties of chaos. Texas was going back to basics. "Let's put it this way," says Princeton's Professor DiIulio, a student of Texas prisons, "the rules of running a prison remain rather simple. Locking, counting, moving and knowing what's going on inside. If you don't have that, you're going to have problems."

But nothing is simple anymore in TDC. McCotter's iron-fisted reform challenges DiIulio's proposition: how does Eastham lock, count, move and protect men who have been thrown into the new, improved prison hole? In the old days, inmates identified as bad actors were assigned to hard labor in the fields and the untender mercies of inmate overseers. Now troublemakers find themselves shipped to administrative segregation — ad seg as it's known — where they may be held for their entire sentences but possess a list of entitlements: decent food in a well-lit cell complete with a toilet, access to reading material and a schedule of regular exercise. It's the job of Gary Gomez, now promoted to captain, to fulfill that wish.

The obstacles are formidable, not the least of them the inmates themselves. Last May Officer Kevin Crooms carried two pitchers of iced tea down and seg's A block. When he reached the last cell, he saw inmate Rickie Smith sitting on the edge of his bunk next to the bars. Smith sprang first, thrusting a spear fashioned from a broom handle and a 10-spike into Crooms's belly, slashing his lower bowel, ureter and an artery. After two hours of surgery, Crooms survived.

Now all the ad-seg cells are being covered with wire mesh. Inmates are strip-searched and handcuffed before they're escorted down the long, narrow hallways. And two guards slide a protective metal panel along the cell block, shielding the inmate — but not the guards — from other prisoners. Under the court order, inmates are entitled to 7 to 12 hours of recreation a week; but the process of taking them out of their cells, one by one, is so time consuming and labor intensive that most get one hour every four or five days. "It's bad, 24 hours a day in a 9-by-6 cell," says Darrell Adams. "It's degrading, humiliating, it's sick."

The only thing as bad as being confined to ad seg is working there as a guard. With nothing but time on their hands, the prisoners craft weapons from available resources: shivs are made from toothbrushes or pieces of metal bunks. The inmates, with little other sport, routinely curse passing guards. And when they're annoyed or go stir crazy, they fling cups of urine or feces or boiling water. "Having stuff thrown on me is getting to be an every-other-day thing," says guard Gregory Judge as he walks the ad-seg line. As he passes, an inmate shouts, "Hey, you yellow-assed nigger." Judge just keeps moving. "It means you're doing your job."

Gomez remembers a time when a guard didn't have to keep his cool: in the old days the BT's would have attacked any inmate who assaulted a guard — unless the guard got to the man first. Gomez is locked behind the same walls as the inmates and, like most everyone else in Eastham, all he sees is justice denied. "These inmates are getting new rec yards, new towels, food brought to them, and they don't have to work," he says with some bitterness. "It's not right that millions are spent for convicts who refuse to respect anyone. It gets to me that I'm working 12 to 14 hours a day and the inmate is doing nothing. And then he throws piss in an officer's face and I have to tell that officer to bring that inmate his food tray."

Gomez carries his stress with him back into the free world. "I drive my wife crazy," he says. "I don't like her to shower unless the curtain is open because I want to see what's behind it. I wouldn't be half as jumpy if I didn't work here. Don't ever come up behind me and tap my back because, if you do, you're going to get hit.''

The Pursuit of Excellence

The killing had stopped in Eastham but last November another serious problem loomed. Special Master Vince Nathan threatened to shut the prison for other reasons. The only kitchen was a stinking, dilapidated mess. Inmate disciplinary hearings were running a month behind. The telephone system didn't work, the law library was often closed and the roof leaked badly. As a remedy, TDC Commissioner McCotter pledged to do better, and offered up George Waldron, Eastham's fourth new warden in the last five years. A plain-spoken psychologist, Waldron was as concerned with the state of Eastham as Nathan—he had first refused the job, preferring to stay at another unit, but headquarters had insisted.

With that leverage, Waldron became Eastham's first real manager. He had cells painted and the windows replaced. He pulled out years of back orders for supplies and demanded that headquarters deliver. He opened the library, cleaned the kitchen and even cut the paper backlog.

At the same time, he was cultivating the dispirited staff. "This is a place that's done a lot of suffering," he says. "Nobody has ever given these people a break." He came to work in a white cowboy hat and practiced a deliberate informality unless VIP's were in town. When an inmate flung urine on a new guard, Waldron charged into the cell block to take a dose himself—and then ordered photographs to use at the hearing. Under the court order, the inmates got expensive new exercise equipment for the rec yards; Waldron reconditioned the officers' baseball field and upgraded their clubhouse. Structural problems remain: the roof leaks and the nursing staff is too small, but Eastham will remain open.

Waldron is experimenting with techniques of control. Like other wardens, he uses a SORT (Special Operations Response Team) unit of helmeted, padded guards to deal with unruly cell blocks. But he's also created another team—one male guard, one female guard and a chaplain— who will try to persuade inmates to cooperate before force is necessary. This is a gentler approach and, each time it works, Waldron won't have to file reports on a violent incident. "Eastham always had a history of bucking," says Gary Gomez. "But we don't think that way anymore. The feeling now is 'We gotta do it, so let's do it'."

But there are problems in Eastham beyond Waldron's control. The place is too crowded. Besides the 18 cell blocks, Waldron governs open dormitories in cavernous rooms where 80 inmates sleep barracks style. The deadline to build partitions and guarantee 50 square feet per man is next

September but Waldron doubts it will be met. William Bennett Turner, the inmates' lawyer, is tired of waiting.

During the summer Turner asked Justice to hold the state in contempt, citing among other things the overcrowding, the inadequate staffing and the lingering problems in ad seg. Justice is expected to rule later this year, and may fine the state. Waldron has little patience for these tactics. "I understand the game," he says. "They can drive us to the point that they're defeating their own purposes and ours, which is inmate welfare. We've entered some agreements that we haven't met. But I can't shit recreation yards or guards, and neither can the system."

That Was Then, This Is Now

David Ruiz, the man who started it all, is back in prison again, this time on a perjury rap. He's doing his time in the federal pen at Leavenworth, Kans., because Texas couldn't guarantee his safety. Earlier this year he wrote Judge Justice, offering to help with the case that bears his name, but thus far the judge has passed.

Justice won't formally comment out of court on the impact of the case. Friends say he was anguished by the inmate deaths but add that he doesn't feel personally responsible. In his view, TDC failed. "One thing is certain," he declared in a recent speech, "if governmental organizations are... prepared to work *with* courts in the vindication of constitutional rights and not *against* them, then some degree of judicial restraint will be in order." Until that millennial day, Justice intends to keep up the pressure.

Gov. Mark White is running for re-election and scrambling to keep the prison issue from boiling over into the campaign. Justice rebuffed his last idea, proposing to transfer 300 prisoners to an abandoned National Guard post to ease the crowding. White's still trying, he says, but he always reminds his audiences that the prisoners "were not sent up for having dirty faces in Sunday School." Many legislators feel the same way, especially during the tight budget days of the Great Texas Oil Bust of '86. Why haven't we appealed? they demanded at a recent meeting. We did, explained Assistant Attorney General Scott McCown, and we lost.

William Bennett Turner keeps winning in court. He's received a Justice-ordered $1.2 million fee and he's proud of his achievements. But sometimes he wonders if circumstances may yet overmatch a good lawyer's skill. "They [the inmates] don't have room to turn around because of the press of bodies," he says. "Over all it's a little better, but it's a close call. Unless they beat the crowding problem all this won't be worth having done."

George Waldron, too, is a man who lives with ambiguities. On a yellow sheet he tallies up seven Ruiz-inspired improvements—including medical care and staff accountability—and eight debits—including the murderous violence and a dizzying array of procedures. "The old system was tough," he says, "but look at that lockup down in ad seg, with no way of ever getting out. Is that more humane? I don't know, the verdict just isn't in yet." Last week Waldron's hard pace caught up with him: he suffered a mild heart attack and will be on leave for at least four weeks.

For all his frustration, Gary Gomez plans to hang on at Eastham, hoping to climb further up the ranks. He wants his men to get some respect. "The bosses are now seen as the bad guys, stupid, carrying clubs," he sighs. "But a lot of us are good. The court monitors are worried about recreation and showers, and I'm worried about security and saving lives."

And the costs of change? "The problem with the notion that reform brought murderous violence is that you get to a 'So what?'" says David Arnold, one of the court monitors. "We phased the building tenders out and we phased in staffing increases. You just can't do it all overnight." But Steve Martin is still tortured by the thought that the state could have cooperated sooner, moved faster and saved 52 lives. He's finishing a book on Texas prisons with sociologist Sheldon Ekland-Olson and he's joining an Austin law firm. "But first I'm a corrections man," he says. "I'd love to run a system under the current 'constraints.' I hope to prove it can be done someday."

Ronnie Roland is still a corrections man, too, living in one of Eastham's dormitories, "bumping knees" with the inmate in the next bed. "I'm not goin' to say it's a plantation, 'cause when I first rode up that's exactly what it was," he says. "And I'm not goin' to call it a country club, either. What this is is a prison."

Darrell Adams has been moved to a prison out of state because he's agreed to turn state's evidence in the upcoming Robideaux murder trial. Now he won't be a hit man himself, but a target for Texas Mafia retribution. "I've put a snitch jacket on myself," he says, using inmate slang for taking on a reputation. "I'm No. 1 on the hit list."

Jerry Ray Bolden is still looking out for number one, doing his time peacefully in an Eastham dorm with 45 other inmates. He works as a porter, pounds a heavy punching bag and hopes for a parole in 12 years. Meanwhile, he's not worried about inmates seeking revenge on him. "I'll stop them any way I can," he says. "When the federal court sent these punks their nuts, it didn't take mine away from me."

Keith Price has been rewarded for his performance in Internal Affairs by becoming a warden, now assigned to Darrington, one of TDC's other hard cases. He says he's found God and contentment and only looks back when he's asked. "The difference between me and some of my colleagues at Eastham is that I changed," he says. "That's called survivin' in the world. It's why the dinosaurs didn't survive. Our organization evolved and I simply changed with it, which seems to me to be the only thing that a thinking man would do. It doesn't have anything to do with loyalty or how I feel about either model of [inmate] control. It's simply a matter of pragmatism. They're the dinosaurs. I'm the new man."

Such are the disorderly lessons of reform, several steps forward and different steps back, many lives helped, others damaged and some lost. In other words, reform imitates life, demanding will and zeal — and humility. But resignation seems a less desirable alternative, ethically and practically. For prisons that operate utterly isolated from view, by abhorrent codes of conduct, can become dark and vicious places. And that's reason enough to promote order and change in institutions that lock in cages men who will eventually return to our streets.

17

"This Man Has Expired": Witness to an Execution

Robert Johnson

The death penalty has made a comeback in recent years. In the late sixties and through most of the seventies, such a thing seemed impossible. There was a moratorium on executions in the U.S., backed by the authority of the Supreme Court. The hiatus lasted roughly a decade. Coming on the heels of a gradual but persistent decline in the use of the death penalty in the Western world, it appeared to some that executions would pass from the American scene [cf. *Commonweal*, January 15, 1988]. Nothing could have been further from the truth.

Beginning with the execution of Gary Gilmore in 1977, over 100 people have been put to death, most of them in the last few years. Some 2,200 prisoners are presently confined on death rows across the nation. The majority of these prisoners have lived under sentence of death for years, in some cases a decade or more, and are running out of legal appeals. It is fair to say that the death penalty is alive and well in America, and that executions will be with us for the foreseeable future.

Gilmore's execution marked the resurrection of the modern death penalty and was big news. It was commemorated in a best-selling tome by Norman Mailer, *The Executioner's Song*. The title was deceptive. Like others who have examined the death penalty, Mailer told us a great deal about the condemned but very little about the executioners. Indeed, if we dwell on Mailer's account, the executioner's story is not only unsung; it is distorted.

© Commonweal Foundation 1989.

Gilmore's execution was quite atypical. His was an instance of state-assisted suicide accompanied by an element of romance and played out against a backdrop of media fanfare. Unrepentant and unafraid, Gilmore refused to appeal his conviction. He dared the state of Utah to take his life, and the media repeated the challenge until it became a taunt that may well have goaded officials to action. A failed suicide pact with his lover staged only days before the execution, using drugs she delivered to him in a visit marked by unusual intimacy, added a hint of melodrama to the proceedings. Gilmore's final words, "Let's do it," seemed to invite the lethal hail of bullets from the firing squad. The nonchalant phrase, at once fatalistic and brazenly rebellious, became Gilmore's epitaph. It clinched his outlaw-hero image, and found its way onto tee shirts that confirmed his celebrity status.

Befitting a celebrity, Gilmore was treated with unusual leniency by prison officials during his confinement on death row. He was, for example, allowed to hold a party the night before his execution, during which he was free to eat, drink, and make merry with his guests until the early morning hours. This is not entirely unprecedented. Notorious English convicts of centuries past would throw farewell balls in prison on the eve of their executions. News accounts of such affairs sometimes included a commentary on the richness of the table and the quality of the dancing. For the record, Gilmore served Tang, Kool-Aid, cookies, and coffee, later supplemented by contraband pizza and an unidentified liquor. Periodically, he gobbled drugs obligingly provided by the prison pharmacy. He played a modest arrangement of rock music albums but refrained from dancing.

Gilmore's execution generally, like his parting fete, was decidedly out of step with the tenor of the modern death penalty. Most condemned prisoners fight to save their lives, not to have them taken. They do not see their fate in romantic terms; there are no farewell parties. Nor are they given medication to ease their anxiety or win their compliance. The subjects of typical executions remain anonymous to the public and even to their keepers. They are very much alone at the end.

In contrast to Mailer's account, the focus of the research I have conducted is on the executioners themselves as they carry out typical executions. In my experience executioners—not unlike Mailer himself—can be quite voluble, and sometimes quite moving, in expressing themselves. I shall draw upon their words to describe the death work they carry out in our name.

Death Work and Death Workers

Executioners are not a popular subject of social research, let alone conversation at the dinner table or cocktail party. We simply don't give the subject much thought. When we think of executioners at all, the imagery runs to individual men of disreputable, or at least questionable, character who work stealthily behind the scenes to carry out their grim labors. We picture hooded men hiding in the shadow of the gallows, or anonymous figures lurking out of sight behind electric chairs, gas chambers, firing blinds, or, more recently, hospital gurneys. We wonder who would do such grisly work and how they sleep at night.

This image of the executioner as a sinister and often solitary character is today misleading. To be sure, a few states hire free-lance executioners and traffic in macabre theatrics. Executioners may be picked up under cover of darkness and some may still wear black hoods. But today, executions are generally the work of a highly disciplined and efficient team of correctional officers.

Broadly speaking, the execution process as it is now practiced starts with the prisoner's confinement on death row, an oppressive prison-within-a-prison where the condemned are housed, sometimes for years, awaiting execution. Death work gains momentum when an execution date draws near and the prisoner is moved to the death house, a short walk from the death chamber. Finally, the process culminates in the death watch, a twenty-four-hour period that ends when the prisoner has been executed.

This final period, the death watch, is generally undertaken by correctional officers who work as a team and report directly to the prison warden. The warden or his representative, in turn, must by law preside over the execution. In many states, it is a member of the death watch or execution team, acting under the warden's authority, who in fact plays the formal role of executioner. Though this officer may technically work alone, his teammates view the execution as a shared responsibility. As one officer on the death watch told me in no uncertain terms: "We all take part in it; we all play 100 percent in it, too. That takes the load off this one individual [who pulls the switch]." The formal executioner concurred. "Everyone on the team can do it, and nobody will tell you I did it. I know my team." I found nothing in my research to dispute these claims.

The officers of these death watch teams are our modern executioners. As part of a larger study of the death work process, I studied one such group. This team, comprised of nine seasoned officers of varying ranks, had carried out five electrocutions at the time I began my research. I interviewed each officer on the team after the fifth execution, then served as an official witness at a sixth electrocution. Later, I served as a behind-the-scenes observer during their seventh execution. The results of this phase of my research form the substance of this essay.

The Death Watch Team

The death watch or execution team members refer to themselves, with evident pride, as simply "the team." This pride is shared by other correctional officials. The warden at the institution I was observing praised members of the team as solid citizens—in his words, country boys. These country boys, he assured me, could be counted on to do the job and do it well. As a fellow administrator put it, "an execution is something [that] needs to be done and good people, dedicated people who believe in the American system should do it. And there's a certain amount of feeling, probably one to another, that they're part of that— that when they have to hang tough, they can do it, and they can do it right. And that it's just the right thing to do."

The official view is that an execution is a job that has to be done, and done right. The death penalty is, after all, the law of the land. In this context, the phrase "done right" means that an execution should be a proper, professional, dignified undertaking. In the words of a prison administrator, "We had to be sure that we did it properly, professionally, and [that] we gave as much dignity to the person as we possibly could in the process. . . . If you've gotta do it, it might just as well be done the way it's supposed to be done—without any sensation."

In the language of the prison officials, "proper" refers to procedures that go off smoothly; "professional" means without personal feelings that intrude on the procedures in any way. The desire for executions that take place "without any sensation" no doubt refers to the absence of media sensationalism, particularly if there should be an embarrassing and undignified hitch in the procedures, for example, a prisoner who breaks down or becomes violent and must be forcibly placed in the electric chair as witnesses, some from the media, look on in horror. Still, I can't help but note that this may be a revealing slip of the tongue. For executions are indeed meant to go off without any human feeling, without any sensation. A profound absence of feeling would seem to capture the bureaucratic ideal embodied in the modern execution.

The view of executions held by the execution team members parallels that of correctional administrators but is somewhat more restrained. The officers of the team are closer to the killing and dying, and are less apt to wax abstract or eloquent in describing the process. Listen to one man's observations:

> It's a job. I don't take it personally. You know, I don't take it like I'm having a grudge against this person and this person has done something to me. I'm just carrying out a job, doing what I was asked to do. . . . This man has been sentenced to death in the courts. This is the law and he broke this law, and he has to suffer the consequences. And one of the consequences is to put him to death.

I found that few members of the execution team support the death penalty outright or without reservation. Having seen executions close up, many of them have lingering doubts about the justice or wisdom of this sanction. As one officer put it:

> I'm not sure the death penalty is the right way. I don't know if there is a right answer. So I look at it like this: if it's gotta be done, at least it can be done in a humane way, if there is such a word for it. . . . The only way it should be done, I feel, is the way we do it. It's done professionally; it's not no horseplaying. Everything is done by documentation. On time. By the book.

Arranging executions that occur "without any sensation" and that go "by the book" is no mean task, but it is a task that is undertaken in earnest by the execution team. The tone of the enterprise is set by the team leader, a man who takes a hard-boiled, no-nonsense approach to correctional work in general and death work in particular. "My style," he says, "is this: if it's a job to do, get it done. Do it and that's it." He seeks out kindred spirits, men who see killing condemned prisoners as a job—a dirty job one does reluctantly, perhaps, but above all a job one carries out dispassionately and in the line of duty.

To make sure that line of duty is a straight and accurate one, the death watch team has been carefully drilled by the team leader in the mechanics of execution. The process has been broken down into simple, discrete tasks and practiced repeatedly. The team leader describes the division of labor in the following exchange:

> The execution team is a nine-officer team and each one has certain things to do. When I would train you, maybe you'd buckle a belt, that might be all you'd have to do. . . . And you'd be expected to do one thing and that's all you'd be expected to do. And if everybody does what they were taught, or what they were trained to do, at the end the man would be put in the chair and everything would be complete. It's all come together now.
>
> So it's broken down into very small steps. . . .
>
> *Very small*, yes. Each person has *one* thing to do.
>
> I see. What's the purpose of breaking it down into such small steps?
>
> So people won't get confused. I've learned it's kind of a tense time. When you're executin' a person, killing a person—you call it killin', executin', whatever you want—the man dies anyway. I find the less you got on your mind, why, the better you'll carry it out. So it's just very simple things. And so far, you know, it's all come together, we haven't had any problems.

This division of labor allows each man on the execution team to become a specialist, a technician with a sense of pride in his work. Said one man,

> My assignment is the leg piece. Right leg. I roll his pants' leg up, place a piece [electrode] on his leg, strap his leg in. . . . I've got all the moves

down pat. We train from different posts; I can do any of them. But that's
my main post.

The implication is not that the officers are incapable of performing multiple
or complex tasks, but simply that it is more efficient to focus each officer's
efforts on one easy task.

An essential part of the training is practice. Practice is meant to produce
a confident group, capable of fast and accurate performance under pressure.
The rewards of practice are reaped in improved performance. Executions take
place with increasing efficiency, and eventually occur with precision. "The
first one was grisly," a team member confided to me. He explained that there
was a certain amount of fumbling, which made the execution seem intermi-
nable. There were technical problems as well: The generator was set too high
so the body was badly burned. But that is the past, the officer assured me.
"The ones now, we know what we're doing. It's just like clockwork."

The Death Watch

The death-watch team is deployed during the last twenty-four hours before
an execution. In the state under study, the death watch starts at 11 o'clock
the night before the execution and ends at 11 o'clock the next night when
the execution takes place. At least two officers would be with the prisoner
at any given time during that period. Their objective is to keep the prisoner
alive and "on schedule." That is, to move him through a series of critical
and cumulatively demoralizing junctures that begin with his last meal and
end with his last walk. When the time comes, they must deliver the prisoner
up for execution as quickly and unobtrusively as possible.

Broadly speaking, the job of the death watch officer, as one man put it.
"is to sit and keep the inmate calm for the last twenty-four hours—and get
the man ready to go." Keeping a condemned prisoner calm means, in part,
serving his immediate needs. It seems paradoxical to think of the death watch
officers as providing services to the condemned, but the logistics of the job
make service a central obligation of the officers. Here's how one officer made
this point:

> Well, you can't help but be involved with many of the things that he's
> involved with. Because if he wants to make a call to his family, well,
> you'll have to dial the number. And you keep records of whatever calls
> he makes. If he wants a cigarette, well he's not allowed to keep matches
> so you light it for him. You've got to pour his coffee, too. So you're
> aware what he's doing. It's not like you can just ignore him. You've
> gotta just be with him whether he wants it or not, and cater to his needs.

Officers cater to the condemned because contented inmates are easier to keep under control. To a man, the officers say this is so. But one can never trust even a contented, condemned prisoner.

The death-watch officers see condemned prisoners as men with explosive personalities. "You don't know what, what a man's gonna do," noted one officer. "He's liable to snap, he's liable to pass out. We watch him all the time to prevent him from committing suicide. You've got to be ready—he's liable to do anything." The prisoner is never out of at least one officer's sight. Thus surveillance is constant, and control, for all intents and purposes, is total.

Relations between the officers and their charges during the death watch can be quite intense. Watching and being watched are central to this enterprise, and these are always engaging activities, particularly when the stakes are life and death. These relations are, nevertheless, utterly impersonal; there are no grudges but neither is there compassion or fellow-feeling. Officers are civil but cool; they keep an emotional distance from the men they are about to kill. To do otherwise, they maintain, would make it harder to execute condemned prisoners. The attitude of the officers is that the prisoners arrive as strangers and are easier to kill if they stay that way.

During the last five or six hours, two specific team officers are assigned to guard the prisoner. Unlike their more taciturn and aloof colleagues on earlier shifts, these officers make a conscious effort to talk with the prisoner. In one officer's words, "We just keep them right there and keep talking to them— about anything except the chair." The point of these conversations is not merely to pass time; it is to keep tabs on the prisoner's state of mind, and to steer him away from subjects that might depress, anger, or otherwise upset him. Sociability, in other words, quite explicitly serves as a source of social control. Relationships, such as they are, serve purely manipulative ends. This is impersonality at its worst, masquerading as concern for the strangers one hopes to execute with as little trouble as possible.

Generally speaking, as the execution moves closer, the mood becomes more somber and subdued. There is a last meal. Prisoners can order pretty much what they want, but most eat little or nothing at all. At this point, the prisoners may steadfastly maintain that their executions will be stayed. Such bravado is belied by their loss of appetite. "You can see them going down," said one officer. "Food is the last thing they got on their minds."

Next the prisoners must box their meager worldly goods. These are inventoried by the staff, recorded on a one-page checklist form, and marked for disposition to family or friends. Prisoners are visibly saddened, even moved to tears, by this procedure, which at once summarizes their lives and highlights the imminence of death. At this point, said one of the officers, "I really get into him; I watch him real close." The execution schedule, the officer pointed out, is "picking up momentum, and we don't want to lose control of the situation."

This momentum is not lost on the condemned prisoner. Critical milestones have been passed. The prisoner moves in a limbo existence devoid of food or possessions; he has seen the last of such things, unless he receives a stay of execution and rejoins the living. His identity is expropriated as well. The critical juncture in this regard is the shaving of the man's head (including facial hair) and right leg. Hair is shaved to facilitate the electrocution: it reduces physical resistance to electricity and minimizes singeing and burning. But the process has obvious psychological significance as well, adding greatly to the momentum of the execution.

The shaving procedure is quite public and intimidating. The condemned man is taken from his cell and seated in the middle of the tier. His hands and feet are cuffed, and he is dressed only in undershorts. The entire death watch team is assembled around him. They stay at a discrete distance, but it is obvious that they are there to maintain control should he resist in any way or make any untoward move. As a rule, the man is overwhelmed. As one officer told me in blunt terms, "Come eight o'clock, we've got a dead man. Eight o'clock is when we shave the man. We take his identity; it goes with the hair." This taking of identity is indeed a collective process—the team makes a forceful "we," the prisoner their helpless object. The staff is confident that the prisoner's capacity to resist is now compromised. What is left of the man erodes gradually and, according to the officers, perceptibly over the remaining three hours before the execution.

After the prisoner has been shaved, he is then made to shower and don a fresh set of clothes for the execution. The clothes are unremarkable in appearance, except that velcro replaces buttons and zippers, to reduce the chance of burning the body. The main significance of the clothes is symbolic: they mark the prisoner as a man who is ready for execution. Now physically "prepped," to quote one team member, the prisoner is placed in an empty tomblike cell, the death cell. All that is left is the wait. During this fateful period, the prisoner is more like an object "without any sensation" than like a flesh-and-blood person on the threshold of death.

For condemned prisoners, like Gilmore, who come to accept and even to relish their impending deaths, a genuine calm seems to prevail. It is as if they can transcend the dehumanizing forces at work around them and go to their deaths in peace. For most condemned prisoners, however, numb resignation rather than peaceful acceptance is the norm. By the accounts of the death-watch officers, these more typical prisoners are beaten men. Listen to the officers' accounts:

> A lot of 'em die in their minds before they go to that chair. I've never known of one or heard of one putting up a fight. . . . By the time they walk to the chair, they've completely faced it. Such a reality most people can't understand. Cause they don't fight it. They don't seem to have

anything to say. It's just something like "Get it over with." They may be numb, sort of in a trance.

They go through stages. And, at this stage, they're real humble. Humblest bunch of people I ever seen. Most all of 'em is real, real weak. Most of the time you'd only need one or two people to carry out an execution, as weak and as humble as they are.

These men seem barely human and alive to their keepers. They wait meekly to be escorted to their deaths. The people who come for them are the warden and the remainder of the death watch team, flanked by high-ranking correctional officials. The warden reads the court order, known popularly as a death warrant. This is, as one officer said, "the real deal," and nobody misses its significance. The condemned prisoners then go to their deaths compliantly, captives of the inexorable, irresistible momentum of the situation. As one officer put it, "There's no struggle. . . . They just walk right on in there." So too, do the staff "just walk right on in there," following a routine they have come to know well. Both the condemned and the executioners, it would seem, find a relief of sorts in mindless mechanical conformity to the modern execution drill.

Witness to an Execution

As the team and administrators prepare to commence the good fight, as they might say, another group, the official witnesses, are also preparing themselves for their role in the execution. Numbering between six and twelve for any given execution, the official witnesses are disinterested citizens in good standing drawn from a cross-section of the state's population. If you will, they are every good or decent person, called upon to represent the community and use their good offices to testify to the propriety of the execution. I served as an official witness at the execution of an inmate.

At eight in the evening about the time the prisoner is shaved in preparation for the execution, the witnesses are assembled. Eleven in all, we included three newspaper and two television reporters, a state trooper, two police officers, a magistrate, a businessman, and myself. We were picked up in the parking lot behind the main office of the corrections department. There was nothing unusual or even memorable about any of this. Gothic touches were notable by their absence. It wasn't a dark and stormy night; no one emerged from the shadows to lead us to the prison gates.

Mundane considerations prevailed. The van sent for us was missing a few rows of seats so there wasn't enough room for all of us. Obliging prison officials volunteered their cars. Our rather ordinary cavalcade reached the prison but only after getting lost. Once within the prison's walls, we were sequestered for some two hours in a bare and almost shabby administrative conference room. A public information officer was assigned to accompany us and answer our questions. We grilled this official about the prisoner and the execution procedure he would undergo shortly, but little information was to be had. The man confessed ignorance on the most basic points. Disgruntled at this and increasingly anxious, we made small talk and drank coffee.

At 10:40 P.M., roughly two-and-a-half hours after we were assembled and only twenty minutes before the execution was scheduled to occur, the witnesses were taken to the basement of the prison's administrative building, frisked, then led down an alleyway that ran along the exterior of the building. We entered a neighboring cell block and were admitted to a vestibule adjoining the death chamber. Each of us signed a log, and was then led off to the witness area. To our left, around a corner some thirty feet away, the prisoner sat in the condemned cell. He couldn't see us, but I'm quite certain he could hear us. It occurred to me that our arrival was a fateful reminder for the prisoner. The next group would be led by the warden, and it would be coming for him.

We entered the witness area, a room within the death chamber, and took our seats. A picture window covering the front wall of the witness room offered a clear view of the electric chair, which was about twelve feet away from us and well illuminated. The chair, a large, high-back solid oak structure with imposing black straps, dominated the death chamber. Behind it, on the back wall, was an open panel full of coils and lights. Peeling paint hung from the ceiling and walls; water stains from persistent leaks were everywhere in evidence.

Two officers, one a hulking figure weighing some 400 pounds, stood alongside the electric chair. Each had his hands crossed at the lap and wore a forbidding, blank expression on his face. The witnesses gazed at them and the chair, most of us scribbling notes furiously. We did this, I suppose, as much to record the experience as to have a distraction from the growing tension. A correctional officer entered the witness room and announced that a trial run of the machinery would be undertaken. Seconds later, lights flashed on the control panel behind the chair indicating that the chair was in working order. A white curtain, opened for the test, separated the chair and the witness area. After the test, the curtain was drawn. More tests were performed behind the curtain. Afterwards, the curtain was reopened, and would be left open until the execution was over. Then it would be closed to allow the officers to remove the body.

A handful of high-level correctional officials were present in the death chamber, standing just outside the witness area. There were two regional administrators, the director of the Department of Corrections, and the prison warden. The prisoner's chaplain and lawyer were also present. Other than the chaplain's black religious garb, subdued grey pinstripes and bland correctional uniforms prevailed. All parties were quite solemn.

At 10:58 the prisoner entered the death chamber. He was, I knew from my research, a man with a checkered, tragic past. He had been grossly abused as a child, and went on to become grossly abusive of others. I was told he could not describe his life, from childhood on, without talking about confrontations in defense of a precarious sense of self—at home, in school, on the streets, in the prison yard. Belittled by life and choking with rage, he was hungry to be noticed. Paradoxically, he had found his moment in the spotlight, but it was a dim and unflattering light cast before a small and unappreciative audience. "He'd pose for cameras in the chair—for the attention," his counselor had told me earlier in the day. But the truth was that the prisoner wasn't smiling, and there were no cameras.

The prisoner walked quickly and silently toward the chair, an escort of officers in tow. His eyes were turned downward, his expression a bit glazed. Like many before him, the prisoner had threatened to stage a last stand. But that was lifetimes ago, on death row. In the death house, he joined the humble bunch and kept to the executioner's schedule. He appeared to have given up on life before he died in the chair.

En route to the chair, the prisoner stumbled slightly, as if the momentum of the event had overtaken him. Were he not held securely by two officers, one at each elbow, he might have fallen. Were the routine to be broken in this or indeed any other way, the officers believe, the prisoner might faint or panic or become violent, and have to be forcibly placed in the chair. Perhaps as a precaution, when the prisoner reached the chair he did not turn on his own but rather was turned, firmly but without malice, by the officers in his escort. These included the two men at his elbows, and four others who followed behind him. Once the prisoner was seated, again with help, the officers strapped him into the chair.

The execution team worked with machine precision. Like a disciplined swarm, they enveloped him. Arms, legs, stomach, chest, and head were secured in a matter of seconds. Electrodes were attached to the cap holding his head and to the strap holding his exposed right leg. A leather mask was placed over his face. The last officer mopped the prisoner's brow, then touched his hand in a gesture of farewell.

During the brief procession to the electric chair, the prisoner was attended by a chaplain. As the execution team worked feverishly to secure the condemned man's body, the chaplain, who appeared to be upset, leaned over him and placed his forehead in contact with the prisoner's, whispering urgently. The priest might have been praying, but I had the impression he was consoling the man, perhaps assuring him that a forgiving God awaited him in the next life. If he heard the chaplain, I doubt the man comprehended his message. He didn't seem comforted. Rather, he looked stricken and appeared to be in shock. Perhaps the priest's urgent ministrations betrayed his doubts that the prisoner could hold himself together. The chaplain then withdrew at the warden's request, allowing the officers to affix the death mask.

The strapped and masked figure sat before us, utterly alone, waiting to be killed. The cap and mask dominated his face. The cap was nothing more than a sponge encased in a leather shell with a metal piece at the top to accept an electrode. It looked decrepit and resembled a cheap, ill-fitting toupee. The mask, made entirely of leather, appeared soiled and worn. It had two parts. The bottom part covered the chin and mouth, the top the eyes and lower forehead. Only the nose was exposed. The effect of a rigidly restrained body, together with the bizarre cap and the protruding nose, was nothing short of grotesque. A faceless man breathed before us in a tragi-comic trance, waiting for a blast of electricity that would extinguish his life. Endless seconds passed. His last act was to swallow, nervously, pathetically, with his Adam's apple bobbing. I was struck by that simple movement then, and can't forget it even now. It told me, as nothing else did, that in the prisoner's restrained body, behind that mask, lurked a fellow human being who, at some level, however primitive, knew or sensed himself to be moments from death.

The condemned man sat perfectly still for what seemed an eternity but was in fact no more than thirty seconds. Finally the electricity hit him. His body stiffened spasmodically, though only briefly. A thin swirl of smoke trailed away from his head and then dissipated quickly. The body remained taut, with the right foot raised slightly at the heel, seemingly frozen there. A brief pause, then another minute of shock. When it was over, the body was flaccid and inert.

Three minutes passed while the officials let the body cool. (Immediately after the execution, I'm told, the body would be too hot to touch and would blister anyone who did.) All eyes were riveted to the chair; I felt trapped in my witness seat, at once transfixed and yet eager for release. I can't recall any clear thoughts from that moment. One of the death watch officers later volunteered that he shared this experience of staring blankly at the execution scene. Had the prisoner's mind been mercifully blank before the end? I hoped so.

An officer walked up to the body, opened the shirt at chest level, then continued on to get the physician from an adjoining room. The physician listened for a heartbeat. Hearing none, he turned to the warden and said, "This man has expired." The warden, speaking to the director, solemnly intoned: "Mr. Director, the court order has been fulfilled." The curtain was then drawn and the witnesses filed out.

The Morning After

As the team prepared the body for the morgue, the witnesses were led to the front door of the prison. On the way, we passed a number of cell blocks. We could hear the normal sounds of prison life, including the occasional catcall and lewd comment hurled at uninvited guests like ourselves. But no trouble came in the wake of the execution. Small protests were going on outside the walls, we were told, but we could not hear them. Soon the media would be gone; the protestors would disperse and head for their homes. The prisoners, already home, had been indifferent to the proceedings, as they always are unless the condemned prisoner had been a figure of some consequence in the convict community. Then there might be tension and maybe even a modest disturbance on a prison tier or two. But few convict luminaries are executed, and the dead man had not been one of them. Our escort officer offered a sad tribute to the prisoner: "The inmates, they didn't care about this guy."

I couldn't help but think they weren't alone in this. The executioners went home and set about their lives. Having taken life, they would savor a bit of life themselves. They showered, ate, made love, slept, then took a day or two off. For some, the prisoner's image would linger for that night. The men who strapped him in remembered what it was like to touch him; they showered as soon as they got home to wash off the feel and smell of death. One official sat up picturing how the prisoner looked at the end. (I had a few drinks myself that night with that same image for company.) There was some talk about delayed reactions to the stress of carrying out executions. Though such concerns seemed remote that evening, I learned later that problems would surface for some of the officers. But no one on the team, then or later, was haunted by the executed man's memory, nor would anyone grieve for him. "When I go home after one of these things," said one man, "I sleep like a rock." His may or may not be the sleep of the just, but one can only marvel at such a thing, and perhaps envy such a man.

18

Removing Children from Adult Jails: A Guide to Action

Community Research Forum
University of Illinois

Who Are the Children in Adult Jails

It is estimated that 500,000 juveniles a year are held in adult jails and lockups in the United States. The Children's Defense Fund states that even the half-million figure is "grossly understated." Although federal legislation requires the separation by sight and sound of juveniles and adult offenders, they are confined together in many states and local communities. In some places, "sight and sound separation" has resulted in juveniles being placed in solitary confinement for long periods.

Most of the children in jails are confined for property or minor offenses. Eighteen percent are in jails for acts such as running away, or being incorrigible—status offenses which would not be crimes if committed by adults. A recent study by HEW of 755,000 juvenile runaways shows that many were not seeking adventure but were fleeing emotional, physical, and sexual abuse:

> A growing number of teenagers were what the bureau describes as *throwaways,* young people who are forced out of their homes.

This document was prepared by the Community Research Forum of The University of Illinois under grant no. 78-JS-AX-0046 awarded by the Office of Juvenile Justice and Delinquency Prevention, Law Enforcement Assistance Administration, United States Department of Justice. Points of view or opinions stated in this document are those of the Community Research Forum and do not necessarily represent the official position of the U.S. Department of Justice. © 1980 The Board of Trustees of The University of Illinois.

We're finding in programs that we're seeing an increase in the number of kids that are being pushed out of their homes, or they leave their homes at 15, 16 years of age by some kind of mutual agreement between the parent and the young person.

When the young are forced out of the homes, we're talking about adolescent abuse, sexual abuse; we're talking about the destruction of the family unit being such that the young people are just told to go out and make it on their own.

The National Youth Work Alliance, a national organization of community-based youth services in Washington, states that "there is another kind of *throwaway,* the teenager who is forced out of his home for economic reasons."

With inflation in general and the housing market in particular, people are living in smaller and smaller units with less and less space, sort of like, just how many little birds can fit in a nest?

Well, somebody gets pushed out and you see this particularly in large cities with minority young people where they just don't fit in the apartment anymore; that seems to be an increasing factor of a lot of homeless youth.

Perhaps the most penetrating examination of children in adult jails was conducted by the Children's Defense Fund. Their nine state study found that children, including status offenders, frequently "are placed in cells with adults charged with violent crime." They discovered that:

- A 15-year old girl was confined with a 35-year old woman jailed for murder.
- A 16-year old boy was confined with a man charged with murder, who raped the boy on three occasions.
- A 16-year old boy, arrested for shoplifting, was confined in a cell with a man charged with shooting another man.
- A 16-year old boy was confined with five men. One was AWOL from the military, one was charged with assault and battery, one was an escaped prisoner from another state, one was in jail charged with murder of his wife, and one was charged with molesting three boys on the street.
- A 14-year old girl was confined in a cell with two women charged with drug use, who constantly cut themselves with pieces of glass.
- A 16-year old boy was confined in a cell with a man charged with murder.
- A 15-year old boy was confined with three adults, two were charged with drunkenness and one with murder.

Inadequate separation also means that children are held in cells

with the mentally disabled. We learned that juveniles are regularly mingled with inmates who are mentally ill or retarded or
with inmates awaiting competency hearings.

Rape, other forms of physical abuse and harassment, and suicides are
among the most grievous and predictable consequences of confining
juveniles with adult offenders.

Many of the county jails and municipal lockups in which juveniles are
held are in deplorable condition. In *Under Lock and Key,* a juvenile court
judge described such a jail:

> When the total picture of confinement in the Lucas County Jail is ex-
> amined, what appears is confinement in cramped and over-crowded
> quarters, lightless, airless, damp and filthy with leaking water and
> human wastes, slow starvation, deprivation of most human contacts,
> except with others in the same subhuman state, no exercise or recrea-
> tion, little if any medical attention, no attempt at rehabilitation, and
> for those who in despair or frustration lash out at their surroundings,
> confinement, stripped of clothing and every last vestige of humanity...

In *Jails,* the author notes:

> Since most jail employees are law enforcement personnel, often unin-
> terested in or hostile to their assignments to guard inmates, people in
> jail are...placed in the hands of those who are least likely to teach or
> exhibit (respect for law and order)...the least qualified and the poorest
> paid employees in the criminal justice system, the jail guards.

The *Youngest Minority,* a publication of the American Bar Association
asserts:

> Besides deliberate and intentional infliction of discipline in a cruel
> manner, punishment can also imply a wrong in institutional manage-
> ment that is not erased by good intent and lofty purposes. For example,
> a 14-year old juvenile was serving 90 days on a chain gang for petty
> larceny. He was shot in the face by a trusty guard and lost both eyes
> and suffered brain damage.

Adult jails often lack the most basic medical services. In the questionnaire survey of "medical facilities" in 1,431 jails, the American Medical
Association found that 759 provided "First Aid Only." Further investigation revealed that many of the "medical facilities" listed were nothing but
first-aid kits.

A recent study by Yale University researchers found that three-quarters
or more of the violent children in a Connecticut reform school "had been
seriously abused by their parents or caretakers." This included being hit
with a belt buckle or whip, and being burned and beaten with a stick.
Ninety-six percent of this group were "found to have brain or neurologic

disorders or psychiatric problems.''

In adult jails and lockups, the mental and physical ailments of juveniles, including drug reactions and diabetes, often go unnoticed. This neglect can and does lead to unnecessary deaths.

Adult jails are not required to provide educational, recreational or indeed any services or programs for juveniles. According to the last National Jail Census, many states had no visiting facilities. In an interview with a Children's Defense Fund staff, a 12-year old confined in a jail cell in the men's section, said:

> ...all steel and you can't see nothing. There was nothing to read, nothing to do at all. I did nothing. I screamed at the cops. It's the only thing to do. Then sometimes they'd push me around. The thing — it was boring. You could be dying in there and they wouldn't even know. Once I ripped a handle off the wall. I wanted to see if they would see me in the camera. But no one came. Another time I smashed a great big hole in the wall and they didn't know.

Self-reports of juvenile crimes show that nearly 98 percent of *all* adolescents will commit at least one criminal act which will go unreported to police. But it is poor children, unable to marshall the support of parents, lawyers, or other resources, who are most likely to be jailed. In *Jails: The Ultimate Ghetto of the Criminal Justice System,* Ronald Goldfarb points out:

> The flexibility of the delinquency concept has aggravated the tendency, already severe, toward class and race discrimination in the administration of juvenile justice. Offenses by young people are common, but, generally, poor children in trouble end up in jails and other correctional institutions. Minority group children are disproportionately represented, while children under-represented.

While recent survey findings indicate that the extent to which children are held in adult jails and lockups may, in fact, be declining. The current situation can only be viewed as abysmal, at best. Poulin, *et al.,* in *Juveniles in Detention Centers and Jails: An Analysis of State Variations during the Mid-1970's* provides perhaps the most comprehensive comments regarding children in jails.

> During the mid-1970's approximately 120,000 juveniles were detained annually in adult jails. Juvenile detentions in jails were distributed disproportionately as well. Ten states (Idaho, Illinois, Kentucky, Minnesota, New Mexico, Ohio, Oregon, Texas, Virginia, and Wisconsin) accounted for over 50 percent of the admissions to jails. However, in all but eight states, some juveniles were held in adult jails. Variation among states in rates of jail detentions per 100,000 juveniles ranged from zero to 2,733. Reliance on adult jails for detaining juvenile offenders during the mid-1970's was greatest in the western United States.

The statistical data which continues as the missing link is the extent to which juveniles are held in municipal lockups. While the Children's Defense Fund study *Children in Adult Jails* estimates the overall county jail and municipal lockup admission figures to be in excess of 500,000 per year; none of the studies noted above have surveyed municipal lockups. The great potential for personal destruction inherent during the early hours of confinement illustrates the critical importance of further examining the practices of these facilities.

Myths About Children in Adult Jails

A number of myths are associated with the jailing of juveniles. We hear most often that these children are dangerous and "the community must be protected." The truth is that while serious lawbreaking receives a great deal of publicity, only about ten percent of delinquent youth who appear in court are violent. A 1978 report to the Ford Foundation, *Violent Delinquents,* reveals that "violent acts by juveniles account for 10-11 percent of all juvenile arrests...repeated violence by juveniles is not a common phenomenon," and "simple assault is the most common violent crime committed by juveniles." A survey by the Children's Defense Fund found that of 162 children for whom jails had recorded charges, only 19 (11.7 percent) were in jail for alleged dangerous acts. In a study of 1,138 juvenile offenders in Columbus, Ohio, the Academy for Contemporary Problems learned that "Youths arrested for violent offenses constituted less than one-half of 1 percent of juveniles born in Franklin County, Ohio in 1956-68, and less than 2 percent of all such persons with a pre-adult police record."

In *Children in Jails: Legal Strategies and Materials,* the National Juvenile Law Center reported that:

> ...a recent NCCD study, conducted in Upper New York State, revealed 43 percent of the children in local jails were alleged PINS (persons in need of supervision), none of whom were charged with any crime. A Montana survey found that dependent and neglected children were routinely held in jails; at over half of the jails, children were confined as a deterrent, even absent formal charges against them. The census reported that two-thirds of all juveniles in jail were awaiting trial. In 7 states, all children detained are held in jail and in 21 states, more children are held in jail than in equally available juvenile detention facilities. Analysis of correctional programs in 16 states revealed that 50 percent of children between 13 and 15 in these programs, had previously been in jail one or more times.

A report on juvenile correctional reform in Massachusetts, prepared by the Center for Criminal Justice at Harvard Law School, compares an "old system" in which all detention was in secure settings, with a "newer system" of detention in open settings, such as shelter care. The report concluded that "In the newer system, since around 80 percent of the youth are in relative open settings with relative low recidivism rates, the policy implication is clear. It is possible to put the majority of youth in open settings without exposing the community to inordinate danger."

To protect children from themselves or from dangerous home environments is another rationale for jailing juveniles. The Children's Defense Fund reveals that,

> In the name of protecting children, we found many youngsters in the filthiest, most neglected and understaffed institutions in the entire correctional system. One child was in jail because her father was suspected of raping her. Since the incest could not be proven, the adult was not held. The child, however, was put in jail for protective custody.

The President's Crime Commission was told of "four teen-age boys, jailed on suspicion of stealing beer, who died of asphyxiation from a defective gas heater, after being left alone for eleven hours in an Arizona jail." In Indiana, a 13-year old boy, veteran of five foster homes, "drove his current foster father's car to the county jail and asked the sheriff to lock him up. The child was segregated from adults pending a hearing for auto theft. A week later his body was found hanging from the bars of his cell; a penciled note nearby read, 'I don't belong anywhere.'"

A recent study of North Carolina jails found young males arrested on drinking charges are particularly prone to suicide — usually within the first 24 hours of incarceration.

For children who are abused or self-destructive, being caged with dangerous offenders, in inadequate facilities lacking sufficient or trained staff, is a life-threatening situation. In 1979, the National Coalition for Jail Reform, comprising 29 organizations including the American Correctional Association, the National Sheriff's Association, the National League of Cities, the American Institute of Architects, and the National Council on Crime and Delinquency, unequivocally endorsed the goal "that no child should be held in an adult jail," and stated that, "confinement in an adult jail of any juvenile is an undesirable practice. Such confinement has known negative consequences for youths — sometimes leading to suicide, always bearing life-long implications." The National Coalition for Jail Reform is in accord with the National Assessment of Juvenile Corrections' assertion that:

> Throughout the United States conditions in jails and most detention facilities are poor; they are overcrowded and lack the basic necessities for physical and mental health; supervision and inspection are inadequate, and little or no in-service training is provided. Lack of continuing supervision is especially problematic for jailed youth, since they can be abused by adult prisoners.

In a four-year study conducted by New York State's Select Committee on Child Abuse, a "definite link" between child abuse and neglect and juvenile delinquency was shown. Reviewing this, and similar findings in other studies from across the nation, the National Council on Crime and Delinquency concludes, "If children first visit court as victims and receive no assistance, they return to the same problems and develop survival skills that often cause their return to court as the accused."

Children are also put in jails "to teach them a good lesson." However, this lesson often backfires. In their Dangerous Offender Project, a three-year effort funded by the Lilly Endorsement, the Academy for Contemporary Problems discovered that, "Incarceration seems to speed up, rather than retard, the recidivism of the 'violent few' among juvenile offenders." The researchers charge that "Juvenile court dispositions swing from a total lack of punishment at the beginning of a criminal career to overly harsh incarceration a few crimes later on." Early on, "A youth learns that he can break the law and not be punished. He is unimpressed with the seriousness of the law." When finally put behind bars, he is likely to regard it as merely "the luck of the draw." The study concludes that "Legislators and judges ought to devise intermediate sanction measures that will make incarceration less frequently necessary. Among these might be restitution, community service orders, restrictions to a group home, and other losses of liberty designed to show that the court means business."

The lavishly praised "Scared Straight" program, in which prison inmates brutally try to frighten youngsters out of careers as lawbreakers by sneering, making homosexual advances, and offering tales of how men are crippled in jails, has been shown to be a failure. A recent study by Rutgers' Professor James O. Finckenauer traced 46 juveniles who had graduated from the Rahway prison sessions and set up a control group of 35 similar youths who had not attended them. "Contrary to televised claims that 80 to 90 percent of the project's alumni had stayed out of trouble, Finckenauer found that only 59 percent of his subjects avoided arrest; in contrast 89 percent of the control group had not been arrested. Worse yet, of 19 youngsters who went to Rahway with no criminal record, six later broke the law." It is not surprising that many authorities express shock that unacceptable prison conditions, instead of being corrected, are being touted as a remedy for youth crime."

Children *are* terrified by jails. They associate them with abuse—homosexual abuse, abuse by guards and abuse by other prisoners. As a result, they learn they cannot trust adults charged with carrying out the law. They learn to hate. The National Council on Crime and Delinquency, states:

> The fact that murders and other violent crimes are committed by children does not make the criminal justice system any more suited to the task of control and rehabilitation of young people. Every study of

prisons for adults has demonstrated the disabling effects and inappropriateness of prison environment for bringing about positive change in attitudes and behavior. The intensive, specialized efforts needed for the serious young offender have a better chance to evolve from programs and experimentation within the juvenile system.

The act of remanding violent young offenders to the criminal courts is often a surrender and a cop-out by otherwise responsible public officials. In too many cases it is a political ploy to appear tough on crime rather than face up to the need for an intelligent attempt to cope with serious crimes by children within the juvenile justice system and to contend with the causes of such crimes.

It is ironic that leaders in the juvenile justice field choose to push the most serious offenders into the criminal courts and to devote their resources to truants, runaways, and unruly children, who were pushed into their laps by education, welfare and mental health systems which also prefer to appear tough rather than smart.

Law enforcement officials and judges often regret jailing children, but justify their actions in the belief that, "Juvenile detention facilities are unavailable, overcrowded or inappropriate." The fact is that even where detention centers are readily available and existing legislation prohibits the jailing of juveniles, children are still placed in jails. In seven out of eight states where surveys were conducted by the Community Research Forum of the University of Illinois, it was found that the availability of detention centers did not in itself preclude children from being placed in jails. The Children's Defense Fund discovered that several thousand children were confined in adult jails every year in a Texas county with a large detention center. Where the practice of jailing children is permitted legally, or through lack of enforcement of statutory prohibitions, jails will be used to hold children.

Overcrowding of juvenile centers should not be used as an excuse for jailing children, since many could be released or held in a community-based setting pending trial. A survey of the effects of an employees' strike, which resulted in the furloughing of many juveniles from state training schools in Pennsylvania, found that "of 426 young people released for a period of two days to three weeks, nearly all returned without incident."

In *Confronting Youth Crime,* a report by the Twentieth Century Fund, it was concluded that preventive pretrial detention is "inappropriate and unjust," and that community supervision, rather than detention, should be utilized to insure that young defendants appear for trial. However, the Supreme Court, which has broadened the rights of children charged with delinquent acts, has yet to act at all on procedural guarantees for young people facing legal sanctions for "misbehavior or uncontrollability."

Children who are mentally ill or seriously retarded, and difficult to place are also put in jails. The Children's Defense Fund team discovered children in jails who were on waiting lists for mental hospitals, along with children who simply had no place to go. "One boy's mother had been hospitalized, and because no relative or neighbor had been able to take him the sheriff took him to jail." *Under Lock and Key* notes that in Montana where dependent and neglected children were held in jails "when necessary," "Juveniles could remain in jail for indefinite periods since only a few counties or cities had procedures for controlling the maximum number of days they could be held."

The final myth concerning the jailing of children is that it is appropriate to "jail children who have been waived from juvenile court to adult criminal court," a practice which is increasing. Guided by public fears and pressures, many broad statutes are being enacted to permit juveniles to be tried in criminal courts. Disturbed youth and juveniles who have committed simple assaults are swept up with those who murder or rape. "All these laws will do is lock a few kids up for a longer period of time," states the ACLU's Children's Rights Project. More than that, they will legally subject juveniles, including less serious offenders, to the risks and harms of commingling with adult criminals.

In Florida, a 16-year old boy was waived to an adult court for purse-snatching. He spent 201 days in an adult maximum security facility, much of it in solitary confinement, while his case was repeatedly continued in adult court. He became increasingly disturbed, telling an officer he would set the place on fire if he was not let out.

> The officer reported this to the supervisor and was told to watch the prisoner's conduct carefully to determine if additional solitary confinement procedures should be used. Within five minutes, smoke was coming from polyurethane mattresses stored outside the cell, which the prisoner apparently ignited by throwing lighted newspapers near them.

One officer and ten prisoners, including the boy himself, lost their lives in this fire. Yet in 1978, Florida enacted a law permitting states' attorneys to prosecute in adult court any 16 or 17-year old who has previously committed two delinquent acts, one of which is a felony. Felonies may include such acts as auto theft and selling marijuana. Having been deprived even of a waiver hearing, the juvenile may then be tried and handled in every respect as if he were an adult. Similar statutes are being enacted despite official crime statistics which show juvenile crime lessening in many areas.